AS I SEE IT

AS I SEE IT

DOUGLAS HARDING

articles

selected by Richard Lang

THE SHOLLOND TRUST

Published by The Shollond Trust
87B Cazenove Road
London N16 6BB
England
headexchange@gn.apc.org
www.headless.org

The Shollond Trust is a UK charity reg. no 1059551

Design: rangsgraphics.com and Richard Lang
Cover photograph of Douglas Harding by Tom Blau.

ISBN: 978-1-908774-51-4

CONTENTS

Preface ix

1 Engineering 1

2 Man No Animal 7

3 Are Angels Superfluous? 13

4 On Having No Head 21

5 The Pot-Bellied Angel 25

6 Grounds For Hope 33

7. The Progress Of Ignorance 41

8 The Thinking In Us 47

9 Heavens Above 53

10 Notes For A Defence Of Angels 63

11 A Living Universe 73

12 The Conflict Between Science And Religion 89

13 Embodiments 97

14 Thirty Questions 111

15 Spontaneous Awakening 119

16 Addendum 133

17 Home Truth 137

18 Preface To On Having No Head 139

19 The Caller.. 141

20 What Am I?.. 145

21 What Is Self-Realisation?............................. 147

22 In This Six Foot Body................................... 153

23 Face To No-Face.. 159

24 The Serious Question................................... 161

25 Masked Ball... 165

26 Making A Good Impression 167

27 What Deludes Is What Enlightens 171

28 The Great Game Of Pretending 183

29 The Wild Hypothesis 191

30 The Answer To "Who Am I?" 221

31 The Headless Way 227

32 Eleven Tests For Buddhists 231

33 How To Be Spontaneous 237

34 Perseus And The Gorgon 243

35 On Trial For My Life 253

36 The Evidence Of Where Thoughts Belong 265

37 The Evidence Of Where Feelings Belong 271

38 The Evidence Of Architecture 275

39 The Evidence Of The Results Of Self-Realisation 279

40 The Sailor, The Ship And The Sea 283

41 Ramana Maharshi And The Availability Of Self-Realisation 291

42 Who Made The World? 299

43 On Logion 29 303

44 Ramana Maharshi And How Not To Grow Old 307

45 What I Owe To Ramana Maharshi 317

46 Seeking The Miraculous 323

47 Alan Watts: Sage Or Anti-Sage? 339

48 Enlightenment For Peace 345

49 Confrontation: The Suicidal Lie 365

50 Confrontation: The Game People Play 367

51 Facing The Yellow Flowers 401

52 The Prince Or Princess, The Tadpole And The Frog 419

53 The Four Fatal Lies 439

54 Mayday Call 481

55 My Special Friend 485
56 The Tunnel 487
57 Whatdunnit 499
58 Harding's List 509
59 The Door 523
60 Fate And Freedom 533
Notes................................. 541
Bibliography........................ 547

Preface

Sometimes people criticised Douglas Harding, author of *On Having No Head*, by saying he was like a record whose needle had got stuck. His reply was that at least his needle was stuck in the Centre! The Centre being the eternal, all-embracing Heart of oneself, one's True Self, the Stillness which is the hub of the turning world, the infinitely small Point that is all the while exploding into Everything. No bad place to be stuck!

The articles in this book, arranged in chronological order, span the period of Harding's life (1909–2007) from the early 1940s to the late 1990s. And though they are the sound of a needle stuck on one subject—the changeless subject of our true identity—the only Subject!—they reveal something of the wide repertoire Harding composed, inspired by that single, silent, mysterious, nearer-than-near, nothing-that-is-everything. These writings also demonstrate how Harding's understanding developed over many years as he explored in different contexts the meaning of what he saw himself to be, in contrast to what others made of him.

Harding first saw Who he really was in India in 1943, after some ten years of study and writing. The important point being that in this year he *saw* his true Self rather than simply entertained yet another *thought* about it. Harding spent the rest of his long life writing about and devising ways to share the experience and meaning of Who we all really are. (For the story of Harding's life, see the graphic biography, *The Man With No Head* by Richard Lang and Victor Lunn-Rockliffe.)

As I See It is not a collection of all of Harding's articles but of those not in print elsewhere, either in the three collections of articles already published (*Look For Yourself*, *To Be & Not To Be*, and *The Turning Point*), or in my book *Seeing Who You Really Are*—where you'll find the article *On Being Aware*, and articles on sex and Seeing and the benefits of Seeing. (I have also included a few poems in this selection.) After Harding died in 2007 I took care of his books and papers. In 2016, wanting to make available all of Harding's work, I sorted out the articles no longer in print. Easier said than done. Even whilst reading through a late draft of this book I discovered that one article appeared twice—hidden by having two different titles and introductions. Then I found that this article was itself already published—under yet another title—in *Look For Yourself*. I'm still not completely sure there isn't some other duplication somewhere. The reason for this duplication is that from time to time Harding recycled his articles. The same article might appear, for example, first in the Ramana Maharshi Ashram journal *The Mountain Path*, with quotations from Ramana, and then at a later date in the London Buddhist Society's journal *The Middle Way*, with quotations from the Buddha—slightly adjusted for a different readership.

Over the years Harding wrote many articles for these two journals—*The Middle Way* and *The Mountain Path*. In the late '50s Harding had discovered Zen Buddhism through reading D. T. Suzuki. After many years on his own with Seeing, Harding at last felt he had found friends—Buddhist Masters from China and Japan who, though long dead, spoke of their Original Face and of being headless. Which of course was the same timeless and faceless Original Face that Harding found where he was. But most importantly, these Masters were not just *talking about* their True Nature, they were also *seeing* it. As was Harding. Then, soon after finding Zen, Harding read *Talks With Ramana Maharshi*. Ramana's repeated declaration that awareness of the Self is the fundamental solution of all problems, and his insistence that the Self is available now—easier to see than a piece of fruit in your hand—inspired Harding. Following his discovery of Zen and Ramana, Harding began writing for *The Middle Way* and *The Mountain Path*. (In the *Notes* at the back of this book I've provided information about where articles were first published, and when.)

Looking through Harding's papers, I also discovered writings not published before, so it's a pleasure to bring these into the light of day as well. I've identified these previously unpublished writings in the *Notes*.

When I first met Harding in 1970 he was always focused, always working on some project—he lived, breathed, ate and slept Seeing. He was almost always writing something. Visiting him you would invariably be treated to the current version of his latest project—as if this was the best thing yet he'd written. As you'll see from the articles in this collection, his focus changed over the years. In the '50s he was still drenched in the ideas he had presented in *The Hierarchy of Heaven and Earth*, so in early articles he's primarily focused on the many-levelled living universe, including the existence of 'angels'—hopefully that piques your interest! Then in the '60s come articles where he is simplifying his approach and language, focusing more directly on the experience of Seeing—though awareness of the sacred, many-levelled living universe is never far from the surface. Harding was also now sharing Seeing with a growing number of people—a loose-knit circle of Seeing friends was emerging. (The article *Spontaneous Awakening* describes the first time Harding really shared Seeing.) After a 'winter' of more than twenty years alone with Who he really was, sharing Seeing with others and receiving such encouraging feedback came like a surge of exhilarating Spring energy in Harding's life. In the '70s, increasingly being asked to give workshops, Harding found himself developing his experiments—the 'skilful means' that make sharing Seeing so quick and easy. Harding also explored the implications of Seeing in a variety of contexts: in the field of psychology—as a remedy for alienation, depression, fear and anxiety; in the field of politics—as a remedy for the conflict between nations, power blocs, races... And Harding's profound respect for and love of Christ—he was raised in the fundamentalist Plymouth Brethren—is obvious in *Harding's List*.

Harding's writings radiate a deep appreciation of Being: the simple, self-evident fact that one is—that the One is. Harding wonders why there isn't just nothing! I AM! By 'I AM' he's not referring to himself as a person but to himself as the One. How astonishing to BE! You—Who you really are—have happened! You are happening NOW—an incredible ongoing success story unfolding moment by moment at the very heart of your life! Given that the One you are is Self-Originating—which by the way includes, without batting an eyelid, creating billions of universes all in working order—after such creativity, please tell me what is not possible! Harding's appreciation of, his surprise and delight about 'the impossible achievement of Being'—the One managing to carry off this magnificent conjuring trick of hoisting itself by its own bootstraps from the darkest night of non-being—Harding described awareness of this as "the joy that casts no shadow". This is the intoxicating thrill, the wildfire burning—out of control—at the heart of Harding's work. At the end of that very great book *The Hierarchy of Heaven and Earth*—in fact it's the last sentence—Harding wrote: "If this book quenches the feeblest flame of awe, of direct awareness, in myself or anyone else, then it were better never to have written it." Far from quenching any flame of awareness and wonder in me, that book set off a blaze. The articles in this collection come from the same powerful bellows. They too fan the flames of awareness and wonder, and indeed of worship, in me. And of trust. As Harding often said, "If you can't trust This, what can you trust?" I hope these articles inspire you too.

Read these articles in chronological order or jump about randomly… My hope is that each will guide you along a unique path to the Home you never left, the clear frameless Window you are looking out of now—this wider-than-wide single Eye; this boundless, infinitely charming, incomparable No-face; this so so still and peaceful Hub of the always-busy world…

As a way of concluding this Preface I feel inspired to say a prayer for you!

I pray that in this moment you find yourself profoundly stuck… Stuck in the Centre!

Which is seeing you are blessed beyond your wildest dreams, here and now, just as you are.

Richard Lang

Chapter 1

ENGINEERING

I have been handed a formidable list of various branches of engineering with the suggestion that it may serve as a basis for my talk tonight. This list includes mines, and ship-building, and harbour works, and land reclamation, and building construction, and reservoirs, and bridges, and much else. Now there are three good reasons why I am not going to unload on you tonight a lot of information about these subjects: firstly I haven't the time; secondly, I haven't the knowledge; and thirdly, if I had the time and the knowledge I doubt whether I could make such technical subjects really interesting to listeners.

What I do propose to talk about is a very general aspect of engineering—an aspect so general that most engineers are, I think, quite unfamiliar with it.

Let us try to see engineering from the point of view of a visitor to this planet from the outside world.

I think one of the first things you would notice would be the way we are making the Earth artificial. The planet is being *fabricated* by man more or less as he fabricates a lump of clay or a bit of wood. Of course the fabricator is very small compared with the material he is working upon, and another complication is that the fabricator is sitting on his material and is actually a bit of it himself. But the fact remains that man is gradually building a new Earth out of the raw

material which is the old Earth. Man is, for instance, not content with
the natural geography of the old Earth, and is making a new artificial
geography. In Holland he has made many hundreds of square miles of
sea into land. Canals, which are artificial rivers, now span continents,
and artificial rivers are so superior to the natural kind that they can
be stepped up over a mountain range, and stepped down the other
side. Even natural rivers are very often artificialised by dams and
embankments, so that we can make them behave, more or less, as
we want to. We prevent the sea from having its own way entirely
with the land, by means of groins and breakwaters and so on. We
re-arrange the order of the Earth's strata by means of mines. We drill
holes through mountains for our railway lines, and throw tongues of
dry land over wide rivers.

Slowly we are artificialising the Earth, and not only Earth's
geography. Our domestic animals and flowering plants and food
plants are highly artificial or man-constructed. A bulldog and a
pouter-pigeon are quite unnatural: we have made, by selective
breeding, what they are. Man himself is, physically, the least artificial
of the domestic animals, but it is probably only a matter of time
before he is forced to take a hand in his own evolution.

We have only just begun the work of moulding a planet according
to our desire. Our descendants will take up the work thoroughly,
and will redesign the Earth's surface as a man now redesigns his
back garden. Artificial lands and seas, artificial animals and plants
of greater use and beauty, artificial weather, and artificial men, will
be found in this terrestrial garden of ours. But we will not be content

with re-fabricating the surface. I have no doubt we will explore and use the Earth's interior as thoroughly as we now explore its crust. We will really use the Earth, take possession of it, move in. We will artificialise the Earth till it really lives through and through with man.

But apparently this can't go on for ever. According to astronomers our sun is cooling down and our Earth is doomed along with our sun. The sun's energy is giving out, and in so many millions of years' time life will not be able to exist on this Earth. If man hasn't succeeded in wiping himself out by then, what will happen to him? Will he perish with his Earth? Or will he escape?

Will his engineering save him? And if so, how? By that time man may have learned to use the Earth's energy to propel the planet through space, away from our sun, to a younger star, which we could adopt as our new sun. Olaf Stapleton has made this suggestion in his brilliant fantasy called *Star Maker*. Another possibility, suggested by J.D. Bernal in his equally exciting forecast called *The World, The Flesh, and the Devil*, is that man will learn to build space-ships which will take him away from our dying planet. These space-ships are envisaged as vast metal spheres propelled, if I remember rightly, by the controlled disintegration of matter into energy. *There* is an engineering problem compared with which our stickiest problems are child's play. We are only amateurs at artificiality. We have only made a tentative start at re-designing our environment: it is still very natural.

Engineering is, then, for our present purpose, the creation of an artificial Earth that shall be more to our requirements than the natural one. By artificial I mean man-made fabricated. But of course if we were to look at the Earth as complete outsiders, as super-human observers, all the works of man would be as natural as a sunset or a flower or a bird's nest.

And so, from this broader view-point, they are. A bridge is as natural as the river it spans. Your coat is as natural as your skin. A submarine is no more artificial than a fish, or an aeroplane than a bird. Engineers are Nature's agents and are simply the means by which Life is changing this Earth and taking it over. Engineers are the means by which Life is able quickly to evolve myriads of new forms. We call these forms artificial, mechanical, unnatural, but that is a narrow viewpoint. The truer, larger, outside view is that human engineering is only a bit of Life's engineering, of Cosmic engineering. One must regard the whole of things as natural, or the whole of things as artificial. Any other view is quite arbitrary.

Perhaps it is not quite clear to you how engineering works are really natural things. Let us try to see them impartially, as if for the first time, from a distance. Let us imagine we are up in the sky looking at the Earth as a whole. Up here, at this height, we can't see little things like men and animals, nor are we interested in them. What we can see are big things—the continents and oceans, rivers and deserts and snowfields of the Earth. And we can see, spread over the Earth's surface, a curious object somewhat like a Creeper—a network of fine stalks that are gathered together at intervals into dense masses of all sizes.

Now if we try to forget that this network is, in detail, a system of roads and railways and canals (with the buildings that line these communications) and try instead to see the network as a whole that wraps the Earth, we shall discover a remarkable thing. This network or Creeper is *alive*. How do we know that? Because it does all the things that living creatures do; it eats, it drinks; it breathes; it gets rid of its waste matter; it grows; it withers; in places it dies. This extraordinary network, which covers most of the Earth, eats coal and iron and manganese and copper and tin, and stone and brick-earth and lime, as well as plants and animals. It drinks at oil wells and lakes and rivers. It breathes the air. It eliminates its waste through a variety of bowels, of which our drainage systems are the most familiar. It grows by pushing new stalks over the Earth's surface and forming new stalk-clusters: in other words it grows by sending out new roads and new railroads and canals, and by forming new towns at intervals along these lines of communication.

See how our closeness to this object blinds us to its livingness, even to its reality. Of course drains and bridges and roads and buildings and canals and so forth are not alive separately and in themselves, any more than the particles in your body are alive as separate things. But the whole lives. This creeping network really is a living creature—not in a manner of speaking, not metaphorically, but in sober truth it is as alive or even more alive than you.

Engineers then are really physiologists. They are the physicians and surgeons of social organs. An inventor is an instrument by which these organs evolve. A construction engineer is an instrument by which they grow. A maintenance engineer is an instrument by which they are maintained.

As I See It

We belong within a creature called Man, and Man's body is a fine network that encircles our planet. Our bodies are part of this Body of Man, and the most important part. But what we call the artificial parts of Man's Body are also of vital and increasing importance. Man (this vast creeper-shaped creature) is largely the work of engineers. Engineers have, all unknown to themselves, played a key part in the making of the body of a living creature. That is their job. Biologists study life, engineers build it. We are what we are in mind and in body by virtue of what we are and do, and, in particular, of what engineers are and do. Their mines, and railroads and tunnels and factories and canals and all the marvels of modern technology are, seen from the broad viewpoint, the natural organs of the creature Man in whose being we share.

Giordano Bruno said that your hat is alive when you wear it. He was right. If he can see us now he's probably remarking upon two marvels—the wondrous livingness of our engineer-made social organs, and the wondrous blindness of engineers who know not what they build.

* * *

Chapter 2

MAN NO ANIMAL

Our forefathers were made in the image of God; we are made in the image of a Gibbon or a Spectral Tarsier. More ingenious and baleful than the other primates, we are still their second cousins; and if we repudiate them our very bones rise in witness against us.

Now of these antipodal estimates of man, I take the first to be the truer, even at the biological level of discussion. For a man's real physique is nothing like an ape's, and no more simian than his mind.

It is true that at the core of his physique there can be found an animal's. But this nucleus is an organ rather than an organism, and by itself incapable of any specifically human function, even of life. For example, this five-fingered hand is no true hand, but only a stump, an animal limb-bud from which human hands may presently burgeon, a socket for whatever limb-ending the human occasion requires, a universal joint to which every kind of human organ—spade, plough, hammer, pneumatic drill, brush, violin-bow may be fitted in an instant, and as quickly removed. Again, this tender and pallid skin is no true epidermis, but the mesoderm underlying colourful and ever-changing human skins of wool and cotton and silk. Well may Bramston exclaim: "Without black velvet breeches what is man?" To undress is to unman. There are many layers to a human being, all of them vital. An unhoused man is less a man than an unhoused snail is a mollusc. Amputate his reaper-jaws browsing in another

7

continent, his factory-stomachs digesting his food stage by stage till at last it is fit for the innermost animal stomach, his water-main-mouth sucking at the reservoir in the hills, his drain-bowel voiding into the sea, his library-brain holding his memory and guiding his thought—amputate these and the rest of his extended physique, and only a corpse is left on the operating table.

Clearly this luxuriant human growth—this peripheral development which makes men of us is very unlike the animal growth which it prolongs. But it is none the less animate and animating for that. Through it we are more active, and so more actual; more alive to more, and so more alive. Nor is it a set of appendages. For learning how to use a tool is learning how to incorporate it. Till my pen is so ingrown and grafted to me that I feel the grain of the paper against the nib, till my chair-legs are so much mine that I am no longer a biped sitting but a quadruped standing, till I am so continuous with my tail and wing-tips that it is I who thrust and slice the upper air, till I am so thoroughly in the ship that I am in the sea, till I am so comfortable on the car-seat that I am not on it but on the road—till then I am only partially embodied. The expert is bigger than the novice. He no more holds on to the wheel or the joystick than his shoulders hold on to his arms: all are absorbed into his total body, his organism-for-the-time-being.

Moreover this new evolutionary departure, so far from negating the old, carries on its works much more swiftly and effectively. It is the sudden and deliberate flower of the other's root, obeying the same basic laws of growth all the more loyally for becoming aware of them. As ages ago our trunks grew fins and our fins grew feet, so now—but at how different a pace—our feet grow shoes and our shoes grow hobnails and skates and rubbers. For all such human gear, like the animal gear it extends, arises from a few great mutations and many small variations—novelties which, when sifted by changing environments, produce every kind of adaptation. Man is immeasurably more adaptable than a beast because he is immeasurably more adapted: with each of his thousand unique hands he grasps a unique world. The counterpart of his life's richness is the richness of the body with which he lives it.

There is even a sense in which the tool is more alive than the arm it terminates. This new physique means new freedom—freedom to use countless materials and devices denied to the old, freedom to invent and not merely to adapt, freedom to start again, freedom to plan ahead, freedom to experiment without risk of extinction—and greater freedom exercised is intenser life lived. Now it is no longer the organism which goes to the scrap-heap, but only the organ. As often as our hand offends us we may cut it off and fit another. Indeed its handiness lies more in the ease of its amputation than of its growth. My telephone would be a death-dealing and not a life-giving organ if it were a permanent system of ears and vocal cords, a thing of flesh and blood to be dragged around and never painlessly shed, a net of nerve fibres instead of wires, irreplaceable and unrepairable and unimprovable equipment born and dying with the rest of us. Aluminium wings serve life better for being dead and featherless: as detachable, they are all the more firmly joined to the living whole.

They are the true wing, of which the bird's are only prototypes.

Prototypes—and deformations. For every specialized animal limb-ending—wing, talon, flipper, hoof, paw—is in its way a malignant growth, a tool which has seized the user, a constriction of the organism and therefore of its universe. Man alone remains an unspoiled animal, uncommitted by his flesh to any narrow way of life, and that is why he is also no animal. Each of the others has impatiently taken on some human tool, and that is why it remains an animal. It is a prematurely expert man—a masterly aviator, or sailor, or runner, or social organizer, or hunter, or dandy—but the price of becoming permanently human in one respect is staying permanently subhuman in all others. He, on the other hand, is content to remain the universal amateur, able to ride countless hobby-horses because none rides him. Animals are consistently up-to-date, and therefore live in the past; he is always falling behind the evolutionary times, and therefore moves with them and moves them. They stick to their jobs (or rather, their jobs stick to them); they have made up their minds, and are never lazy and incompetent and poor. He alone bungles, and forgets his job, and takes time off, and changes his mind and his body. To rise above these human limitations is to fall into animality. It is when modern man is only modern that he is the inferior of his ancestors.

The measure of his mind, then, is not so much his giant body as his power of putting off this body, his faculty of reversion; for human nature includes the necessity to divest itself of human nature. The mere animal becomes and unbecomes every animal, and therefore is no animal.

Here is our answer to those who argue from our animal past to our animal present, from the shape of our skeletons and embryos to the shape of our minds, from our little craniums to our little souls. Man is not what he seems. He is the elastic organism, the brain which adds to itself and subtracts all other brains, the body which grows and shrinks to match the situation, the deciduous world-tree. You know where an animal ends and its world begins, but you can never by external inspection tell a man's extent. For to think and feel as a human being is to think and feel your way into and out of many worlds, and to have godlike immensity.

* * *

Chapter 3

ARE ANGELS SUPERFLUOUS?

My encounters lead me to suppose that the educated Christian's belief in angels rarely exceeds his belief in centaurs and unicorns. Of course it is true that his Old and New Testaments and Prayer Book and Hymnary have many clear and striking passages about the host of Heaven, true also that he repeats these without much conscious insincerity. But his angels are dead. It is not that he has anything against them—indeed he finds them charming, especially in carols and stained glass windows—but rather that there is something quite fatal to them in our modern air.

But it would be a mistake to suppose that our inability to take angels seriously comes from either superior knowledge or profounder thinking. Indeed I am sure the matter is the other way round, and that our disbelief is due much more to poverty of imagination than wealth of reason, to human parochialism than universal enlightenment. In what follows I shall try to set down a few of my reasons for holding this opinion.

What, in fact, has happened to our angels? To answer this question we need to see them in their setting: we need to ask what has happened to our universe—to the cosmos in which they used to play so vital a part, and in which they are now superfluous.

Perhaps it is impossible for us to imagine what it was really like to live in the sort of universe which confronted men at the beginning of the Christian era. It was altogether too alive; the spheres above a man's head were overpopulous, haunted, crowded with a vitality at once magnificent and terrible, full of threat and of promise. The later Jewish literature described a great company of angels who were God's courtiers and ambassadors and the administrators of nature, and other angels who were the heavenly bodies themselves, the Watchers, living stars. The whole Hellenistic world was fascinated by the divine sun and planets and stars: sublunary beings were not more but less animate and intelligent than the rest of the universe, and a man had only to lift his eyes to look into Heaven, into a Country whose splendour and divinity increased with its distance from himself. He knew his place. He lived below-stairs, under the very eyes of his betters.

This cosmos became part of the Christian inheritance. Clement of Alexandria taught that the heavenly bodies are all living creatures, and Origen described them as rational and moral beings capable of sin: the sun, though desiring to be freed from the body, is content to pursue his path in the spirit of service. Two centuries later St. Augustine did not definitely rule out the possibility that the sun and stars are angels, and as late as the 13th century St. Thomas Aquinas himself conceded that to believe celestial bodies have souls is no heresy. In general, however, the mediaeval universe was populous not with living bodies but with spirits—finite incorporeal substances without sensitive or nutritive faculties, but capable of temporary association or even union with material bodies—a great hierarchy of supernatural intelligences directing the great hierarchy of natural processes and steering the stars in their courses. The universe was still alive, but its mind and body had parted company.

Mediaeval man robs the angels of their bodies; renaissance man robs them of their functions; modern man robs them of their existence—he adds the finishing touch. Every advance in science has thrown an angel out of work, or else compelled him to dress up as a Tendency which bodies observe, or a Law of Nature which they obey, or a Force to which they submit. And now these last angelic disguises have worn thin and been seen through: compulsive laws and forces are reckoned almost as mythical as their winged originals.

Nor are we left with so much as a dead universe. For one by one its sensible qualities have been gathered in from the object over there to its perceiver here. The sun's warmth and brightness and colour, his beauty, and even his motion, are no longer his but ours: they belong to the beholder's eye and not to Heaven's. And finally the sun's bare matter or physical substratum has been reduced almost to nothing but a set of mathematical formulae. Apart from us our cosmos is not even an engine or a firework display: all that it seems to be, we read into it. It is our projection. Our sun is first a god, then a corpse impelled by a wraith, then a mere corpse adrift in the blue sky, then a few fast-decaying remains, and in the end something less than thin air. And the fate of our sun is the fate of all the stars. We have changed places with the universe: we who used to be its desert are now the oasis.

It has taken us a millennium thus to disprove our angels, and we have done so with immense thoroughness. All that was above our heads is now drawn into them—divine order and intellect, the science of sidereal navigation, the entire furniture of that high and beautiful country. As the body of our expanding universe is centrifugal, so its mind is centripetal. What once we attributed to the principalities and powers in the heavens we now claim as men on earth. The truth is not that we have grown out of our angels, but that they have grown into us. They have come down and converged upon us and possessed us, though it is plain that in the course of their descent they have greatly changed for the worse.

Indeed our refutation of angels has been altogether too thorough: it has become something like their demonstration. For if this is a disproof of the life above us then eating is the disproof of food and learning the disproof of books. The only way that we who are terrestrial and solar and galactic can begin to show that our earth and our sun (our developed star, the solar system) and our galaxy are dead is by committing suicide at once: for so long as we (who are our own samples of them) are alive to their lifelessness they live in us, and so long as we are conscious of their unconsciousness they are conscious in us. They have passed from transcendence to immanence, not passed away. They have migrated, not absconded—how can their visit here, to this corner of the universe, be their exit from it? If they have been reduced to an absurdity, then we are that absurdity. We are always forgetting that man is not only man, and that in him every hierarchical level from the lowest to the highest is at least potentially present. It is our vice to try to isolate ourselves (as if we could!) from all our life-sources—not only from our Source, but from every stream that flows down to us from It. No wonder our planet and star and nebula are dead, when directly they put forth a limb (and we are their limbs) we amputate it, and directly they show any intelligence, any science, any love, any goodness, any wickedness (and of these we all have first-hand knowledge) we call them accidents and anomalies and intrusions in a world that is prejudged to be incapable of anything of the sort. We suffer from the insane delusion that we have been parachuted into the universe from outside, and are therefore clues only to what the universe is *not* like. We leaves are sure our Yggdrasil Tree is dead—because it is so obviously not a leaf.

Such an outlook is in the long run disastrous as well as silly, for the centripetal mind that possesses us, the angel who in us has come to deny the transcendent world and all other angels and every trace of divinity but its own, is well on the way to becoming a devil. We are inspired with a knowledge and purpose that are hellish rather than heavenly, because they lack nearly all objective reference and natural piety, all wonder and awe and humility, all reverence for what lies beyond ourselves.

Yet there are signs of our conversion. Little by little we are being rid of our superstition that all which is not human is infra-human. We have begun to suspect that other species are not necessarily sunk in primitive stupor—witness the recent discovery of the bees' language; that other planets—Mars in particular—may be far ahead of us; that other stars and galaxies may well have a life compared with which our life is merely vegetative. This is a great awakening at once for us and for our night-world. But it is no more than a first opening of the eyes at early dawn. We have still to join the mind we have found to its body, and to see the life in the stars as the life of the stars instead of something parasitical. We have still to awake to the fact that heavenly bodies are not cosmic cannon balls infested with men, any more than human bodies are skeletons infested with cells.

The signs are that at last, after so many centuries of contraction, a huge expansion is about to begin: we are ready for the tremendous vision of a hierarchy of mind and meaning that lies altogether outside ourselves. Our angels are already trying their wings for that long outward flight which will make them angelic again, and I think that before very long we shall once more look up into a visible Heaven that is in every sense above us. Then it will come as a revelation and a revolution that we have never ceased to look right into the realm of the bright angels, and that we really are in Heaven all the while.

And after all even common sense is on the side of the angels without knowing it. Is it likely that the structure of the universe is so ill-balanced that all is orderly and filled and complete up to our human storey, and that thereafter there is just emptiness till we get to the roof? Between ourselves and the physical substratum—a packed hierarchy of particles and atoms and molecules and cells; between ourselves and the Apex of the hierarchy—nothing. It is incredible. Incredible also that we should fail to see in our obsession with the infra-human and denial of the supra-human a defect of imagination, or an obstructed view due to our half-way position in the hierarchy. Doubtless my particles and cells never suspect the existence of any levels above their own—and still less are aware of how their present acts issue in the writing of this sentence about them—but that is no reason why my lower levels should infect the higher with their blindness.

For the Christian this question of hierarchy is crucial. Plainly the mediaeval universe was top-heavy, just as ours is bottom-heavy, and plainly hierarchical symmetry is what we need. But this means that our angels must come to life again. Without them, as Richard of St. Victor says, our universe is acephalous, *quod est inconveniens*. And ungodly also. For disbelief in angels is near atheism. Machinery that makes and runs itself has no need either of managerial staff or of Inventor, and certainly our leveled-down and proletarian cosmos has no need of a King. If His angels are superfluous, He also can be spared. But a hierarchy, a full and symmetrical hierarchy of Heaven and earth, implies a Head. In truth our self-glorifying war against the Court of Heaven has been aimed at its Sovereign, and our resubmission to it is a part of our resubmission to Him.

* * *

Chapter 4

ON HAVING NO HEAD

We are the victims of many illusions about ourselves, but I know of none more startling, or more fundamental, more productive of further illusions, than the belief that we have heads.

Allow me to introduce you to yourself. Let me describe you as you really are at this moment. You are a pair of hands and forearms, portions of a lap, stumpy legs with very small feet, and a trunk which fades into nebulous shoulders. But the shoulders carry no head. Instead, there is only this page of print—and thrown across it a pink shadow which you call your nose, and perhaps round it a cloudy oval frame which you call your glasses, and on it a double blot which you call your pipe. And when you look up from this book you will find that you are still without a head, and that presented in its place are the fireplace and a hearthrug, the picture over the mantel, the window, the house opposite, the sky, the evening star. Yet all your life, till you read this paragraph, you thought you were like other men and women, and had a head!

Of course you may find all manner of goings on—tastes, aches, roughnesses, itches, warmths, pressures—in the region where you thought you kept a head. But to pretend that these make up a head, or make up for the lack of a head, or are remotely like the turnip-shaped thing you find on other men's shoulders, would be absurd.

The fact is that there exists, not one sort of human being, but two utterly different sorts. The first, of which you meet countless instances, have a head apiece; the second, of which you have just met the only instance (but numbers, the counting of heads, carry little weight here), has lost a head and gained a world. In other words, the view out *from* a man is quite unlike the view *in* to him. And till you clearly recognise this, and know when you speak of man which kind of man, which view of him, you mean, you will never begin to make head or tail of him.

The first great mistake springing from this misunderstanding, this failure to distinguish between the headed and the headless, is a mistake about your size. You thought you were an insignificant animal creeping on an insignificant planet, which circulates about a commonplace star, which is only one of thousands of millions of stars—that, in short, you were lost in a world so terrifyingly vast that you might as well not exist at all. Now this could be true of the *other* man, of the man-with-a-head, of the view-in-to-a-man, but never of *this* man, of the headless man, of the view-out-from-a-man. If it happens to be a clear night, you can put down these pages and go across to the window and take in—and take upon yourself—a skyful of stars, so that instead of being lost in them they are lost in you. It is no mere part which finds itself containing the whole.

The second mistake is the belief that you are chained to this one spot, imprisoned here for life. But this spot you call Here is for you as extensive as the universe; and you may, without moving a step, pass at one stride from earth to the highest heavens. When the furthest star can be present to you in an instant, it is ungracious to complain about your lack of travel facilities. Other men—the ones with heads—may reasonably do so, but not you.

The third mistake is to suppose that you are only a man. You imagine that you belong to the same species, and genus, and order, and kingdom, as the bipeds around you. But this is evidently not the case. You are so unlike them that to call you by their name is an abuse of language. For you lack their constant human heads, and they lack your variable non-human substitutes-for-heads—stars, trees, men, this page, a pinhead, or anything else you like or dislike. There is no equivalence between the headed creature that is comprehended, and the beheaded creature that comprehends. How can the fraction be confused with the totality? If your first-hand experience of what it is like to be yourself is any guide at all, then you are not one thing but a home for all things, some of them much greater than a man and some much less. Observers who are taken in by what they can see of you are deluding themselves: they are really observing something else.

The fourth member of this family of illusions, offspring of the same parent, is the belief that, because you are shut up in this present moment of time, you are shut out of all other times—out of the whole past and future. But in fact it is the very nature of your Now to enclose every Then, just as it is the very nature of your Here to enclose every There. How can so much as the idea of history occurr to you, unless it is gathered up into this moment of history? How can you contemplate all time and all existence except as present time and present existence? This head-substitute of yours, this capital consolation prize, is as immense in time as in space. Through it, the life-span you acquire may be less than a mayfly's and greater than a galaxy's.

Therefore it will not do to speak of you as a mere mortal, whose term is eighty or ninety years. For in one respect your lifespan is no time at all: in the Now-instant from which you can never escape you can never find time to be or to do anything. Indeed it does not take a doctor to explain that in your headless condition you cannot survive for a minute. Obviously, the only life you can enjoy is that of the objects you enjoy. But it is limitless. In so far as you are occupied with your neighbour whose years are threescore and ten, that is the extent of your existence; in so far as you live in and for the things of today, today you live and today die; in so far as you make way for One who, including and transcending all time, is eternal, you enter into eternal life. You cannot drink the medicine of immortality in teaspoonfuls, over the years, but in one dose, now. Nor are there any half-cures.

There remains what is perhaps the greatest illusion of all—the illusion that, since you are a mere man with a head, a finite thing bounded by other finite things, so, even more certainly is your neighbour. And consequently he is there to be used like any other thing. But once you really awake to your own headlessness, you cannot stop there, but must wake to mine and every creature's. Putting yourself at my centre, you see me as I am—boundless and deathless—because I am the habitation of the One who is boundless and deathless, and in the last resort there is only Him.

* * *

Chapter 5

THE POT-BELLIED ANGEL

You meet two kinds of cranks—those that force their King Charles' Head on you in the first five minutes, and those that keep it cunningly hidden till they have scraped an acquaintance with you, and then let it out so gradually and disarmingly that you find yourself taking the thing seriously: or at least seriously enough to argue about it. In the end, of course, you see the monstrosity for what it is: the sparkle of enthusiasm in your companion's eye is revealed as the horrid glare of fanaticism; your rejoinders dwindle to embarrassed monosyllables; and you get away as soon as you decently or indecently can. But for a time you are almost taken in.

It was on a crowded air-liner that I collected my most remarkable specimen of this second species of crank. He was shown at the last minute into the seat at my side, and there was no escape. To tell the truth, I had no wish to avoid him; for he looked agreeable enough, with his boy's face under an old man's brow and hair, and his engaging smile. Besides, I was in the mood for conversation.

Our newspapers provided the topic—the Loch Ness Monster had cropped up again. That led us on to whales, giant squids, and the colossal animals of earth's past. I reeled off something I had read about the limits which nature sets to a creature's bulk: if it is too big it just can't survive.

"That's true of a creature crawling on a heavenly body," he said.

"But suppose it took off—I mean more thoroughly than we have just done—and, leaving its parent altogether, set up as a heavenly body on its own account. Then it could be any size it liked." He seemed to say this half-jokingly, and I (who make a point of letting my imagination have its fling sometimes) was ready enough to play his game.

"You're wrong there," I replied. "It would need to wrap itself in its own atmosphere and keep a firm gravitational hold on it; and if the creature weren't as big as a planet it could never do that." I felt I had made a point, and he seemed to look at me more keenly, with a new interest.

Anyhow he accepted the correction eagerly (so eagerly that I should have been put on my guard at once), and then we went on constructing this celestial giant of his. "Obviously," I said, "it wouldn't need wings to fly; and arms and legs would be more of a hindrance than a help for getting about in the sky. A nose and ears would be no use at all—the heavenly spaces aren't noisy or scented. In fact its anatomy would be entirely different from any earthly creature's... But what would it live on? Meteorites?"

"A poor diet. Why not sunlight, like the plants?"

"Why of course," I said, unwisely warming to the game. "I can see a kind of cosmic Vegetable, with its whole skin lapping up the sun's energy. But then you wouldn't look for a mouth, and still less for a stomach or bowels or an anus. I doubt whether it would have a head: all the same it would need to be a nimble and cautious vegetable, to avoid being either frozen or baked to death. Actually it would die both deaths at once if it failed to keep turning a new part of itself to the sun, like sidereal meat on a spit."

"Now I wonder," said my companion (just as if the idea had never struck him before) "how such a creature—wingless, armless, legless, as you say—would manage to stay the right distance from the sun. Because, you know, it wouldn't help much to revolve on your axis if you were all the while either falling into or away from the sun."

I plunged still further into the trap—"No difficulty there. Provided it started off on the right foot, at a tangent and with some impetus of its own, it would go on circling round the sun indefinitely, just as the earth does." He gave me a queer look as I said this, but let me ramble on. "A dull life it would lead. Nothing to do but imitate a child's top."

"Oh I don't know," came the casual-sounding reply. "The creature could still *see*. That sense at least wouldn't be out of place, because if there is a country where the views are good and long it is the heavens. I shouldn't be surprised if it were to grow eyes all over its skin—rather like Ezekiel's wheels—and spend its time watching the dance of the stars and planets. Your vegetable would be a cosmic wallflower… But no: we've decided it must join in… And, with more-than-binocular vision, it would see the nearer dancers in full perspective; and, if it grew very clever, it could work out the distances and motions of the others. It might fall in love with some of its celestial companions, sing songs about them, give them names. And even if it began life as a creature of blind habit, it could still grow more and more alive to its own actions, so that all its spinning and swaying in the stars' ballroom became in the end perfectly deliberate and calculated. It might well grow up to be a brilliant mathematician and astronomer."

When a man gets rhetorical, I get cautious. "Where would it find the instruments?" I asked.

"It would grow them. That's the usual way, after all. If it were as fitted to its heavenly environment as we are to the earthly, it would develop huge eyes capable of seeing much further into space than you and I can, and sense organs we lack altogether. It would be sensitive to many radiations we never feel, though they rain on us from the sky all the while. In every way such a creature would be well placed to live a superhuman life… I think your celestial cabbage is beginning to look more like an angel."

"A pot-bellied and wingless one. It would be more like a…"

"Well?" he prompted, slyly.

"A planet," I admitted, with reluctance. The truth was that I had glimpsed King Charles' Head. For the first time there was a pause in the conversation.

"Of course this is all nonsense," I said, like a fool, instead of shutting up there and then. "It's clear there aren't any of these monsters about, and the biggest creature you or I are likely to see is the whale at South Kensington."

The sky was already dark, and a few stars had come out. "Suppose there were one out there now," he said, pointing to the window at my side. "How would you tell it? From its looks and behaviour?"

"No," I said firmly. "We've agreed it would have to act as if it were a planet—like Venus there. You couldn't recognize it at all from this distance, but would have to get quite close to find out that it wasn't a planet after all, but a living thing. And since that's out of the question, we might as well drop the subject."

But he was relentless. "There are other ways, you know. You might listen to it—I mean listen *in* to it. If you could hear it on your radio, singing to itself, chatting away about itself and its companions, or even telling the universe that it was dead and a fiction, then you would be sure it was neither."

To this new fancy I declined to reply. There was a long silence— if you can call the roar of six engines silence. I began to scheme ways of escape. Hanging from the seat in front of us was a pair of radio head-phones, provided for passengers in need of extraneous entertainment. I think he saw my glance, even if he didn't guess my little plan. Anyhow his hand was on the instrument before mine.

When he had listened for a few moments, he handed it to me. "Do you know what that music is?" he said.

I held the thing to my ear. "No," I replied. Put off by this sudden change of topics—or of tactics—I feebly handed the head-phones back to him. He replaced them.

"*Das Lied von der Erde,*" he said.

Now music is one of my weaker subjects, but I was sure that the few bars I had heard were *not* from Mahler's Earth-song. I thought it safer not to argue, however.

He went on: "You can't trust your ears, perhaps, and you decide to take a closer look at this musical and talkative sphere. What do you find? As you approach, you lose sight of the whole, and see instead a part of the surface anatomy, the patterned skin, circulatory systems, great complexes of organs for using solar energy, vital rhythms...

Nearer still, even this physique goes, and you are left with the separate components—some alive and others dead, some mobile and others fixed, some intelligent and others stupid. Among the intelligent ones you may find a handful who see their life and intelligence as no private possession, but fragments of a greater. As for the others, it will be no use appealing either to their reason or their imagination: because of course if you look at anything closely enough it is abolished; and they live, not on top of but inside the creature whose organs they are. Their minds are wingless."

King Charles' Head was now quite unveiled. The man was no longer talking with me, but at me: his whole manner had changed. My boredom and his zeal kept pace. Fortunately there was no need to look for another red herring to draw across his trail: we were banking and about to come down. I pointed out to him the delicate tracery of city lights framed by the window, like a bedewed and sparkling spider's web on the other side of the pane. As we descended I could make out the moving lights of the traffic, the flux of the main thoroughfares, the continuous glow at the city's heart. And presently this too had gone, and we were racing along the runway. In the cosy bar of the airport I reflected, over a long drink, how comfortable it was to get down to earth again, in mind and body.

But I was not to escape the clouds so easily. He started again almost as soon as we were back in the plane and off the ground.

"Look here," I protested, making no effort to hide my annoyance, "you talk as though this monster were possible. It is more absurd than an archangel. To mention only one objection—nothing half so big could take off from this or any other planet."

"It could take off from the sun."

Patiently I pointed out that no living thing could survive in that furnace. But there is no arguing with such people. His reply was: "Of course it is dead when it leaves the sun, but gradually, over millions of years, it comes to life and mind. After all, wasn't earth herself just a tongue of fire when she broke loose from the sun? And look at her now." He pointed to the dwindling web of lights.

I gave up. He went on and on, of course. Because I refused to encourage him by raising any more objections, he must needs raise them for me—objections on the score of free will, political expediency, the Christian religion, our separate selfhood, teleology, time, and common sense—and then (as he thought) knock them down. In the end I shut him up by closing my eyes and pretending to snore. The last thing I remember him saying was that his views were, after all, traditional as well as reasonable and that I would find them in the poets...

We were due to make another call that night, and when I woke he had gone. But not without leaving a souvenir. On his seat I found a crumpled envelope, and on the back of it scribbled in pencil, with many corrections, these words:—

Is she a garden of flowers, or their Seed?

Is she the body of her limbs, or their dance floor and then their mortuary slab?

Is she blind, and the eyes that look out of her at the stars not a star's, but the parasites of a star?

As I See It

If she is a man-infested stone, man is a cell-infested skeleton.

*If his thoughts of her are not hers, neither are they his but his brains',
and neither are they his brains' but their particles'.*

*Man is no brain-cell, but he is not therefore witless; her face is no
woman's but she is not therefore a clod.*

*Where you are settles what you are: to live in the heavens you need
a heavenly body; to live in a heavenly body you need an animal body;
to live in an animal body you need a cellular body—and you live in
them all.*

Our geology is geocide.

The science of life that ignores her life is the science of death.

The original envelope is in the keeping of a psychiatrist friend
of mine.

* * *

Chapter 6

GROUNDS FOR HOPE

We are in trouble, of course. We always have been, and probably always shall be: it is the human condition. But just now, the prospect looks particularly black. Our many present-day reasons for despair don't need listing or underlining: they're painfully obvious.

Not so the equally valid—I believe, more valid—reasons for optimism. This is a pity, because the least hopeful aspect of our present state is perhaps our lack of hope; for anxiety creates situations which create more anxiety, and so the vicious circle revolves. Here I want to show that this gloom of ours is not altogether justified.

Reacting against Victorian faith in Progress, we have come almost to equate pessimism and realism, and to suppose that facing the facts is always facing the worst and never the best. This is because we look only at the surface facts. We appraise superficially, at one level—the merely human—and take all the others for granted.

First and most of all, we take for granted that altogether preponderant item on the credit side of the cosmic balance sheet— the achievement of Being, the fact that *something* has actually come to pass. Incredibly unobservant, we overlook the supreme and perpetual miracle which reduces all other miracles to child's-play—namely, the existence of anything to look at and of anybody to look at it, the amazing fact that there is not just nothing. It is really incredible; yet this tallest of tall stories happens also to be true. Most unnaturally and absurdly, there is an Occurrence, and we are (at least) part of it. Here's an unlikely thing, an irregularity, an insult to common sense, and marvel enough for many lifetimes! Let us then begin by enjoying—or at any rate acknowledging—the wonderful That, before we too hurriedly take it to task for being What it is. The impossible has already happened and is happening all the while, and the immense superstructure of the world and ourselves is balanced upon that pinpoint. After such a start, and such a sustained performance, who dare call anything impossible? It would be odd if, with existence to its credit, the existent were at any time without further promise.

And when, turning from the That to the What, we examine what has occurred, we can scarcely complain either of its poverty or its dullness. If the first surprise is that anything exists, the second is that so much of it exists, and is so unspeakably lavish and elaborate. We may like neither the world nor ourselves, but let us give credit where it is due, and confess that the universe is built on the grand scale, making all our adjectives tremendous, profound, fantastic, awe-inspiring—sound quite inept. There are millions of millions of suns, and probably millions of inhabited Earths, some of them no doubt far more advanced than our own. This planet alone carries many millions of species and countless individual organisms, each enclosing an immense world.

This human body—to go no further afield—is itself a kingdom whose billions of living citizens (we call them cells) are busy leading their own varied lives; and each is in turn a kingdom of particles, and a kingdom of kingdoms of particles. To be this island universe called "a man" is not something we understand or supervise, though we often talk as if we do; it is not something to be sniffed at, or of less importance and interest than anything one is likely to hear on the six-o'clock news. It is even something to be thankful for. No doubt this organism is imperfect; but the wonder is not that occasionally something goes wrong, but that anything ever goes right, or goes at all. We have eyes only for the surface disturbance, for the ripple and glint on the ocean, and the unfathomable depths and heights might as well not be there. An idiot, a madman—yes, even his rotting corpse— is still an infinite nest of miracles, and the miracles are sustained. The universe shows no sign of flagging. Why take all this for granted? After all, it's quite "unnatural" to wake up every morning to a world, a universe bravely carrying on: the "natural" thing would be for it to have given up the effort long ago, or rather, never to have started. Does it have to be? If so, kindly explain why! Only the exceptionally mean-minded can avoid exclaiming: well done!

We are like a man who, having been left undisputed millions plus a doubtful ten, spends the rest of his life miserably in frenzied lawsuits over the ten. If we had once been granted the sight of a rose or the stars, if for an hour of one spring morning we had been happily in love, if we had overheard one plainchant ending—that would be immeasurably more than we have any right to expect. Do we *deserve* to be human? Have we somehow *earned* the universe? If we hold the title deeds to such property, let us produce them. Indeed it's time we took the advice (not half as trite as it sounds) of the old hymn, and began to count our blessings. It wouldn't be long before we lost count.

As I See It

Very unreasonably, we aren't a bit interested in the innumerable blessings we enjoy already, but only in the one or two we are in the process of gaining or losing. However much we have, the slightest loss is agony, and the slightest gain our only joy. And nowadays we have little hope of real gain. Advance in one respect involves retrogression in another. The more intelligent and observant we are, the less we believe in real Progress. No wonder we aren't happy.

You, who look around desperately for any sign of amelioration, however slight: look in your mirror, and then think of yourself twenty, forty, sixty years ago, as a youth, child, baby, foetus, embryo, ovum. Aren't you a Success? You began your career as the inferior of your dog and your cat, of the fly on the window, of most of the animalcules you can see with your microscope swimming around in a drop of pond-water: and look at you now! Each of us started life as a jelly-speck, as a beast beside which a mouse is a god in glory; and now it is we who are gods in glory beside the mouse. If this isn't Progress (and Progress safely in the bag, too) then what is? If such a past holds no promise for the future, by all means let us hear of one that would.

What we call the facts of life are not facts at all for us, but the emptiest of theories. We cannot face what we have been. Nor do we have to: it's conveniently tucked out of sight. But if, like crabs or butterflies or fish and so many other creatures, we happened to grow up as comparatively big larvae outside our mothers instead of little embryos inside them, we shouldn't now so easily pretend we've been human all our lives. It's only a kind of biological accident which enables us to avoid noticing that our real offspring are so lowly, and

36

that our children are wormlike and fishlike and apelike before ever they are manlike. If as amateur fish they had preferred the public ocean (or aquarium, or laboratory bottle) to the private sea of the womb, if as amateur apes they had made their nests in trees instead of in women, we should perhaps be prouder of them. Surrounded by our own history in the shape of our beast-children, it would surely dawn upon us that the dullest in his own lifetime piles success upon success and pulls off immense victories. And, made to live with such a past, we might naturally entertain the brightest hopes for a future to match it. In any case, it is a tragically huge joke that any man—who manifestly is the world's wonder, the success story incarnate, the great show-piece of progress—should ever come to deny all progress and lose all hope.

Repressing the depths from which we have come, we repress also the heights to which we may go, and cut off our future along with our past. And our excuse is much the same. The higher levels are as invisible as the lower. We meet (and it's a pity) neither gilled and tailed embryos nor winged angels in the street. They are there, all right, but concealed, interior. For just as the humanity we mix with is hiddenly invaded by animal life of all evolutionary stages, so also it is hiddenly invaded by godly life of all degrees of excellence. There are those amongst us who reach planes as far above man as fertilized ova are below him—men who, without ceasing to be men, take all creatures to their heart, and by love and understanding are transformed. They are not little men; they are truly great, great-hearted. These magnanimous ones are as extensive as the world they are at one with; they are capacious of the universe, while outwardly the minutest fragments of it. The contemporary saint is the promise of our future as the contemporary foetus is the register of our past. In fact, there is nothing in our total history which is not to be found summed up in our total present—the Now which is nothing if not a web of anachronisms. We don't advance by turning our back on the past and forging ahead into the future, but rather by exploring the altitudes of the Now which contains every Then.

Our prospects really are black so long as we take them to be merely prospective. Well may we despair of horizontal man, that monstrous abstraction which denies its animal antecedents and divine destiny. But of vertical man, in whom is presented at this very moment every level from particle to Whole, and all history, there is more than a lively hope. There is realization here and now.

These are comforting reflections, no doubt; but supposing the lot of us, embryos and men and saints as well, were blown sky-high tomorrow, what good would they do us? So long as that mushroom shaped fate hangs over us, what real hope is there?

There is every hope still. For, firstly, each has to die sooner or later, and sooner and together couldn't be much worse than later and alone. Secondly, life always has been, and presumably always will be, more or less nasty and precarious, now from one menacing cause and now from another; but it goes on in spite of—and even, because of—this essential insecurity. Indeed, it may take the worst situation to bring out the best in us, and prevent stagnation; after all, some of the finest moments of history have been responses to desperate circumstances.

Of course we should like heroism without danger, good men without wicked ones, intelligence without stupidity, light without darkness; but this is asking for the impossible. And thirdly, even if our planet should go quite mad and destroy herself, she will only be anticipating by a few hundred million years her inevitable doom. And meantime, no doubt, life will continue upon countless other planets—insecure everywhere, often shifting ground and playing hide-and-seek with itself, but still carrying on with undiminished creativity and zest, interminably.

But all this is rather by the way, and may well sound less like hope than resignation. The real grounds for hope are quite different. They require us to face the grim facts, not glossing over a single one. We really are in trouble. It is a desperately dangerous thing to be human—fortunately. For if we, along with all the visible things of our life, were perfect and everlasting and happy, or even moderately satisfactory, then we should never need to penetrate to their invisible Source within ourselves, to that indwelling infinite Self which, in contrast to our outer and finite selves, is perfect, changeless, undying, and blissful. If it were quite safe to be a man, we should never be driven to find out what else we are. Everything perishes but God, and we shall go on perishing till we find our life in Him. The sooner we do that, and give up hope in everything else, the better for us and for the world.

For those of us who cannot bring ourselves to believe in Him, or in any underlying Reality or Source or Essence, the outlook is necessarily bleak indeed. Yet in this, too, there is hope. It is the very hopelessness of the situation, of this condemned cell where our Executioner stands over us night and day, which sooner or later will drive us to Him. We aren't going to be comfortable, or let alone with our false hopes: this phenomenal world will never work out. Despair of the imitation will in the end force us to the true. We should indeed have reason for despair if it were otherwise, and Paradise could be built upon Earth, so rendering Heaven superfluous. It is the hopelessness of all things short of our one Hope which ensures that we shall find it.

Meantime, we may refuse to learn by experience, and hope against hope that things will not turn out so badly, after all. Perhaps we can put off the evil day for some time yet. But in the end we shall be made to see that all hopes are false that aren't centered in unchanging Reality. That is the message of every great saint and sage, and of every great religion. It is the ultimate pessimism—and the ultimate optimism. It is the secret of peace and lasting joy.

To this, a footnote may be added. The source of most of our current miseries is our attempt to cure them at their own level alone. We let Hell loose on Earth by trying to *build* Heaven here, where it can never be, instead of *finding* it where it always is, within ourselves. If we gave up this futile endeavour, sought our real Heaven and expected little of our Earth, we should stand a good chance of having some pleasant surprises. This world is at its best when it is seen as no end in itself, but a mere by-product of Heaven.

* * *

Chapter 7

THE PROGRESS OF IGNORANCE

Nowadays we are fond of telling ourselves that we are naughty children who know more than is good for us, that our information has raced disastrously ahead of our morals. Thus we are able, while pointing self-accusingly with one hand, to give ourselves small (but slightly reassuring) pats on the back with the other. "No doubt our parents lived more sensibly," we seem to say, "but then they were so ignorant; at least we lack their illusions, and face the world and human nature as they really are. Wicked we may be, but not stupid."

And in one sense, of course, this is as true as it is trite. But in another and deeper sense it is the very opposite of the truth. Our troubles are not due to excess but defect of knowledge, to our growing ignorance of the universe. The progress of what we are pleased to call science has become the regress of Science (if that word is to keep anything like its original meaning) and we know less and less than is good for us. For a millennium our universe has been sinking—not steadily, but with many ups and downs, and many brave attempts at rescue—towards the unlit ocean-floor of absolute meaninglessness. And we have gone down too, for plainly we must share its fate.

Let us admit how proper and natural it is that science should take the world to pieces to find out what makes it go. Unfortunately, however, it is equally natural that in so doing science should *lose* what makes it go, and should be left in the end with nothing but 'go', with raw energy. This way of seeking the reason for and in events is, as a matter of fact, the graduated denial of their reason, and their reduction to sub-brute force. Yet our immense systematic effort thus to make nonsense of the universe is the indispensable counterpart of any wounds on himself. The subject cannot surpass the object, or thrive at its expense. While Heaven lay about man, he was Heaven's child; now it lies only within, he is worse than orphaned. So long as he ranked a little lower than the angels, he was crowned with glory and honour; now that he ranks himself several stages higher—since he contains them all—both he and they are much more like devils. Their descent into him is their Fall.

The fact is that, having let go of the suprahuman, we cannot hang on even to the human. No macrocosm, no microcosm. Man recognizes no superior, and therefore is inferior. He is no longer man, but only a clever mammal; and the mammal is reducible to cells which are the most elementary of creatures, and the cells to particles which are so elementary that to call them 'particles' is to flatter them. And the self succumbs with its body. The greedy psyche, having sucked in all the gods and the goods it used to live amongst, finds them quite indigestible if not actually poisonous, and itself emptier and hungrier than ever. Here is what must be the oddest of all fictions—one written, and then written off, by itself—a ghost self-invoked, self-haunted, and self-exorcized. In short, our undoing of matter and of mind keep pace; and both, in seeking what is absolutely basic, seek absolute vacuity.

Of course there were the best of reasons for this fatal descent into the void on which the world is built. Before the rise of experimental science, thinkers had worn out their ingenuity in the effort to construct an adequate world-habitation for man. It was only after their very limited range of materials had been tried out in every combination that the architects called a halt to building, and began the serious study and collection of building materials. That work has been wonderfully successful. But it has also been a deplorable failure, because we have so fallen in love with our mounting stockpiles that their purpose—house building—has long been forgotten.

Worse than this, we find ourselves sitting on an exploding ammunition dump, instead of quietly at home. We have gathered a prodigious supply of building materials for a world, but all the while they have been growing less and less inert, till they are now unbuilding materials. The finer we mill them the more combustible they become: the portland cement of the universe not only refuses to set, but dries out as gunpowder. What should have held the bricks together drives them apart with subatomic force. In other words, as synthesis without sufficient analysis led to the sterility of the Schools, so analysis without sufficient synthesis has led to the virulence of the Laboratories; and the second of these is lethal. The further we take the machine down the more likely it is to blow up. Indeed the universe cannot be recommended as a safe toy: it hits back. Not surprisingly, the more violence we offer it the more we find, till nothing else is left. The working parts have no safety valve but the whole, which is the first thing we strip. For the bonds of matter are not to be found at the level of matter, at the base of-the hierarchy where nothing is left intact: they exist only at the higher levels, which alone are the unity of the lower. A man is the peace, the reconciliation of his warring organs and cells, just as the cell is total shape and agreement of its molecules and atoms, and the atom of its particles. In fact it is not till we reach the Whole, the apex of the hierarchy, the One who is the pacification of the Many, that the universe hangs together, and there is a universe at all instead of a multiverse.

Our acosmism is, to be sure, no mistake. The universe really is a myth so long as we break up its time and its space. What we find in it is a question of the room and the opportunity we allow it: without the chance to prove itself, it can do nothing and be nothing. Cut up a man's space into the comminuted space of his particles, and nothing human —indeed nothing alive, or even solid—is left; cut up his time, and you cut up his space also, and the result is the same. For all space takes time, and human space takes human time. At this instant, and at every other instant, there is just nothing, not even an electron or room for one. An atom is not the work of a moment; still less is a molecule or a cell. When you divide our own history into separate years, days, hours, minutes, its achievements progressively vanish. The slower effects, the structures that take centuries to build, the large shapes—all that is valuable goes, and the tale is only of the destruction which takes almost no time, of sudden catastrophe, of violent death. What is worth while invariably takes a long while. On the other hand, when deprived of its time-span, the solidest object melts into moving bodies which show by their agitation that they are not all there; and they in turn melt away into mere forces—

into the motions which are the left-overs, the merest coprolites of a universe. All history is indeed shapeless, sordid, violent, if you judge it piecemeal. If you take it as "one damned thing after another" that is precisely how you will find it. But if you take it as one damned thing *with* another, as all damned things together in their proper places and relations, then they are no longer damned; and the whole of it may well be called blessed.

In our modern Hell we all suffer from short sight. This is a Dark Age in which visibility is almost nil, and the very near view is the only view: in fact it becomes more and more the hallmark of intellectual respectability to attach meaning to less and less. We have de-verified all but the smallest and briefest and inanest things. But stand back, give Hell's furious particles the room and the time to show what they can do with their fury, and there is a chance you will one day find yourself in Heaven. Conversely, if you go on taking Heaven's completed order apart, you will surely land in Hell, where the only reminder and remainder of what you have destroyed is your own frenzy and your companions'. Hell is Heaven's amplitude undone, the divine pattern unpicked, the still waters dissolved into their Brownian Movements. Here everyone is in a devil of a hurry, knocked about like Paolo and Francesca by cruel and never-resting winds, always getting around but never getting around to anything. In other words, Hell is wilful (but admirably 'progressive' and 'scientific') ignorance of itself. If we could look past ourselves to its whole expanse, instead of examining on strict positivist principles only what lies beneath our noses, we should in fact be enjoying the long vistas of Heaven. Hell is a very snug and exclusive rendezvous, where the nicest distinctions are made. Heaven includes Hell, while Hell is so small it ends by excluding even itself. For, in the last of its innumerable analyses, at the lowest point and infernal fundament, it is self-eliminating; it reduces to nothing at all, to the lie which finally gives the lie to the liar, and the fraction which cancels out. And this is the true ground of optimism.

* * *

Chapter 8

THE THINKING IN US

It is a consoling reflection that whereas what we *do* is increasingly other people's business, what we *think* remains our own. We feel assured that we can still—thank Heaven!—keep our thoughts to ourselves, and others' thoughts from ourselves. You can't find out what I'm thinking unless I choose to tell you; there's no risk of your waking tomorrow to find your memories of today gone, and mine in their place. However involved we may become in our exterior and public life, we can still lead private inner lives which (so far, at any rate) are better hidden than our most intimate bodily functions.

There is, of course, much truth and precious truth in this. But in some ways it is the very reverse of the facts. The evidence for telepathy and clairvoyance and mediumship, for mental invasions and involvements of all kinds, can no longer be explained away; and it forbids us to go on speaking, without qualification, of distinct and atom-like minds. And if we are still unconvinced, there is the witness of common speech and experience—we think and act for one another; we sympathize; we put ourselves in each other's shoes; we have fellow feeling; we see in the chief figures of history not merely individual men, but the agents and spokesmen of their time. Whatever theories we profess, it is difficult to escape the conviction that behind and somehow continuous with the great statesman is his nation, that the true prophet does not vainly claim to be the

47

vessel of still more august powers, that the inspired artist really is used (often at huge cost to the man) by something vastly more than his private personality. Who, indeed, bothers to listen to one who speaks (or, more likely, pretends to speak) for himself alone? Man's traditional estimate of himself is that he is and yet is not one man alone, but the organ or representative of many men, and of all men, and of quite other orders of being. His vehicle is the seat of endlessly diverse drivers; he is the channel of strange waters rising in unknown countries, an edged tool in the hands of cosmic artificers. In short, he is liable to possession—both by what is above and what is below, by good and evil powers, by the divine and the demonic. "Not I," says St Paul, "but Christ liveth in me." He speaks with the voice of suprahuman authority; therefore we listen.

Many of us write off half this sort of thing as superstition and the other half as metaphor. It is less easy, however, to account for our experience of what it is to grow up to full manhood, acquiring the mental and moral capacity that is expected of us. What is this growth but learning to take up others' points of view, while allowing to our own no more than its very humble due? For instance, looking out of my window now, I see a creature smaller than this pen, one-armed and one-eyed, making his way slowly along a threadlike pavement. Yet—so thoroughly do I discount this private view in favour of his and all men's—he is for me five-feet-ten, even when he has dwindled to a point in the distance; he is always two-armed and two-eyed no matter how, by turning this way and that, he is deformed; and everywhere he treads, at ordinary walking pace, ample pavements.

I see the world through his eyes more than my own, and through all men's eyes more than his. Born with binocular vision, I am not human till I have grown more eyes than I shall ever see. Every man is Argus, surnamed Panoptes.

Again, when I write this I mean it to be true, and by true I mean as true for you as for me, and as true for non-human observers as for human. To use language at all is to speak for all reasonable beings everywhere and at all times, to be their mouthpiece. And when I approve or condemn your conduct, I do so whether I (and my family, and even my nation and my species) stand to gain or lose by it. From the very start our judgments of what is true and good and beautiful claim to hold universally, and our education is the graduated staking out and substantiation of this claim. We learn to see our partial and temporary selves from the standpoint of Humanity as a whole, our specialized Humanity from the general standpoint of Earth's creatures (which are her organs), our eccentric Earth from the more central standpoint of the Sun, our moving Sun from the more stable standpoint of the Galaxy. Such is the natural history of the mind that is in us. The more we think the less we think of and for ourselves alone; the more we know the less it is simply human knowledge of human things; the more of the world's problems and joys and sufferings we take on ourselves the less we take them on as mere men. Who looks depends on how far he looks. Who it is that thinks, knows, feels, wills, depends on what is thought, known, felt, willed. The subject cannot be capacious of the object without being, in a certain sense, raised to its rank.

Nor is there any duplication here. If we take a Sun's-eye-view of our terrestrial motion, then that view exists, and we may not go on speaking of a mindless Sun. For as a man has no barriers against my feeling for him, no door to shut me out, so also the Sun has no means of killing the life we come to live in it, no defences against invading mind: it is occupied territory. We really become as much and as little of the world as we happen to be thinking and feeling for. Man is one phase of an infinitely elastic organism.

In a hundred ways we admit as much. Who or what (to take the nearest example) is writing this paragraph? A man, certainly. But also the Humanity that uses him, for no one man can claim the thinking that goes on in him. On the other hand I learn that it is really my brain that is now thinking, or rather my brain cells; and that in the last resort these reflections are a function of my electrons and protons. It is they that are now composing and recording this account of their performance. Now the truth is that all these levels of organization—with many more above man and below him, yet all within him—are involved in everything he does. As man, he is powerless either to initiate anything or to put it into effect; for all is settled at the top of the hierarchy, worked out at the intermediate levels (which include the human), and done at the base.

The saints desire to be to God what his hand is to a man. In fact, and in the longest run, this is a fate which none of us can escape. The hand may be clumsy, all thumbs, palsied, but eventually it does what is wanted of it. Nevertheless it is no machine. We are free, within limits, to leave our mark on all that is done through us. More than this, we are free to realize what is done through us, and who does it. But the hand that knows it is a mere hand is no longer a mere hand; the organ that is alive to its subordination to the whole body is alive to the whole body, and alive in the whole body. Thus to be free and effectual, a man must know that, alone, he is neither; that any work done through him (in so far as it does not cancel out) is God's work; that he must submit to the rule of the transcendent divine before he can enshrine its immanent freedom. To the extent that these words are worth reading, they are not written merely by this pen-nib or this pen, by this hand or arm or man, by this species or some still greater instrument, but by the Author who stands over all these, and in whose hand they lie. Nor have the words meaning, except in the Whole Story. When we concentrate upon them and ignore it, when we have eyes only for the calligraphy, for the grain of the paper and the colour of the ink, such is our world and such is our status in it: we are only writing materials. But when we begin to read we begin to share the life of the Writer for whom alone the completed tale exists.

* * *

Chapter 9

HEAVENS ABOVE

Enlightened Christians recognize two Heavens: one of them good, the other... well... indifferent. Holy saints and angels inhabit the first, entirely secular planets and stars the second; and between them there is no bridge. The Heavens of the theologian and of the astronomer lie so far apart that neither throws the least light upon the other, and even their languages are different. There is no chance at all of the Archbishop of Canterbury and the Astronomer Royal putting their heads together to draw a composite picture of Heaven.

Or rather—to *re*draw it. For their Heavens were not always so incongruous. There was a time in the history of our race, and perhaps in our own individual history also, when there existed for us only one Heaven—a Heaven which was (so to speak) at once astronomical and theological. Certainly when I was a child I believed that the angels shared the sky with the stars, diving and soaring overhead like religious birds of paradise in God's aviary. And of course I took the gospel story of the Ascension quite literally. If Heaven lay about me in my infancy, then its general direction was upwards. But I was soon made aware of my childish mistake, and warned that, though the Heavens may declare the mathematics of God, for His glory I must look elsewhere. I was more likely—so it seemed—to find traces of divinity among my neighbours in the street than among my more luminous neighbours in the sky. And now Heaven's angels are displaced persons; indeed they have been evacuated and hounded out of space altogether. It is even considered much to their credit that they have no room or home of their own, however temporary, in the physical world. We don't doubt that when Dante populated the spheres of the moon and planets and stars with the blessed, he was writing poetic nonsense. So was Shakespeare, in those magical lines about the orbs "still quiring to the young-ey'd cherubims". So, again, were Plato and Plotinus and the other ancients who in rapturous language described the stars as immortal and happy gods, and their motion as the grand dance or procession of the universe. So was the author of the *Book of Job*, when he said that "the morning stars sang together, and the sons of the gods shouted for joy".

All such ecstatic talk about the Heavens above we now know to be nothing but beautiful white lies, so patently false that nobody bothers to expose them. The founders of our civilization thought they lived in a world which grew more and more lively and intelligent and divine as you worked outwards from man and earth at the centre; and now we, their heirs, are sure that the world is arranged the other way round. Modern man has not only turned his garment the universe inside out, but is convinced that this is the only way to wear it.

I think he is wrong. It's true, of course, that science has bartered many outworn fancies about the universe for shiny brand-new facts, and that cheerfully undisciplined guesswork has given place to cautious observation of detail. And of course this is admirable— so far as it goes. But it doesn't go half far enough, and certainly not as far as a total picture which makes sense. When we look up at the stars and see nothing but so many tons of superheated material, or something like a badly organized fireworks display in slow motion, we are no nearer the truth than our ancestors who looked up into bright Heaven itself, into the dear country they came from and hoped to go back to. Indeed I believe that, on the whole, it is not they but ourselves who are wrong. I believe that the ancient vision of a tremendously living universe is not only noble but substantially true, and that science has actually done more to confirm and complete it than to destroy it. In the rest of this talk I want to give some of my reasons for holding these beliefs, or (if you prefer to put it that way) for being so dreadfully out of date.

Let me begin by very briefly recalling the story of man's idea of the universe. It happens to be a murder story, with an exciting *dénouement*—a thriller so long and complicated that I can summarize only a little of it now. Our part of the tale starts with a universe that was very much alive—indeed alarmingly so. Clement of Alexandria and Origen (two of the greatest early Fathers of the Church) saw the sun and stars as living and intelligent creatures capable of sin, patrolling the skies of their own free will, and governing natural processes here below. And now for us, eighteen centuries later, they are not merely stone-dead and buried in the unconsecrated ground of the space-time continuum, but decayed almost beyond recognition.

How have we managed to do away with them so effectively?

Now it's obvious you can't dispatch heavenly bodies as quickly and easily as earthly ones. You have to attack them, not with physical weapons, but with the sword of the intellect, and first you have to sever your victim's mind from his body. The star then ceases to be a god, and is degraded to a thing—the plaything of a spirit. Heaven above becomes an angelic ball-game, the magnificent prototype (you might almost say) of all our earthly ball-games. Once an indivisible body-mind, the star is now a mindless body steered by a bodiless mind, a corpse goaded into action by a ghost, a celestial zombi. The mediaeval universe is not so much alive as haunted.

You might think that this would content the killer in our story. But in fact his lethal work is only begun. His attack is now two-pronged—aimed at the stellar corpse, and equally at the ghost which agitates it.

Let's begin with the ghost. It is first an angel, a pure spirit capable of taking up a definite position in space, and even of assuming, temporarily, the appearance of a body. Then science moves in to the attack, and what was a godlike ruler of Nature is reduced to so many rules of Nature, to physical laws, forces, tendencies. And finally, in our own time, even these angelic remains are got rid of, and compulsive laws and forces and tendencies go the way of their more majestic originals. The stars are no longer guided in their courses. They merely take the path of least resistance. The ball-game plays itself.

While we have thus been laying the ghost of our heavenly victim, we have been busy getting rid of the body—again, by the well-tried method of chopping it up. That is to say, by analysis. We take each of the star's attributes—such as its beauty and its twinkling and its brightness and its colour —cut them off piecemeal, and remove them as far as possible. We bring them down to earth, to ourselves here. In fact we deny that they ever really belonged to the star at all. Even its apparent motion is now ours.

Nor is it enough for us that the deceased is now stripped of every sensible quality, a bare lump of matter, unrecognizable and indeed inscrutable. This too—the very stuff of the stars—must go. The corpse is now, we are told, mere empty space sparsely dotted with particles, and not even the particles may be thought of as solid or material. If anything at all is there to correspond with our formulas, nobody can say what it is.

Surely this is a plot which for thoroughness far outdoes all the trunk murders and acid-bath murders of our own century's fact and fiction. And the villain's skill is matched by the detective's dullness. So far from unmasking the criminal, we have scarcely detected the crime.

Nevertheless murder—however brilliantly committed—will out: and indeed it would be strange if the death of a universe could be hushed up indefinitely. Our story moves to an astonishing climax. The victim turns up, and turns up in the least likely place of all— inside the killer himself!

No function or quality torn from the universe is lost: we have taken them all upon ourselves. The solidity and brilliance and colour, the astronomical science, the beauty, the divinity—everything we once found in the sky above our heads we now find in them. Like the savage warrior who eats the heart of his enemy in the hopes of acquiring his strength, we have absorbed our victim. It is as if we had fed upon the gods. No wonder we have mental indigestion.

The remedy is to conclude our crime story, at once learning and enacting its happy ending.

As I See It

We have now to see that, in fact, what seemed to be a murder tale is nothing of the sort. The victim not only turns up, but turns up alive and well. For when we slowly pulled the living universe apart, taking upon ourselves one by one its attributes, we were not taking them out of the universe. We were only shifting them from one part of the universe to another. Man the executioner is an organ of the world he executes; therefore he is not really an executioner. Though he has drawn all the life and meaning of the surrounding universe into his own head, his head (however swelled) still lies within the universe (however depleted), and is in fact his chief and most reliable sample of what that universe is really like. The most he could do towards proving the world dead would be to commit suicide at once, by severing any one of the innumerable arteries which unite him to the world and feed his life. After all, he has not been parachuted here from Limbo. He is not a parasite which the universe has somehow picked up, nor a visitor who has somehow dropped in. He is much more like a bud on the tree of the universe. And when in spring the sap rises and the bud bursts, the tree is not dying. It is indeed a silly leaf that calls the branch dead—because it isn't a leaf!

Take for instance our own heavenly body, the sun—by which I mean this developed star that we call the solar system. Don't we figure in that development? Is the intelligence in the sun an anomaly, a mere by-product of its real industry, which is energy-production? The trouble is that we are *determined* to prove our star dead, and to hug all its life and intelligence to ourselves. And so, of course, no evidence whatever of vitality (such as myself speaking here, and you listening

58

there, and the BBC which brings us together) can be evidence of the sun's vitality, but only of its infestation. None of the life *in* the sun can ever be the life *of* the sun—because we have settled the question in advance, by including lifelessness in our definition of the sun. It is the easiest trick in the world to prove the most lively creature dead, if as soon as it puts forth a limb we mentally amputate it, on the principle that it is unlike the trunk and therefore cannot belong to it. When we take a collection of the sun's particles as they were, say, a million million years ago, they are our clue to what the sun is like; but when we take those same particles now, after they have at last—by virtue of inconceivably intricate processes become organized into ourselves talking about those processes—why then they are our clue to what the sun is *not* like! Again, sunshine and sunspots are solar, but—by some miracle—sunbirds and sunflowers and sun-myths and sun-poems aren't solar! To detach any part or function from this star of ours it is enough to show that it is alive. Thus do we insist on remaining millions of years behind the solar times.

What nonsense this is! We have sucked in, not only from our sun, but from the whole universe, everything worth while, and the result is quite absurd. The only sensible thing to do is to put it back again—by putting ourselves back again. We have to redistribute the intelligence and vitality that we fondly suppose are concentrated in us. We have to open up. We have to see ourselves as channels of life rather than its reservoir.

And not the only channels either. Scientists are starting to talk about millions of solar systems, many of them no doubt with planets very much like our own earth. And we are told that wherever the conditions of life ripen, there life itself will follow. In short, contemporary scientific theories tend to suggest that the universe is the home of abundant life. And it would be strange if none of that life were so far ahead of ours as to merit the name of angelic.

Moreover the chances are that, to find the higher ranks of this angelic life, we should need to look further and further afield from our earth-centre. The realm of the nine (or so) planets is plainly not such promising country as the remoter realm of the stars—the hundreds of millions of stars of our own galaxy; nor is this a millionth part so rich in celestial possibilities as the still remoter realm of the galaxies, with their unthinkably great star-population. In fact we now have some excellent reasons for looking up to the stars, instead of merely looking up *at* them and looking down on them. And some excellent reasons for once more matching physical height to spiritual status.

And so we come back again to the start of our murder story— with the great advantage of knowing how it turns out. Again, but this time less fancifully, we can reckon upon the Heavens becoming more heavenly the further we look into them. We can know our place again, as a little lower than the angels—and angels which enliven rather than haunt the universe.

And this conclusion, however upsetting to our ingrained habits of thought, is after all rational enough. I see no reason why the bulkiest living creatures in the universe should be the Big Tree of California and the Greenland Right Whale, or why the most intelligent should be certain featherless bipeds with an I.Q. of, say, 170. Surely it is mere parochialism and meanness of imagination to suppose that below us in God's hierarchy there is every grade of creature down to (and far below) the worm, while above us there is nothing at all till we get to Him, to the dazzling Crown of the hierarchy, and the Heaven which lies beyond all space and time.

Nor is the natural impiety which contemplates a dead and murdered universe necessary to the spiritual piety which contemplates its living Creator. Thinking more of God isn't thinking less of His creatures. Rather the reverse. The Heavens do not declare the parsimony of God, but of the man who thinks poorly of them. And we never need fear that our picture of His universe isn't mean enough, or that our imagination could beggar the reality.

And really it is ridiculous—even for the most earnest of materialists—to go on talking about the universe as if it were a vast slag-heap. It is the chief dogma of his faith that all he holds dear is everywhere potential in the raw stuff or energy of the universe, and only awaits the conditions in which it can reveal itself. And when he reduces all life and mind and values to functions of this stuff or energy, he doesn't get rid of them. Quite the opposite. He universalizes them. He can't reduce the divine to electrons without raising electrons to divinity—every one of them. The materialist who makes sneering remarks about the Christian's 'pie in the sky' is the very one who insists that even the dust and debris of the universe entertain angels unawares.

* * *

Chapter 10

NOTES FOR
A DEFENCE OF ANGELS

We live in an age of myths and fantasies. And one of them is that we have got rid of myths and fantasies. We imagine that it is we and not our ancestors who face the truth about the universe without flinching, that at last we are stern realists. In particular, modern man takes for granted that the professional scientist has exploded the traditional Christian universe, and that he is himself an amateur scientist who knows how the charge was placed and the fuse lit. I shall give some examples to suggest how little substance there is in these popular assumptions.

A central Earth
Consider, first, the shape of the mediæval universe, with Earth and man at the hub, and the vast angel-populous spheres of the planets and stars turning about him. We go on supposing that Copernicus and Galileo made final nonsense of this geocentric scheme, and it has still to dawn upon us that they did nothing of the kind. The principle of relativity allows us to take for our 'fixed' point of reference, for our central observation post, whatever spot we like in the universe— Earth, Sun, or any other—which point we choose being a matter of convenience. And (we are entitled to add) what could be more convenient, more proper for us, more natural and indeed inevitable

in practice, than to take our own planet for centre?

The mystery of matter
But what do we gain by reinstating Earth at the hub of the revolving universe, if that universe is merely a throw of dice without a Thrower (and almost without dice), if it is a senseless jostling of energies, and no longer magnificently alive, no longer the tiered and jewelled choir-stalls of the angels, no longer even God's starlit machine shop, but a refuse heap? The divine works have been blitzed, and we find ourselves in fragments on the bomb-site. For we are informed that science has taken everything, from the furthest and sublimest heavenly body to the nearest and dearest earthly one, and somehow reduced all to the inane to-and-fro of particles, and the particles themselves to practically nothing whatever. Religion and art, and science itself—and indeed the scientist himself—are reported to be simply the sort of thing that happens when these particles chance to arrange themselves in certain unusually intricate patterns, as sooner or later they are sure to do.

But who can take seriously the science which spends its time sawing off the branch it sits on? And if it is not, in fact, undermined by this kind of argument, neither is religion.

Besides, what is the scientist really telling us here? In effect, he says that the life and the intelligence, the science and art and religion, all the treasures of this most astonishing world, are somehow potential in its meanest dust, and only wait for the conditions in which they can show themselves. This despised and ubiquitous matter or energy is the precious seed of every flower that opens in our life. The very dirt of the universe is pregnant with gods. So far, then, from sterilizing the world of all that is worthwhile, the scientist finds the infection to be universal. He cannot deflate the openly divine to a point without leaving the point hiddenly divine. Indeed he is not very far from the needle's eye which is the gate of Heaven, and the God whose centre is everywhere and circumference nowhere.

Matter and mind

In any case, the honest physicist does not pretend to know what his particles are 'in fact' or 'in themselves'. He has eyes only for their remote effects upon his instruments. The impenetrably hard billiard-ball atom was shattered long ago; and now—for all the physicist can tell to the contrary—each of its fission-products may well be something like a mind, or a godling, or even the shrine of an omnipresent Deity.

But we try to have it all ways. We admit we know nothing about matter; then flatly contradict ourselves by denying that it can be mind travelling incognito; and then contradict ourselves again by saying that mind 'inevitably' and 'naturally' arises from it.

I am not, however, without reliable and inside information about these particles. Of one collection of them I have first-hand knowledge, for I am that collection. And I am a mind.

Other life in the universe

Another objection may be put here. What is the use of a mind— or even of a Mind—which is hiding in matter, if it is so rarely in evidence, and perhaps peeps out nowhere at all except briefly upon our quite insignificant Earth?

Again it is the scientist himself who suggests the answer. He is coming round to the view that our solar system is unlikely, after all, to be a cosmic freak and deformity, and that among the hundreds of thousands of millions of stars in our own Galaxy alone there may well be thousands or millions which are ringed with planets as our own star is ringed. And he goes on to suppose that whenever the conditions of life arise upon a planet then life will follow. One eminent physicist has remarked how odd it would be if the universe could not put up a cricket eleven capable of beating the Australians. And surely it is mere sclerosis of the imagination which prevents us from adding that it would be odder still if nowhere in the sky of galaxies and of stars is there to be found a life which, though still creaturely, is angelic and even seraphic compared with our own.

The angels and distance

And the chances are that, to find the higher ranks of this cosmic life, we should need to look further and further afield from this Earth-centre. Evidently the nine or so planets are not nearly such promising country as the teeming realm of the stars, nor this a millionth part so rich in celestial possibilities as the still remoter realm of the galaxies, whose star-population has been calculated in millions of millions of millions. And if—in spite of our human parochialism—we are not so Earth-bound that we cannot thus reach out to these super-human beings, how much more should they be able to reach out to us, to look down upon us in angelic pity and wonder and love, and indeed to sustain us in ways we can scarcely imagine. Who can tell what we do not owe them, or what disasters they are now averting? Can we be sure, indeed, that they have neither knowledge of nor hand in even such an inadequate commentary upon them as this one?

Yet it is the agnostic scientist who, in spite of himself, is pointing the way back to the concentric universe of our Christian tradition, in which remoteness is proportional to divinity; while the Christian, anxious not to seem altogether behind the scientific times, points uncertainly in the opposite direction.

The status of life in the universe

But what is the real significance of this cosmic life if— to judge by our own sample—it does not add up to more than a few sandgrains in the desert of the world? Are not organisms the least typical pieces of nature, occasional green-fly on the stars? The needle—let alone its eye—is quite lost in the cosmic haystack.

This objection really is too naive. When was mere bulk ever the measure of value, or littleness a sure sign of triviality? A diamond mine is still a diamond mine, and not a débris mine, no matter how heavily the débris outweighs the diamonds. Equally the living are more rather than less important and alive for the fact that they have—and must have—so much 'dead' material to live on. Moreover, what we live on we live in and through. For such material, when it is indispensable to life and involved in vital processes, is a true limb of the living. To live *is* to quicken the dead. It is not merely that to live we need to drag so much of outer nature into the circle of our life, but rather that the degree to which we do so is the measure of our liveliness. In fact, it may well be that the highest life of all is the one which leaves nothing inert and unregenerate, and that the deadness we find around us is only the symptom and projection of our own depravity. Angels—and may angels not be a higher form of cosmic life?—may be expected to do better.

Let me put this another way. Is it not quite arbitrary to say of any creature that he stops at his skin, and so to cut off from his individual physique all those common organs of nature and of artifice without which he could not survive for a moment? I need my Sun more than my eyes, my Earth more than my right arm, my atmosphere and house and tools and clothes more than a great deal of my flesh-and-blood organization. These are not the lifeless circumstances of my life, but its vital embodiment. And if Earth is our organ, equally we are her organs. Ours are the hands she holds up in prayer to her Maker, ours the eyes she opens to see the stars, ours her outlook upon angels and then upon no angels.

But we live under the illusion that we are mites infesting this Dutch cheese of ours or lice in Mother Earth's hair. She is alive only in the verminous sense. And of course no heavenly body can be anything more than a clod (or at best a ball-bearing in the cosmic engine) so long as we cling to our superstition that the life upon it can never be of it, that its organs are only its parasites, its intelligence mere possession. We regard ourselves as unnatural, the grand exception, gate-crashers at the cosmic party. It is as if, having killed off our angels, we try to take their place, rushing in fearlessly to fill the vacuum they have left. And the joke is that the science whose name we invoke professes to wage total war upon the supernatural!

Science and angels
Evidently this science needs watching: her sleight of hand passes so easily unnoticed. It is rarely long before the traditional truth, having been slung out at science's back-door and left for dead, is welcomed again at the front, renamed and in modern dress. Thus science is less lethal than she seems. The teachings of religion enjoy greater expectation of life than hers, because they have such a cunning way of surviving in them. By the time we have seen through our stained-glass angels, they have already taken double-flight from the church window into the skies they came from and the men they came to: and in both they escape detection. But psychologists are now talking in terms reminiscent of mediæval demonology and angelology. And even the Prince of the Power of the Air should seem to us less fabulous, now that newspaper stories of unearthly flying objects are at least as commonplace at breakfast as bacon and eggs, and now that our own science has winged those aerial legions whose behaviour has so little to learn from him.

It is a serious thing absent-mindedly to have attempted to murder a universe. Let us get out of our mental easychairs on to the stool of repentance. Or rather, let us cease falling between two stools, between two worlds—the mediaeval one which called its angels angels, and the modern one which calls them by many other names. Why make the worst of both worlds by taking neither seriously? A little science is as dangerous a thing for angels as for men. It has cost us a universe unnecessarily. In every way we should be better housed in the old-fashioned cosmos than in our half-modernized cosmos, which is neither the one thing nor the other. Not science, but popular science, is the enemy of religion.

The angels and reason

Certainly the Christian need no longer blushingly apologise for his angels, as if they were some childish habit he has not yet broken himself of. They are not pious toys left over from the nursery, or pretty fictions like Santa Claus and his reindeer. Not only are they important ingredients of the Christian revelation and the Christian tradition, but belief in something of the kind belongs to our universal human heritage. Moreover, no scientist was ever armed or able to do them real injury; and now he sometimes wonders whether he really is, after all, the most aristocratic tenant of the many mansions his telescopes have shown him. As for the theist, whether Christian or not, why in Heaven's name should he find ranged between himself and bare matter every grade of being, yet between himself and his God no being at all? This immense hiatus, this absurd gap, is surely a gap in the human imagination rather than in the order of things. And certainly it is no compliment to the Creator to suppose ourselves his finest work, or loyalty to our King to degrade all his nobility. What could be more disingenuous than to guillotine the court of Heaven, while pretending to do homage to the Throne?

Of course we must change our infant ideas of angels, distinguising between the essentials and the accidents. The holy and innumerable company of Heaven must be stripped of their wing-holed nightdresses, of their charming but equally comic wings, of their human faces and figures, of their ninefold hierarchies as tradition too-precisely imagines them, before they can become for us the vividly actual and majestic beings they once were. But this stripping is properly an unveiling, and the very reverse of fatal. Such accretions never were more than picturesque visual aids. And now that they have outlasted their usefulness, and become stumbling blocks even to children, they must go, leaving the true angelic splendour to shine forth.

Nevertheless the real trouble is not that we are too rational to believe in angels, but that we are not rational enough. God's Heaven and the astronomer's will remain poles apart, and the star-haloes of the angels will never be anything more than Sunday hats, till we begin to use and respect reason as the Seraphic and Angelic Doctors— Bonaventure and Aquinas—used and respected it.

* * *

Chapter 11

A LIVING UNIVERSE

We have heard much of the conflict between science and religion in the modern age, but little of their underlying agreement. Their common ground, their shared assumptions, remain for the most part unexplored. I suspect, however, that the future historian will find in these assumptions of ours the real clue to our time. The most significant evidence for him may well be, not the questions which agitate us, but those which we suppose were settled long ago, and not worth raking up again.

For instance, almost all of us—Christian and non-Christian, scientist and layman, materialist and anti-materialist—hold much the same opinion of the universe. Our basic cosmology (if anything so little examined, so much taken for granted, can be dignified by the name of cosmology) needs no defence, for it is never attacked. It is true, of course, that the vastly different world-views of Plato, or Plotinus, or Dante, or Shakespeare, interest and charm us; but it never occurs to us to take any of them seriously, as a possible challenge or alternative to our own. In this field, intellectual experiment and adventure are felt to be somehow improper, and certainly a waste of time.

What is this world picture that we all carry about with us? Very briefly, our universe may be described as a huge space thinly dotted with balls of very hot material, one of which (and probably many of which) are ringed with much smaller balls of cooler material. On the surface of at least one of these smaller bodies there occur still smaller lumps of matter—complex systems called organisms. These, in contrast to the rest of the universe, are said to live; and some of them are said to have 'minds'—or else they are said to behave in such a way as to give rise to that kind of talk. Such, more or less, is the natural order contemplated by theist and atheist alike; and almost the only important difference is that the one says that God made it, and the other says that it made itself, or that it happened by chance.

In this paper I shall give some of the many reasons why I cannot accept this world-view.

Of course there is a great deal of truth in it, and still more utility, but I think it leaves out so much that what remains does not make sense. Our picture of a lifeless and mindless world, in which living things hardly figure at all, in which they are (as it were) sub-microscopic anomalies, is a false picture. At least, every time I try to examine it with any care, I find that I cannot understand it, and a quite different picture emerges.

I must begin by attempting a definition. What is a living thing? I am reliably informed that it is a piece of matter in a state of ceaseless change, having interdependent parts that make up an indivisible and self-contained and self-perpetuating whole; and that this whole tends to develop from a less complex to a more complex state, to absorb alien material, to reproduce its kind, and then to perish. If we find a material system with most or all of these characteristics, then we say that it is alive.

Note that this definition says nothing about the *size* of a living creature. We take it for granted that the biggest organisms in the known universe are the whale and the Big Tree of California. But are they the biggest? That is the first question we are to consider.

Unfortunately it is not enough just to look round for some bulkier creature; for if we do not know what kind of thing we seek we shall not know it when we find it, and therefore we shall not find it. We must sketch in the main lines of the portrait before we can hope to discover its subject.

Biologists tell us that there are natural limits to the bulk of a living creature, so that if it is too big it is unlikely to survive. Now this is no doubt true of one that lives on this planet or on some other heavenly body, but it would cease to be true of one that took flight and set up as a heavenly body on its own account. Then it could be very big indeed.

Or rather, it would *need* to be very massive; otherwise it could neither conveniently carry its own atmosphere and water-supply about, nor keep a firm gravitational hold upon them. And without oxygen to breathe, and something like an atmosphere to protect it from meteor showers and dangerous quantities of radiation and undue heat and cold, it could hardly live for long in the heavens. We should look, then, for a massive creature wrapped round with a thick cloak or skin of air.

By itself, of course, this skin would not be enough to save it from death by freezing or roasting: indeed our creature would die both deaths at once unless it kept turning a new side of itself to the sun, like meat on a spit. Again, these revolutions would be useless if it were all the while falling either into the sun or away from it. The only practicable way of keeping a safe distance would be to sweep out an orbit round the sun. And both movements—the spinning and the circling—would be altogether fitting because, once begun, they would go on effortlessly: the laws of physical motion and of physiological need would here work in perfect accord, and to comply with the one would be to comply with the other. By such easy and economical obedience our hypothetical creature saves its skin.

And by saving its skin makes its skin: for we should expect it to live upon sunlight. It seems that we must look for something like a cosmic Vegetable, with the whole of its surface lapping up the solar energy, rather than for some overgrown mammal. Certainly wings— to say nothing of hooves, fins, claws, hands, feet—would in the sky be encumbrances fit only for a comic turn, and even a head would be absurdly out of place. As for the spinning torso, we should naturally look for some globular or lens-shaped thing.

The heavenly spaces are neither noisy nor scented: here a nose and ears are as anomalous as a pair of red lips, and rows of teeth, and streaming hair, and a stomach and bowels and an anus. Does our creature then live a dull life? Not necessarily. There is still vision—the most 'intellectual' of the senses. That at least would not be out of its element, because if there is a country where the views are long and fine it is the heavens. Imitating Ezekiel's wheels, this creature might well grow eyes all over its surface, and pass the time watching the dance of the stars and planets. But we have already seen that our observant Vegetable can be no wallflower of the sky: to live at all it must join in the dance. And, gifted with more-than-binocular vision, it could see all the nearer heavenly bodies in their proper places; in time, perhaps, it could learn to judge the sizes and distances and evolutions of the remotest. Might it not also fall in love with the more brilliant of its celestial companions, compose songs in their praise, name them? And even if it were at first merely brutish, yet it could gradually awake to its own behaviour, so that all its spinning and circling became in the end perfectly calculated. The skies have been our own best schoolroom and laboratory: is one that has made them its home unlikely to equal our mathematics and astronomy? To be as fitted to the celestial environment as we are to the terrestrial it would need to grow huge eyes capable of seeing much further into space than we can, and sense organs that we lack altogether. It would be sensitive to radiations we never feel, though they rain on us from the sky all the while. In many ways such a creature would be well placed for leading a superhuman life. Indeed our celestial cabbage is beginning to look much more like an angel—though a profane and pot-bellied one.

So much, then, for the kind of thing we might reasonable look for. Of course there are countless other possibilities—beings wholly unlike ourselves, independent of solar energy, with another kind of metabolism altogether, with senses and modes of thought we cannot conceive. But this is unprofitable guessing. I have been content to take the biological pattern of earthy life, and to change it only so far as heavenly circumstances seem to require.

Now evidently this living creature—if it exists—is likely to look and behave very much like a dead planet. How, in that case, could we distinguish it from one?

First, we could try listening to it. If we could hear it singing, or talking about itself and the stars, or even telling the universe that it is the lifeless satellite we took it for, then we should be sure it was nothing of the sort.

Unable to trust our ears, we decide to take a closer look at this talkative and musical sphere. We circle it in our spaceship. What may we expect to find? The view of the whole has been left far behind, and we see instead part of the patterned skin, circulatory systems, coordinating fibres, great complexes of organs for using solar energy in its many forms, vital rhythms and pulses, growth and decay... Nearer still, even this detailed physique vanishes, and we are left with the separate corpuscles—some of which we should no doubt call alive, and others dead, some mobile and other sedentary, and all of them very different in form and function from the whole body. We might find some behaving intelligently, and perhaps among them a few who have awakened to their strange condition, and describe their intelligence as no merely private possession, but part of a greater. As for the rest, it will be little use appealing to their reason or their imagination: because of course if you look at anything closely enough it is for you abolished; and they live right inside this creature whose organs they are. Their minds are wingless. They *know* that nothing much larger than a corpuscle like themselves can live and await their discovery. *They* are the pattern and measure of all life, and you are a crank if you doubt it.

One last question: from what heavenly body could such a massive beast take flight? From one of the major planets, or—more likely—from the sun itself. Nor is it a sufficient objection that no living thing could be born or survive in that heat: though inert at first, it might yet (once out of the fire) slowly awake to life and mind. *Has not Earth done just this?*

We have painted our rough portrait, and found its subject—our planet, Mother Earth, our own heavenly body. In every particular—in parentage, weight, figure, constitution, behaviour, sense organs, speech, science—she fits our description; and we, her corpuscles, think of her as we were warned we should think. For us she is not the Seed of her flowers, but merely their garden; not the Body of our limbs and hers, but only their dance floor and then their mortuary slab; not the Mind of her astronomers or even their common body, but their platform. For us it goes without saying that, because the eyes which look out from her to the stars are *our* eyes, they cannot also be *her* eyes; and that, because her radio speech is English or French or German, it cannot possibly be *her* speech. That geological specimen which is called a geologist claims his geology for himself alone and allows none to her—somewhat as if my eyes were to claim that only they, and not I, now see you, or as if my tongue were to claim for itself exclusively the speaking of this sentence, or as if my right hand were to set itself up as the author of these written words. Such evidences of her life as this college and this meeting and this body and these remarks are not, in our view, evidences of *her* life at all, but only of her infestation.

Yet we must admit that, according to the definition of a living creature that we began with, Earth is very much alive. In fact we must go further, and admit that if to be more alive is to be more complex and complete and self-contained and self-perpetuating and long-lived, then she is more alive than any of her parts. But of course, if we *define* a living creature, not as I have done, but as a piece of protoplasm ranging in size between a bacillus and a certain Californian tree, and described in biological textbooks, then we *confine* the phenomena of life, keeping them within our conventional bounds. Similarly, if we *define* Earth as a ball of inert matter, that is what she will remain. For our definition requires that, directly she shows the least sign of life, it shall be a sign only of the life that lives on her. It is scarcely surprising that this globe is dead, when every limb it puts forth is immediately amputated; and stupid, when every idea it has is immediately another's. So long as Earth is by definition a clod, she will dutifully play the part of a clod.

No doubt it is a useful convention that we should pretend that we are the reverse of autochthonous, that we have been dropped upon this planet from Limbo, and are evidence only of what she is not like. Eleven hours out of the twelve our effectiveness as her organs requires that we deny that we are anything of the sort; but there remains the twelfth when we should do well to come to our senses by seeing them as hers. As Meredith observes,

> Till we conceive her living we go distraught,
> At best but circle-windsails of a mill.

But the idea of Earth as a piece of cosmic machinery, an enormous heavenly ball-bearing, is so firmly fixed in our minds that seriously to question it is to cause embarrassment (or even anxiety) amongst our friends, and to invite the contempt of our enemies.

Therefore let us leave this awkward part of our subject for the moment, and begin our inquiry over again. This time, let us start at home, with ourselves, our own bodily organization. We are looking for the living creature called man: that is to say, we are (according to our definition) looking for the *Whole* of him, for a self-contained system. Anything less than this is more properly called an organ than an organism.

Where does this vital equipment of ours end, and its non-vital background begin? Where shall we find the boundaries of the living function, the spot where it meets the non-living? I cannot find them anywhere. This skinful of blood and flesh is not a living whole, and when we call it the total human body we are, once more, taken in by our conventions. For by itself this body is incapable of any human task. What we call a human hand is really not so much a hand as a wrist, from which may sprout a thousand truly human hands— spears, axes, knives, spoons, forks, brushes, scissors, saws, and so on indefinitely. Again, what we call a human skin is more like an endoderm, the raw flesh underlying the true skins of wool and silk and cotton. It is impossible to give an intelligible account of a man's behavior so long as you treat the flesh-and-blood nucleus as the whole of him, and regard as merely external devices his aeroplane-wings and paddle-fins, his bootsole-hooves and pincer-claws, his hammer-fists and pen-fingers, and all the rest of his extended body.

Now these are not fanciful metaphors. We really do have the experience of incorporating our clothes and tools; for while they remain for us distinct things discontinuous with our flesh, we do not yet know how to use them. They have to be worn in, absorbed into our physique, otherwise we carry our clothes as though they do not belong to us, and have not mastered our tools. The craftsman is not in contact with the handle of his tool, but with the wood parting beneath his blade; the expert horseman is not a biped sitting on a quadruped, but a temporary quadruped; the cyclist is not *safe* till his body includes his machine, and he feels the macadam against his tyres. Each of you has grown four additional legs since entering this room. It is characteristic of a comfortable chair that it ceases to be furniture and becomes physique—though of course, when I remind you of the fact the physique becomes furniture again. We are infinitely elastic—at one moment we have taken on the body of a world embracing giant, and the next moment we have shed all but the core. It is very difficult to tell by looking at him just how big a man is. Indeed he is liable to take *you* in.

Of course our fabricated organs are very different from the natural organs which they extend. Indeed it is their departure from the earlier pattern—their 'deadness', if you like—which makes them so vitally effective. Taken piecemeal, they are not alive; fully integrated with the body which they prolong, they enhance and share its life. The life of the whole is what it is because each part, natural and artificial, does what it does. Just as the glass of water I have drunk at dinner is now living in me (and thus part-commentator upon itself) so was the glass, while I held it, living in me. As Bruno said, the stable is alive when the horse is in it, and our hats are alive when we put them on—and by alive he did not mean lousy. And if you object that a dead thing cannot become a true part of a living, I reply, firstly, that every meal contradicts you; and, secondly, that if you take any living thing to pieces you will soon find only dead parts. To the observer who is small and short-sighted enough we are all of us stone-dead. On the other hand, to an observer who is big and long-sighted enough, we are not only alive to our fingertips, but far beyond them. For only a Proteus, an infinitely variable monster, can live a human life. This is charmingly put by a Chinese sage of the third century B.C.— "Although to be patterned in the form of a man is something to be more or less pleased about, the source of joy beyond all reckoning lies in the fact that a thing like a man's body has a myriad transformations, and there never has been any limit to them."

There is indeed no limit to them. Once we admit these manufactured outer things into the circle of our physique, we cannot stop with them. For we are seeking a living *whole,* remember, a self-contained organism in contrast to a dependent organ, a complete man. He must include those preliminary stomachs which we call kitchens and shops and factories and farms, those distant mouths which we call reapers-and-binders and fishing nets, those extended bowels which we call drains and sewers, those outer shells which we call his house and town and country, and countless items of natural equipment besides. He must include the planet itself. Amputate a man's right arm, and he may still live and flourish; amputate his atmosphere, clouds, ocean, soil, rock, and what have you left? Are not these the indispensable apparatus of that life which is lived in us, its very minimum physique or embodiment? If you say, "here in this room life is now evidently being lived, but the physical basis of that life extends beyond this room", then, before very long, you will find yourself dragging in the whole planet. In other words, a full description of any one of us, of our physique and behaviour, would turn out to be a description of Earth. She is the whole of every part of her.

We have come back, by a different route, to our previous conclusion—that Earth is not merely alive, but the only kind of creature which is fully equipped to live in the universe as it is.

Still, perhaps, we feel that this conclusion is absurd. Let us then, once more, change our approach. Let us put this objection: are we not, in confining our remarks so far to the biological level (more or less), leaving out what really matters, namely experience? Earth may well, in spite of her magnificent vital physique, have the mind of an idiot, of a vegetable, or even no mind at all. In any case, how can we ever hope to settle the question?

Well, we are not without clues. Man is his own sample of the universe, his own piece of inside information. Of certain systems of organized material we are entitled to speak—namely, of those systems which we comprise—and these we find to be, in fact, systems of experience, or minds. Now it is surely safer, when we come to consider other systems of organized material, to suppose that they are not utterly different from ourselves: it is safer to think of them as minded than as mindless. Of the two—an Earth which is mere matter and an Earth which is also mind—the first is the wilder hypothesis. In fact, to speak strictly, I am not at all sure that it is conceivable.

Moreover this parcel of matter, of which a man has first-hand and inside information, has many sizes. A man, as I have said already, is elastic. Sometimes I have the experience of narrowing down to one or another part of my body, so that the rest becomes environment. I am no longer a whole man. If I go on doing this improperly and to excess I am in danger of disintegrating—of becoming what Mr. Lewis has called a fountain of vermin, a rabble of organs. At other times I have the opposite experience of widening out till I include, not merely the whole of my fourteen stone, but my clothes and house and car, and my family, profession, town, country, race, and even the planet itself. For instance, when I think of a possible war between Earth and Mars, I feel for Earth, or at least feel as though I am feeling for her. I take up a point of view which really does seem to be more hers than mine in any private sense. I find my sympathy widening to include all that is hers. Now I take this experience seriously. I think the simplest explanation of it (and perhaps the only one that works) is that this portion of Earth called D. E. Harding feels and thinks, occasionally, for the whole of it: that in him and through him Earth is aware of herself and her celestial companions. And if it is silly to say that *Earth* sees Mars when I see Mars, then I think it is just as silly to say that I see you when my eyes see you. Do let us try to be consistent.

But it is a mistake to suppose that our difficulties here are intellectual ones. They lie very deep. It is perfectly *obvious* to the modern mind that heavenly bodies are dead bodies, and the sky a graveyard. Yet we should remind ourselves that, perhaps for most men most of the time, the opposite has been equally obvious: the consensus of human opinion is that the universe is not only the theatre of abundant life, but much of that life is of a higher order than ours—though we may after death (or even now) come to share in it. It is possible, of course, that we are right and they are wrong; but mere assertion that this is so is not enough.

The whole question of the status of life in the universe needs to be reopened. And directly we give it our attention we see how unlikely it is that human life should be the highest kind of life, that there should range between the electron and man many grades of being, and above him no grades—except, possibly, the Supreme Being. Surely this is cosmic provincialism, parochialism, meanness of imagination. I quote your President again: "We feel quite sure that the first step beyond the world of our present experience must lead either nowhere at all or else into the blinding abyss of undifferentiated spirituality, the unconditioned, the absolute. That is why many believe in God who cannot believe in angels and an angelic world... I cannot now understand, but I well remember, the passionate conviction with which I myself once defended this prejudice." And Mr. Lewis goes on to say how he rejected without trial any rumour of floors or levels between the Unconditioned and the familiar world.

To this I should add: if these levels exist, then Earth—the planetary level—is well fitted to constitute one of them.

A Living Universe

What about the others? In this talk I have taken Earth as my example for convenience' sake, and I must now do something to correct the false emphasis that I have given her. I have argued, you will remember, that hers is the only body that is self-contained and fully equipped for life in our universe. But of course she is just as dependent upon the solar system as man is upon her. Nothing less than a star—and our solar system is a fully developed star, a star in full bloom, so to say—nothing less than such a heavenly body can claim to be a living *whole,* an entire organism. Nor can we stop even here. This search for the complete equipment of our life can only lead us on, through the Galaxy and systems of galaxies, towards the only true Whole, that is at last independent and free from accident and self-contained and self-existent—the only whole that is not also a part.

Now let me remind you that scientists have, on the whole, ceased to think of our solar system as a solecism or a celestial monster. There may well (so I am told) be thousands or even millions of stars in our own Galaxy alone which have unfolded into planetary rings. Possibly it is the star which never grows into a solar system that is abnormal. I am further informed that a planet like ours *must* ripen to life and mind as soon as physical conditions are ripe for their emergence. We are invited to think of planets at all stages of development—and it would be extremely odd if our own were the highest. With a fairly easy scientific conscience, therefore, we may presently leave this room and look up at the stars over Oxford, and feel confident that we are looking, not merely into scenes of life, but of life that is in part truly heavenly. But I doubt whether it will be the tremendous and thrilling experience it might be, unless we can see the life *on* heavenly bodies as the life *of* heavenly bodies, as the stars' organs rather than their bed-bugs. Heavens that are alive only in the verminous sense do not worthily declare the glory of their Creator. On the other hand, I am sure the experience will have grave dangers unless we remember that the true end of every intelligent creature in Earth and Heaven is the enjoyment of God, the ineffably transcendent One, who is not one God amongst many gods, or some super-super-system of galaxies, but the ground of all existence. Nevertheless we do not enjoy God more by enjoying creatures less: to think meanly of creation is not to think highly of the Creator. Rather the reverse. It is our pride, and not our loyalty to the King of Heaven, which has led us to degrade and liquidate all his nobility.

Nor does man himself escape the same fate. Addressing this Club earlier in the year, Mr. Owen Barfield said that since Christ's coming we have been busy depriving nature of inwardness. And he added: "Because there is only one inwardness we cannot treat nature, or any kind of outwardness, in this way, without reducing our own inwardness to zero."

* * *

Chapter 12

THE CONFLICT BETWEEN SCIENCE AND RELIGION

Well-meaning denials are no good: there is real conflict between our science and our religion. And the struggle will go on so long as the contestants are not all they should be. In other words, it will go on so long as there is man on earth.

Ideally and in principle, however, there can be no conflict, provided we grant that the aim of pure science is to discover part of the mind of the same God that religion worships. If science is concerned with the revelation of God in the universe, and religion with his revelation in man's heart, then any ultimate discrepancy between them could only mean some ultimate discrepancy in God himself—or at any rate in his work: either he is divided against himself, or else his creation is divided against itself, and so spoiled by the Fall that it is more a revelation of Satan's mind than of God's. I believe neither of these propositions, though some Christians seem to do so. This article is not written for them.

Unless, then, we are Manicheans (or dualists of some milder and more respectable variety) we must locate the war between science and religion in ourselves rather than the nature of things. Accordingly our best hope of peace is to rectify our science and our religion, till they are no longer incompatible.

As I See It

Rectifying our science
Our Science has two equal and opposite defects: we have at once too little of it, and too much.

Notoriously, a little science is a dangerous thing—and certainly dangerous for religion. We all know the self-styled 'rationalist' who, having read a little popular science, professes atheism. He imagines that the doctrine of biological evolution through survival of the fittest organisms disposes of their Creator, that the resolution of the physical world into particles or energies or wave-motions disposes of Mind, that the discovery of the pre-Christian prototypes of Christian beliefs and practices disposes of Christianity, that the linking of religious experience with sexual instincts disposes alike of that experience and of its Object, and so on. And it is not only the 'rationalist' who has these delusions: most of us are touched with them. If we knew more science we would be in danger of knowing also that we know almost none, and that when we refer phenomena back to their primitive stages we deepen the mystery instead of dispersing it. The scientist's pursuit of 'explanations' and 'causes' is a necessary and exciting wild-goose chase, which only the merest novice could excusably mistake for the progressive triumph of secular enlightenment over faith.

Too much science, on the other hand, is equally damaging—too much (I mean) of one department, to the exclusion of the rest. In fact, the scientist who forgets more and more about other fields as he learns more and more about his own (and maybe prides himself on the discrepancy), is really not a scientist at all in the strict sense of the word, but an obscurantist, a professor of a species of ignorance. Nor is it any defence to plead that Science is the totality of its proliferating departments, unless there exist some persons who can appreciate the grand total. Besides, the more the specialist narrows his aperture, and cuts off his chosen glimpse of the universe from the whole picture, the dimmer and more distorted his pin-hole vision is likely to be. In the end, to lose the whole is to lose the part also. Fragmented science discloses a fragmented world. It ceases to be the pursuit of truth and tends to become mere peeping tom-foolery. No wonder it is dangerous for religion.

We need, then, a synoptic view of the universe—one which studies the trees in sufficient botanical detail, and a few of them minutely, without losing sight of the wood. No doubt this is terribly trite advice: it is what almost everyone says and almost no-one acts on. How hard do we try to rediscover that lost Science of the sciences, whose aim is to make sense of them by unifying them in a single world-perspective? Yet this difficult—but not impossible—task is essential if our science and our religion are to begin to come to terms. Let me suggest a few of the results which would follow.

We should take in time instead of being taken in by time. We should no longer fondly imagine that what happens slowly is understood, or that what happens to be distributed amongst many of science's departments does not happen at all. It has taken (so I am told) many billions of years for these atoms which I comprise to reach such a pitch of organization that they can now get together and record the fact on this sheet of paper, but this achievement—physical, chemical, vital, and psychological—is neither less remarkable nor less mysterious than if it had taken a split second. If anything, it is more wonderful. Again, we should cease believing that, by tracing man's history back and back (individually in his mother's womb, and racially in his ancestors) to the simplest forms of life, we are somehow reducing him to their level; on the contrary, it is not man who is degraded, but rather the primitive cell that is ennobled by wonderful potentialities. Ultimately, we are often informed, everything boils down to the agitation of particles or waves. But when we attribute the sensible behaviour of well-known living creatures to the senseless behaviour of almost unknowable dead ones, we still have it on our hands, and two miracles instead of one. In fact, countless billions of miracles. For each electron comprising the brain that is now thinking these thoughts is reputed to be just like all electrons everywhere and at all times: so far, then, from showing life and mind and values to be strangers in the world, we find them lurking everywhere, like a universal Jack-in-the-box waiting for the button to be pressed.

Really we have no excuse for our infernal superstition that the most complex things in the world are its accidents, and the least complex its essentials. Why the devil (the devil that is the high-priest of such unrealism) should the present activity of my particles taken one by one reveal more of the universe's nature than their behaviour taken as a whole, in the writing of this article? Let us try to be a little less inconsistent and fanciful. We do not judge a rose by its roots or its seed, a man by his embryo or his red corpuscles or his metabolism, a house by its individual bricks, an old master by the chemistry of its pigments, yet we judge the universe by its physical substratum—as if we knew what that is! As if, having 'explained' the mysterious by the incomprehensible, we had illuminated all! No doubt the more elaborate parts of the universe are late and rare and small, but they are not needles lost in the cosmic haystack: at least some of them are aware of the haystack, and in that sense contain it. And who would deny the existence and unity of a plant on the grounds that for a million large spring leaves it bears one small summer flower, which should therefore be ignored—or rather, hastily plucked, on the absurd theory that it must be a parasite? It is probable that values do not appear till well on in the world's story, but in what tale are the long opening chapters all that matters, and the climax—however brief—irrelevant? Again, it is true that the higher living creatures are relatively detached and mobile, and do not rise like waves or hills from the surface of our Earth. But my blood is not less mine because it circulates in me, and neither are we less Earth's because we circulate in her. Quite the reverse: man is more intimately united to her than any rock or stone could ever be, for he depends upon her in countless new ways, while she depends upon him—her most effective and sensitive organ—for countless new functions, expressing through him her nature at its prime. But evidently the limb must mistake the body for a corpse, so long as it goes on mentally amputating itself, on the crazy principle that no part of the planet is a geological specimen till it is stone-dead and fossilized. How can we expect the cosmic party to be anything but deadly dull, if we forbid its life and soul even to gate-crash its way in?

None of this is to deny, of course, that the discoveries of physical science are immensely thrilling and important—provided they are put in their place. That place is near the base of the hierarchy of being, where the whole lies in pieces. As we mount this hierarchy, from the physicist's particles, through atoms and molecules and cells and organs, to man himself, we find at each level functions and qualities not to be found below, yet all levels are united by innumerable upward and downward processes. Thus a man is not 'really' particles, or 'really' cells, or 'really' a unique and quite separate human personality above and beyond these, or 'really' a planetary organ, or 'really' an aspect of the whole universe, but all of these things and many more at once—a vast and busy hierarchical complex, which can in part be read horizontally by the separate sciences as they now exist, vertically by integrated Science as it might become.

The hierarchy above

Now it would be strange if this hierarchy were to reach up to man and stop with him; and still more strange if it were, after rising by easy stages to his level, suddenly to leap at one bound to the highest level of all. Yet this is what most of us have come to believe. If you take angels seriously your friends are liable to send for the doctor. Nevertheless tradition has nearly always found as many levels above man as below him—devas and star-gods and archontes and ninefold ranks of angels, for instance—and common sense itself suggests that to suppose ourselves the loftiest and most inclusive of living creatures is more likely to be a trick of perspective (due to our station in the hierarchy), and the blindness of human pride, than true insight. My cells (which are quite distinct organisms) may be excused for never suspecting that they comprise a man, but the man has no excuse for never suspecting his membership of still vaster beings.

Who or what are these beings? I confine myself here to two or three examples familiar to all Christians. If the Angels of the Seven Churches of the Apocalypse are not the 'collective personalities' of their members (or something of the kind), what are they? Again, and at a very different level, if the Parable of the Vine and the Branches, and the Pauline doctrine of the Church as the Body of Christ, do not mean that in him we are one, yet at least as distinct from one another as leaves from fruit and hands from feet, what can they mean? How can we reject them and call ourselves Christians?

It is science itself, with its tale of the manifold levels below and within man, which points towards those manifold levels above him that religion has hitherto stood for, but now neglects at her peril. The hierarchy below man is the proper study of science, the hierarchy above him is the proper study of religion, and without either he is incomplete. So far from being sworn enemies, science and religion at their best are the interdependent halves of one whole.

We need to make this discovery. Our science which concentrates upon the very lowest subhuman needs to see it as the many-levelled sacred vehicle and expression of the superhuman; and our religion which concentrates upon the very highest superhuman needs to see it as the many-levelled container and saviour of the subhuman. Together, their business is to fill out the universe that they have, between them, reduced to the hollow shell of itself.

* * *

Chapter 13

EMBODIMENTS
Architecture As A Bodily Function

Vitruvius begins his *De Architectura* with a formidable list of the branches of knowledge with which an architect ought to be familiar. They include philosophy, music, medicine, and optics, as well as painting, sculpture, and mathematics. A few architects, and among them some of the greatest, have approached this ideal of versatility: familiar instances are Michelangelo, Bernini, Vanbrugh and Wren—the last was actually appointed Savilian Professor of Astronomy at Oxford. Modern architects may plead, of course, that the renaissance master did not have to wrestle with the innumerable technicalities which beset us. To which he might reply, with justice, that his difficulties, though unlike ours, were no less formidable, and that we are narrow specialists because that is what we want to be.

We are so busy being architects that we have no time to wonder what it is to be architects. This has its advantages. If the Garden Spider (that designer of genius) were to stop to consider how and what and why he builds, he would probably find himself leg-tied and incapable of building anything at all. Similarly, it seems, some human designers need to work in a kind of specialist's daydream. To rouse them would be to risk breaking the fine thread of their thought, and might end in paralyzing entanglements

There are many others, however, who are ready to pay the price of fuller self-awareness—namely, some loss of time and perhaps even of efficiency—in the hope of greater efficiency in the end, and in the certainty of greater pleasure now. This essay is written for them.

Architecture makes man

What does the architect do for man? What is his real job? Is it merely to set man in a beautiful and convenient environment, to contrive the best possible devices for him to live in?

Not at all. The architect does not make man's trimmings. He makes man. He does not design containers for the human body, but its indispensable extensions or outgrowths. He contrives a large part of that vital equipment lacking which a man is not a man at all, but an animal or even less than an animal. For the naked human body, whittled down and pared of home and furniture and clothes and tools, is no longer a truly human body. It is incapable of any specifically human function, and even of survival. My hands and feet are not so much organs as organ-holders, or limb-buds from which some truly human limb-ending—pen-finger or hammer-fist, bootsole-hoof or pincer-claw, plane wing or oar-fin—may be grown whenever it is needed. My life extends far beyond my skin, which is little more than the raw surface of animal flesh upon which must be grafted such human integuments as my shirt and jacket, my wallpaper and two-coat plaster, and the skins of my 10-inch cavity well. Well may Samuel Butler complain: "If those who so frequently declare that man is a finite creature would point out his boundaries, it might lead to a better understanding." [1]

1 *Life and Habit,* p. 104. Cf. Goethe: "When to my car my money yokes six spankers,

Embodiments

In a manner of speaking, man is chiefly not-man, and the not-man chiefly architecture. And the whole lives. You cannot meaningfully say of this whole that it is alive here and dead there, any more than you can meaningfully say of my life-blood that it is a dead juice in which living corpuscles are swimming for their lives and for mine. What at once makes and is made by vital functioning is itself vital functioning. "Man is a tool-using animal," wrote Carlyle. "Without tools he is nothing, with tools he is all." [2] They are a part of his human nature.

No, a house is not a machine for living in, but an organ for living through. The client comes to his architect seeking an organism rather than a convenience, for the unhoused and the underhoused are to some degree disembodied or disorganized. The architect treats and cures partially-Invisible Men. He bodies them forth, helping them to grow the healthy physique which makes solid and well-formed humans of them. He is much more like a plastic surgeon or a physical culturist or a midwife than a tool merchant. [3]

Nature and artifice

It was all very well for Emerson to say "These temples grew as grows the grass," [4] but he was not their architect, and certainly not one of

are their limbs not my limbs? Is't not I on the proud racehorse that dash by? Mine all the forces I combine, the four-and-twenty legs are mine!" Faust (Anster's translation), I.4. And A.N. Whitehead asks: "Where does my body end and the external world begin?" *Modes of Thought*, p. 155.
2 *Sartor Resartus*, I.5.
3 "Although to be patterned in the form of a man is something to be more or less pleased about, the source of joy beyond all reckoning lies in the fact that a thing like man's body has myriad transformations, and there never has been a limit to them." *Chuang Tzu Book* (E.R. Hughes' translation), VI. This was probably written in the third century B.C.
4 "The Problem."

their sweating masons. Yet he was right. The Parthenon is as truly a natural specimen, a piece of natural history, as Emerson himself.

Of course you may say, if you like, that the designer's work is to extend and fulfill nature by art, so long as you add with Shakespeare that "the art itself is nature." [5] It is natural for man to be not only an artificer but artificial—to be nine-tenths his own artifact. All you can mean when you distinguish his works from nature's is that in them nature is waking to intention and awareness, is coming at last into her own. If anything, buildings are (like Alice) "as real as life, and twice as natural." Here, in their designing, is that small part of the total design of the universe which we may well claim to understand, seeing that it is done by us and for us and through us. Yet, paradoxically enough, it is precisely our inside knowledge of this piece of nature called a building project, our first-hand information about it and our control of it, which seems to remove it from nature. Whereas in fact it is just this special intimacy which should make it for us the most revealing of all instances of nature at work. To be an efficient designer is to live in the very bud and growing point of the evolutionary tree, and there to enjoy real insight into its most vigorous thriving. And certainly not even the most rugged individualist among us is employed as an *outside* architect by nature. We are all on her staff, salaried men of

5 "Yet nature is made better by no mean,
But nature makes that mean; so, over that art
Which you say adds to nature, is an art
That nature makes...
...this is an art
Which does mend nature,—change it rather;
The art itself is nature."
—*The Winter's Tale,* IV.8.
Cf. Browne: "Art is the perfection of Nature." *Religio Medici,* I.16.

hers. At least occasionally, then, it should be true of the architect as of the hero of *Notting Hill*, that "the artificial city had become to him nature, and he felt the curbstones and gaslamps as things ancient as the sky." [6]

The Extension of the body

You may object that this latest kind of growth, this new departure in evolution which man controls, is a crude substitute for the old; that its organs are loose and optional and inert and mere appendages or makeshifts, bloodless and insensitive; that (in short) this so-called growth is not growth at all, but only addition.

You would be wrong: the facts are the other way around. A man—the total organism—would be less alive and not more alive if his drain-bowel were a mere trailing outgrowth incapable of painless amputation and regrafting as often as he pleases, if it were made of living tissue instead of 4-inch and 6-inch and 9-inch salt-glazed stoneware pipes jointed in cement mortar, if it could never be rodded and smoke-tested and water-tested and grubbed up and relaid to proper falls without an anesthetic, if it were liable to diarrhea and dysentery, if it took millions of years instead of hundreds to evolve from its beginnings to its present form. If it were more alive, he would be less alive. The deadness of the part promotes the life of the whole, and shares in it, and so is raised from the dead. By themselves and cut off from their users, drainpipes are of course stone-dead stoneware; but as continuous with their users they are living stones, hardware come to life. Doubtless the architect must mentally amputate and

6 G.K. Chesterton, *The Napoleon of Notting Hill*, III.1.

so kill these organs when he is specifying and inspecting them, but that is no reason for never pausing to think what he is really up to. Butchery is not his only business.

In any case, *all* our building materials are dead, whether they make up flesh or its extensions. If you take the components of any creature one by one, and ignore the whole, you will sooner or later come upon nothing but lifeless matter. Our saliva, the lymph of our bloodstreams, our atoms—these are no more alive than our drains. Life is not a ghostly presence haunting organisms, but a function of their wholeness, of the total pattern, of the togetherness of their lifeless parts which include outer artifacts no less than inner chemistry. D.H. Lawrence's wish that "cities might be as once they were, bowers grown out from the busy bodies of people," has never really lacked fulfillment.

The house comes alive

It is a disturbing (and possibly inspiring) thought that when your client moves into the house you have built for him he moves into every part of it, from the tips of his television-antenna to the soles of his footings, and that in the man thus enlarged the whole of your work springs to life. For he is little more than a lodger or a caretaker until he feels co-extensive with the structure, and its cube is his, and he is sensitive to its slightest injury, and hurt when it is hurt, and praised when it is praised. The psychology here is no less than the proper counterpart of the physiology, seeing that this brick-and-mortar physique that you have cultivated for him, this outgrowth, contributes far more to his life-pattern and life-history than a great deal of his flesh-and-blood physique can ever do. He does not live in the house; it lives in him.[7] You have not designed a receptacle of life, but a way of life. Now he has more reason to fear the loss of a few shingles than a few hairs, and a lesion of the extended bowel may be as dangerous as a lesion of the unextended. Again, he can spare his appendix sooner than his downspout, toenails than roofnails, a finger-joint than a truss-joint.[8]

Indeed, your client is now a very complex creature, quite unlike any mammal. He lies right outside the vegetable and animal kingdoms in a third kingdom—the human. This kingdom is your province. As planner, you have seen to it that every organ of his extended body has its proper spatial relation to the rest; as constructor, that it has its proper physical constitution; as heating engineer, that it has its proper temperature. For example, take the last, and consider the system of body-temperatures which are normal in your now well-developed client. His blood-system is maintained at a steady 98.4 degrees, his hot-water system around 160 degrees, his refrigeration-system around 25 degrees, his warm-air system around 68 degrees, his foundation system (if he stands on clay) at not less than 32 degrees. And his outer skins have been designed as a superior kind of insulating fur or feathers, with a view to maintaining these body

7 The philosopher Giordano Bruno (1548-1600) claimed that the stable was alive when the horse was in it, and his hat was alive when he put it on—and by *alive* he did not mean *lousy!*

8 "Often if an accident happens to a gentleman's legs, they can be mended; but if a similar accident happens to the legs of his pantaloons, there is no help for it... Dress a scarecrow in your last shift, you standing shiftless by, who would not soonest salute the scarecrow?" Thoreau, *Walden*, "Economy."

temperatures at a minimum cost in calories.

Language itself bears this out. It is no mere oddity of speech that we credit the house and parts of the house with human functions, referring (for instance) to the dining room instead of the dining-man room. The inhabited room dines—you have planned it so—and its mouths are the service hatch and the tradesman's entrance. Your living room is a *living* room, and your dwelling dwells. It is good sense as well as good idiom to say that the house *sleeps* at night and *wakes* in the morning, and *overlooks* its neighbors, and *faces* the south, and is *fed* with gas and electric current, and has good (or bad) architectural *manners.* For it is nothing else than your enlarged client doing all these things. Sleeping men include as well as need sleeping clothes and sleeping rooms and sleeping houses and sleeping cities.

The total organism

"A man's Me is the sum total of all that he can call his, not only his body and his psychic powers, but his clothes and his house… his lands and his horses, and yacht and bank-account." [9] Indeed, he extends far beyond all his private property, and covers many square miles. Like any cow, he feeds on the land at one end and excretes on the land at the other; only his two ends may be a thousand miles apart—as far apart as the farm where his reaping-machine jaws are feeding, and the farm where his sewage effluent is finally returned to the soil. Like the cow, he needs more than one stomach; only he may run to scores of stomachs—stomachs of that new (but, nevertheless, quite 'natural') sort which we call threshing machines and mills

9 William James, *Textbook of Psychology,* p.177

and factories and bakehouses and kitchens. Like the cow, he must drink; only instead of walking up to the lake he prefers to grow up to it, and drink without moving—his iron mouth sucks permanently at the reservoir. Like the cow, he can see and hear only what is in sight and within earshot; only he grows new ears and eyes wherever he needs them, and spares himself the trouble of moving about to discover what is happening—every telephone instrument and television camera is his sense-organ, potential or actual. Thus man is not so much a nimble biped as a sedentary myriapod, thanks to the engineers and town-planners and architects who, during the last 10,000 years, have been redesigning him.

Growth and amputation

But if this were the whole story—if the designer were concerned only with the growth of bigger and better human organs—then he would in fact be doing man a terrible injury. For ungrowth rather than growth is the mark of a human being. It is even more important to be able to amputate your four bed-legs in the morning (at the first attempt if you can, and without too much pain) than to be able to grow them at night.[10] The bedridden have not advanced, but in their own way reverted to the quadrupedal state, to the condition of the animal that stupidly clings all its life to a single set of tools. Unable to move to a new house, the snail is injured and dies with it, whereas the man merely calls in the demolition contractor and the architect to set him up with a healthier integument. In a sense, every *permanent*

10 It was not so long ago when a German peasant would put a chair-leg in splints if one of his sheep broke a leg—sympathetic magic, of course, but there is some sense in it.

outer skin and limb-ending and sense-organ is a cancerous growth, morbid tissue, a tool that possesses its user.[11] If you cannot shuffle off your television set or your house, it has become a truly mortal coil. The too house-proud man is like a giant snail or limpet; he is miserably vulnerable because inordinately attached. House-ridden he becomes inhuman, distorted, monstrous. His architect is guilty of having cultivated a morbid growth upon him.

The fact is that to be human is to be *less* than animal—to lack the lobster's claw, the spider's spinerets, the swallow's wing, the horse's hoof, the tortoise's armour, the moth's antennae, and almost all the immense range of nature's instruments. It is to be feeble, naked, inexpert, incurably amateurish—and unspoiled. It is to be a species of universal joint, a socket for innumerable tools. And the reward of man's age-long restraint, of his refusal to grow any one particular set of animal appendages, is that eventually he grows them all, after his own fashion. In his ancestors he was content to wait while, impatiently, corals outbuilt him, and fish outswam him, and every other animal outdid him in some special skill. And now he outdoes them all, incorporating in his great body all the fins and flippers and wings and claws and shells that are distributed piecemeal throughout the world.

Like an octopus or an Eastern god, he is many-limbed; only his arms are not held apart in space so much as in time. His house is something between an armoury and a Blackbeard's chamber, where

11 This is true even of our 'natural' organs: we have to learn to amputate them mentally. Thus Marcus Aurelius: "As for thy body which as a vessel, or a case, compasseth thee about, and the many and curious instruments that it hath annexed unto it, let not them trouble thy thoughts. For of themselves they are but as a carpenter's axe, but that they are born with us, and naturally sticking unto us." *Meditations*, X.38.

his amputated limbs are hanging in readiness for re-incorporation. As he goes about the house he is, accordingly, transformed, and reborn a new creature in every room. To be a man bathing and then a man telephoning is to have slipped out of one embodiment into another so easily that the metamorphosis passes unnoticed.

The evolution of artifacts

Clearly, then, the effectiveness of this new kind of human growth lies in its immense difference from the original organism which it extends. Nevertheless, because the tool-bud is functionally united to the limb it grows on, and is no makeshift or orthopaedic device, the main laws of its development are those of all life. Let me give some examples.

The so-called artificial organ, like the natural, develops by *adaptation* to a changing environment. For instance, just as my feet are fins progressively adapted to travelling on the land, so my footings are walls progressively adapted to resting on the land. Such adaptations arise from *variation*. Many kinds of feet and of foundations have been hit upon and tried out—some of them important new departures or mutations which change the course of evolution, and others which are trivial. But, whether important or not, these variations are all the while subject to *selection*—first a blind sifting by circumstances and economic pressures, and then a conscious sifting in the light of experience. (Architects, who have weeded out innumerable characteristics of the house, are only carrying on the work of nature which has weeded out innumerable characteristics of the householder—the main difference being that only in the first case can the organ be scrapped without scrapping the organism.) And selection often leads to *exuberance,* when some organ goes on developing much further than practical needs seem to require; and conversely to *degeneration,* when the organ survives, in a useless and vestigial form, long after it has been superseded. Examples of the first are the peacock's tail and fan vaulting, and a woman's hair and hairstyles and hats; of the second, the whale's hind legs (now deeply buried in its body, and shrunk almost to nothing), the dummy half-timbers which are still planted on to suburban gables, and the dummy buttonholes on a man's sleeve—vestiges of his once turned-up cuff.

Here, then, in tailoring and planning his outer body, man is continuing more economically and swiftly and intentionally the natural processes which have produced his inner body. Architecture is biology brought up to date.

Practical conclusions

Such considerations cannot help but change our attitude to our job, giving us a new vision of it and respect for it and delight in it. Henceforth we shall be more alive, because more alive to our vital (and, indeed sacramental) office.

Perhaps we shall be more sensitive, also, to the individual needs of the men and women we at once build for and build. To design a fitting body for your client you must know his mind, so that the one shall match the other—or, at the very least, shall do no violence to it. Obviously it will not do to fit up the professional wrestler and the mystical poet with the same type of extended physique. We shall be inclined to think again about large repetitive housing schemes, and all planning which reckons in terms of income groups or classes of people instead of unique individuals. When we plan dwellings for persons we neither know nor try to know, are we not mistaking the function of the architect, treating the house as the standard dead-pan mask instead of the unique living expression of its unique family? Are we not apt, by standardizing the outer man, to promote the standardizing of the inner man, and by imposing our architecture (however excellent) upon him regardless of what he is, to impose upon him body and soul? Architects make men. The question for us is: what kind of men? And how many kinds? Architecture is one of the most important ways in which human beings vary. And appropriate variety is more than the spice of life: it is the main dish.

* * *

Chapter 14

THIRTY QUESTIONS

"God's in, we're out." Eckhart

"It's too clear, so it's hard to see." *The Gateless Gate*

What, after all, is Awakening, Enlightenment, Realisation? Awakening from what? Enlightenment as to what? Realisation of what?

It is waking up from all your dreams and imaginings and preconceptions, becoming enlightened as to the given facts, realising what you clearly are in your first-hand experience right now. It is being perfectly honest to yourself about yourself, at last. It is having the courage and effrontery—even the idiocy—to go by what you see, instead of by what you are told. It is questioning all mental habits and conventional assumptions, however common-sensible or sanctified. It is total open-mindedness, transparency, simplicity, and taking nothing for granted. In one word, it is discovery.

What is to be discovered is your own nature. Who are you? Only you are in a position to find out, because everyone else is elsewhere, off-centre. Only you can investigate what it is to be you. This article, therefore, is intended to stimulate your enquiry and not to dictate its results. In fact, if your self-discovery is genuine, it will find unique expression, and no existing formula will quite fit it.

It may be helpful to expand this rather vague question—who or what are you?—re-phrasing it in numerous ways in order to bring the enquiry down to earth and make real discovery less difficult. Accordingly, it is suggested that you ask yourself the following thirty questions, and try to answer them without reference to what you have read, or what people say, or what you have thought up to now. As far as possible, make a clean break with memory, and put these questions to yourself as if you had this moment arrived in the world, knowing nothing. Pick a time when you are not hurried or anxious, and then if only for half an hour, allow yourself to be quite childlike, content to be made a fool of by the facts. Stop thinking, just look, and be prepared for anything. You have no idea whether you are God or man, angel or animal, everything or nothing. It all remains to be seen.

1. In the place you now occupy, sitting in your chair and wearing your spectacles, do you find a human being? Is what you observe roughly the same shape as the people you observe out there, complete with head, neck, back and so on?

2. You are surrounded by solid objects, lumps of matter. At their centre, are you, too, a solid lump? Does what you find here feel dense, or light and airy? Is it like earth, or water, or wind, or more like empty space?

3. Have you any evidence, *at this moment*, as to how many eyes you own, and their colour and shape? How many ears and noses and heads can you now detect? If not, what's in their place?

4. Where is the man who is called by your name? Is he out there, where people and animals and cameras and mirrors register him? Or at the centre, where nothing registers him? If he's always out, who's

in? If you're in, who are you?

5. Is what you observe over there in your mirror at all like what you observe where you are? Are there two men given or only one, and where is he given? Is he in your bathroom, or the other bathroom behind the glass? Does your glass, then, show you what you are, or its opposite?

6. You are sitting in this chair, your friend in that. Look and see whether you are equals, members of the same species or genus or kingdom. Or, walking beside him, is it a case of two men walking, or one-and-a-half men, or one man, with some sort of presence floating alongside? Notice whether your relationship with another is ever symmetrical.

7. When you explore with your fingertips, do you find your face to be like his—coloured, solid, opaque, blocking the view?

8. You are now looking at this printing. Can you make out any distance between yourself and it? Observe the space between two stars. Can you find any similar space between them and yourself?

9. Can you find anything at all on your side of this page, anything added to this black-and-white pattern? Any seer or seeing?

10. How tall are you, how thick? Where do you find yourself stopping and the world beginning? Try pointing out your boundaries to yourself.

11. You see men in the world. Do you really see yourself in the world, or the world in you?

12. A man, as a small part of the universe, becomes less and less mysterious as science discovers more and more about him. Is this true of you? If the reverse is true of you, why?

13. Try destroying and re-creating the world at will. Then compare the operation with what happens to the world when the man over there closes and opens his eyes, or goes to sleep and wakes up again. Why not take your powers seriously?

14. You observe the birth and death of creatures around you. Do you observe your own birth and death? And anyhow, in the place you occupy, can you trace anybody who could be born, or grow older, or die?

15. Do you find yourself at the centre of the universe always, or sometimes, or never? Can you get away from the centre? How many centres can you find?

16. Have you found any real companion, anyone at all out there who is like yourself where you are? You note innumerable bodies, but how many minds? Can the universe do with more than one?

17. Men are evidently not free, but at the mercy of their environment and their bodies. Can you find anything outside yourself to bind you, or anything inside yourself to be bound? If you aren't built for freedom, suggest some improvements. Don't you feel you have free will, anyhow?

18. At table, you watch alien substances being pushed into holes in people's heads, and this is called eating. Is your eating like that?

See what happens to the food on *your* fork.

19. How many kinds of seeing are there? Is it the *absence* of eyes and brain and head which enables you to see (since they would block the view), and their *presence* which enables others to see? How do you know they see the world? Of how many seers have you clear evidence? How is it possible to see a thing if one is a thing?

20. You observe men and animals and even inert objects reacting to sounds. Do you observe them *hearing* sounds? Can one who has ears hear?

21. You can see that men are often hurt and troubled through and through, because they have no invulnerable core. Are you like that? Do you find the world can upset what lies at its centre?

22. What place or function can be found in a man for anything supernatural, such as God, the Kingdom of Heaven, the Holy Spirit, the Atman, the Buddha-nature? In yourself, can you find anything else?

23. Work is always being done around you, by those things, those men, those two hands and feet. Is the centre busy, too? See if you aren't bone lazy.

24. Most hands are attached to human bodies. Without moving, see what yours are now attached to.

25. However many views you take of a man over there, you will never see all of him. Do you find this true of yourself? Are you, perhaps, the only one who is what he looks like, and altogether visible?

26. Man is rarely satisfied. See if there is anything you lack, or any part of the world which, if you were God, should be rearranged.

27. Lying awake in bed in the dark, can you for a few moments be at peace and without thoughts but intensely aware of awareness? When in this state, what are you?

28. Other lovers are face to face. Does your beloved's face confront yours, or abolish it? Do you find room for two?

29. Can you see anyone or anything clearly without loving them in this way, and deliberately dying so that they may live in you?

30. If, after having answered these questions *on the evidence before you*, you still suspect you are only a man after all, then say what else is needed to establish your divinity. And then look and see whether that, too, isn't plainly given.

Of course these thirty questions are leading ones. They aren't precisely the questions you would ask, or phrased precisely your way, but they will do to illustrate the radical spirit of this enquiry. If you really *want* to find out who you are, then your own slightly different questions, your unique way of looking within, will infallibly occur to you, and the search will be no mere duty or practice, but irresistibly fascinating and urgent, and therefore successful. Your life will not have been wasted.

Is there, perhaps, a Liberation which is not a matter of self-discovery, one which is concerned, not with the facts as they are now given, but with somehow improving upon them? First see who you are now. Then you will surely find that only the truth sets you free, and it is all of it clearly presented at this moment, if only you stop thinking about it, and look, and take seriously what you see.

One who really looked for himself wrote: "Perceiving then, O man, all this in thyself, that thou art immaterial, holy, light, akin to him that is unborn, that thou art intellectual, heavenly, translucent, pure, above the flesh, above the world, above rulers, above principalities, over whom thou art in truth, then comprehend thyself in thy condition and receive full knowledge and understand wherein thou excellest: and beholding thine own face in thine essence, break asunder all bonds... desire earnestly to see him that is revealed unto thee, him who doth not come into being, whom perchance thou alone shalt recognise with confidence." [1]

Like all other scriptures (incidentally, this is a third-century Christian one, innocent of Zen) its proper use is to encourage us to look at the place we occupy, and not to tell us what to see there. Otherwise it will just block the view.

* * *

---

1 Acts of Andrew.

Chapter 15

SPONTANEOUS AWAKENING

This is the first article to be published about a very remarkable (yet outwardly very unremarkable) young Englishwoman. It is a brief description of how her life has, almost without warning and practically overnight, been altogether revolutionised, written by a friend who has throughout been her close companion and sole confidant. Its purpose is to encourage all serious spiritual seekers, and particularly those who imagine that true Illumination is necessarily a long way off, or almost impossibly difficult, or the preserve of some particular sect or religion, or indeed the product of any religious discipline at all. The case of Helen Day Scrutton shows that you never can tell. It brings home to us afresh, in our own time and circumstances, the tremendous reality of what Masefield calls the "glory of the lighted soul", demonstrating in the most concrete and vivid way the joy and splendour that await us all just around the corner of our life: no, press right in upon us here and now, as we read these words. We can't be too often reminded, not only of the existence of our Infinite Treasure, but also of its perfect accessibility and naturalness, its homeliness and handiness and immense practicality, and above all its aliveness. To remain satisfied with anything less than This just doesn't make sense.

It was about four years ago when I first met Helen. Since then we've worked very closely together all the while in the same organisation, seeing a great deal of each other during the day, and increasingly when off duty. I should know her fairly well.

Let me try to describe the first impression she made. (If this sounds like an employer's testimonial, why that's what it is, after all—but with what a difference!) I saw Helen as a lively, healthy-minded and healthy-bodied, very intelligent but not at all intellectual woman in her late twenties. In repose, her face was on the stolid side, with splendid eyes, but what brightness when she smiled! She proved quick to learn all the complex details of her job, practical and level-headed, conscientious after her own independent fashion, humorous, tactful and easy with people as a rule, and unusually patient and self-controlled when things went wrong. In short, a Treasure! No nonsense about Helen—not even powder or lipstick (that I've detected, anyway)—athletic, clear-complexioned, scrupulously turned out, good-looking in an unobtrusive way, not pretty. The ideal confidential secretary and a charming friend.

But I still felt obliged, in the end, to take Helen to task. It seemed to me that she didn't know her own value. Her job, though a responsible one, could lead nowhere, and she was clearly capable of something much more creative. Her interests—tennis, swimming, fairly wide but desultory reading (which included few religious books and certainly no mystical ones), listening to all kinds of music, some youth-club work (neglected in recent years), regular but unenthusiastic Church-of-England attendance, and the sort of superficial friendships such a cheerful and popular young person would naturally make—these seemed not to reflect her true character and potentialities. I had the cheek to tell her so, rather often. She offered no comment. But she did, eventually, make serious plans to train as a probation officer. And a wonderful one she would have made.

We were fond of each other, without seeming to make any deep contact. Inevitably she got to know about my concern with spiritual matters, but no pressure at all was exerted: I had no desire to steer her in that or any other direction. And certainly she seemed a most unlikely subject—altogether too normal and down-to-earth, not a spiritual type at all! (In a certain sense, I still think she isn't, thank God!) Besides (and how unlike so many of us, how spiritually unfashionable, almost reprehensible!) Helen solemnly assured me that she'd loved and been loved by her admirable parents, led a happy childhood, enjoyed her grammar school (she must have been a fine head prefect), and found her office work pleasant enough. Her most testing experience was the loss of her fiancé; and in fact death, or some other insuperable obstacle, has intervened to break no fewer than three engagements. (The significance of this seeming tragedy isn't lost on her, of course, and she is now more than happy to remain single and quite unattached to any man.) No, Helen is altogether too well-balanced a young woman, lacking almost all the current credentials—no tangled complexes, no awful history of suffering, no prolonged and bitter struggle—to be what in fact she is, a most gifted mystic. (I suspect, really, that the best masters of the spiritual life were, like Ramana Maharshi, specially sane and healthy, the reverse of abnormal.) Yet when she typed for me some article about mystical religion she scarcely seemed interested, and had less than usual to say. It's true that when she came to our house for an evening, or to stay for a day or two, she got into the habit of picking up one of my books on Vedanta or Sufism or Zen and reading it; and I noticed that she'd always finish what she'd started, however difficult or dull the author. She also read my own little book *On Having No Head*—but made nothing of it, I now learn. At the time, she was too polite to say so.

This brings me to the real beginning of the story—to May, 1964, and what we sometimes call the "Ten Days that Shook the World". Helen was off to Eastbourne for the Whitsun holiday, and anxious to take some of my books with her; I remember these included Aldous Huxley's *Perennial Philosophy*. Evidently she had become really interested. Something was happening.

A new Helen came back, deeply stirred and now eager to talk. "Douglas," she said (and I think I can quote almost the exact words: after all, it was only a few months ago), "I've just realised something: all this applies to me! And of course absolutely nothing else matters!" She explained how the whole thing had, after a few weeks of inward search, accompanied by increasing concern and tension, become perfectly clear to her: now it made sense, she'd taken it in, taken it to heart, and this was quite overwhelming. Those evenings that followed, when she walked alone for hours in the park, wearing dark-glasses so that people shouldn't see that she was crying for joy at the wonder of her discovery, the transformed world, the colours that positively sang, the exquisite beauty of everything (yes everything, including the 'rubbish' in those wire baskets)! Morning after morning in the office, I was to hear from Helen this kind of story. Often—indeed, usually—it was: "No sleep at all last night, Douglas: time just flashed by: again it was just joy, oneness, clarity, from the time I lay down to when I got up for breakfast, fresher than if I'd slept the whole night. The extraordinary thing is I never feel tired." I remember her explaining how she left home, and presently found herself at the office half a mile away, and the interval was just brightness, no-thinking, with no recollection of having walked at all. I remember also her trying to explain how, on other occasions, her walking was "just like taking the dog for a walk"—her legs and their movement had been like the dog's, nothing to do with her. It was a wonderfully free-and-easy feeling. Yes, Indeed!

Many other surprises were in store for us. Helen's tennis, always goodish, immediately became quite remarkably good, to the astonishment of the members of her club—and their greater astonishment and disappointment when she announced that she wasn't going to play anymore, after completing the games that had already been fixed for her. Those games she won brilliantly, automatically. To me, her explanation was that she did nothing, her racquet did it all, the game played itself—with a skill and ease she'd never known. Part of the secret (we agreed) must have been that whereas before she had always wanted very much to win, now she had no feelings at all one way or the other, and the resulting relaxation naturally helped her performance. But she insisted that she didn't do anything: again, she was the onlooker. (And, lest anyone should suppose she'd been reading Herrigel's book on Zen archery, I happen to know she still hasn't done so.)

All ambition, all other interests, had gone. The probation-officer project was dropped at once. In fact, Helen even discussed with me the possibility of getting a routine job, such as a copy-typist's, which would interfere as little as possible with her new life. This idea, however, was soon scrapped because she found that her work, however complicated, practically did itself if she didn't interfere. More remarkably, it did itself (I noticed) even more accurately and rapidly than before. (It *had* to: we spent so much time in the office on other business, on our real business!) "Just let things happen," she said, "and they turn out perfectly. Do them deliberately, plan ahead, and they go wrong." Before, she'd generally been pressed for time: now, she had all the time in the world.

I'm sure everyone in the office noticed the change in her. One man who (somewhat unreasonably, I thought) she hadn't much liked, was now "quite nice really, and it was all Helen's fault." It was plain how happy she was. People asked what had come over her: she looked like a cat that had just had kittens, someone remarked. Not that she was changed beyond recognition: thank goodness the old, charmingly informal Helen, with most of her personal quirks was still with us. There was nothing odd or unnatural or spectacular about the change in her: if anything, she was more truly normal and natural than ever. (So much so that some who don't know Helen very well, but have preconceived notions of the outward effects of Illumination, naturally doubt whether anything more than a psychological reorganisation, akin to those religious conversions which are common enough, has occurred in her. And, of course, one cannot find in Helen, or in any other, what one hasn't begun to find in oneself.) Her ego had never stuck out very far; now it was imperceptible—except, perhaps, for occasional irritation with some particularly difficult client, or employer! "No, it comes back occasionally," she confessed to me, "but now I see clearly when it's there." (Lately, I think even this rare and trivial ego-symptom has disappeared, though she remains capable— we've just discovered—of momentary anger.) Obviously she no longer had moods, but was permanently happy whatever happened. And she had no need to tell me about her changed feeling for people. Her heart really went out to them; she enjoyed and loved them, not equally (it's true) but far more than she'd ever done before. How many times she's walked into my office exclaiming: "What a *wonderful* person so-and-so is, Douglas!"—and her glowing face and shining eyes were eloquent of her feeling. At the same time she no longer saw us through the distorting spectacles of self-interest, but as we really were: and in some instances this shocked her. Unsuspected weaknesses and meannesses were now quite plain. Hidden motives showed themselves. She was no longer deceived.

And Helen had no time for the old social round, no time for idle chatter or hobbies or amusements—no time at all except for the one thing that mattered, and all her time for that alone! She somehow got out of those (always rather pointless) little lunch parties, all reading (including newspapers) except for books on *the* subject, her tennis of course, and even her swimming in the end.

It was the swimming that warned us that her tremendous spirit might be asking too much of her body. One evening in late July I drove Helen to her beach-hut, and as we parted something made me beg her to be very careful. She wasn't. Next morning at the office she told me how rough the sea had been, and how she'd got out beyond the breakers only to become mixed up with a large stinging jellyfish, and then (to cap it all) realised the strength of the current pulling away from the shore. She remained perfectly calm and content (these are roughly her own words) and just waited to see what would happen. Without any effort on her part, her body somehow took her shorewards, where a large wave just picked her up and deposited her quite gently on the beach. There she was surprised to find herself trembling and exhausted.

Helen had become much too careless of her health. She walked and walked goodness knows how far, though always with that unhurried, loose-limbed, easy gait of hers, which is almost like the lope of some animal. She ate too little and irregularly, and rapidly lost weight. Night followed night without sleep—her new-found happiness was so great. (When, however, she did at last sleep it was, from then right up to now, always dreamlessly. This surprised her, because she had been used to dreaming a lot. It interested me, too, because, unlike her, I knew that one of the marks of the illumined is that they dream little or not at all.) After a few weeks of living like this, no wonder she went down with an attack of her old complaint of anaemia, and had to take it easy—physically. Spiritually, things continued to get better and better, though she couldn't understand how that was possible! If she then read and talked much less, this wasn't because she was tired, but so spiritually fresh that talking and reading books about It had become rather pointless. She was their Author; she was It.

Spontaneous Awakening

The weeks following Helen's return from Eastbourne had been a time of ecstasy. Let me quote her own words, typical of that period, hastily scribbled on a scrap of paper without regard for grammar or punctuation, and only just rescued from destruction by me:

Light dazzling pure light clear brilliance

A feeling of being carried away weightlessness

11.00—5.30 time non-existent endless eternity

No physical tiredness sleep out of question feeling of exhilaration and peace. Happening for the first time like fog or a curtain dropped completely away

This is all that matters for always

There must be a heaven on earth

Why explain? Words are useless and unnecessary, but the knowing constant.

(26th May, 1964)

I did suggest, at the time, that this phase of Helen's illumination (we called it the "gorgeous technicolour" phase) would develop into an even profounder, more natural, and virtually permanent state. And this soon happened, in fact. Is it possible for me to describe that state?

Perhaps it would be useful to summarise here by mentioning the four aspects—or moments, or stages—into which we have often divided (artificially, for the sake of description) the essential experience:

1. The VOID. This is the KEY, the indispensable basis. It means clearly *seeing*, at will, even all the time, that right here one is totally

headless, bodiless, mindless, and in fact Nothing whatever.

2. LOVE. The result of this absolute contraction is an equal and opposite expansion, a great outward surge which leaves nobody and nothing out.

3. The ALONE. As thus all-embracing, one is the One, quite solitary, free, independent. These foolish words can give no idea of the Homecoming.

4. MYSTERY. Thus actually to be the Alone, Self-originating and Self-sufficient, is unspeakable wonder.

These four may give some slight clue to an Experience which is, of course, neither Helen's nor mine, but that of the One who is our Self; but really they won't do at all—they only import complications into what is perfect Clarity and Simplicity. Between this Clear Seeing, and the finest description of it, there must always remain an infinite gap. It isn't merely that words can't reveal It: they're what hide It.

Of course a certain amount of talk helped at the beginning. Just being with Helen, ready with encouragement and understanding when she needed them, and the occasional explanation of some puzzle, did make a good deal of difference. And I was able to put her on to those few—but very few—books which have been written out of first-hand experience, and protect her temporarily from the thousands that have not. I introduced her to Eckhart, Ruysbroeck, Rumi, the Upanishads, Sankara, Ramana Maharshi, Lao-tzu, Huang-po and Hui-hai: notice I was careful not to plug any one tradition: it was imperative that Helen should find her own affinities. In fact, she was unable to pick and choose between them: each displayed for her an indispensable aspect of a single clear pattern.(Only, perhaps I should add, Ramana Maharshi has a very special appeal for us both.) Helen devoured these books, ignoring always the merely geographical and historical accidents and grasping the common essence. She had no real questions to ask me then, none at all.

A miracle it remains for us both, how suddenly and completely this wonderful thing has happened. But even miracles have some background, and obviously this one called for further investigation. How was it possible for Helen so rudely to jump the spiritual queue? We thought of the years of anxious searching, of austerities, marathons of meditation, which are traditionally reckoned the price of any real Illumination, and we marvelled. Was Helen one of those very rare exceptions to the rule? Then we discovered—not, of course, an explanation of her gift and her grace, but something of its history. She'd been a dark horse all along. Understandably, there'd been, throughout childhood and youth the flashes, the brief but lovely previews of heaven; but in addition something much more remarkable and significant. From her earliest schooldays onwards, she'd been in the habit of going off on her own, swimming, rambling, just sitting; and this solitude became more and more an essential part of her life-pattern. Latterly, her beach-hut had provided a convenient retreat where she used to sit, quite alone for hours, on summer evenings and at weekends. I asked what she had thought about. She replied—bless her!—just as if it were a stupid question to have asked: "Why, nothing! I just sat!" "Dozing?" I enquired. "Of course not. Quite wide awake, with an empty mind." Just like that! It's true the fact that there was something odd about this behaviour had already dawned upon her: her friends were inclined to regard it as self-indulgent, or even morbid. Not that this had at all deterred Helen: the pleasure of merely sitting there was its own reward, and increasingly necessary to her well-being. But certainly it never occurred to her that this state of no-mind might have some religious or mystical significance, or was much more than an idiosyncrasy. If anyone had told her then—as I did later—that after months and years of sitting meditation a *yogin* would be doing well if he could avoid all wandering thoughts for a few minutes, whereas Helen was able to shed them for as long as she liked—why, if anyone had told her this she would have thought he was just teasing! I don't mean to imply, of course, that this strange accomplishment of hers was 'sitting meditation' in the full sense of that term, or spiritually mature: it was, as yet, far from Self-aware. But what better rehearsal for the Self-awareness she now enjoys could be imagined?

Well, that is Helen's story to date, in brief. It will be pointed out, of course, that having got off to a wonderful start, she still has a long, long way to go. In one sense, it's true: there's no end to This. But in a much deeper sense it's *the* lie. She has nowhere to go. She's where she has always been—HERE. What's more to the point, she has the nerve to see it, and to say she sees it, and to live every moment accordingly. That's all that matters.

For all genuine seekers, and particularly for us in the West, Helen should prove a huge encouragement. She doesn't want to be known—or unknown, for that matter—and is virtually indifferent to praise or ridicule.

But she agrees that others should take heart from her story—from this account of what can happen to a quite 'ordinary' person (in fact, of course, none of us—and certainly not Helen—is quite ordinary), and has happened so recently right here, under our noses, where almost everyone interested in these things suffers from a chronic spiritual inferiority complex. We all know the sort of thing: "It can't be done here. You have to go off to some cave in the Himalayas, or some Japanese monastery, and there you have to spend months just learning how to sit and breathe properly, and then you have to sit in meditation for perhaps the rest of your life, under the guidance of the right Master (and how difficult he is to find) before you can hope for Enlightenment. Even then the chances are you'll miss it. Well, at least you'll get off to a flying start in your next life, or the next but one…"

Helen is splendidly *confident*. Only once, right at the start, has she entertained the slightest doubts regarding her illumination, and then they passed very quickly. (Comparing the immense efforts of certain Zen monks to gain some glimpse of their Original Face, with her own apparently effortless and clear seeing of It, she didn't know what to think—understandably enough.) Her confidence doesn't arise from what she understands, but from What she sees—and anything, anything can be doubted except This.

How many more Helens there are I don't know. Even if there's only one who, reading her story, finds the courage to follow her over the brink of the precipice she will bless Helen, infinitely.

* * *

Chapter 16

ADDENDUM

Notes made in November 1966

During the past year a number of new cases [of 'seeing'] have occurred. Generally, these confirm the foregoing Notes [published in *The Turning Point* under the title '*The Headless Way in 1965*'], but some new points have arisen.

1. Is the seeing real when it 'lacks all impact'?

There have been some cases of highly intelligent young men, interested in these matters, who have said, in effect, "Yes, of course I see this Absence of flesh and blood right here. It is obvious, and makes scientific sense. A 'thing' is a Central Emptiness giving rise to innumerable regional effects which are picked up by its observers and mistakenly projected back upon the Centre. I see I am this Emptiness here, and my human form is only one of its regional effects out there. This is clear, but it lacks all impact. Even when first seen, it is matter-of-fact, uninspiring, flat. No satori, no mystical experience, no thrill. And no noticeable improvement in my mental condition. This can't be It."

The short answer is that It is even duller and flatter than you think. It is absolute Poverty, absolute Inaction, absolute Stillness. The trouble is not its lack of Impact, but your feeling that it ought to have some. Any quality we impose upon It, naturally destroys It.

A more detailed answer runs like this:

(i). Like so many other books, *On Having No Head* unintentionally gives a very wrong impression concerning the experiences which commonly accompany and follow seeing. These depend on all sorts of accidental factors and obey no rules. Their occurrence is not a measure of the clarity and depth of the seeing. Literally, they are quite beside the Point. The Point is seeing Nothing, feeling Nothing, thinking Nothing, being Nothing.

(ii). It is seeing the perfectly simple Truth which sets us free, not having feelings about it. Nobody who takes a laboratory experiment seriously would imagine its validity to depend upon his mood at the time. An ounce of curiosity about what I am is worth tons of religious feeling or mystical experience. These are the normal products of seeing; when they are expected to produce or accompany seeing, they block it.

(iii). All the Masters say nothing is gained and the Void is really void. It follows that seeing what we are is a total emptying or dying, and this is disagreeable. So we tell ourselves that this miserable Vacancy must instantly be filled (even before we have clearly seen It) by some splendid experience. This way we succeed in postponing our seeing.

(iv). It isn't that we can't see (in fact, we do see) but that we don't wish to—yet. With good reason we fear that if we allow ourselves to see This we shall soon be interested in nothing else. We cannot force the issue, but we can allow our curiosity about ourselves to grow, and we can remember when things go wrong that (according to all the

Masters) only Self-seeing leads to happiness and a truly full life. To
the degree that we are Poor right here, the riches flow out from here.
So long as we remain at the still and empty and infinitely tiny Hub of
the universal wheel, we command every spoke. But when, craving the
glitter and movement and colour of one spoke or another, we move
out towards it, we lose all.

2. What is the connection between seeing and depth-psychology?
Seeing does not dispense with the need to face the whole of one's past
and to undo its knots by exposing them to the light of consciousness.
The more analytical work that has been done before seeing, the clearer
and steadier the seeing is likely to be. Nevertheless such analysis does
not itself lead to seeing, nor does neglect of it rule out seeing. No
doubt in all cases of seeing there remain hidden conflicts. (In one or
two recent cases, the trouble seems quite severe.) How should these
be dealt with? Not now at the psychological level, but instead at the
deepest level which is seeing itself. Our sole task is just to go on seeing
who we are. The necessary situations will then arise, quite naturally,
in which we may re-enact the essential aspects of our buried past,
so ridding it of its menace. (This is presumably the significance of
the Buddhist belief that Enlightenment involves the recollection of
one's total past.)

Temporarily to neglect our seeing, therefore, in favour of some
kind of self-analysis, in the mistaken belief that we shall thereby see
still more totally, would simply be to revert to our old blindness,
and the analysis would just go on and on. Seeing itself is the only

truly profound and final analysis, and it may be trusted to clear up (quickly, if we allow it) all our psychological problems. It is the one answer to all problems, because all problems are, basically, failure to see who we are.

3. Is sitting meditation necessary?

Meditation is even more essential for seers than for non-seers, though it is now increasingly an enjoyment instead of an effort. The only essential thing is to see until seeing becomes quite habitual. Each must find his own way of bringing this about. For some, sitting meditation may be extremely helpful, if not absolutely essential. The same posture, time, place, and circumstances, each day, produce a cumulative effect. As for the subject of meditation, this is the Subject himself, this Absence of body-mind here. Generally, this seems to work best when the eyes are half open, and the something out there stands in contrast to the Nothing here, giving It special vividness.

(One or two friends find it useful to wear, for meditation, a towel over the head, projecting a few inches in front of the face like a monk's cowl. The just-glimpsed edges of the towel are then seen to frame—one's Real or Original Face.)

It is important to come to each meditation in a state of total openness, importing nothing from last time. Then each occasion will have its own unique and unpredictable flavour.

* * *

Chapter 17

HOME TRUTH

When I stop overlooking this looker
and start making odious comparisons
I see that the one I'm looking out of
Is nothing whatever
like the one I'm looking at—
the former so plain, the latter so interesting.
Yet it is because he and I have nothing in common
that this emptiness here is full of him,
my shapelessness taking on his shape,
my colourlessness beautifully stained with his pigments,
my house his home. Here's hospitality for you!
Where I view myself from
settles what I view myself as.
Viewing myself from where you are, 6 feet away,
I discover an elderly gentleman,
distance lending that much enchantment.
Viewing myself from where I am, 0 feet away,
I find 0—this terrifying Home Truth.
However, viewing itself from here, this 0, this nobody,
innocent of distance, incapable of pushing anybody off,
sees it is everybody it sees, including that elderly gentleman
who keeps staring through the glass into my empty bathroom.

This is the end of terror.

* * *

Chapter 18

PREFACE
to the 2nd edition of
ON HAVING NO HEAD

This new edition provides a welcome opportunity to correct certain misapprehensions, and also to mention some of the further developments and findings of the past six years, since this little book was first published.

Chapter 1 is misleadingly dramatic. Seeing one's Original Face is seeing one's absence; so far from being uplifting, it is a kind of dying, a total humiliation or deflation. (That is why it is 'difficult'.) Also it is extremely matter-of-fact, and not at all religious or mystical. Suzuki's description—prosaic, non-glorious, grey, unobtrusive, unattractive— is exact. The famous tears and sweat and uncontrollable laughter that we have come to associate with Satori are incidental, and only what might be expected from sudden success in any endeavour—such as winning the Pools—after years of anxious trying. Such inevitable reactions throw no more light on the nature of Satori than they do on the nature of affluence. When there has been no long build-up of tension, there follows no violent release of tension: the experience is cool and ordinary. This does not mean it is shallow.

Enlightenment is quite free and available instantly. However desirable, spiritual maturity is not an essential prerequisite: we don't have to remodel our human nature before we are capable of seeing our real Nature. Nevertheless dedicated practice, sooner or later, is indispensable. In a very real sense, we get nothing on the cheap, though there are alternative modes of payment. It's like buying a car: you may take delivery now and pay over the next two years; or you may save for the whole two years and purchase outright at the end. In the last instance, the car is yours for keeps; in the others, the firm will distrain if you don't keep up your instalments. It is only too possible, if one's seeing has come early and easily, to undervalue and therefore neglect it, with the result that it fades away.

* * *

Chapter 19

THE CALLER

George: What is Enlightenment?

Henry: Hello! Is that you, George?

George: Yes, it's me.

Henry: Where are you? Where are you speaking from?

George: Right here, of course.

Henry: (tapping George's forehead) You mean you are in here?

George: Where else?

Henry: (tapping George's forehead again) Well, George, you've got a visitor, knocking at your door. May I come in?

George: Don't be silly. No admittance.

Henry: So you're short of room in there, are you? Crowded?

George: Well…

Henry: All right, George. You're in, I'm out. I'm standing outside here on your doorstep, calling on you, not allowed in, but very curious about what lies indoors. Just tell me what it's like in there, shouting your answers through the letterbox. (Points to George's mouth.)

George: What do you want to know?

Henry: Is it stuffy in there, oppressive, hot?

George: Not at all. It feels quite fresh and airy.

Henry: These two small windows in your facade, George: do they really let in enough light? Is the glass clean? What colour and shape are the window frames, looked at from your side? Honestly, now...

George: Well... Now I come to look: how extraordinary! There's only one window, and it's huge, huge. No frame round it, and no glass either. Absolutely clear!

Henry: Brilliant natural daylighting throughout the house, no dark corners at all?

George: None.

Henry: Well, the walls must indeed be far apart to take a picture-window like that! How big is this room of yours, really? After all, it's for living in, and your inside story is what matters, not my outside impression.

George: Endlessly wide and tall and deep. No walls at all! No floor, no ceiling!

Henry: (taking hold of George's nose) What about this?

George: How curious! It's a sort of transparent pink cloud dangling there in mid-air, with nothing at all my side of it.

Henry: Nothing at all? What about George, the Inhabitant of this house? What's he like? Who's answering these questions?

The Caller

George: No trace of him at all! Nothing here but room, vast emptiness.

Henry: Life must be terribly dull in there, in a home so unfurnished? —bare even of a tenant.

George: Quite the contrary! This place is all picture-window, which means all view? All view-out, with no view-in and no viewer. And the view totally invades the room, which is thus marvelously furnished.

Henry: 'No admittance', you said.

George: What madness, not to mention discourtesy! Everyone's admitted—everyone except George! It's he who's out, you who are in. Just now, Henry's face fills and floodlights this room, leaving not an inch of it in shadow. This is your house because it never was mine. You fit in here so beautifully because I don't fit in at all. Welcome home!

Henry: You were asking about Enlightenment.

George: If this is Enlightenment, why I've been Enlightened all along, without noticing it. And so has everybody else.

Henry: You see.

George: But can it be as simple and obvious as this? Tell me the rest.

Henry: The moment you think that there must be something else, and that seeing your total Emptiness is not enough, then you have stopped seeing it and are thoroughly unenlightened. But once you have really looked into the place you occupy (and found you don't occupy it!) you can always drop thinking and look in again, at will.

As I See It

The thing is then to will to look more and more often, till you see all the while What you are.

* * *

Chapter 20

WHAT AM I?

A: I keep on enquiring *What am I?*

B: What for?

A: I hope one day to see clearly my non-existence.

B: But the question *What am I?* assumes the I's existence! Isn't it like shouting for silence, or furiously denying ill temper?

A: What's to be done then?

B: Why not try scrapping all such labels as *I* and *you*, *self* and *others*, *mine* and *his*, *here* and *there*, and see what happens? Instead of imposing these question-begging distinctions, why not humbly submit to the facts just as they given, and be prepared for anything?

A: What facts?

B: Well, what presents itself now?

A: Only these hands.

B: They'll do, so long as they're stripped of labels.

A: Hands are all much alike.

B: All?

As I See It

A: Well, no… Among the many hands that come and go, only two feel heat and cold and pain and roughness and smoothness… And stay more or less the same size…

B: Go on, go on!

A: …and fade out around the elbows, and are attached to no…

B: Ah! Now you see!

* * *

Chapter 21

WHAT IS SELF-REALISATION?

In order to answer this question as clearly as possible, let us distinguish six progressive stages:

Steps

	(1) Ignorance—not knowing What one is
(1) to (2) Gradual	
	(2) Understanding—knowing What one is
(2) to (3) Abrupt	
	(3) Seeing—catching sight of What one is
(3) to (4) Gradual	
	(4) Illumination—steadily seeing What one is
(4) to (5) Abrupt	
	(5) Self-Realisation—being Who one is
(5) to (6) Gradual	
	(6) Full Self-Realisation
	—steadily seeing What one is
	—steadily being Who one is
	—steadily realising That one is

This table is subject to variation in individual cases. For instance, Understanding (2) may come later than Seeing (3), and Illumination (4) may come later than Self-realisation (5). Again, some of the stages may be telescoped, though not actually avoided. And, of course, the titles chosen for the six stages are rather arbitrary and will not suit everybody. In fact, having set up such a scheme, it is easy (and, in the end, necessary) partially to demolish it. Before we do that, however, let us see to what extent it can clear up misunderstandings about the nature of Self-realisation and how it may be arrived at.

(1) Ignorance—not knowing What one is:
The marks of this stage are that one believes the world is real in its own right, that one is a body which is a part of the world, and that one's consciousness is dependent upon the body.

The activities which normally go with this stage are the pursuit of pleasure, and when that disappoints the pursuit of possessions and power, and when those disappoint the pursuit of reputation and fame.

(2) Understanding—knowing What one is :
It is a decisive step in one's life when one turns from the surrounding world to oneself at its Centre, and asks What lies here. More or less gradually one comes to understand that one is not the body but Consciousness or the Self, that one is not a thing among things but that unique No-thing which is the Source and Ground and Container of all things. One comes to know, and in the end whole-heartedly to believe, that the Real is not what is experienced, but the Experiencer, the One who is not in the world, but in whom the world is.

Profound intellectual work is characteristic of this stage. It takes the form of ever-renewed discrimination between the object or not-Self there, and the Subject or Self here, with the result that one becomes progressively detached from the world and identified with the Reality it depends on.

Also appropriate to this stage are talking and reading about spiritual matters, and the practice of systematic meditation. All this leads to growth of one's desire for Self-realisation, directly experienced.

(3) Seeing—catching sight of What one is:

Though it is a useful preparation, no amount of understanding the Self will ever build up to seeing the Self. And for a very good reason: seeing the Self is quite incompatible with thinking about the Self, and is a much simpler and more direct experience. Instead of *knowing* that right here, on the Spot one occupies, is this brilliant Clarity without so much as a speck of body-mind, one actually *sees* this Clarity, and sees it more sharply and convincingly than one sees anything else whatever. The Self here sees itself to be perfectly lucid, transparent, obvious. In fact, mere objects out there are, by comparison, hardly seen at all: only very limited aspects of them are perceived, remotely and one at a time, and in the spatio-temporal gap between observer and observed all kinds of errors are certain to creep in. Not so Self-seeing, where Seer and seeing and seen are one and the same, coincident, unseparated by any interval of time or space, with the result that there is no possibility of error. Moreover, because this Self-seeing is seeing what has no parts or aspects or history, it is always a total and perfect seeing: one cannot half see it, nor can one see half of it. To see the Self at all is to see it entire—while the seeing lasts.

This Self-seeing is true Liberation, the decisive step. Or rather, it is a sudden, unpremeditated leap in the dark: not the result of intention or training or merit, but the free gift of a Grace which is not to be commanded. Nevertheless this first seeing is, as a rule, a sudden flash which does not at once issue in a steady state. It fades immediately it is not attended to, and needs constant renewal. In a sense, therefore, this third stage is only the beginning of the true spiritual life.

(4) Illumination—steadily seeing What one is:
One's seeing needs to be practised and stabilised, till it goes on all the while. Actually, 'practised' is misleading: 'enjoyed' is nearer the mark, because seeing is so very easy, natural, and agreeable. All the same, it can be neglected, and total dedication is indispensable. Normally, it will take years of more-or-less deliberate seeing before seeing becomes quite automatic, in all the circumstances of daily life. In the end, there will be no occasions which are unfavourable to Self-seeing.

(5) Self realisation—being Who one is:
Just as there is no footbridge between understanding the Self and seeing the Self, so there is no footbridge between seeing the Self and being the Self: the transition is a sudden leap, powered by Grace. No amount of seeing clearly *What* one is—namely, this Emptiness of body-mind—will automatically lead to the first-hand experience of being *Who* one is—namely, the One, the Sole Reality, the Alone. Certainly some progress in stabilising one's Self-seeing will make Self-realisation rather more likely. But they are distinct and independent orders of experience, and it is perfectly possible to advance in one

bound from one's initial seeing of What one is to being Who one is, without any practice of the former. This radical shift of consciousness, of identity, comes out of the blue, when it wills.

The mark of this stage is that, instead of merely *thinking about* and *seeing* the One, one actually *feels* like the One. One answers to this Name, as before one answered to a human name. One directly experiences what it is to be the All and the Source of All.

But again, this realisation is not, normally, constant, but a series of realisations, flashes of the Supreme Identity separated by periods of Self-forgetfulness.

(6) Full Self-realisation—steadily being Who one is:
Again, it is certainly not practice as a task or a duty, but as ever-renewed enjoyment, which leads to the permanent establishment of the Supreme Identity.

And probably, long before that Identity is uninterruptedly enjoyed, it will be seen to include, besides seeing *What* one is, and being *Who* one is, realising *That* one is. In other words, though the experience of this sixth stage is in the last resort perfectly simple and indivisible, yet it must somehow include a total amazement—amazement at the 'impossible' fact that one has actually occurred, that anything exists at all, that the Self actually is. Here, one says 'I AM !' and that is enough. Not *How* I am or *What* I am, but *That* I am: not what I look like, or embrace, or do, but the simple and astounding fact that I ALONE AM—this incredible achievement of having, without help or reason or cause, raised Myself out of the chaos of non-existence and nullity into BEING. This alone is true spiritual knowledge—the knowledge of the unknowable Mystery, which is the Self's own wonder at Itself.

The fact that some exceptionally gifted souls may be able to combine two or more of these six stages, thus abbreviating our table, does not make nonsense of the table. For most of us, it is essential to sort out our confused ideas about Self-realisation, and cease (for instance) confusing the mere understanding of Stage 2 with the seeing of Stage 3, or the seeing of Stage 3 with the being of Stage 5; otherwise, we are likely to rest satisfied with a partial realisation, or (in the case of Stage 2) with no realisation at all, but only an intellectual grasp of the truth. Moreover, unless we recognise the difference between the stages of gradual progress, where systematic practice is appropriate (not to say essential), and the stages of sudden break-through, where practice is meaningless and only Grace counts, we are in danger of misdirecting our energies.

The only way to *see* the Self is to be interested enough just to look, once and for all, at the Spot one occupies. And the only way to *be* the Self is to submit, once and for all, to the experience of Aloneness. These two essential leaps in the spiritual life cannot be commanded or worked up to, or occur in slow motion. They are mysterious, unpredictable gifts. On the other hand, they are eminently worth knowing about, because they are more likely to be conferred upon those who have heard of them, and earnestly desire them. Grace gives no command performances, but has been known to respond to an urgent and heartfelt invitation.

* * *

Chapter 22

IN THIS SIX FOOT BODY

Thou canst not by *going* reach that place wherein there are no birth, no ageing, no decaying, no falling away, no rising up elsewhere in rebirth… For, my friend, in this very body, six feet in length… I do declare you are the world, and the origin of the world, and the ceasing of the world, and likewise the way that leadeth to the ceasing thereof.

Anguttara Nikaya

How can we get to this marvellous Goal? Or rather, since the Buddha says we are already there, and the goal lies within our very body, how can we enter and look into our own organism? How can we see what it is really like here at home, right on this spot? It is worth trying anything that promises to help us to this insight: hence the following suggestions.

We have no difficulty in seeing what it's like to be in our *bricks-and-mortar* home. This very ordinary and accessible experience, then, may possibly give us some clues to that seemingly more difficult experience—seeing what it's like to be in our *flesh-and-blood* home. In other words, let us find out whether our outer habitation can throw some light on our inner one, our house illuminate our body. Let us take seriously the significant fact that our body has universally been pictured as a kind of house we are somehow inhabiting.[1]

---

1 The aptness of the metaphor derives from the fact that, functionally, the body and its housing are one. My house, including its many services, is my body extended, its

As I See It

Beginning with the bricks-and-mortar house, the first thing to be noticed is that it has two aspects. Evidently for the owner it is one kind of thing, and for the milkman and postman quite another kind of thing. I distinguish clearly between my house's interior and exterior, between my experience of it from inside and others' experience of it from outside, between my outlook and their inlook, between my view of the *other* houses in the street when I'm at home and my view of *this* house when I'm standing on the pavement opposite. Indeed, I'm in no danger of confusing these two aspects, for it is the vast difference between them—a difference of kind and not of degree—which makes this house my home, a place to live in. Thus it is perfectly obvious, when I'm indoors, that my house is amply spacious but presents no façade (though the shadow on this side of the street and the reflection on the other side, in the windows opposite, may give hints); and perfectly obvious, when I'm outdoors, that my house presents plenty of façade but no living space. It is closed against me. To open it up, I stop admiring the front elevation and go in.

When at last I care—and dare—to look, I find that all this applies not only to my house but to its occupant, to my body. It, also, has two contrasting aspects—interior and exterior, my experience of it from inside and others' experience of it from outside, my outlook and their inlook, my view of the *other* bodies when I'm in this one and my view of *this* body when I'm out there seeing myself from their point of view.

---

outgrowth and needful development; and the kind of life I live can only be lived by and in both together, as a single 'biological' unit. It isn't surprising, therefore, that they should have similarities.

And again, the difference between these two aspects, and the importance of not confusing them, cannot be exaggerated. As with my house so with my body, when I'm at home I find ample room but no façade or face here (my shadow and what I see in the mirror are over there, and the wrong way round anyhow); and when I'm out (as I think) I find my face or façade but no room, no interior living space. This body's accommodation is concealed from and closed against all outsiders. I must take up residence and view the property the other way round. I must discover the inside story. Then I find plenty of room.

In fact, the interior of my flesh-and-blood house is immense: here is an ultra-contemporary design, an open plan indeed, bare of furniture and the walls glass everywhere—all view and no privacy, no hiding place, no dark corners, no shadows. The inside and the outside story are not so much contrasting as incongruous. How odd that an elevation so small and opaque and complicated should give on a ground-plan so huge and luminous and uncluttered! How odd that one structure should incorporate two such incompatible architectural styles!

These two aspects are, however, by no means of equal status: the inside matters most. Houses are for living in and looking out of rather than for living out of and looking at, and this is emphatically true of my flesh-and-blood house. Anyway I can't get out. I'm housebound, a lifelong stay-at-home.

Now the astonishing thing is how I made believe quite the opposite of this: how I pretended to myself, crazily, that there was only *one* aspect of this body, only *one* view of it—the outsider's. It's as if I were dreaming I had locked myself out and were doomed to shiver there in the street all the rest of my life; and all the while I was safely indoors and tucked up in bed. Or it's as if, sitting at home and seeing the façade of the house opposite, I pretended I was also sitting in the house opposite and seeing the façade of this house, so that the two houses were simultaneously seen as alike, façade to façade, and neither had any room inside. In short, I was 'seeing things'. Sane on the comparatively unimportant subject of my bricks-and-mortar home, I became quite insane on the all-important subject of my flesh-and-blood home.

But now, coming to my senses, I find that making myself thoroughly at home here in this body, enjoying its unsuspected immensity and openness, is the easiest, the most natural thing imaginable. In fact, so far from being that one spot in the world which is inscrutable, this living space of mine is the one spot in the world which I know directly and through and through, for here is no gap between seer and seen: in me, now, they coincide. I can be wrong about all other people's homes (in fact, they *must* be different over there from what they look like here) but not about mine—once I bother to look. I am this dwelling's sole inhabitant—no visitors allowed—and I alone have inside information about it. Only I am in a position to say what it's like here. The saints and sages, the philosophers and scientists, are all of them elsewhere, and therefore unqualified to tell me what I shall find when, in all simplicity and honesty, I notice not only the premises I'm looking at, but also these very different ones I'm looking out of.

All the same, it is delightful to read the words of other home-lovers:

> Observing that this body is like froth, observing that it is like a mirage, breaking the flowery shafts of Mara, he (the disciple) goes where the King of Death cannot see him.
>
> *Dhammapada*

> I realised the Essential Nature of my body-mind, that it was like the fluidity of the oceans of fragrance surrounding the Isles of the Blest. I came to realise that I had all along been throwing the broken shards of my thoughts of personality into the pure limpidity of my Essential Nature.
>
> *Surangama Sutra*

> In the place where no man is I will put my hand to my forehead and watch for you... I will wait and look out for you where no man speaks, that is in Maitreya's land, where no mouth or lips are needed.
>
> Pai-chang

> Thou art as a mirage in the desert that the thirsty man taketh to be water until he cometh unto it and findeth it to be nothing, and where he thought it to be, there he findeth God. Even so, if thou wert to examine thyself, thou wouldst find it to be naught, and there wouldst thou find God... and naught would be left of thee but a name without a form.
>
> Shaikh Ahmad Al-Alawi

As I See It

He saw a city set upon a hill sloping to the south, that to his sight when it was measured was no more of length and of breadth than a rood.

But as soon as he was brought into the city and looked about him, then thought him it was wonder mickle... Then was this wonder to him, how this city within was so long and so large, that was so little to his sight when he was without.

Walter Hilton

To thyself a Tenant be,

And inhabit safe and free.

Say not that this House is small,

Girt up in a narrow Wall.

Joseph Beaumont

O! that this too, too solid flesh would melt!

William Shakespeare

* * *

Chapter 23

FACE TO NO-FACE

At large O at large this huge brilliant morning
nothing at all here my side of that touchable sky
my side of those cauliflower clouds and those dinky firtrees
my side of those toy cars and lilliputian children playing
my side of this skyscraping grass
my side of your world-eclipsing face
nothing at all here, nothing whatever, nothing
no-face to no-face this brilliant morning
face to no-face this huge morning—morning for just looking

When easily now I stop overlooking this looker
and start making far-from-odious comparisons
I see the one I'm looking out of
is nothing like the one I'm looking at
the one so plain and the other so complicated
this face so blanched blank barefaced
that face so filled in so many coloured counties for exploring
Thank you O thank you

Face to no-face this just-for-looking morning
It's because you and I have nothing in common
(vive la différence) that I am you, am you, am you
my emptiness brimming over with you
my shapelessness shapely shaped by you
my snow stained rainbow with your rainbow blood

As I See It

my house your home—here's hospitality for you—O welcome
O face to-no face this huge brilliant no-thinking just for looking morning
Thank you O thank you

* * *

Chapter 24

THE SERIOUS QUESTION

The main reason for Ramana Maharshi's widespread and continued appeal in the West is his insistence on asking: "Who am I?" This is really the crucial question for the modern world. It crops up everywhere, not merely in philosophical and religious circles. Psychiatrists find their patients—dimly aware of the place where healing lies—obsessed with it. It is one of the chief themes of the more intelligent pop singers—Petula Clark, for instance, has a song actually entitled "Who am I?", and, though the answers are inconclusive, at least the question is relentlessly insisted upon. Young people are particularly concerned, as never before in history, with the problem of personal identity and the meaning of their own existence. It is not surprising, therefore, that Maharshi should interest them.

A fair proportion of these young people (and some older ones, too) are really serious about this all-important question: they feel it is not merely for asking, but for answering also. It is not for them a rhetorical question or incantation or pious formula expressing some vague aspiration, but a matter to be settled now. Life is short and precarious, and it would be negligent to die before one had made time to ask who it is that is alive. If *this* question isn't interesting and central and urgent, what question is? If I'm serious about it, if I mean business, I shall demand a clear and prompt reply.

— As clear and prompt a reply as if I were asking the question,

"*Where* am I?" Suppose I have lost my way in a strange city: I don't shut my eyes and ears and recite the words "Where am I?" till I die of hunger and exhaustion. I hurriedly consult a map and street-names and passers-by till I succeed in locating myself. I put my question clearly, expect a precise answer, take that answer seriously, and act on it without delay.

"*Who* am I?" is a far more vital question than "*Where* am I?" Fortunately, the answer also is far more straightforward and simple and accessible—according to Ramana Maharshi, and our own experience if only we will attend to and trust it.

There is no doubt about what I *appear* to be. Stationed out there, my observers see me as a man. And there is no doubt about what I *am*. Stationed here, I see myself as not a man, not an animal, not a plant, not a thing of any sort, but as this simple No-thing, or Clarity, or Void, or Essence, or Light—the names are many, the experience one and simplicity itself. What lies right here is for me brilliantly obvious and wholly accessible—accessible not to thought, but to direct inspection.

To the question "*When* can I thus see who I am?" Maharshi answers "Now!" I can find no record of his ever having said to anybody: "You aren't ready yet to see who you are. Go away and discipline yourself, practise this or that kind of meditation for so many years, and then come back to me." Instead, and whatever the disciple's condition or problem, he says, "The answer to your problem is to see who has it, now. What are you waiting for? You *are* the Self, and never have been anything else."

The Serious Question

To the question *"How* can I thus see who I am?"* Maharshi answers
"There is nothing to do but be yourself, and what could be easier and
more natural than that? Just stop thinking and see what it's like being
you, and not being the body which others see. The only reason you
aren't enlightened about who you are is that you *think* yourself out
of it." Or words to that effect.

If I have the sense to take Ramana Maharshi seriously, if I have
any real respect for his teaching, if I attend to what he actually says
rather than the human personality the message comes through, if I
genuinely want to discover who I am and am not frightened to death
of doing so, if I am at all sincere in the inquiry—then I shall just look
and see. And, once having seen, I shall not dishonestly pretend I don't
see. Just as the lost traveller, having been shown exactly where he is,
briefly expresses his thanks and goes his way, so I (if I am equally
sensible) say, without embarrassment or mock-modesty, "Thank you,
I see," and get on with my seeing—that Self-seeing which is from now
on my true meditation.

May this meditation be practised in the Sri Ramana Auditorium!
In other words, may its users be true devotees. Who is the true
devotee: the one who in all simplicity does what the Master tells
him, or the one who so adores the Master that he wouldn't presume
to follow in those holy footsteps?

* * *

Chapter 25

MASKED BALL

When at last I get tired of making faces at you
and bother to look here
I am perfectly transparent to myself
(whatever could you be staring at,
what's so interesting about this blank wall behind me?)
then I positively delight in being seen through by you
and in thereby seeing through you also
through the deception of your countless opaque appearances
to the one reality behind them
—or rather in front of them, my side of your face—
to the unmasked face here, where I love you because I am you.

Conversely when I pull faces at you
(however kindly I make them they are all rude, really)
when I refuse to look here
when I insist on trying to save my face
by taking myself at face value
when I put on the act
of putting up this tragi-comic mask here to hide behind
then you also are hidden from me, O tragically defaced stranger
and we are all dancing in the masked ball which is Hell.

Hell is keeping up appearances and pretending they are real
identifying with one's own appearance
and refusing to see through others'

to where all appearances come from, to what they are appearances of.
Hell is mutual impenetrability, non-recognition,
density, solidity, opacity, thickness, separation, alienation,
mask confronting mask symmetrically,
all third persons together and no first person singular in sight.
In short, imaginary.

Heaven isn't waiting till the beautiful starry clock chimes twelve
celestial lights up, all masks off, true faces shining out at last. No, the
clock is running slow and the ball will never be over. Heaven is this
mask off, disclosing the one bright and charming Face now.

* * *

Chapter 26

MAKING A GOOD IMPRESSION

Nowadays one hears so much about the need to become fully aware of how one strikes other people, and one even meets groups deliberately practising the art of self-presentation or projection. In my own experience, however, the need is all the other way round, and concern about self-projection is our main trouble.

Certainly as a child I had to learn how my behaviour looked to others, and how it required constant adjustments in the light of their reactions. Even more certainly, I had to discover that whereas, for myself as 1st person, I wasn't so much in the world as the world was in me, this was not at all how the world viewed me. As 3rd person, I was very small and local and unimportant. Indeed my growing up was really my cutting down to size, my inevitable shrinkage from cosmic dimensions to merely human ones, as I learned slowly and painfully to see myself as others saw me—or as I feared or hoped they did. But the tragedy was that I learned this necessary lesson only too well, and by the time I approached manhood I had altogether lost sight of what it was like being myself here at home, unprojected from this Centre. I had become truly eccentric and Self-alienated, and this gave me hell. Agreeing with society that I was that little, solid, opaque, boxed-up thing they saw and nothing else, I virtually became my appearance at (say) 6 feet; and What this was an appearance of, at 0 feet, the central Reality from which my myriad appearances stem,

I was determined to overlook. I was sick, with a sickness that is all the more serious because it is practically universal, and all the more insidious because it is practically un-noticed.

When I don't see What I really am here to myself, I inevitably waste much time imagining how I appear to be over there to others, what they are making of me, how I'm going over, the face I'm presenting to them. And my self-concern, my lack of genuine interest in them, my anxiety to make a favourable impression, are enough to ruin that impression. Moreover my behaviour follows suit: my reactions grow bungling and nervy, and the self I present is worsened further. I'm very aware that I'm projecting badly. The whole enterprise is miserably self-defeating.

But when I do see What I really am here to myself, I find myself ceasing to care how I look over there. All that interests me now is what I actually find instead of what I imagine: I take myself exactly as given—as mere capacity or empty room—and others exactly as given—as filling this room with their fascinating shapes and colours and movements and speech. Now my new-found attention to and enjoyment of these others, along with my lack of anxiety about myself, ensure that my responses shall be much more sensitive, swift, spontaneous, and (in the long run) appropriate. No doubt the others are better served now, but how I'm going down with them is none of my business. My business is what impression they are making here, and upon Whom.

The problem of social relationships is solved by seeing Who I really am. Satisfactory projection goes on out there only when it's allowed to look after itself, and I look after its infinitely resourceful Source right here. Such is my own experience, and I doubt whether I'm exceptional.

* * *

Chapter 27

WHAT DELUDES
IS WHAT ENLIGHTENS

*The tools that assembled the personality-box
are the very ones for dismantling it.*

Mrs General: "If Miss Amy Dorrit will direct her own attention to,
and will accept of my poor assistance in, the formation of a surface,
Mr. Dorrit will have no further cause for anxiety."

Dickens

The notion that a man has a body distinct from his soul is to be
expunged; this I shall do by... melting apparent surfaces away, and
displaying the infinite which was hid.

Blake

WHAT sort of universe do we find ourselves in—one that is out
to delude us, to put up every obstacle to our Enlightenment? Is its
essential Nature, which is our own also, withheld, deeply buried, or
heavily camouflaged? Is the saving Truth so untruthful about itself
that only the most industrious and gifted of detectives—by dint of a
whole lifetime or many lifetimes of relentless interrogation—could
hope to wring it out at last?

How fortunate for you and me that the sages give a resounding
NO to these questions, and go on to assure us that the boot is on the
other foot! All is given now (they say) to the simple, the childlike;

and what veils the Great Secret is its own blinding obviousness. It is precisely our busy ingenuity, our interfering imagination, our meanly suspicious attitude, our fearful rejection of the unvarnished Truth as it presents itself to us, which coat that Truth with layer upon layer of falsehood and inevitably make our lives a sham. Once we stop varnishing just long enough to notice what we are trying to cover up, we find in it all we need. This present moment and place require no re-surfacing. Our Nature is on view. All we have to do is look, trust what we see, and go on looking and trusting.

And surely, when we are quite well, we have a hunch that the sages are right. It is true we meet people who seem sure the universe is a gigantic confidence-trickster determined to catch them out; but such people, we feel, are sick—often very obviously so. As for personally putting the question to the test, when have I ever trusted the Nature of things too much, or been too open to it? What lets me down is not how things are but what I do to them. I find that whenever I have the grace and the good sense to submit to what is freely presented at this moment, without trying to improve upon it, the Clear Light of What-I-am (and therefore what everything else is) blazes forth. Better even than this, I'm always finding that *what I took to be a massive stumbling-block proves on inspection to be a wide-open gateway leading straight Home.* The worst obstacles to Self-discovery turn out to be the best aids to it. The Universe proves after all to be helpful candour itself and transparently honest (inviting us to take after it); it wears its Heart on its coatsleeve; without hesitation it comes down on the side of the unsophisticated. And small wonder that it should be so strewn with clues and advertisements about its own Essence, that it should indeed be built for Enlightenment, if (as the sages have assured us) its very reason is Enlightenment, and if its own Self-knowledge is what the cosmos is all about.

Let us now observe how these principles work out in everyday practice. Enlightenment I shall take to be seeing clearly that *here* I am no-thing whatever, that *here* form is void (without eyes or ears or nose or mouth, or any thing or function or quality whatever), that here my Original Face is absolutely featureless. What was it, then, that tricked me into believing otherwise, that told me I was looking out at the world through two windows in a box, that at the centre of my world lay my acquired human face instead of my Original non-human Face? Four wilfully misinterpreted messages did me that disservice—(1) what my mirror told me, (2) what other faces told me, (3) what my fingers told me, (4) what scientists told me. The rest of this article seeks to show how these same four messages, taken seriously just as they come to me, will now (if I allow them) reverse their meaning, will undeceive and Enlighten me; or, in other words, how *the same four tools I used for knocking together the (illusory) personality-box are all I need for knocking it apart.*

(1) What my mirror tells me

The question isn't whether I have a human face (of course I have!) but where I keep the thing. My mirror shows me. Now I look in it to see what I'm *not* like here: the contrast between my face out there on the far side of the glass, and my no-face here on this side, is vivid and total. Now my glass, no longer misused for making a thing of me here, is used for unmaking me; now it removes like a powerful magnet the last particle from this Spot, leaving it perfectly vacant. Now I see that my mirror never deluded me: it was I who, self-deluded, was blind to its truly Enlightening message.

(2) What other faces tell me

Those other faces, so often turning towards me, soon persuaded me that I must be like that. Too successfully they insisted on my joining the club and becoming one of them. Staring, peering in this direction, frowning, smiling, hinting in a thousand ways at what they made of me, and often telling me outright, they won me over to their viewpoint and most thoroughly faced me up. I imagined what it was they must be looking at, and how they felt about it, till in the end I took it to be myself; and what I saw myself to be right here became of no account whatever. Thus I was led to commit the double absurdity of ignoring what was given and manufacturing what wasn't given—at what a cost in confusion and anxiety! It was as if, more than anything else in the world, I feared and hated the obvious.

But now, going by what I plainly see, I see those faces as so many coloured and moving shapes curiously punctured and hair-fringed—shapes which don't begin to be haunted by any kind of spook, still less by spooks with notions about me. I no longer have the uncomfortable feeling of being under inspection by those eyeballs.

The relief, the negative benefit, is great, the positive benefit much greater. Your face over there proves just the thing to strip me of mine here and show me what I really am. I notice that whereas those two other people conversing over there are, for us here, face to face, you and I are not: we are—marvellously, hilariously, lovingly—face to no-face. Your face hits me in the face so hard it knocks mine clean out of existence.

Our asymmetry is superbly brought out—nose there, none here; pinkness there, colourlessness here; motion there, stillness here; opacity there, transparency here; and so on indefinitely. In short, the face there that used to put a face on me here, now obligingly takes if off me, instantly and completely.

(3) What my fingertips tell me
My third face-building tool, my third method of attempting to assemble a head here on my shoulders, was feeling—in particular, exploring this region with my fingertips and finding here what I thought was a nose, mouth, eyelids, and all the other standard features. This was an elaborate piece of self-deception, because what I felt, had in fact no colour or opacity, or even shape, at any one moment and apart from memory (keeping my fingers still, almost no information comes through; moving them, what information there is vanishes behind as fast as it grows in front). The most I could truthfully claim was that, inhabiting the nearer regions of my universe, is a spectral and evanescent succession of touch feelings, plus various itches, aches, tastes, tensions, and so forth. Not even the sum total of these, however, at their most obtrusive, could ever begin to build a box here, and certainly not the sort of coloured ball

I notice on other people's shoulders and in my mirror. However busy my fingers I remained unballed, unboxed, free, at large—whenever I cared to look.

But how to look here, how to cease overlooking this Spot and its essential voidness? One of the best-known aids is attending to what is going on round and about this Spot. It isn't always convenient to be 'fingering my face' (as others would describe it) but I can't avoid breathing; it's always there for the noticing. Attending to the slow rhythm of my breath 'passing in and out of my nostrils' (again, not my story) is accordingly *the* traditional exercise leading towards Self-realisation. Assiduously practised, it turns me *round* (rather than on); it directs my attention away from the external world to what lies at the Centre; in the end, it can see me Home.

Or, if I prefer it, exploring this Spot with my fingertips can have the same result. For instance, 'feeling my left cheek with my left hand' and simultaneously 'feeling your left cheek with my right hand', I notice the immense difference—notice how the former experience emphasises my no-face while the latter emphasises your face. Or again, I can notice that the only human face I can never touch is my own; for when I try to do so by stretching out my hand to my mirror, I encounter only smooth glass, and when I try to do so by retracting my hand and exploring here, I encounter only something like rough glass—transparency unlimited, containing a tiny area of felt texture. Yet again, I can 'hold my ears' (as the outsider would say) and observe the blank space that lies between. Or simply attend to whatever sensations happen to be given in this region now, without naming or interpreting them. All such exercises, with others one can devise as needed, have one purpose and one effect: they reverse the out-pointing arrows of attention, they point my way to the Home I have in fact never left, they bring me to myself. They lead in to the Centre—to this untouchable, invisible, colourless, formless, silent, tasteless, odourless Receptacle of all my sensations, to this unbounded Absence in which all things are presented.

(4) What scientists tell me

My rediscovery of the obvious, of how it is here, would perhaps have come sooner and made better sense when it came, if I had not been intimidated by science—by such questions as: if I have here no eyes, retinae, rods and cones, optic nerves, visual cortex, what are they for, and how do I manage to see without them? I see, therefore I have eyes—so runs the argument. Even if the other three messages (coming from my mirror, from other faces, from my fingers) were not enough to plant a head on these shoulders, the scientist's message (so detailed, so consistent, so proven in medical and optical practice) clinched the matter: firmly and finally it located here no mere meatball (so to say) but the most complicated mechanism known to man, a balled-up universe or world-in-miniature. So far from being headless or empty-headed, it seems I am more elaborately headed than I can ever imagine.

This story is specious but it doesn't, as it stands, make sense at all. The scientist cannot observe how I present myself here at the Centre; all he can do is observe how I present myself over there.

He is in a position to register the immense variety of my regional appearances, but never the unique central Reality they all stem from. And what he makes of me depends on how far he stations himself from me. At, say, 10 feet he makes me out to be a man ; at 3 feet a torso ; at 1 foot a face (or, if he is a surgeon, perhaps an area of brain); at less than 1 foot (when equipped with the necessary apparatus) he finds, as he approaches me, tissues, cells, cell-structures, molecules, and so on, till there's nothing to see at all. His close-up tale is of colourless, formless, unimaginable energy-packets separated by comparatively vast empty spaces: here, he reports, I'm reduced to the thinnest of thin air, to almost nothing. On his observational journey towards me, all my boasted qualities—human, vital, material—are progressively left behind: I am systematically undone, abolished. Penetrating through veil after veil of outward manifestation, he comes very near indeed to the Truth of what lies right here—the inside story of what I am.

But only I, who alone am right here, am in a position to confirm and complete his story. *Here* I am indeed abolished. *Here* are no eyes or brain, no colour or form, no substance or motion (I swear it!), but only Emptiness, Absence of all I thought I was. So his story and mine fit perfectly: I only add the tailpiece—'Here, form is void'.

But how, in that case, do I manage to see you? The question is resolved as soon as we notice that the verb *to see* has two antithetical meanings. When we observe two people conversing, we say that each *sees* the other, and we notice the symmetry of the set-up—on each side a face, a pair of eyes, a nose, etc., and between them a distance of a few feet. But my seeing you is nothing like this at all: the set-up is absolutely asymmetrical. There is nothing here in your way: you fill my void. Yet (such is our obtuseness and dishonesty) we use the same word—*see*—for these two wholly dissimilar operations; and, of course, the same word means the same thing! You see equals I see; 3rd person seeing equals 1st person seeing! The truth, obvious once glimpsed is that only the 1st person, present tense, sees—or, for that matter, hears, tastes, smells...

What, then, is the relevance of the scientist's story of how seeing occurs? All of it—involving the sun, light waves, eye-lenses, rods and cones, impulses running along optic nerves, events in the visual cortex—all of it is true, not of 1st-person seeing, but of 3rd-person communication, which is a very different matter. The story is of a chain of events in a physical world, a chain which is nowhere broken into by anything like a Mind, or Consciousness, or Seeing: any such 'mystical' intrusion would be quite unscientific and useless: it could do nothing, explain nothing. On the contrary, it poses such insoluble problems as how matter can produce mind, how it can be acted upon by mind, at exactly what point in the chain of physical events the non-physical intervenes, and how the vast and brilliant world I experience can be packed inside my head. All these puzzles are meaningless once I stop thinging this No-thing, heading this headless one, 3rd-personing this 1st person. I see, not because I have eyes here, but because I haven't—they would only block the view. The sages are agreed:

As I See It

I look and listen without using eyes and ears.

Lieh-tzu

By what means do this body or mind perceive? Can they perceive with the eyes, the ears...? No. Only one's own Nature, being essentially pure and utterly still, is capable of this.

Hui-hai

Thou seest them 'looking', but they are like the pictures in a bath house: they do not see... The form appears, O worshipper of form, as though its two dead eyes were looking.

Rumi

It is the Unborn which sees and hears.

Bankei

Only God has seeing, hearing.

Al-Arabi

There is no seer but Him, no-one to hear but Him, no-one thinking or aware but Him. He is the Self, the Ruler within, the One Immortal.

Brihadaranyaka Upanishad

Once more, the enemy of Self-realisation turns out to be its servant. Only pseudo-science, applied to the question of my Nature, deludes me: science Enlightens me. Taken seriously, it removes any lingering doubts about my voidness.

So I really am tooled-up for Enlightenment, since I possess

these four handy claw-hammers (my mirror, other faces, touch, and science) which are even better at pulling apart the box here than they were at putting it together. Handled one way round, they slowly and painfully built delusion; handled the other way round, they can now swiftly and easily demolish it.

The universe which produces such a dual-purpose toolkit is surely much to be congratulated. Is this ingenious beneficence part of a more general trustworthiness? Could it be true that, in the long run, *all* that happens, the way *all* things are, is geared to the great enterprise of Enlightenment? Anyhow the sages are sure that, to one who sees *Who* he is, nothing comes amiss, the darkest cloud is big with refreshing rain, the deadliest sword is already a life-saving ploughshare, *all* stumbling blocks are really stepping-stones on the way Home. If I want to test this I don't wait and see, but see and wait.

* * *

Chapter 28

THE GREAT GAME
OF PRETENDING

Maharshi: There is no greater absurdity than this—that we seek to gain the Reality that we are... It is ridiculous. A day will dawn when you yourself will laugh at your past efforts. What will be on that day is also here and now.

Disciple: So it's a great game of pretending?

Maharshi: Yes.

It is an odd and very significant fact that, ever since man became fully human, he has queried his humanness and asked himself who he really is. And the more mature and self-aware he becomes the more insistently the question comes up. Why this curious doubt, this seemingly inescapable obsession, this universal problem about his identity?

On the face of it, no such problem exists; or, if it exists, it's no more than a semantic muddle. How could a man fail to be a man? If I'm not the person described in my passport, who on earth could I be? What alternatives offer themselves? Well, obviously, if I am a thing at all, I am a man, and not a beetle or a stone or a plant or a star or an atom. In practice, accordingly, there are only two serious alternatives: either I am this man-thing or no-thing. Or (to put the alternatives rather more traditionally) either I am in reality the human being

I appear to others to be, or else I am not a human being, or any kind of being or thing whatever, but that undifferentiated Being or No-thing which has variously been called the Void, Clarity, the One Light, the Self, Brahman-Atman, Spirit, Reality, Consciousness, the Kingdom of Heaven, and so on—however you name it, it's as non-human as it's possible to be. Such is my two-way choice, for I can find no credible third possibility. Certainly there is no vagueness about it: the contrast is as sharp as it is immense. On the one hand I am offered a small, local, mortal, faulty, boxed-in thing, a minute and brief fragment of the world; while on the other I am offered the unlimited, changeless, qualityless, perfect Source and Container and Essence of the world, with the world itself thrown in for good measure. More briefly; shall I be part or the Whole? Am I to be in the universe or is the universe to be in me? This is no trivial matter. It's bound to make all the difference in the world to me which of these two I choose, which of them I elect to be, or rather discover myself to be; and to put off for another day this crucial decision would be irresponsible and absurd, even suicidal. Of all the many varieties of madness this surely is the maddest—refusing or neglecting to go into and settle this clear-cut question of who I am—especially now the question has been plainly put to me, and the alternatives have been reduced to two, thus making the issue quite definite.

Nor can I delegate my responsibility. The issue is one which I have to settle for myself, since no-one else is in a position to say how it is with me right here. Others lack inside information; I have it because I am it, I coincide with myself. I am the sole and final authority on what it's like being this 1st person singular, present tense. Therefore I have to put aside all I've read and been told, and just look, as if for the first time in all honesty and simplicity, at myself for myself. Encouraging me to do just this are the great sages. Is it hard for me to see who I am? Maharshi replies: "It would be absurd if to look at outside things were easy and to look within were difficult. It's the other way round." Is it then difficult for me to realise what I see? Maharshi replies: "You are it. All that's necessary is to drop the thought 'I haven't realised.' " And what is the nature of this realisation? Maharshi replies: "The absurdity is to think that one is this or that. 'I am' alone is, not 'I am so and so.' When existence is unqualified it is right, when it is particularised it is wrong. That is the whole truth." "Having any form or shape is the trouble: just be yourself: just be." "The thought 'I am a man' is unnatural. 'I am' is natural. Why do you qualify it with 'a man'?" To an enquirer who points out that the Bible teaches that man is born in sin, Maharshi gives a drastic answer indeed: "The man is sin!"

It isn't nearly enough to think, or even to feel, that one isn't this particular man, or any man, or any thing at all. On the contrary, it's thinking which is our trouble, this conceptual fog we work up to hide what is simply given; and anyway what we think today we are quite likely to deny tomorrow. Our task is to stop thinking just long enough to look at who's looking. As for feeling, it varies like English weather: we can rarely have it how and when we want it, and even then it's notoriously deceptive. No, neither thinking nor feeling is reliable or conclusive. Only seeing is believing. That's why the seers are called seers and not thinkers or feelers: they insist that the truth of who-one-is shines forth brilliantly of itself and needs no assistance from the thinking and feeling mind: the Self is self-luminous, as clearly visible as the gooseberry in the palm of one's hand. Thus Maharshi again: "See the seer within." "The Supreme is hearsay but the individual experiences himself directly. You can make use only of direct experience, therefore see who you are." "Leave off all this verbiage! Be as you are. See who you are and remain as the Self, free from birth, going, coming and returning." It is seeing which convinces, and which (unlike thought and feeling) can be had at will. What is to be seen is ever present, and ever able to inspect itself. At no time is it impossible, or even difficult, to see who one is—provided one wants to.

The trouble is that the 1st person has become so used to—so terribly good at—putting on this act of 3rd person and playing the part of being a man that it is very hard to 'come off it' and become perfectly sincere and natural again. The game starts very early in life. The small child soon starts impressing upon his central Formlessness—which is quite neutral, fluid like molten wax—features which aren't his at all but belong out there to his companions. One of the main reasons is that he fears being odd, being excluded from the club. Thus the two little girls who were brought up by wolves near Midnapore were persuaded they were wolves and behaved just like the other members of the pack, just as (conversely) animal pets reared solely by humans become members of the family and have little time for their own species. In A. A. Milne's poem, Christopher Robin has four chairs in his nursery: in the first, he is an explorer; in the second, a great big roaring lion; in the third, a ship at sea; and in the fourth, just for fun, a human being:

> Whenever I sit in a high chair
> For breakfast or dinner or tea,
> I try to pretend that it's my chair
> And that I am a baby of three.

In the other chairs, apparently, it was quite easy being a lion or a ship; it was pretending to be human that was difficult! At the age of three or less, Christopher Robin is at least as likely to be a lion pretending he's a little boy as a little boy pretending he's a lion. But the game of pretending to be a boy, of feigning humanity, soon takes precedence, if only because it's the one his parents insist on playing with him. "Now be a good boy," they say. And all too soon he becomes, if not a good boy, at least a boy. He learns to see himself through their eyes and to pretend to be what they expect him to be. And of course this suits his book too, for it progressively conceals the fact that he, as the unique 1st person, is totally different from all those 3rd persons out there. This wandering from his true station in order to become a thing, a human being, is inevitable; it is his passport into human society, and eagerly he grasps it. But the price of socialisation is high and rising all the while. As life goes on, he gets better and better at pretending to be what others see him as, more and more self-deceived and self-alienated, more and more particularised, more and more narrowed down from his first general Being to being a very special person indeed. To start with, he just is; then he is a little boy with a name; then he is a distinctive person—going outside himself he views himself as tall or short, fair or dark, handsome or homely. And then, growing up to manhood, he further reduces to a social type and job-holder, a role-player, a specialist, and perhaps in the end little more than an elaborate actor. Take, for instance, the waiter in a French café, so well described by Sartre. His movements are a little too precise and rapid, his interest in the customers' requirements a little too solicitous, his movements rather jerky and mechanical, the balance of his tray unnecessarily precarious. "All his behaviour seems to us a game… He is playing, he is amusing himself. But what is he playing? We need not watch long before we can explain it: he is playing at being a waiter in a café."

Sartre's waiter isn't an unusually false or affected person: in fact, his special trouble isn't that he's pretending but that the pretence isn't quite clever enough—it doesn't convince. But it does serve to point and underline the absurdity all 'normal' civilised adults live by—the absurdity of seeing oneself only as others see one (or rather, as one hopes or fears they do) and refusing to see oneself as one sees oneself, right here and now. Any straying from one's home here, to view one's appearance out there and identify only with that, is to deny the central Reality, to be false to one's intrinsic Nature, and—in a word—to be unreal. Even if I don't regard myself as just a waiter (or butcher or baker or candlestick-maker or whatever), even if I do sometimes think of myself as 'a man for a' that', still I'm making myself out to be what I certainly am not here, in the place where there never has been a man and never will be. The result may not be so painful or ridiculous to others, but it is immeasurably damaging to me, because it is making believe that I am the exact opposite of what l am. It is imagining myself to be a thing, a solid lump, a body, right here—which is impossible. Indeed it is, in Maharshi's uncompromising language, fatal. "The person soaked in I-am-the-body idea is the greatest sinner and a suicide." And how do we get such an idea? We view ourselves as the body by going outside and looking at ourselves from out there. "The body identity is due to wandering of the mind... Seek your Source, merge in the Self and remain all alone."

The true disciple does what he's advised to do, and looks for himself at himself without prejudice. He minds his own business, which is his own Reality situated precisely where he is, now—perfectly obvious and perfectly accessible to him and to no outsider. And what does he find?

Well, I can't answer for anybody else. What it's like being you is your affair and not for me to tell you. What I have to do is see how it is here, just now. And I swear I can find here no-thing whatever, no solid object at the mid-point of my universe, no flesh-and-blood house or box here in which I'm shut up, but only this marvellous Emptiness or Absence or Light or Clarity or Openness. And this Wide-openness, so far from being mere vacancy, is at this moment visibly full to the brim with the clouds and trees and flowers outside my window, and the chairs and tables and carpet in this room, and these legs and this arm and hand and pen and paper on which these words are now forming themselves. Insofar as I am at all, I am at large in this familiar scene, replete with this assembly of coloured and moving shapes that is now presenting itself: all these are in me, are me.

What I am here for, the purpose of my life, is to stop the great game of pretending, just look, and be Myself. Nothing could be simpler, or more urgent.

* * *

Chapter 29

THE WILD HYPOTHESIS

"Closer is He than breathing and nearer than hands and feet."

Notes on how to test it.

The Hypothesis

The most persistent and consistent of rumours—put out by saints and sages and poets and philosophers from the dawn of history, and believed by countless ordinary people—is that inside man dwells a mysterious Inhabitant who is none other (some would say) than God himself. The many names for this non-human Occupier or Core include Atman-Brahman, the Buddha Nature, the Void, the Tao, the Kingdom of Heaven, the Inner Light, Spirit, the Holy Ghost, the Godhead… However named, It is alleged to be quite central to me, more real than my human nature, more me than I am myself. And if I ignore and overlook It, or fail to find It, I am in trouble. So runs the story.

Is the story true? On the face of it, one can hardly imagine a more fantastic, more unlikely tale. Isn't a man plainly a man, as a stone is a stone through and through and a tree is just a tree? Is there room in him for God? Does the human body contain accommodation at all suitable for such a Tenant? If so, where? What are the outward signs of this extraordinary Pregnancy, this truly Interesting Condition?

And what does it feel like here, playing host to this divine Parasite?

Well, absurd hypotheses have a way of being true—what could be more crazy than the little round Earth, careering and spinning through space? In the present instance, the timeless universality of our more-than-Copernican hypothesis, the immensity and imaginative splendour of its claim, the practical issues at stake, not to mention ordinary curiosity about what I might be—all demand that I test it without further delay. How could I hope to deal with life's problems if I'm deeply deluded about who entertains that hope? I am my own tool for living, and if I have no idea what that tool is I'm as sure to hurt myself and others as if I mistook my saw for a hammer. If this wildest of hypotheses is true, it stands to revolutionize my life. If it is untrue, let me now be done with it—indeed it's time the age-old confidence trick was finally seen through. This article, accordingly, describes a set of procedures for putting the matter to the test and coming to a definite conclusion.

How to test the hypothesis

Stating our hypothesis is one thing, making up our minds how to test it is quite another thing. The laboratory conditions, the set-up, the actual program, are all-important—even decisive. Fortunately the experts, the accredited propounders of our hypothesis, those who have put it into practice, have dropped plenty of useful hints. They have indicated what to look for, where to look, when to look, how to look, what qualifications the looker needs; and, for good measure, they have indicated what other senses he may employ in his search, what novel powers his discovery may endow him with, what new understanding, what practical benefits. Or, to be more precise:

1. What to look for

There is a story of a famous scientist who, when asked to look down a microscope at an interesting phenomenon, objected: "How can I see it unless you tell me what to look for?" Equally, if I am looking in man for this strange Occupier or Core, I must have at least some idea of what It may be like. And I'm told It is (a) no-thing, empty, void, speckless, qualityless, simple, absolutely transparent; (b) analogous to light, air or breath (pneuma, spirit), pure and still water; (c) vast, without edges, unbounded; (d) unchanging, indestructible, unaffected by time; (e) so filled out with all manner of particular and changing things that It is them, without distance or separation; (f) once seen, blazingly obvious, self-luminous, indubitable; (g) aware of Itself as all this. Whatever I make of these indications they certainly should be enough to go on. At least I know more or less what to expect and stand a good chance of recognizing It provided It's present at all.

2. Where to look

I have, according to the Buddha, to turn my attention inwards to this fathom-long body—the body which, says St. Paul, is the temple of the Holy Ghost. The great seers urge me to look right here, to look within at this Looker, to see Who or What is looking. Particular heed is to be given to the upper half of me, and as a rule to the region of my head, face, eyes. (Thus Zen invites me to notice what my True or Original Face looks like to me, and identifies It with my Buddha Nature. Thus—if I am to take Jesus at his word—I shall find the Kingdom of

Heaven within, and my body filled with light, when I exchange my two eyes for one. Thus Hinduism suggests that I see with my Third Eye; and it tells the story of the seeker who could never find the Pearl of Liberation because he looked everywhere for it except on his own forehead, where it was suspended all the time. Thus for Sufism Illumination is the unveiling of the Face which is featureless: "Behead yourself!" exclaims Rumi, "become seeing, seeing, seeing!" As for Taoism, the Chinese character TAO—the Way, Heaven, Reality—is itself made up of the characters for HEAD and GOING...)

3. When to look

While the authorities admit that, in practice, prior mental or spiritual discipline may in some cases be required before one is ready and willing to see What is plainly on view here, they hasten to add that, in fact, It is ever-present, and any preliminaries are for removing the mistaken idea that they are needed. There is really nothing to do but look, *now.* The experience is inaccessible to memory, anticipation, imagination, thought; it will not keep; it requires renewal from moment to moment. And, indeed, with many of the most expert seers the seeing came first and the lifelong discipline afterwards: it was the initial seeing which made the subsequent discipline possible and meaningful—and even then it wasn't discipline aimed at some future attainment but enjoyment of the perfection which is always present.

4. How to look

I am informed that I shall see It clearly, not when I have acquired some understanding or knowledge or skill or maturity, but on the contrary when I give up all these acquirements and become quite simple like a little child. Above all I have to trust what is given, to go by what I can see for myself and not by what I think or remember or read or am told: in this manner I have to look at myself as if for the first time and I were newly arrived in the world, unprejudiced and clueless, without the faintest notion as to my nature. It sounds so difficult! But I'm not required to still my mind thus and look inwards for a whole day, or an hour, or even a minute, but only for long enough to see What takes no time at all to scan. A split second will do.

5. Who is to look

About this the authorities are in no doubt: I have to look—look at myself for myself. This isn't a task I can delegate any part of—I am the expert on myself, and the only qualifications I need are truthfulness and confidence. I am the sole and final authority on Who I am here at this instant, on What lies at this the unique centre of my world, and nobody else is in a position to so much as glimpse It. Sages advise me What to look for, but cannot look for me. Only my tale—the inside story of what it's like being this first person singular, present tense—is to the point.

6. What senses to employ

If It were only seen It might perhaps be doubted, but It is said to be accessible to all the senses. The One who lives in man, it seems, is never out of touch or out of reach or inaudible, and may even (so some allege) be enjoyed by a general sense which embraces them all. Nevertheless, sight predominates. Seeing is believing, and it isn't for nothing that the seers aren't called hearers or tasters or smellers—and certainly not thinkers or feelers.

7. What Godlike powers to look for
If I am to believe there lives in me a divine Inhabitant, a truly superhuman Being, I shall need clear evidence of Its godlike faculties, of Its magical powers or siddhis. These are said to include the ability to destroy and recreate at will, to disappear and reappear, to travel great distances instantly, to grow suddenly huge and shrink again, to know all things. These are wild claims indeed, but it is only to be expected that our fantastic hypothesis should involve fantastic corollaries. And certainly if—against all the odds—I were to find even the least of these faculties being exercised here, it should be very clear to me Who or What is responsible for them.

8. What new understanding
According to the sages, seeing Who I am is finding the Master Key, the Pearl of Wisdom, the Clue, the Answer to life's riddle. What's here makes sense of what's there. The meaningless becomes meaningful; previously unrelated facts dovetail; I begin to lose my puzzled frown. It's as if, in discovering It, I discover the central missing piece in the cosmic jigsaw puzzle and everything falls into place around It—yet the underlying wonder and mystery are (how fortunately!) greater than ever. Our hypothesis not only, like all hypotheses that work, claims to set in order many hitherto disorderly facts, but even, in some sense, all facts! If our tests should find these huge claims at all justified, our wild hypothesis will indeed deserve to be renamed the Great Hypothesis.

9. *What practical benefits*

The claim is that when I find my indwelling Reality I shall find lasting peace, genuine happiness, and other good things otherwise hard or impossible to obtain; and I shall become a much better, more useful, more loving citizen. But man as man is quite imperfectible, the world remains much the same, and no Millennium is assured. On the other hand, most of our social evils spring from fear and greed and hate, and these in turn (the sages declare) spring from delusion—delusion as to What one really is, or (as we might say) willful neglect of the hypothesis we are now considering. If even a small (but hopefully influential) minority were to discover and value their true identity, the ameliorating effect could be out of all proportion. Utopia may be dismissed, but not improvement. As the final test, therefore, it is proposed to take some of our worst social problems and discover how far they can be explained and rectified in the light of our hypothesis.

The Tests

The foregoing nine sections are provisional and indicative; they lay down a rough-and-ready pattern of guidelines. It isn't necessary—it isn't possible—to understand this extraordinary hypothesis in all its aspects and implications, or to make sense of all the conditions laid down for testing it, in advance of the testing itself. What matters is that I do now have plenty of hints to proceed by, sufficient general directions for my research, and the rest can await the outcome of that research. But it has to be real research, in which I am free to invent my own up-to-date and down-to-earth techniques and to make straight for the simple Heart of the matter, leaving aside the countless (and often contradictory) complexities which from time immemorial have been accumulating around It. I must add that the following tests are specially devised for carrying out right away, and just reading about them is almost no good at all. For clarity they have been sorted into five main sections: (I) What do I find here? (II) What do others find (on their way) here? (III) What superhuman powers does It exercise? (IV) What does It explain? (V) What use is It?

(I) What Do I Find Here?

Right here under my nose my own Laboratory Specimen—all nicely prepared and set up—now awaits examination by the only qualified investigator, by the one observer who can ever be in a position to find It. I alone am perfectly placed (others can't get within sight of It) and if I don't do this job it won't get done. All the same, the following ten tests aren't merely private and subjective: everyone is urged to repeat them for himself upon his own Specimen, and if he gets quite different results—well, *he* is the sole authority on what It is like where he is! Anyhow he can't complain he isn't up to the task (some of the best scientists I've met in this field aren't in their teens yet), or that he can't afford the equipment, or that the instructions are vague.

1. *"It's in the bag."*

I take an ordinary paper bag about 12 inches deep and 24 inches in circumference (some trash bags are exactly the right size) and cut off the bottom to make a paper tunnel. Standing in a light strong enough to illuminate the inside of the bag, I fit my face into one end of it while you fit yours into the other. I then *count the faces in the bag.*

Alternatively, my task may be described as (a) noting the absolute asymmetry, the immeasurable difference between what's given at the far end of the bag and at the near end; or (b) comparing what I'm looking *at* there with what I'm looking *out of* here; or (c) looking to see whether you and I are face-to-face or face-to-no-face. The lack of ventilation in the bag ensures that we emerge from it after a few seconds, before—let's hope—we have time to think away what is actually presented, and the bag is (so to say) thick with conceptual smog.

The reason why this absurdly simple method is so effective (more so than any meditational device and certainly any book I've ever encountered) is that it cuts out the fallacy on which society as we know it is based—"All *those* feet and legs and trunks end in heads, therefore *these* do." By temporarily obliterating the lower regions where you and I are alike, we are free to concentrate on that upper region where we are not at all alike.

The following additional tests in Section (I) are more-or-less optional: they bring out further details but add nothing essential to what's already in the bag.

However, as a valuable part of my much-needed re-education, they furnish me with a set of handy reminders: they help me to go on rediscovering the obvious—till it really is obvious, all the time.

2. *"It's buttoned up."*
I note how smoothly my gaze travels from the toecaps of your shoes all the way up to your neck and face and hair, without any hold-

up or difficulty whatever. Trying the same procedure on myself and mounting the ladder of my shirt-buttons (or necktie or blouse or whatever) I find myself stopping around *this* button: just here my shirt, collarless and neckless, fades out, and I can climb no further. (To be exact, I *descend* the ladder of my form to reach the formless here, at the unsupported foot of the ladder.)

3. "It's on paper."

I sit on the floor with a sketch-pad between my legs and draw only what I see, starting with my shoes and socks at the top of the sheet and including my arms and legs—and how much else? I take seriously this portrait of the headless first person singular.

(This exercise lends itself to group work. People sit in a circle on the floor, shoulder to shoulder and facing outwards, and make their self-portraits. Then they all get up and move to the side, leaving their drawings on the floor, and note the one No-head from which all these headless bodies are seen to stem, their common Owner and Operator Who is visibly "nearer than hands and feet". Finally, each notes that this floor-pattern is only a beautiful exterior symbol, and What it symbolizes is never out there by a hair's-breadth, but indeed nearer than the nearest.)

4. "It's under my nose."

I observe how your nose is small, opaque, central, continuous with the rest of you and well supported. Then I note how different mine is—large, transparent, twofold, one on each side, where it is mysteriously suspended (so to speak) in mid-air. Under it, above it, behind it, I discover—*What?*

5. *Counting heads*
Looking round the room, I count the number of legs and torsos present, then the number of heads—and I go by what I see.

6. *Spectacles*
Holding my glasses a few inches away, I count the lenses, then slowly put them on (on what?) and count again. How many lenses are given now? Am I looking out of two windows at the world, or one? How big is this window and what shape? Using both hands, I draw its outline in the air. What lies behind this window? Is it dark or small or stuffy or congested in here? Am I not all window, and in no kind of house or box at all?

7. *Mirror*
Just as, when I find my dog out-of-doors, I conclude he isn't indoors, so when I find my face there I cease expecting it here. (By "my face" I mean that oval, opaque, coloured shape—fringed with white hair and simultaneously containing various holes and protuberances—which people call Douglas Harding.) Having no reason to distrust my mirror, I let it show me where I keep my face—a few feet from here—for I certainly don't have two faces, one each side of the glass. And I can let it show me where I don't keep my face: when I bring my mirror up here I lose my face and every part of it.

8. *This side of*
The following is an experiment in "two-way looking"—that is,

simultaneous observation of Seer and seen.

Observing your face, I observe also how, because *my side* of it is Colourlessness, I see its pinkness; how, because *my side* of it is Transparency, I see its opacity; how, because *my side* of it is the Unshaped, I see its form; how, because *my side* of it is Stillness, I see its motion; how, because *my side* of it is the Immeasurable, I see its boundaries. Whatever thing or quality is given on that side, on this side its Absence is even more clearly given. Your face reveals my Facelessness, your somethingness my No-thingness, and *vice versa*.

9. *"Distance no object"*

The purpose of this experiment is actually to measure my Inhabitant, the One Who lives right here. In other words, it is to test the proposition: "Whereas you and he (as second/third person) are in the world, I (as first person) am not in the world—instead, the world is in me. I coincide with my universe; I am as big as it is; I am it.'

As you look round the room at the table, at the window, at the picture, I measure the distance between you and it, noting how you remain distinct in your place and it remains distinct in its place, with this precise number of inches between. Then, as *I* look at these same objects, I measure the distance between each one and me, noting how the result is always zero: for the tape-measure, taken end-on to me, is no length at all. I can clearly see that all its inches have shrunk to nothing. This reading I take seriously. There being no gap between myself and my objects, we coincide, we aren't separate. I go right up to them and they come right into me—even if they happen to be the moon or stars or galaxies. In fact, I can find no observer of them here, and no here distinct from there. I see I am my world and it is two-dimensional: I see I'm immensely deep, in that I include all my objects, yet no depth at all, in that they are all telescoped in me to paper-thinness. And this "I" and "me" refer, of course, to this explosive Inhabitant of mine, Who refuses to be contained even in the universe—yet isn't above using this humble tape-measure to demonstrate the fact.

10. The other senses
The tests so far have been visual ones. I have been looking at What's here, or (let's say) It has been looking at Itself. Can It also hear, smell, taste, touch Itself?

On a quiet night, lying comfortably in bed in the dark, I conduct an experiment in two-way hearing. I listen to the Absence of specific sounds—to the non-existence now of people's voices, of music, of traffic noises, of the patter of raindrops—to the Background against which occasional night sounds (such as the hoot of an owl or the striking of a distant clock) stand out, to the Pool of Silence into which they drop. And I observe that this continuous 'Sound-of-Silence' isn't imagined or thought (and obviously not seen or tasted) but actually heard, and heard more clearly than any 'sound-of-sound' which happens to come and go in it. It alone is never too faint or too loud or badly pitched; it alone is perfectly audible even to the stone-deaf; it alone never stops yet never bores. Of my Inhabitant or Core I can now say: this No-sound is how It sounds, Its Quiet Voice, just as this No-form is how It looks, Its Featureless Face.

And so with the remaining senses: I find each is similarly two-sided. How do I know I'm not tasting strawberry jam just now, or smelling violets, or touching fur, or suffering toothache, or feeling too hot? Only because each sense goes on actively reporting the Absence of any such sensations, pending their arrival. Only because It goes on tasting of Nothing can I tell when the taste of something occurs; only because It goes on smelling of Nothing can I tell when the smell of something occurs; only because It goes on feeling like Nothing can I tell when the feel of something occurs. In short, I find It is unique in being accessible all the time, to all the senses, with unvarying clarity. Compared with This, mere things are shadows! And without This, they aren't even shadows!

For confirmation I carry out the following experiments. (1) Pressing my thumbnail into a fingertip I feel the pain as (a) present there, (b) absent here, (c) absent from there and here now I cease pressing. (2) Tapping the table with my finger I hear the sound as (a) present there, (b) absent here, (c) absent from there and here now I cease tapping. (3) I repeat the test, stroking the table with my finger, tasting a little salt, smelling a flower—with similar results. *This side* of every particular sensing I find It sensing Itself—as the Absence of sensation.

(II) What Do Others Find (On The Way) Here?
The foregoing ten tests are designed to bring home to me what I find at Home. (Normally, I take everybody's word for what it's like indoors—except the word of the only one who ever got in!) They are designed to give me the courage of my sensations, confidence in how

it is here, as this first person singular, present tense. Yet the outsider's view of me isn't altogether irrelevant: though he can't quite get to What's here, he can get very near It. Hence the following experiment.

I stand at one end of a longish room or corridor, and you, facing me with your camera, at the other. Your job is to tell me, without fear or favour, what you make of me, how I strike you. In your view-finder you first discover a man. Then, as you approach, you discover in turn a torso, a head, an eye, and presently a mere blur and practically nothing at all. Or, if you have suitable lenses, you may come, well before making contact, to regions where I'm revealed as a patch of skin, as cells, as particles of descending order, and in the end as virtually empty space. Here, at close range, all my colour and shape and opacity and materiality (whatever that is) have been left behind.

And here, right at the Centre where all these regional effects stem from, the Reality of which they are the appearances now confirms and completes your story. Here It is indeed empty.

Finally, instead of looking *at* me from there, you turn round and look with me from here. Holding your camera as close as possible to me, you find it now frames the far end of the room, the window, the scene beyond. And this too I confirm and complete. Here It is empty of me—and full of my world.

(III) What Superhuman Powers Does It Exercise?

1. Destruction and re-creation. I see you there opening and closing your eyes and I notice the lack of results: nothing happens to anything else in the room, to the room itself, to the world outside the window.

On the other hand I notice how, whenever the One here wishes, everything around is instantly destroyed and as instantly re-created. (You tell me, of course, that I merely shut my eyes and open them again, but you speak of what's out there, of the man, the 3rd person, the regional appearance. I speak of What's here, of the No-man, the 1st person, the Central Reality.)

2. *Disappearing and re-appearing.* I see you look down, then ahead, then up at the ceiling—and still you are all there. I see you turn round—and the room behind you remains intact. But the One here, without moving from this spot, can at will cause this body—and your body, and indeed anything present—to de-materialise and re-materialise. (You rightly say that this man only raises and lowers his head, and turns his back. But I rightly say that the One here has no head to raise or back to turn.)

3. *Astral travel.* I see you star-gazing, and this doesn't make you into any kind of cosmonaut. But the One here nonchalantly blasts off to the constellations and moves around them at will in no time at all. Nor is his journey imaginary: this Spaceman always *goes right up to* his destination.

4. *Growing and shrinking.* At one moment I'm as wide as the sky, at the next as narrow as this page, as this *word*. How different I am from what I look like to you!

5. *All-knowledge.* Concerning only one thing in the world have I complete, reliable, inside, direct knowledge—namely the thing called

my body. Suppose I treat it as a true sample of all the other things in the world. (This is fair enough, seeing that it turns out to include them.) Then I have perfect insight into the true and intrinsic Nature of all men and animals and plants and inert objects. In seeing What I am I see What you and all others are, and I am you and them. This isn't knowledge of appearances (very few of which are worth knowing about) but of What they are appearances of, of Reality.

Note. The popular tradition—unable to distinguish between 1st person and third—is that the adept *as 3rd person* possesses these five siddhis; the truth is that everyone *as 1st person* possesses them. This isn't to deny that, in addition, the adept may sometimes be observed, as 3rd person, to work 'miracles' and call upon 'supernormal' sources of information. But though real enough these powers (the sages agree) are best ignored, and certainly not to be cultivated.

(IV) What Does It Explain?

As a further crucial test of our hypothesis about the hidden Nature of man let us briefly explore how far it explains his psychological development from infancy, makes sense of his seemingly perverse adult behavior, and illuminates his most distressing social problems. If he is in fact What our hypothesis proposes and immensely different from what he seems, then his life from cradle to grave, both individually and socially, should in many ways betray his secret: the inner truth will surely leak out, not so much in his words as in his deeds, not so much consciously as unconsciously. The following summary is presented here as a progress report to date, plus an open-ended program for further research, and by no means as a final or complete story.

1. Infant. All the evidence indicates that the newborn baby is for himself like any animal, faceless and at large. He isn't a thing-in-the-World but unseparate from his world, as big as it is. He is truly first person but without being aware of it. In other words, *the infant's life is the steady but unconscious assertion of our hypothesis.*

2. Child. Many a child, from the age of around two years or less, becomes keenly aware from time to time of his facelessness, of the immense difference between himself as first person and others as third person. "Mum, why don't I have a head?" is a typical exclamation. Or the protest "But I'm not a boy!"—said irritatedly, but confidently, as if it were quite obvious. Even up to the age of nine or more he is apt to leave himself out when counting people present—refusing, so to say, to count the bowl in with the oranges. Or he may tell you with some delight how he sees himself as the space in which things are happening rather than one of those things. In other words, *the young child lives our hypothesis much of the time, and occasionally asserts it quite categorically.*

But training in the systematic denial of our hypothesis, the long and hard work of face-building, starts at a very early age and goes on at least till one's teens. It proceeds by three main methods.

(a) *The mirror method.* At first the infant ignores the face in the glass, then begins to treat it as another baby's. Only gradually does he learn the trick of taking on and wearing that face—a trick involving six impossibilities: 1) reaching through the glass for that face; 2) freeing it from the glass and bringing it forward (say) four feet; 3) greatly enlarging it on the way; 4) rotating it through an angle of 180 degrees; 5) bestowing depth or 3-dimensionality upon its features; 6) attaching it by some miraculous adhesive to the no-face here so that it stays in position all the while.

(b) *The handling method.* From birth the infant's face is built up by means of kissing, patting, fondling, washing, etc. Later, he is deliberately taught, often with the help of nursery rhymes and games, to relate the *felt* features of his own face to the *seen* features of his mother's till the immense difference between the two "faces," as actually presented to him, is obscured and in the end lost. What his fingers are exploring here is eventually read as opaque, solid, pink, all-present-at-once, whereas in fact it is no more than a fugitive array of disembodied feelings which occasionally haunt the nearer regions of his universe and are quite incapable of boxing him up there and solidifying him. No matter how obtrusive and complex and close-knit the itches, aches, tickles and so on may prove, he is still perfectly at large. As first person, he is freer than the wind.

(c) *The stretching method.* To this third and main method of face-building the first two are quite subsidiary. It consists of a kind of self-alienation or ecstasis, an imaginary stretching out to a distance of (on average) six feet and turning round and looking in at oneself from that position, in order to see oneself as (one hopes or fears) others are seeing one, and projecting the resulting self-portrait back upon the sitter here. The outcome of this manoeuver is 1) to discover one's regional thingness or third-personness, 2) to superimpose it upon one's central No-thingness or 1st-personness, 3) to lose sight altogether of the Base of all one's excursions. Grown-ups are quite big: they live about six feet off-centre.

3. *Youth.* Learning thus to play the Face Game is the necessary condition of membership in our society. But the subscription can be very costly. Some, never learning to play at all, are institutionalised. Others, playing incompetently, suffer much distress. This can take the form, common in youth, of extreme shamefacedness, bashfulness, morbid shyness. Alternatively, (or in addition) extreme hatred of one's face. Any feature can be selected for loathing—the nose is the regular one—regardless of its actual appearance. Some of the most beautiful teenagers I have met were so worried about their faces that they were insisting on plastic surgery. And of course they were quite right: their cure (in some cases not only sudden but complete and lasting) was the facelift they were really after—a painless and free lift of some four to six feet, from the near side to the far side of the mirror. The trouble with one's face isn't *what* it is but *where* one puts it: here, it boxes one up; there, it lets one out, and so becomes quite acceptable.

4. *Adult.* Normally the Face Game, once learned, becomes second nature to the adult: he settles down to 3rd-personhood without going obviously sick or crazy. But the effort is often exhausting and the pain severe, and the field is full of casualties. For instance:

(a) *Greed.* Society has cut me down to size, reduced me from being the Centre and Container and Owner of the universe to being this miserable little piece of it. But in my heart I know that society is wrong and I am right: it still all belongs to me, and I will prove it by every means in my power. So I laboriously win back as much of my lost empire as I can—money, goods, power, fame, status: all my life I slave away trying to be as big as I really am. How pitiful!

(b) *Hate.* Instead, I can turn my energies to injuring the society that has so cruelly injured me, that has shrunk me from being practically everything to being practically nothing, that has mounted this chip of a head on my shoulders instead of the world. My revenge can take the form of violent crime, of every sort of delinquency, of ordinary aggression and obstructiveness, of gross selfishness. How understandable a reaction!

(c) *Drug dependence and addiction.* As an infant, I was naturally 1st person—at large, open, spontaneous, loving, unanxious, with all my senses alive and innocent and unclouded. The society that shrank me to 3rd-personhood, thereby depriving me of all this, now has the temerity to deny me the use of those (mind-expanding) drugs which, however temporarily and ineffectively, promise to restore my natural state. So of course I defy that society and its laws—at whatever risk.

(d) *Mental illness.* At root, what is mental sickness but withdrawal and alienation from the world, the breakdown of communication, separateness, lovelessness, loneliness, smallness? So I am a social problem! But hasn't the society whose function is to reduce me from being all the world to being this tiny, faulty, mortal bit of the world—hasn't this society itself made me sick and created the problem? In my unsocialized completeness I was all there, whole and healthy; as this socialized fragment I'm not myself at all, unhappy, confused, full of vague longing for the rest of me. The Wonder is how I remain outside a mental hospital! It isn't mental sickness which calls for explanation so much as mental health. Fortunately, the truth is that, in spite of everything, I am hale and whole: society notwithstanding, I am What I am—this 1st person who isn't in the world, but in whom the World is.

All this suggests that *the great problems of adult life arise from the conflict between our native assertion of our hypothesis and our cultivated denial of it.*

5. *Conclusion.* Enough has been said in this Section (IV) to indicate how useful as an interpretative device, or hermeneutic tool, our hypothesis may be. Do we not have here, in this outline of the process and consequences of self-thinging (of surrendering one's 1st-personhood), a means of bringing together and making sense of many otherwise loose and puzzling (and, mostly, very worrying) facts? Even more important, don't we also have guidance as to what to do about them? In the next Section we shall briefly explore the practical consequences of our hypothesis.

(V) What Use Is It?

l. *The individual.* First, what personal benefits does our hypothesis hold out? Tradition, plus what is observed to happen to one's friends, plus some experience of one's own, combine to tell the following tale. To the extent to which I see clearly and steadily into my own Nature,

into how it is right here and now (and I take seriously What I find)—
to that extent I may expect to enjoy more openness, spontaneity,
love, acute sense-awareness (colours, shapes, textures, sounds, tastes,
smells are apt to take on new brilliance), joy, compassion, energy,
concentration—but the list is endless. Nevertheless, all these, because
they are experience of something, because they have specific content,
are relative and variable; they come and go and are by no means to be
counted on. Human nature as such is (to say the least) imperfectible,
and anyway its setting—the world out there—remains the mixture
as before. The universe, not excluding that fragment of it called man,
will no doubt continue to be made up of ever-changing problems.
Only experience of What I am, of this indwelling Experiencer of the
world and its problems (that is, experience of No-thing at all, the
clear seeing of the Void here that neither comes nor goes nor suffers
any change)—only this is always to hand and complete and problem-
free. This is simple peace of mind, the sober sense of Homecoming,
the settlement of one's basic anxiety, and in the long run its total
plainness is worth more than all the other benefits—colourful,
beautiful, perhaps highly mystical—put together.

All this is presented for testing, not for believing or taking on
trust. The proving begins the moment I first see What I am and goes
on all the rest of my life. All I can do is see and wait, be my Source
and notice what flows from It, give in to this One Power (what other
is there?) and concur with what It does. What the experts say It will
then do for me and through me, and what I observe It is already
doing for and through my seeing friends, is very encouraging, but I

have to see for myself—and go on doing so. Our hypothesis isn't for proving once and for all and then shelving for future reference; it is nothing if not a *working* hypothesis, one to live by all the time, and in practice it ceases to be valid when it isn't being put to the test. The seeing is the proving. As soon as I stop seeing Who is seeing—and hearing Who is hearing, and so on—I am outside myself, identifying with what others see me to be. Taking leave of my senses which so effectively reveal their Ground, I am relying on the thought and memory which so effectively hide It. And so I naturally begin to think of our hypothesis as not only wild but mad. It is fortunate that the resulting misery sooner or later drives me back Home to the sanity of 1st-personhood.

2. Society. Our great social problems spring from fear and greed and hate, and these in turn (as Section (IV) brought out) from delusion—delusion as to Who we really are. If we let ourselves be conned into believing We are what we look like *to others,* mere 3rd persons plural, then we are sure to suffer from feelings of inadequacy, meaninglessness, loneliness, alienation, resentment, self-pity, terror, anxiety, and to behave accordingly: we are beside ourselves, wandering, out of our Mind, distracted, far gone, wool-gathering members of a society intent upon making us that way.[1] The cure is to come to our senses and see What we look like *to ourselves.* This is the only radical and lasting psychotherapy, for the patient to

---

1 It wouldn't be so bad if I knew which thing to be. Unable to reconcile different observers' pictures of me or to decide which to take on here, which mask to wear and role to play, I go crazy. My cure is to un-thing myself. About that man there are as many views as viewers, about this No-man only one.

discover—or rediscover—Who the patient is. This alone is sanity, to stop pretending we are what we are not. Being whole is being the Whole—no less.

It all comes back, inevitably, to the individual. If I see that here, whether I like it or not, I'm built for letting you in, for love, how can I go on trying to shut you out? If I see that I am, in my first-person Clarity, absolutely One with you, how could I go on trying to score over you and put you down, to rob or cheat or injure you in any way? I should only be hurting myself. If already it is my Nature to contain the world, why should I go on clutching at these absurd little bits of it so frantically? If I find that by living the 1st-person life I get all the alleged satisfactions of drug-use safely and more surely, then what use are these drugs to me? If, faceless here, I gratefully take on your face, so that it is now more mine than mine is, how can I object to its colour? Who, when white confronts black, has the black face? If I learn to value instead of to fear the Emptiness here, why should I go on trying to bung it up by smoking,[2] making-up, fidgeting with glasses, chin-stroking and hair-patting, over-eating, or non-stop talking—as if to persuade myself there must be *something* here to stick this great big pipe in, to lay all this powder and lipstick on, to fiddle with, to take in all these snacks and put out all these words. And so on.

In general, seeing What one's behaviour is coming out of is bound to affect that behaviour radically—one's observation of seers amply confirms this—and bound in turn to have its social effects.

2 In a recent British radio programme about cigarette addiction, two of the participants agreed that they smoked "to fill the empty space between their ears".

The question then is: what are the chances of enough people seeing clearly enough Who they are, and doing so quickly enough to change significantly our ailing society? For the following reasons the chances aren't as small as they might at first appear. (a) Among intelligent young people all over the world the sort of view put forward in this paper is quickly gaining ground, and the future lies with them. There is overwhelming evidence that, unlike their elders, they see their facelessness very easily, and that a sizable proportion value it.[3] (And, once having been clearly seen in youth, it can always be re-seen in later life when the need for it has become painfully evident. This isn't a skill which one is liable, by neglect, altogether to lose the knack of.) (b) The ever-growing speed and spread of communications ensures that an idea, catching on today, is everywhere tomorrow. (c) History, the underlying assumptions of a society, the manifest climate of opinion—these aren't changed by vast numbers of people acting in concert: it is always an influential minority, sometimes a very small one, which leads the way. (d) And what governs history, beneath all the show of physical power, is the power of ideas, and specially "the power of an idea whose time has come." (e) And if such an idea can get going in the schools it is well under way. Here, in education, there is much experiment and the

---

3 Witness the words of many songs current among international youth: for instance, the Incredible String Band's EKL 4037, entitled *Douglas Traherne Harding*, with words and music by Mike Heron. It begins:
When I was born I had no head
My eye was single and my body was full of light
One light, though the lamps be many
And the light that I was, was the light that I saw by...

possibility of rapid change.[4] (f) We are too concerned with opinion polls, with mere numbers. The social future of our hypothesis isn't a matter of counting heads but of counting no-heads—and the answer is One. When I see What is here it isn't the case of a man, one of thousands of millions, who is seeing This, but of This seeing Itself in me—*in* this man but not *as* this man. Enlightenment cannot be contained, it must spill over because ultimately it is the enlightenment of all. If this is true it follows that the social influence (deep, hidden, but all the wider and stronger for that) of just one unknown but dedicated seer may be decisive for the world's future.

And, after all, if our hypothesis is true, what could it be but the *raison d'être* of the entire universe? And if the purpose of the One's seeming Self-division into you and me and the others is Its own Self-consciousness in us, then already this marvellous goal has been partly won, and who could believe this to be the end of the story? Has the One shot Its bolt, come to the end of Its ingenuity, exhausted Its energies, got bored with the quest for Itself? Is the world as we know it Its last word? Merely to put such questions is to be assured that no one who entertains our hypothesis can be a real pessimist—not even about human society.

---

4 Of course the idea is already very much in the schools -- for systematically removing! In my own encounters with children of around 8 to 15, they were apt to be ahead of me in appreciation of their facelessness and its implications and value: often they led and I followed lamely: it was great fun—and very serious. Could it be that, before too long, a school should have one classroom—the children's very own—dedicated to unschooling, to a more, childlike version of the *Cloud of Unknowing*, to seeing oneself as one sees oneself, and to seeing the world as one sees the world, instead of seeing what one is *told* to see? A class in which the children themselves keep alive the wild hypothesis which we parents and teachers, and society in general, are inevitably killing?

Conclusion

This paper began by stating our hypothesis (that in man lies this remarkable Core) and went on to enquire precisely how it may be tested. There followed (I) the ten simple tests of *one's own* view of What is here, (II) the single but crucial test of *the outsider's* view of What is here, (III) the test of detecting Its five distinctive functions or powers, (IV) the test of discovering how far our hypothesis fits the facts and serves as an interpretative tool, how well it explains human development and behavior, and finally (V) the pragmatic test, the field test of practical utility.

The last two Sections, though easily the most important in that they bring out the value and social utility of our hypothesis, are of lower status in that they are necessarily imprecise and suggestive rather than exact and definitive. Their function is to indicate lines for further long-term research and practical effort in a rapidly changing social scene: accordingly, they should be treated as elastic and open-ended—and productive of further subsidiary hypotheses for testing in their turn. (As for the philosophical colouring and religious overtones accompanying their presentation here, these will certainly not please everybody: matters of taste or personal preference, they can't be tested like matters of fact.)

But though these two later Sections give point to the earlier ones, our case doesn't rest upon them. It rests on Sections (I) and (II) and (III), which stand or fall on their own merit, for they describe clear-cut tests which taken together are more than enough to determine the truth or falsity of our hypothesis.

The rest is up to my reader. If you have followed this paper so far without actually carrying out for yourself most of these simple tests (they require almost no time or effort or gear) then it has failed to convey its message. These printed pages remain about 18 inches wide of the Mark—the Mark being not what is read but Who is now reading. But if you have made that 18-inch leap and applied these tests, then it is *you* who are in a position to check our hypothesis, *you* are the authority on what it's all about, you check my words against *your* experience and not your experience against my words. It is to *you* I say: does this wild hypothesis make sense? Is it an important issue? Is it proven so far? Is it then worth pursuing further? Is it for living by?

Or is it—as we said at the start it might prove to be—just a hallowed myth, the most ancient of confidence tricks, the dream that humanity is overdue to wake from? I am content with your findings.

* * *

Chapter 30

THE ANSWER TO "WHO AM I?"

There is no answer to "Who am I?" The very asking is the answer.

Ramana Maharshi.

Normally when we ask a question—unless it is a merely rhetorical one—we look for an answer. And in the case of the most important of all questions—"Who am I?"—surely we expect a particularly clear, satisfying and final answer: otherwise, why bother to put the question at all? Yet Maharshi says there is no answer, since the very asking is the answer. And even this no-answer seems to be far from final, since we have to go on and on asking the question.

Why this contradiction, this puzzling or even disturbing paradox? If we can find the explanation we shall be very near the heart of his teaching. If we can't find it, or if we just ignore the paradox, we shall certainly remain far away from that heart.

Let us consider what kind of answer we naturally seek when we ask *Who* we really are.

First, we look for an intellectual answer, a verbal formula, an enlightening phrase or sacred text which appears to settle the question beyond doubt, which satisfies our need to know the truth, to understand the case. When we ask who the President of the USA is we expect a concise and conclusive verbal answer like "Mr Nixon". At another level, when we ask what the purpose of life is we expect a clear (if hardly conclusive) answer like "To discover Who is living it." Similarly when we ask *Who* we really are we expect some such definite verbal reply as "*Atman-Brahman*, or the One, or the Buddha-Nature, or the Godhead". But obviously the words, whether read or spoken or sung (however repeatedly), aren't enough; it isn't mere information we are after. Going along with the words there must be a genuine understanding of their meaning and implications. We have to know what the term *Atman-Brahman* signifies, as well as know that we are, at root, that same Being.

But clearly this understanding is still not enough. Even if we are continually telling ourselves we are *Atman-Brahma* in reality, and have some idea of what this amazing statement means, our question "Who am I?" isn't settled yet. No formula, however sacred, and no accompanying understanding, however penetrating, is much good if we lack the 'feel' of it. There must also be a deeply felt conviction that this is the central truth, that we indeed are, now and for ever and contrary to all appearances, the very Source of all things. We have not merely to say this with our lips and think it in our heads but to believe it in our hearts, so that the whole man is involved. Otherwise, nothing much happens.

But again, this isn't enough. The belief has to be maintained. It's not much good being deeply convinced now that we are, intrinsically, the No-thing which is the Origin of the world, if the next moment we forget it, and think of ourselves as mere parts of that world and essentially things surrounded by other things. There has also to be a steady realisation of *Who* we are.

Yet again, is this quite sufficient? Profound conviction, steadily maintained, as to our true Identity, needs to be actualised in everyday life, to become fully operative in all we do and say, so that we are manifestly living no longer from our imagined human centre but from our true Centre.

So thinking and feeling and living, we might be excused for believing that at last we are truly settling the question "Who am I?". Yet, according to Ramana Maharshi, this isn't so: the question remains unanswered—because it is unanswerable. What can he possibly have meant? What have we neglected to do?

In fact, the kind of answer we have been exploring so far is not at all the kind that he intends, not at all the kind that can really settle our question. We have been going in the wrong direction, working along the wrong lines altogether—along the well-worn lines of the mind, thought, knowledge, feeling, action, lines which branch into ever-increasing complications and make ever-increasing demands upon the traveller. If the discovery of *Who* we are is available only to the kind of person we have been describing, it is only for the very few who are sufficiently intelligent, intuitive, concentrated, dedicated, untiring: in short, it is available to almost nobody. But Ramana Maharshi consistently denied this. He never expected people to become sages or paragons of any sort. Without reservations or conditions he announced: "Whatever your human self may be like, be your real Self. Whatever your problem, the answer is to see *Who* has it, now. What are you waiting for? All the difficulties are imaginary: if you can't see your Self, who can? The reason you aren't Self-realised is that you think you aren't."

Here, then, is the clue to what he means. When we ask the question "Who am I?" in the way he intends, what happens is that no idea, no formula, no sacred text, no intuition, no emotional colouring arises in answer to it. Quite the reverse: all these vanish, and we are left in a state of total clarity, openness, no mind—fully alert, wide awake, but free from any particular experience, empty of all mental content or process.

Knowledge implies ignorance of what lies beyond the known, says Maharshi. "Knowledge is always limited." But seeing Who I am isn't knowledge: it is ever-renewed discovery, fresh, unconnected with past and future, perfectly simple. And it is seeing the Unlimited, the boundless Clarity which has no beyond. Therefore it provides the wholly convincing and satisfying answer to our question. If it contained the slightest verbal or intellectual or emotional ingredient, it wouldn't do at all. We couldn't rest in it, because such ingredients would demand a comment, further study, interpretation, development. The Plainness which lies right here for the seeing, at the Source and Centre of my everyday experience, discovers Itself to be free from all pollution by the world-stream that flows from It. Of another order altogether, this Wellspring remains entirely lucid, transparent, colourless, still, while from It flows with inconceivable abundance the turbid and restless world-stream.

How, then, am I to ask the question "Who am I?" In such a way as to come to that true answer which is no answer? I have just to look right here where I now am, and take seriously what I find. Forgetting what I remember and have been told about myself, I have to take a fresh look at what it's like being me. And when I look at myself here, without preconception or prejudice, what do I find? Darkness, a mass of flesh and blood, a box with two little windows in it, an apparatus or thing of any sort? An observer, a seer, a person? A mind, a system of ideas, feelings, words?

No! When I honestly attend to this very Spot I occupy I find here absolutely No-thing whatever—Simplicity itself, indubitable, obvious, final. This No-thing is the No-answer to the question of Who I am; and paradoxically, the perfect answer too!

* * *

Chapter 31

THE HEADLESS WAY

Over the past thirty years a truly contemporary and Western way of 'seeing into one's Nature' or 'Enlightenment' has been developing—one which seems to appeal specially to young people.[1] Though in essence the same as Zen, Sufism, and other spiritual disciplines, this way proceeds in an unusually down-to-earth fashion. It claims that modern man is more likely to see Who he really is in a minute of active experimentation than in years of reading, lecture-attending, thinking, ritual observances, and passive meditation of the traditional sort. Instead of all this, it uses a variety of absurdly simple, non-verbal, fact-finding tests, all of them asking: *how do I look to myself?* They direct my attention to my blind spot—to the space I occupy, to what's given right here at the Centre of my universe, to what it's like being lst-person singular, present tense.

Five stages of development are distinguished:-

1. Like any animal, the new-born infant is for himself no-thing, faceless and at large, unseparate from his world, 1st-person without knowing it.

2. The young child, becoming briefly and intermittently *aware* of himself-as-he-is-for-himself, may ask his mother why she has a head and he hasn't, or may protest that he isn't a boy (he's not like that at

1 See D. E. Harding: *On Having No Head, Religions of the World, The Face Game* and *First Person Toolkit,* Shollond Publications, England.

all!), or may even announce that he's nothing, not there, invisible. Yet he's also becoming increasingly aware of himself-as-he-is-for-others—a very human 3rd person complete with head and face. Both views of himself are valid and needful.

3. But as the child grows up his acquired view of himself-from-outside comes to overshadow, and in the end to obliterate, his native view of himself-from-inside. In fact, he grows *down*. At first, he contained his world; now, it contains him. Victim of the universal confidence trick, he is 1st-person no longer. Shrunk from being the Whole into being this contemptible part, he grows greedy, hating, fearful, and deluded. Greedy, as he tries to regain at whatever cost a little of his lost empire; hating, as he revenges himself upon a society that has cruelly cut him down to size; fearful, as he sees himself a mere thing up against all other things; deluded, as he imagines, against all the evidence, that he is at 0 feet what he looks like at 6 feet—a solid, opaque, coloured, outlined lump of material.

4. His cure is to take a fresh look at himself and discover Who he really is. Of the many recommended pointers and aids to this Self-realisation (some of which use other senses than vision) the following are typical. (Warning: it's no good just reading about them: you have actually to carry out these simple experiments, for yourself.)

(a) *Pointing here.* Point to your friend's feet, then yours; to his legs, then yours; to his torso, then yours; to his head, then... What, *on present evidence,* are you now pointing to?

(b) *Single eye.* In your own experience now, are you peering through two little holes in a kind of meat-ball? If so, what's it like in there—dark, stuffy, congested? Slowly put on a pair of spectacles (you can make a good-enough pair with your thumbs and forefingers) and notice how those two small 'windows' become one vast 'window'— spotlessly clean, frameless with nobody looking out of it.

(c) *No-mask.* Cut a head-sized hole in a card. Hold the card at arm's length noting the hole's boundaries. Put it slowly on, noting how they vanish into your boundlessness.

(d) *Paper bag.* Get an ordinary bag about 12 inches square, and cut the bottom out. Fit your face into one end while your friend fits his face into the other. How many faces are given in the bag? Dropping memory and imagination, are you face-to-face, or face-to-no-face?

(e) *Mirror.* Observe the region where you keep your face—over there in your mirror, and where it's presented to your friend (who can accordingly tell you about it), and where he finds it in his camera.

(f) *Boxed-up?* By stroking and pinching and pummelling, try to build up here on your shoulders the sort of thing you see over there in your mirror. Now try to get inside it. Now try to describe its contents. Aren't you still out-of-doors, as much at large as ever?

(g) *Onion peeling.* Get your friend to check your faceless emptiness (at 0 feet) by coming right up to you with his camera (a viewfinder consisting of a small hole in a sheet of paper will do). He starts at a place (say 6 feet away) where he finds you to be a man, then comes to where (at, say, 3 feet) he finds you to be a torso, then a head, then an eye, then a mere blur. If he has the right instruments, the blur reads as an eyelash, then as cells, then as molecules, and in the end as practically empty space—featureless, transparent, colourless. The closer he gets to you, the closer he gets to your own view of yourself as No-thing at all.

5. You have actually seen, by conducting such exercises in basic attention, what it is to be 1st-person singular—the No-thing that is nevertheless keenly aware of Itself as the empty Container or Ground of the whole scene. Now your task is to go on seeing your Absence/Presence in all situations, till the seeing becomes quite natural and continuous. This is neither to lose yourself in your Emptiness nor in what fills it, but *simultaneously* to view the thing you are looking at and the No-thing you are looking out of. There will be found no times when this two-way attention is out of place or can safely be dispensed with.

It isn't claimed that this direct method of Awakening is everybody's, or that it is easy. Certainly the initial seeing into one's Void Nature is simplicity itself: once noticed, Nothing is so obvious! But it is operative only in so far as it is practised. The results—freedom from greed and hate and fear and delusion—are assured only while one ceases overlooking Who they belong to.

* * *

Chapter 32

ELEVEN TESTS FOR BUDDHISTS

Following the lead of the Buddha himself, it is often claimed for Buddhism that, in contrast to other religions, it is undogmatic, that its teachings are for testing and not merely taking on trust. A true Buddhist doesn't deal in second-hand goods. He is said to be open-minded, humble before the facts as they actually present themselves, and above all mindful of what is given now, dropping imagination, hearsay, prejudice, and all preconceived views—no matter how sanctified by tradition.

What follows is, accordingly, an invitation to put this open-minded mindfulness into practice, and test some basic Buddhist teachings by finding out how they match up to first-hand experience.

First, a glance at these teachings:

> Do not seek refuge in anyone but yourself.
> You cannot by going reach that place wherein there are no birth, no ageing, no decaying, no falling away, no rising up elsewhere in rebirth... For, my friends, in this very body, six feet tall... are the world, and the ceasing of the world, and the way that leads to its ceasing.
>
> Gautama Buddha

Perceiving that this body is like froth, like a mirage, he (the disciple), breaking the flowery shafts of Mara, will go where the

As I See It

King of Death will not see him.

Dhammapada

Here, O Sariputra, form is void.

Heart Sutra

I realised the Essential Nature of my body and mind, that it is like the fluidity of the oceans of fragrance surrounding the Isles of the Blest. I realised that I had all along been throwing the broken shards of my thoughts of personality into the pure limpidity of my Essential Nature.

Surangama Sutra

This empty, visionary body is no less than the Dharmakaya.

Yung-chia Hsuan-chueh

In the place where no man is I will put my hand to my forehead and watch for you... I will wait and look out for you where no man speaks, that is, in Maitreya's land, where no mouth or lips are needed.

Pai-chang

As long as you are not carried away by external winds, your Nature will remain like water for ever still and clear.
Perception that there is nothing to perceive—this is Nirvana, also known as Deliverance.

Hui-hai

Can you see, for yourself, without the slightest difficulty or doubt, into your Void Nature? In other words, are the above-quoted passages obviously true right now, in your own immediate experience? If so, don't bother to read the rest of this article.

If, again, you neither see what they are on about, nor want to see, there's no point in reading further.

But if, on the other hand, you don't see it, but are willing to try anything that might enable you to do so, then it is suggested that you devote the next twenty minutes to carrying out some simple experiments. Just reading about them is rather worse than useless. They have actually to be done. The following questions are for settling *on present evidence* alone, on what you can find at this moment, when you stop reading things into it:

1. Stand up, look ahead, keep still.

(It helps to get a friend to read the questions out to you, but you don't need to answer them out loud).

How many feet do you now have, so far as you can tell?

Of course you feel sensations, but what are they really like? Do they add up to feet? On present showing, couldn't you just as well have claws or hooves or fins?

How many legs can you find? How many trunks? How many heads? Where are your boundaries? How big are you? How old? What sex? Are you any thing at all, or are you more like the space in which a lot of other things—including various thoughts and feelings—are now happening?

2. Answer the same questions, this time with your eyes closed.

3. Look at your hand. Are you in it, or is it in you? Have you any clue what it's like in there?

4. Keep looking at your hand.

How could you now see its colour, if you were coloured? How would you receive its shape, if you had shape?

How could you register its movements now, except in your stillness? How could you contain it, if you weren't empty?

How could you take in all that detail, except by being absolutely plain and simple?

How could you feel the pain in it (as your thumbnail presses into your finger) if it were not felt against an on-going background of no pain?

How could you hear the noise it makes (as you snap your fingers) if the sound didn't plop into your boundless pool of silence?

5. How many eyes are you looking out of, now you really attend? See what happens when you put your glasses on, slowly. Outline with your hands the extent of your 'Eye'. What's behind it?

6. Point to your feet, legs, belly, chest, then to what's above that. What, in all honesty, is your finger now pointing at? Go on pointing.

7. See if you can get face-to-face with anyone. Isn't it face-to-*no*-face?

8. Make sure where you keep your face. Is it where you *thought* it was? Or is it over there in the mirror, and where your friend is in receipt of it (and therefore can tell you whether there's a smut on your

nose), and where he holds his camera (which can therefore record it, smut and all)?

9. By stroking and pinching and pummelling, try to build up on your shoulders a coloured, opaque, all-together-in-one-piece, bounded *thing*, such as you find on your friend's shoulders. Try to get inside and describe its contents, as now revealed. Aren't you still at large, spaced out, immense?

10. Look at the sky above you. Is your Earth-body now voided, just as your man's body and face and eyes were voided? Isn't it true that 'the whole great Earth is nothing but you' (Hsueh-feng) and that 'the great Earth doesn't contain a speck of dust' (Zen saying)? Isn't what you are looking *out of* always splendidly capacious for what you are looking *at*?

11. You are the sole authority on how it is where you are. But if you don't trust your own findings, get your friend to check, so far as he can, your central emptiness (at 0 feet) by coming right up to you with his camera (a 'viewfinder-hole' in a sheet of paper will do). Doesn't he start at a place (say 6 feet away) where he finds you to be a human being, then come to a place where (at, say, 3 feet) he finds half a human being, then a hand or a head, then a patch of skin, then a mere blur?

(Supposing he had good microscopes, etc., wouldn't the blur read as cells, then as one cell, then as particles of descending order, and in the end as practically empty space—featureless, transparent, colourless, unbounded?)

Isn't it true that the closer he gets to you the closer he gets to your own view of yourself as No-thing whatever?

Can you now see for yourself, beyond all doubt, into your Void Nature? If so, what prevents your going on doing so, whenever and wherever you like, till the seeing becomes your normal way of life? This may not take as long as you fear. In any case you have got off to a good start.

* * *

Chapter 33

HOW TO BE SPONTANEOUS

The article under this heading, in the May '74 number of *Self and Society,* made me look afresh into the question of my own spontaneity, and what (for me) spontaneity really is, with the results that I shall try to summarise here.

But first, the points in that article which started me off. Briefly, they were these:

When someone annoys me, there are four possible levels of response. (1) The worst, I say nothing. (2) Slightly better, I blurt out: *'You are a pain in the neck.'* (3) Better still, I say: *'You give me* a pain in the neck.' (4) The best, I report: 'When you did that, *I felt* a pain in the neck, etc.' Here, at level 4, there intervenes a tiny pause, when my attention is turned inwards to find out how I am actually feeling. This (as I understand the article) enables me to act spontaneously, with my whole self, on the whole situation.

I find there is a fifth possibility: I can notice that the pain I feel right here 'in my neck' isn't *for me* in a neck at all!

In that place where others observe my neck to be, I find nothing of the sort. When I'm really attentive I find here nothing solid, or opaque, or pink or brown or black, or cylindrical, but just space— space in which these pains and tensions are coming and going. In fact, I have difficulty in locating them anywhere at all—let alone inside a column of flesh and blood and bone, about 6 inches in diameter—to be quite honest.

Let me try to describe in more detail what I find happening at this fifth level:

a) I notice that the situation *as given,* vis-a-vis that infuriating person, isn't in fact symmetrical at all. It's not a face-to-face or neck-to-neck confrontation, but neck-to-no-neck, face-there to no-face-here. I observe that, whether I like it or not, I'm wide open to and for him. Not on principle, not as a matter of policy, not in idea or feeling or imagination, but actually, in simple perception, I make way for him. I am room for him to be like that in. Right here, I find I'm built that way. ThomasTraherne puts it well:

No brims nor borders in myself I see: My essence is Capacity.

b) Seeing this total asymmetry, I find thoughts ceasing. There occurs here a kind of 'alert idiocy'. My mind 'goes blank'. I'm perfectly clueless about how to cope.

c) Commonly, though not invariably, I find, along with this cluelessness, a kind of relaxation, in which my body is very alive but very still, and my breathing seems almost to cease altogether.

d) I just wait and see. Or rather, see and wait: see how it is here and await what comes out. I respond to that annoying person unpredictably, in accordance with no plan or conscious level of behaviour: I have no preview of what I shall find myself doing or saying. I may (and very often do) keep silent, or turn tail, or tear strips off him, or even (though this is most unusual) treat him to an account of what he's doing to my neck, etc., supposing I had one right here. Often I'm surprised, occasionally shocked, at what emerges.

e) But whatever my reaction I find it can be trusted—*provided* I'm attending to where it comes from—this inner Emptiness or Clarity or Capacity. It turns out to be (so far as I can judge, with hindsight) the best response possible in the circumstances as a whole, appropriate to the total situation, and certainly never destructive or hating. (Conversely, to the extent that I imagine here a thing instead of no-thing, a solid face and neck to confront him with, I am rejecting him, shutting him out, telling him to keep off. My dishonest attempts to make the set-up symmetrical are a sort of hate—the very basis of all my personal-relationship problems—with the result that those problems get worse and worse).

(f) I may afterwards (but this is optional) attempt to explain to myself why this fifth level alone is, in my experience, truly spontaneous, creative, and workable. My explanation takes the following form:

This Space, or boundless Capacity, which I find here (in which that person is doing annoying things and these pains and tensions are going on) is what I really am as 1st person singular, present tense: it is my inside story. It has, traditionally, many names, from which I may take my pick. They include: the Void, the Buddha Nature, Tao, Atman-Brahman, Being, Consciousness, the One, Spirit, Essence, the Source, one's True and Original Face, the Single or Third Eye, the Kingdom within, the Light that lights every man, the Godhead, the eternal indwelling Christ—the names are many and varied, the fact is one and the same. I know it because I am it: it's the one 'thing' I have inside knowledge of. Whatever label I give it, I find it to be without any limitations or attributes, perfectly simple, indivisible, obvious, and accessible right here at this very moment.

It is me, but not mine. It belongs just as much to that annoying person as to me. It is the inside story of what we both really are. As this, at this level, I am him and he is me. I can, silently, but with total sincerity, say to him: *"Here, I am you. To hurt you is to hurt myself."*

Of course it isn't necessary that he should see the situation that way, and I'm unlikely to burden him with an account of what I'm up to. And even if *both* of us are consciously enjoying this basic unity, it doesn't follow that we shall at once, or ever, cease to give each other a pain in the (no) neck from time to time. But our behaviour towards each other will at least be spontaneous, basically loving, and in the long run mutually helpful. For this seeing What or Who we really are isn't love in the ordinary sense. It goes deeper than that. It is love's basis. It is that conscious identity at the deepest level, which liberates us to enjoy our immense differences at every other level.

A final word about the practice of this fifth way. It sounds complicated: in fact, it is simplicity itself. But it isn't easy. The lifelong habit of taking everybody's word for what it's like right here, except the word of the one who is right here—myself—isn't quickly outgrown. Society's basic confidence trick (that I am here what I look like to you there, a solid thing, neck and all) isn't seen through once and for all. Only I am in a position to say how it is here, but the world has intimidated me, and it takes time to get back my courage to look for myself at myself, and then live by what I find.

It helps to have problems. If I'm having trouble relating to people,

How to be Spontaneous

I have a powerful motive for seeing *Who* is having this trouble. For I find that all my problems—including that of spontaneity—boil down to the problem of my identity. Who am I? It is extremely easy to look and see for myself what the answer is: namely, that I am, as 1st person, just Capacity.[1] It is less easy to go on looking till the social confidence trick—which makes me out to be 3rd-person only—ceases to take me in. But neither is it as hard as it is often advertised to be.

* * *

---

1 For instance, I have only to point here (to the place where I *imagined* that I experienced a neck) to see that my finger is pointing in to empty space. Or I have only to look down at my trunk to see that it stops well short of my neck, and carries, Atlas-like, the world.

Chapter 34

PERSEUS AND THE GORGON
A New Interpretation of the Ancient Myth

Man is wiser, his roots go deeper, than he knows. His Unconscious is always coming up with images, often elaborately disguised, whose function is to redress the imbalance of his conscious mind. A remarkable instance of this hidden wisdom arising from the depths is the ancient Greek myth of Perseus and the Gorgon. No enlightened man or group of men ever made up this story in order to convey, in the form of an easily followed and exciting tale, profound religious and psychological truths that the people weren't ready for. No; the story just grew up along with the ancient Greeks themselves, much as their language and social customs grew up, and got written down and thought about much later. In fact, we are still thinking about the adventures of the Greek heroes. There can be no final and conclusive interpretation of the great myths of mankind. We find in them what we currently need.

In this article we present (1) an outline of the myth as it comes down to us from the Greek poets and dramatists and sculptors. Then we offer (2) our own interpretation in terms of Self-realisation. And conclude with (3) some sayings of Ramana Maharshi, by way of summary; plus (4) a warning footnote.

1. The myth
A typical hero of Greek mythology, Perseus was half divine and half

human—a son of Zeus, the Father of the gods, and Danae, a mortal woman. Danae's father, Acrisius, had been warned that he would be killed by Danae's son, so he took the precaution of shutting her in a brass tower. This did not deter Zeus who, turning himself into a shower of golder rain, came down through the roof and impregnated her, thus begetting Perseus. When Acrisius discovered that his daughter had given birth to a son, he set them both adrift at sea in a chest. However, Zeus caused them to come ashore at Seriphos, where a fisherman rescued them and took them to the king of the country, who befriended the refugees.

When Persues reached manhood the king set him the formidable task of killing Medusa, one of the terrible Gorgon Sisters, whose head was covered with writhing snakes instead of hair—a sight so frightful that one look at her turned everyone to stone. Perseus equipped himself for the adventure with great thoroughness. First, he visited the Weird Sisters who shared one Eye between the three of them, and snatched it as they were passing it round. Then he made them direct him to the Nymphs, from whom he obtained the Winged Sandals (which enabled their wearer to travel rapidly through the air), the Magic Wallet (into which things disappeared and out of which they re-appeared), and the Cap of Invisibility (which gave its owner the power of vanishing at will). Next, Hermes presented him with a wonderful Sword for beheading Medusa. Finally, Athene, the goddess who personified ideal wisdom and power, lent him her Mirror-shield, in which alone Medusa could safely be viewed. Thus magnificently armed, our hero duly tracked down and decapitated the monster without looking directly at her, concealed her head in his Magic Wallet, and got away unharmed from her enraged sisters— thanks to his Cap of Invisibility. Other adventures followed, in which he overcame his enemies by producing from his Wallet the Gorgon's head and freezing them in their tracks.

2. Interpretation

Such, in brief, is the famous legend of Perseus and Medusa the Gorgon. According to the interpretation which follows, Perseus is everyman—in particlar, myself coming to realise Who I really am, my true Identity.

(a) The Divine-human hero

On one side (his mother's) Perseus was mortal; on the other (his father's) divine. My nature is dual. Looked at from outside, I appear all-too-human; from inside, I'm nothing of the sort.

(b) The Fall

Perseus is at sea, abandoned, all hint of divinity gone, in danger of death. So, again, with me. I am lost. I have indeed come down in the world.

(c) The Task

Reaching maturity, Perseus is required to solve the problem, aptly called petrifaction. In other words, solidification, the universal but false idea that one is shut up in a body, entombed, imprisoned, condensed and shrunk into a limited, substantial, opaque, coloured thing, an object like those objects out there. For myself, growing up from infancy, my mother's face, every face I see, becomes in effect Medusa's, forever telling me, "You too are like this: the thing you are looking at is your clue to the thing you are looking out of." My task is to see through this lie. I have to find a way of looking at that face, of somehow coping with it, without letting it pertify me—a way of seeing I'm not like that at all. For this great task I'm already marvellously equiped, as follows:

(1) The Third Eye. for a start I can't do better than, like Perseus, find my Single or Third Eye. The fact is I've only to notice I never looked out of anything else! I have only to count, in all honesty and simplicity, the number of windows my 'house of clay' really has, seen from indoors. And, having counted one, to notice how this huge and speckless Window has no frame and is set in no wall and has no structure at all this side of it. My two-windowed façade exists for others.

(2) The Winged Sandals. Again, as soon as I have the courage and the honesty to attend, I discover that the world is given as two-dimensional—high, wide, and without depth. Distance is a put-up job, a convenient social fiction. I clearly see that I'm no further from that star than from that treetop, and no further from that treetop than this hand. Looking at myself right here, I'm not in the world at all: it's in me. Whereas Perseus, shod with Winged Sandals, gets all over the place, at speed; I am all over the place, instantly.

(3) The Magic Wallet. Like Perseus, again, I'm furnished with the Magic Wallet, the Void here that is forever taking in and producing all the world's treasures. Indeed I am this Bottomless Purse or Horn

of Plenty. My very essence is Capacity, with room and to spare for all the shapes and colours and sounds and smells and tastes and feelings and thoughts that come and go in It.

(4) The Cap of Invisibility. The Cap fits, and I wear it—and find no wearer! Not for others there, but for myself here, I vanish.

(5) The Sword. This is the indispensable weapon in the fight against petrifaction, the keen Vajra Sword for severing Self from not-Self, Reality from all its appearances, Nirvana from Samsara, this First Person Singular from all second and third persons, this Void from its filling, this featureless Original Face from all those Gorgon faces. So long as the cut-and-thrust of my Sword of Discrimination leaves one strand of connecting tissue between subject and object, I remain an object among objects, threatened by them in a million ways, petrified with fear. But when all connection is severed, I see I've always been unconnected, no object but the Space in which objects occur. As such, I coincide with them, I am them all, and their menace is overcome. But it's only when the distinction between the Space and its contents is seen as total that their union is seen as total.

(6) The Mirror-shield. Whenever I look directly at any face there, while overlooking the featureless Space, the mirror-like Clarity here in which that face is presented, I'm thinged, trapped, faced up, petrified. (It's all imagination, of course, but none the less painful for that.) My only protection against those baleful features is, like Perseus confronting Medusa, to turn my attention round from them to my Absence-of-features, to the clear Mirror here which is my Shield from all harm. Seen as if she were self-existent, real in her

own right out there and independent of the Seer here, Medusa turns me to something like stone. Seen from her Origin here, she's not only rendered harmless, but is revealed as a unique and indispensable expression of Who I am, and probably quite beautiful into the bargain. What's more, she's yet another reminder to me to look back at Who's looking.

(7) Medusa's head re-deployed. My task accomplished, the world's a safe place for living in me. I'm its life, and it has none whatever of its own. For now it's my turn, like Perseus exposing Medusa's head to his pursuers, to petrify all comers. There are no embodied minds, no separate consciousnesses around. Only here, where I can find no eyes, no face, no obscuring body at all, is the indivisible Spirit, and none of it is left out there lurking behind those little eyes. No goblins peep through those windows at me. Eyes and faces and bodies are now seen for exactly what they are—decor, interesting scenic features, charmingly coloured shapes as unhaunted as clouds and flowers are, as devoid of menace. I no longer feel under inspection. And in case this should sound as if I'm merely killing everyone off, reducing them to so many walking corpses or mechanical dolls, let me immediately add that the opposite is also true: there's more than enough Consciousness here to go round and bring the whole Universe—including all the officially 'dead' parts—to abundant life again. But this time the life is from here. I AM the life and soul of the cosmic party. There are no others.

3. Summing up

Who could better conclude for us than Ramana Maharshi himself? Most of the following quotations are taken from his Talks, a few from his Translations. They are arranged to correspond with the items of equipment used by our hero in the fulfilment of his great task.

(a) The Third or Single Eye, for really seeing with

The forms perceived are various—blue and yellow, gross and subtle, tall and short, and so on; but the Eye that sees them remains one and the same.

If the eye becomes the Self, the Self being infinite, the Eye is infinite.

Disciple: What is the significance of the spot between the eyebrows? Maharshi: It is mentioned as if to say, "Do not see with your eyes."

(b) The Winged Sandals, for conquering space

Where is the star, in fact? Is it not in the Observer?

The trouble is you see the world as external.

The "I" has no location.

(c) The Magic Wallet or Hold-all

What is not in you cannot appear outside.

Everything is within one's Self.

The idea that one is limited is the trouble.

(d) The Cap of Invisibility, worn by No-body

Anything seen cannot be real.

If you think you are a body the world seems external.

Do not confound yourself with the object, namely the body.

Identification of the Self with the body is the real bondage.

(e) The Sword of Discrimination

Countless scriptures proclaim only discrimination between Self and non-Self.

To qualify for enquiry into the Self, a man must be able to discriminate between the Real and the unreal.

The Self has no sort of relationship with anything.

(f) The Mirror-shield of the Self

Find the Subject, and objects will take care of themselves.

Wonder of wonders... they see phenomena apart from the Self!

Can anything new appear without that which is eternal?

If you know your Self no evil can befall you.

(g) Medusa's head re-deployed: the end of the others

There are no others.

In reality, all these are nothing but the Self.

Nothing can be apart from you.

Phenomena are real when experienced as the Self, and illusory when seen apart from the Self.

4. Footnote

If the story of Perseus and the Gorgon has a defect, it is its very richness: it puts one simple point in so many ways. He didn't really need to collect all that gear: any part of it would have done the job at once. This needs saying in case we should regard the stages of his preparation as a hint that we have to go through similar stages. Of course, if we want to put off dealing with the problem of Medusa indefinitely, we can always plead careful preparation as our excuse. But if we are serious, we shall deal with her now, using any device that's to hand. As actually experienced, there's no real difference between our Single Eye, our Cap of Invisibility, and the rest. One way of escaping petrifaction is as good as another, and the resulting Transparency is exactly the same.

In another respect our myth can mislead. Medusa isn't, in real life, overcome once and for all. She has unsuspected powers of regeneration—and petrifaction—and has to be killed again and again till she stays dead. In plain language, it takes much dedicated practice before one sees effortlessly and unbrokenly into one's Clear Nature. No doubt the initial seeing is the easiest and most natural thing in the world; keeping it up is just about the most difficult. Nevertheless, having once been seen, This can always be seen again. Our hero's armoury leaves us no excuse for not getting on with the job.

* * *

Chapter 35

ON TRIAL FOR MY LIFE
Summary of Proceedings

I. Charge

I am accused of being a man, the penalty for which is death.[1]

II. Plea

Not guilty.

III. Prosecution

The case against me falls into seven parts. Three witnesses—a Philosopher, a Psychiatrist, and a Scientist—are called.

The Philosopher

(1) claims that all say I am a man, and no-one can be found to deny it;

(2) that in fact I, too, see myself to be a man,

(3) and feel myself to be a man,

(4) and do what men do—working no miracles.

(5) And that the deep-seated defects of my character remain. The meagre benefits of my strange belief—that I transcend the human—show how wrong I am.

---

1 *Ramana Maharshi:* The person soaked in 'I-am-the-body' idea is the greatest sinner and he is a suicide.
Disciple: The Bible teaches that man is born in sin.
Ramana Maharshi: The man is sin!
St Paul: The wages of sin is death, but the gift of God is eternal life.

The Psychiatrist

(6) explains my case in pathological terms (e.g., paranoia—an all-too-human condition).

The Scientist

(7) classifies me as an ordinary specimen of *Homo sapiens,* one of the Primates—an order which includes lemurs, monkeys, and anthropoid apes.

Ultimately, I am for him a system of waves or particles whose behaviour reaches those degrees of elaboration called chemical, vital, and human.

IV. Defence

I conduct my own defence, recalling and cross-questioning the witnesses and taking the stand on my own behalf. I deal in turn with the Prosecution's seven counts against me.

(1) The evidence of consensus

The Philosopher, going back on his previous testimony, admits that not everyone says I am a man. He agrees that the Perennial Philosophy, which lies at the heart of the great spiritual traditions, insists that I am really the Self (alias *Atman-Brahman,* the Buddha-Nature, the Void, the Godhead, Being or Consciousness, the Kingdom of Heaven, etc.) and that the whole reason for living is to realise I am This and no man, no thing at all.

He further admits that the experts in this Philosophy are precise about *where* to find my Self ("Closer is He than breathing, and nearer than hands and feet"), and when to look for It ("Now is the day of salvation"), and how to look for It ("Like a little child"), and what It looks like ("Light", "Living Water", "Space", etc.).

Finally, the witness concedes that this Philosophy is the *only* one which has remained intact down the ages. It is the real consensus. No other teaching has proved so independent of history and geography and cultural differences, has so stood the test of time and experience.

(2) The evidence of Self-perception

Appearing in my own defence, I swear on the most solemn oath that I perceive nothing at all right here where I am, let alone a man. For instance:[2]

(a) Looking now at these marks on paper, I'm looking *out of*— what? Not, *on present evidence,* out of two eyes, or even one, but out of this huge oval 'window' without frame or glass, or indeed any looker this side of it.

(b) Looking straight across at that person over there, is it a case of a man observing a man? What is now taking him in here? I find here no present evidence of a body, no structure or solidity, no opacity or colouring, no boundaries where this observer ends and the scene begins, nothing to which a name or age or sex could be attributed. I try to count (while still looking across at him) how many toes I now have... how many fingers... how many legs... arms... heads... In every case I find nothing to count. The idea that I *am* a human body or *inhabit* one, or even own one makes no sense now. What would it be like in there?

---

2 If the reader, too, wants to escape the death-penalty, he should actually carry out, *for himself,* the identity-tests or experiments which form the substance of the Defence throughout.

(c) When I go outside and lie down and look up at the sky, it isn't only my human body but also my terrestrial body—the Earth—that is dissolved without trace into room for the stars to shine in.

(d) Finally, I shut my eyes (that's what people say, not my story) and dissolve all those stars, the Universe itself.

In short, whatever I'm up to, I see that I couldn't be *less* like those fixed, solid, complicated, shut-in creatures called men.

(3) The evidence of Self-feeling

Continuing to testify on my own behalf, I agree it isn't enough that I *perceive* myself to be this elastic, all-dissolving Clarity, this conscious Absence which the Perennial Philosophy describes. What I really am must also be a matter of what I *feel* myself to be, what comes natural. Do I carry on as if I were God, or a mere man, or what?

Levels of identification

Quite apart from realising Who in fact I am, my self-feelings—however confused—have certainly never been those of a mere man.

(a) Sometimes I felt like nothing whatever.

(b) In great physical pain or pleasure, I *identified* myself with one part of my body in distinction from the rest.

(c) Arguing with my brother, I *felt* like one human confronting another.

(d) If a neighbour started encroaching on the family property, I *found* myself reacting for and as the family.

(e) In case of a threat to my sect, or nation, or race, it was as each of these, in turn, that I *faced* the threat.

(f) Imagining my Planet or Solar System to be in danger of invasion by another, I *found* myself thinking and feeling for this heavenly body as against that one.

(g) I *experienced* the anxiety that haunts these intermediate levels, their instability and comparative unreality. But there *occurred* times of great peace when they were left behind, and not a particle in the universe *eluded* my embrace. Then at last I *was* mySelf. I *felt* comfortable. As the Nothing that holds the All I *rested*...

My mistaken identity

In fact, I never *accepted* my supposed 'human limitations'. They never fitted. My trouble *was* that I *tried* to achieve *as man* what I already am as the Self. If I *was* greedy it *was* because I *knew* in my heart that all things are mine. If I *was* self-centred it *was* because I am forever Self-centred. If I *sought* power it was because I dimly *recognised* there is no other power. If I *tried* to evade responsibility it was because I never *got* involved anyhow. If I *behaved* as if I was immortal, it *was* because the One here is deathless. If I *hated* all my limitations it was on account of my profound conviction that in reality I am unlimited. The instinct *was* right; only its expression was wrong, inefficient, partial. In all my deeds and cravings, even the worst, I *was* half-heartedly laying claim to my Self. Throughout all these false identifications I was implying my true Identity.

My True Identity

How does it feel to be the only One, the Alone, the Origin, the self-generating Self? To be this unthinkable mystery? To celebrate not *what* I am but *that* I am—since there is no reason for anything to be at all? Somehow, inconceivably, I arrange my own existence. It's impossible! But who is now feeling this incomparable wonder? How could a man begin to do so? Who but the Self knows this joy? To whom but the Self could it come so naturally?

(4) The evidence of miracles
The Prosecution wants to know why, if my testimony so far is true, am I so powerless, unable seemingly to work a single modest miracle? If I'm not a man but really God why doesn't He occasionally show his hand?

The fact is that to see what I'm up to *I have to be really childlike.* When at last I dare to look for myself, ignoring what I've been told to see, I find, not occasional miracles going on around here, but fantastic miracles all the time—of which the following are random samples:

(a) Whereas men close and open their eyes, I annihilate and recreate the world.

(b) They only stop their ears; I hush the world.

(c) They rotate; I spin the world.

(d) A man holds a bit of red glass to his eye; I paint the sky.

(e) He turns his face to the distant stars; abolishing distance, I coincide with the stars.

(f) The road pays no attention to the human traveller, but for me it widens, closing in again behind.

(g) He walks in the country, moving at one speed in its stillness. The whole countryside walks in me, moving at many speeds in my stillness. I watch him shifting his little body, while I shift mountains, trees, houses—effortlessly, at will.

And so on, indefinitely. Here is no human magician. I, and I alone, perform only miracles—superhuman feats that make the famous *siddhis,* which a few men are capable of, look commonplace indeed.

(5) The evidence of practical results
The Prosecution points out that if I really am God, then living as such should work out better than living as the man I took myself to be; for it would indeed be a strange world in which such stupendous realisation made no practical difference. But in fact (the Prosecution continues) the consequences of my alleged Self-awareness manifestly fall short of its pretensions.

What, then, are the benefits of seeing and feeling and knowing Who I am? According to the Prosecution, they appear negligible. I say they are non-existent! For, firstly, this simple Being here cannot change for better or worse: here is nothing to modify. Secondly, the man which I am not is by nature ever-changing, limited and imperfect in every respect, incapable of any radical reform, and my liberation is my liberation from him—and from all attempts to improve him. So that even if he does seem to pick up a few benefits, these are incidental, irrelevant, not my business, or perhaps a diversion from the real issue, which is my total Perfection. In any case, these supposed benefits are nebulous and fleeting. Having come, they will go; having no substance, they melt on inspection.

Yet there is something that must be added. Paradoxically, I find that his failure to find any certain gain, or rather this loss of interest in this whole matter of human improvement, is itself the greatest gain!

It is the indescribable peace of resting in my true Nature.

(6) The evidence of psychology
Recalled to the witness stand, the psychiatrist is questioned about
my case-history, the background of my denial that I am a man. The
following developmental stages emerge:

(a) As a new-born infant I was, like any animal, unself-conscious—
no-thing for myself, faceless, at large, unseparate from my world.

(b) As a young child, becoming on occasions aware of myself-as-
I-am-for-myself, I wanted to know why my mother had a head and I
lacked one, or protested that I wasn't a boy (I wasn't like those solid
people at all!), or announced that I was nothing, absent, invisible. [3]
In other words I saw, however rarely and briefly, into my true non-
human Nature. Yet I was also becoming increasingly aware of myself-
as-I-am-for-others—a very human and special person, complete with
head and face. Both views of me were valid and needful.

(c) But as I grew up my socially acquired view of myself-from-
outside came to overshadow, and in the end to obliterate, my native
view of myself-from-inside. In fact, I grew *down*, I collapsed. At first
I contained my world; now it contained me—what little of me was
left. Intimidated, I took everybody's word for what's here where I am,
except my own. I was out-voted by thousands to one. So I shrank
from being the all-embracing Subject into one of its myriad objects,
into a cut-off, closed-in body, into a thing whose nature is to be up
against all other things, into an alien in an alien universe. Into a

---

3 Listen to young children, and you will find that (till they are laughed out of it by
grown-ups who 'know better') they really do talk like this.

'case' calling for an alienist or mind-doctor, since mind-sickness is essentially alienation, separateness.

(d) But one day, daring at last to look within this 'case', I found no patient, no man, no thing but Space for things to happen in, and no separation from them whatever. And this discovery, so far from constituting my disease (as the witness first maintained) was my cure.

(7) The evidence of science

Up to this point, the strength of the Defence has lain in its appeal to my own direct, first-hand experience of What I am, my Subjectivity— seeing that no one else can speak for me here. From the Prosecution's view point, however, this subjectivity is precisely the weakness of my case. But there remains the Prosecution's last shot, its final and most impressive witness, the Scientist who tells the outside story of me. And his evidence, though external and therefore powerless to upset my inside story, may at least claim to be objective and impartial and well-tested. As such, it is important, though not critical, for this trial.

Well, does his tale really contradict mine?

On oath I assure the scientist that right here, at a distance of 0 inches from myself, I find—Space. And I invite him to come here and see for himself whether I am speaking the truth.

Accepting my invitation and approaching me—armed with cameras, microscopes, and so on—he takes careful pictures of me at each stage of his inward journey, and lays the evidence before the Court. It turns out that what his cameras make of me, what I register as at each stage, depends upon his *range*. Thus his distant portrait of a man is soon replaced by a nearer one of a face or a limb, then by a skin-patch, then by cells followed by one cell, then by molecules followed by one molecule, and so on, till—very near the point of contact—I figure as virtually a blank. My approaching observer has lost me on the way to me—leaving behind in turn my humanness, my life, my materiality, my colour and opacity and shape—and come, *almost*, to empty space.

But not quite. Still an outsider, he has to leave the last step to me, the insider. But it is the natural completion of all the steps he has taken towards me. Thus we agree. My story fits and rounds off his.

And not only in its conclusion. The place where my travelling observer discovers a man in his view-finder and on his film, is the place (say, six feet away) where I find him in my mirror. Again, where he finds only a *face* is where I find it (say, two feet away) in my mirror. We agree that not right here, but over there, is where those human appearances belong.

And if he were now to recede from me (by helicopter and space-ship) instead of approaching, he would make me out to be, in turn, a city, a country, a continent, a planet (the Earth), a star (the Solar System), a galaxy (the Milky Way), and, in the limit, empty space. Or rather, *almost* empty space, as when he came up to me.

I am the Subject of all these portraits. What they are pictures of, the Reality behind every one of my appearances. And as *all* these regional manifestations, ranging from electron through man to galaxy, I testify on oath that each is, intrinsically and viewed from their common Centre here, the Self seeing itself as Capacity. When the Scientist, accordingly, labels me as 'waves or particles in space', or an 'animal', or a 'man', or any other grade of thing, his own researches indicate that I am *every* grade of thing, and beyond all things their Core and Periphery of No-thingness.

V. Prosecution summing up
The prosecution has nothing material to add to its case, but is content to appeal again to sober common sense, and call for a verdict of GUILTY, and the penalty of death.

VI. Defence summing up
Traditional wisdom, my own Self-seeing and Self-feeling, my unique powers, my practical needs, my health of mind, the account which physical science gives of me—all seven have one message I'm *not the man I seem.* In their different ways they announce my true Nature.

VII. Judge's direction to the jury
Only when you have tried out *for yourselves* the basic 'Self-seeing' tests on which the Defence rests its case, are you qualified to pass your verdict.

Having sincerely carried out at least a few of these simple experiments, you may go on to consider whether, in the course of the trial, each of the Prosecution's seven points hasn't been turned into a Defence point. And, if it has, what their cumulative value is.

VIII. Verdict?

* * *

(Note: Chapters 35—39 are excerpts from the unpublished book *On Being God* (or *Man v. God*), which later became *The Trial of the Man who said he was God*.)

Chapter 36

THE EVIDENCE OF WHERE THOUGHTS BELONG

Witness No. 7—the Common-sense Philosopher—maintains that, supposing I do succeed in dismissing my *body* as 'not me', it isn't so easy to dismiss my *mind*.

Observing my behaviour, the Witness finds every indication here of a normal mental life going on, of a typically rich and certainly unique nucleus of human experience and human thinking. I'm a self contained in a not-self, a mind here surveying matter there, an inner world encompassed by an outer. And for me to disown this inner world, or any considerable part of it, in the interests of a comforting mystical notion of myself as 'God', or 'Empty Space', or 'Pure Spirit', is self-delusion. To the extent that I succeed, I really am 'out of my mind'.

The obvious fact, according to the Witness, is that I'm nothing if not a mind, and this mind is nothing if not human.

The Defence replies: What is this mysterious entity the Witness calls 'my mind'? Everyone seems to take it for granted, but does it really exist? Can I find a *something* here—possibly something like an immense, shadowy computer or memory bank or reference library— into which I feed information and out of which I draw information? Or do I find a *nothing* here, a bottomless abyss into which information vanishes without trace, and out of which information emerges without warning? An infinitely receptive and productive Void or Blank which itself remains speckless and characterless, and which I am?

What do I find happening when a thought arises? Let me take a letter of the alphabet and think of three words beginning with that letter, *observing where they come from and go to.* The letter is L…

I find the three words just popping up out of the blue, out of this Blank, and proceeding at once to the scene where they belong, out there in the world. They have objective reference, not subjective. Certainly they don't hang around here, cluttering their empty Source, or helping to form or maintain a mental nucleus of any sort.

I try again with another letter, M…

And get similar results. If I have a mind at all it is—or at least is at large in—this encompassing universe, seeing there's Nothing here at the centre to keep hold of it and prevent its outward flight.

My thoughts are others' property. Whenever I try to conjure up an idea that is my personal possession, one that is wholly internal and private and unrelated to the world, I come to total Idiocy, to Mindlessness, to this Blank once more. My thinking, if it is at all genuine, is about others and not about myself. Just as I taste marmalade and not a tongue, and smell toast and not a mucous membrane, so my astronomical observations are observations about the stars up there in the sky, and not about the observatory or the observer down here. I'm *into* the constellations, as the current expression happily puts it. Whatever its field, my thinking always breaks down when it cuts adrift from the object thought, and tries to cling to the thinking Subject, so-called—to this I whose sole business is mindless Being, Self-aware. My *world* is mind enough.

The Witness warns me I won't find it easy to *dismiss* my mind. Superfluous advice! Essentially centrifugal, it has already taken leave and made off in all directions. Insofar as I have a mind at all, I'm assuredly not small-minded. It's none other than this many-levelled universe, and no more human than it is sidereal or atomic, terrestrial or molecular: it finds itself perfectly at home at all levels. In its miraculous origin from this mindless but conscious Blank, in the majesty of its cosmic scope and energy and penetration, in the wealth of its contents of every grade, it is immeasurably more, and immeasurably less, than human.

To claim here a human mind, any mind of my own, is to ask for trouble within and without. Abstracting my thoughts and feelings from their rightful stations and holding them here, I progressively reduce the universe to a mindless concatenation of particles, and build myself up into what the Witness euphemistically calls this 'rich nucleus of human experience'—which nucleus grows so confoundedly affluent at the world's expense, so clogged and swollen and near to bursting, that I'm driven to seek psychiatric help in letting some of the stuff out again. My relief is the world's refurbishing. My swelling and the world's wasting were two sides of one disease, and have one remedy.

That remedy is to *come clean*, restoring to the universe these stolen goods which have gone bad on me, this huge collection of loot I call my human mind or self or personal psyche. And then it transpires

I'm innocent after all! I never owned a thing. The inside story is that there never has been an inside story!

So the Prosecution's charge against me will not stick: there's nothing here to fasten it to. Idiots cannot be taken to Court, and neither can universes. I'm much too big to be placed under arrest, and much too empty-headed and scatter-brained to be tried by any Court whatever.

* * *

Those who cling to the notion that there is a world outside the mind go on rolling themselves along the Wheel of Birth and Death.

Lankavatara Sutra

Only have no mind of any kind: this is undefiled knowledge.

Huang-po

Buddhahood is attained when there is no mind to be used for the task.

Hui-chung

This ground is so desert and bare that no thought has ever entered here.

Tauler.

Our souls live in the surrounding world.

Heracleitus

The Evidence Of Where Thoughts Belong

The inward and the outward become as one sky.

Kabir

As he gets to be more purely and singly himself… the astronomer is out there with the stars, rather than a separateness peering across an abyss at another separateness through a telescopic keyhole.

Abraham H. Maslow

A Bodhisattva should develop a lucid mind which fastens on nothing whatsoever. This may be likened to a human frame as large as the mighty Mount Sumeru (the Cosmos).

Diamond Sutra

* * *

(Note: Chapters 35—39 are excerpts from the unpublished book *On Being God* (or *Man v. God*), which later became *The Trial of the Man who said he was God*.)

Chapter 37

THE EVIDENCE OF
WHERE FEELINGS BELONG

Witness No. 8—The Close Relation—having known me intimately most of my life, has no doubt about what makes me tick, what I'm like at heart. My claim to be empty—changeless, cool, neutral, a featureless no-man's-land—she regards as just a pose, not to be taken seriously.

The landscape here is much more interesting than that, says the Witness. She finds me to be warm-hearted but often strangely cold-hearted and petty beyond belief. And so on, without end. What a mass of contradictions, not without its recurring patterns! The human heart, and mine is no exception, is an inexhaustible storehouse of feelings 'good', 'bad', 'indifferent'. If any part of *me* is more me, more central than the rest, it is this.

Ideas, opinions, principles and lack of them, trains of thought— these I *have* in plenty: I entertain them: they are around all the time. But this core or heart of feelings I *am*: they take me over: I'm stuck with them: they run so deep there's no getting beneath them.

Anyway, why should I wish to get beneath them? How can I deny my human-heartedness without denying love itself, and pretending to be what (to the Witness's certain knowledge) I'm not – a cold fish, icy, unhuman, if not actually inhuman?

The Defence replies: The only way to settle this hugely important

271

issue is to clear one's mind of prejudice and search within afresh, right now, for this alleged private core of feelings. After all, not even the Witness has any access here: no outsider is in a position to pronounce on what's inside.

I search for *love* here. Not love for him or her, but love itself, the love I have in my heart, my love... And find none at all.

I look for—I try to experience—at least the faint beginnings of *curiosity*. Not curiosity about someone or something, but curiosity itself, right here at this moment... and again fail utterly.

I invite joy. Not joy in another, but just joy... and nothing happens. I remain as before, neither joyful nor sad.

And so on, conscientiously trying to discover in myself at least a passing shadow or tiny seed of pleasure... pain... hate... anger... distaste... compassion... with always the same negative result. Throughout these simple experiments (which, to mean anything at all, must actually be carried out) all I find here is an unvarying Sameness, a cool and indifferent and certainly non-human Blank— which, again, is nevertheless keenly aware of itself as Blank.

Am I then incapable of these feelings? Have I no capacity for love, joy, the rest? I am capacity itself, empty for love as a cup is for water. The moment I cease searching for love here in myself, and turn to one I love, there's no question about the feeling or its location. *There* is my treasure, and where my treasure is my heart is also. And doubtless that's why I'm in the habit of calling her 'my love' and 'my dear heart'.

And the moment I cease trying to detect the faint beginnings of curiosity here, and glance at Mr Jones yonder, there's no doubt about the fact of curiosity, or where it occurs, or whom it sticks to. Mr Jones *is* a curiosity. And the moment I cease trying—and failing—to feel joyful, and remember my friends, my joy is in them. It comes alive there, wrapping itself around them. They glow with it.

And when I breakfast off hot toast and marmalade, and then venture out into the bitter weather, the pleasure of the one and the ache of the other are around all right—and it's the *food* that tastes and smells so good, and the *wind* that feels so cold.

It's the same with all the other feelings I miscall mine: only insofar as they qualify their objects are they real. When 'she's adorable' lapses into 'I'm so in love', when 'his need' lapses into 'my compassion', when 'it's a sad, sad world' lapses into 'I suffer from depression', I'm ceasing to attend to what's clearly given, and building instead this shadowy illusion called 'my human heart'. The feelings that I strip from the world and gather to myself are misplaced, falsified, distorted: the love, mere sentimentality. They are stolen goods which give me endless trouble till they are returned to their owners.

In short, the Witness got her facts inside-out. Heartless at home, my heart goes out to the world.

* * *

The Sage has no heart of his own.

Lao-tzu

The soul lives in that which it loves.

St John of the Cross

As I See It

The mind abides nowhere.

Hui-neng

Every thing and quality is felt in outer space.

William James

Whatever there be of feeling... one should realise this does not belong to me, this am I not, this is not myself.

Buddha

* * *

(Note: Chapters 35—39 are excerpts from the unpublished book *On Being God* (or *Man v. God*), which later became *The Trial of the Man who said he was God*.)

Chapter 38

THE EVIDENCE OF ARCHITECTURE

The architect's concern is with space.

He has to sense and feel himself into space, to map out and organise space, to create new spaces, to wrap himself round the shapes of things as the air does, to embrace creatively in a lifelong love-affair the forms that make up the human scene, so bringing to birth new forms—unique, need-meeting, economical, elegant.

Now who is better qualified to do all this—that man you see, that tiny, private, boxed-in portion of space, excluded from the rest: or this no-man I am, who realises himself as boundless space?

Who is more likely to have a feel for space, to be sensitive to the contours and structure and functioning of its occupants—the form that now confronts you in the dock, which is at best in external relationship to other forms; or the formless and form-fitting ambience I find myself to be, and which is even now consciously enfolding all the forms on display in this Court?

Who is in a better position to mould things creatively—that man-shaped thing whose nature is to exclude all other things from the volume it occupies; or this unshaped no-thing whose nature is to include all things?

Just to ask these questions is to answer them. I'm built for architecting, as no man could ever be! Denying my constitution as this all-inclusive presence, I disqualify myself professionally.

Whether it's a question of architectural creation or architectural appreciation, a man is indeed handicapped. I observe him facing the cathedral, his tiny face or façade to that huge façade, and a hundred yards between. Whereas with me, it's no-façade to huge façade, and no distance between. Absolutely devoid of human features, I take on absolutely that wealth of architectural ones. Again, entering the nave, I observe how low and insignificant a thing a man is in this vastness, how unbeautified by this beauty, how stuck with himself. In total contrast to him, I explode into and fill out this vastness: it fits me like a gigantic glove. I'm high and wide and mediaeval; groin and vaulting rib—all is my anatomy; every moulding moulds me; I glow and burn with the glass and sparkle with candle-light and silver and brocades. I wear all this gothic splendour and shapeliness as if it were tailored for me alone. A clear liquid, I am instantly poured into this jelly-mould. This is to enjoy architecture, by supplying its space.

Let me sum up in another metaphor the tale of my dealings with space. At first I was the boundless, wave-filled ocean, making and unmaking an endless flux of heaving, tumbling, iridescent forms. Then the tide ebbed. I found myself reduced to a rock-pool, and the flowing ocean to a rigid ocean-bed whose tide-marks were the only reminder of my lost immensity. No longer co-extensive with my world, I became isolated in a corner of it; no longer actively at play all over it, I became its passive observer from a distance… And then I woke up to find that it was all a dream. I never was anything else than the shoreless ocean.

The Evidence Of Architecture

In plainer language, when I was very young all space was my space. I filled it out creatively, peopling it, structuring it, decorating it. I was a natural visualiser, and space readily took on the shapes I gave it. But then I lost space, I collapsed. It was my very ability to play with space that proved my undoing. Learning first the trick of standing aside and viewing myself from a distance, and then mistaking that view for the real me, I contracted to the dimensions of that person. And along with my space I lost the power to fashion it, my faculty of visualisation. Having passed outside my jurisdiction, space was— naturally enough—no longer amenable. I lost the art of feeling and thinking centrifugally and expansively. I grew small-minded. My life was a centripetal process. I shut myself in a box, a talking box or gramophone substituting recorded words for flowing actualities. I believed the symbols even when they flagrantly contradicted the realities they were supposed to stand for. At the age of 8 or 9 the switch from visual to verbal thinking was well under way...

Much later, waking from my word-dream, I came to my senses again. The rock-pool discovered it was the ocean after all. The fugitive from great space became the space maker again, the natural designer.

And if I now have any capacity as an architect, it's because I'm alive to myself as capacity itself and no longer one of its inhabitants.

* * *

(Note: Chapters 35—39 are excerpts from the unpublished book *On Being God* (or *Man v. God*), which later became *The Trial of the Man who said he was God*.)

Chapter 39

THE EVIDENCE OF THE RESULTS OF SELF-REALISATION

The Prosecution finds no saintliness, no unusual virtues: nothing to suggest I have transcended the human or am anyone special. No doubt I take the opposite view though, and consider that social norms do not apply to one who looks down upon man from so great a height.

The Defendant replies: It comes as no surprise that the fruits of seeing and feeling and knowing Who I am appear negligible to the Prosecution. To me, they appear non-existent!

How could it be otherwise? For, firstly, This-which-I-am cannot change for better or worse: here is nothing to modify. Secondly, that man-which-I-am-not is by nature ever-changing, incomplete in every respect, incapable of radical reform, and my liberation from him is liberation from all attempts to improve him. Attempts which, insofar as they succeed, would only lead to more and more self-satisfaction, reinforcing my false identity at the expense of my true Identity. Even if that man does pick up a few incidental benefits, these are irrelevant, more others' business than my own, and certainly they are nebulous and fleeting. Having come, they go. Having no substance, they melt on inspection. No human ever transcended the human by a hair's-breadth.

I am no kind of man. No wonder, then, I was never much good at being a satisfactory one. Indeed it was my constant and many-sided failure to be a man, and make something of myself, which drove me at last to discover Who I already was. And now it isn't the *fruits* of this tremendous discovery which hold me to it (the awesome *facts* will do!) but rather the lack of fruits. For the only possible improvements would be trivial adjustments of a nebulous personality, tending always to divert me from the splendour of my true Being.

And now for a paradox! One's failure—and the Prosecution's—to find any real gain, together with this loss of interest in the whole enterprise of self-improvement, turns out to be the greatest gain! It is the indescribable relief of resting in one's everlasting Perfection. In this sense, the fruits of Self-seeing, are, after all, infinite.

To the Witness's accusation that I put myself above the law and more-or-less do what I like, I again plead guilty but go further! Of course the *man before you* is subject to the law, and that's why he's standing here in the Dock today. But the *no-man I am* is subject to nothing, unaccountable even to himself—for He does nothing, decides nothing (right or wrong), and suffers no consequences. His business is just Being. Accordingly, He isn't in this Dock and Court: they are in Him. I don't believe this: I see it!

But the question remains: though awake to myself-as-Him do I find myself-as-man misbehaving? The answer is: Often! I observe him flouting convention, committing offences against the civil law, and even against the moral law as generally accepted. These codes are indispensable and a price is paid for breaking them, but they are for ignoring when they conflict (as they often do) with that higher Code—the Precept of Identity which lays down no rules whatever. I have no preview of the actions that may follow from Seeing-Who-I-Am, but since this is also Seeing and Being Who-You-Are, it means evidently I can't hurt you without hurting myself, for at root I am you and I am all creatures.

This is the Rule to end all rules. It is the only genuine Freedom and Spontaneity, and it is God's alone.

* * *

(Note: Chapters 35—39 are excerpts from the unpublished book *On Being God* (or *Man v. God*), which later became *The Trial of the Man who said he was God*.)

Chapter 40

THE SAILOR, THE SHIP, AND THE SEA

When we return to the Root we gain the meaning;
When we pursue external objects we lose the reason.

When the deep mystery of one Suchness is fathomed,
Suddenly we forget the external entanglements;
When the ten thousand things are viewed in their oneness,
We return to the Origin and remain where we have always been.

The Third Patriarch of Zen: *'On Trust in the Heart'*

There was once a lone sailor becalmed in mid-ocean, facing death by thirst and exposure. At first he was a mass of self-pity. His sole concern was himself and his personal predicament, his smallness in this pitiless expanse, his isolation and likely fate. It was as if in his suffering he withdrew further and further into his solitary self, becoming ever more dense and leaden, more shrunken and closed in, till the outer world of ship and ocean scarcely existed for him at all.

Then, as he grew weaker, something gave, and in a flash of illumination he noticed a fact that was as obvious as it was astonishing: he didn't exist at all! The lonely sailor—the 'too, too solid flesh' he had imagined himself to be—dissolved into thin air. The idea that he had ever been shut up in a body seemed quite ridiculous to him;

the supposed physical nucleus of his Universe vanished; the centre of things dropped out leaving only the things. For a whole day and night (despite the cruel heat of the one and the equally cruel cold of the other) he enjoyed an extraordinary freedom from care, an expansion and a lightness, a blessed sensation of release from the dark prison of his separate human identity.

At large now, he started taking a lively interest in the details of whatever presented itself for his inspection. The grain of the blistering woodwork, the rust stains like wounds slashed across the once-white paint, the faded blue of his tattered trouser legs, the hairs on the back of his blackening hands, the acrid smell of the brine, the slap-slap of ripples against the hull and their flickering reflections on the underside of the boom: everything was more intense, more actual, more vivid, more peculiar, more insistent upon its uniqueness than he had experienced since early childhood, and all because he was no longer present to get in its way. The sailor had gone absent without leave, had relaxed into the ship, had become the ship, and there remained nothing but these flopping sails, slack ropes, creaking deck, and the rest: and even these weren't identified and named by him, but wordlessly announced themselves. Only this scene was real. Real, and quite without meaning or purpose: no-one was around to give it any. He was ready to die now, because for himself he had already passed away.

Or had he? Already the mood of release was beginning to evaporate. He couldn't help suspecting that somehow he had been cheated. Cheated, for a start, of his religion—such as it was. Before, in the earlier and more hopeful days of his mid-ocean loneliness, he had sensed within and around him a diffused Presence, a Power embracing all powers, a Resource that in the end would not forsake him. And now that last support, shadowy but strong, was cut away, leaving only these unsupported sights and sounds and smells and pains. It was a loss that he could ill afford at this time, of all times. He told himself that he had sold what little faith he possessed for a cold and barren unbelief, and done so at the moment of his greatest need. He was left with no self great or small, no Essence or Root or Origin, no Suchness, no Reality—and he lost heart, because he could find no Heart to lose or re-discover. In spite of the heat he found himself shivering violently.

Or was it that he found, not *himself* shivering, but just a shivering? What had become of him? Surely he had sold himself short. He began to realise that he had traded a person for so much ship's chandlery, for this pitiful array of now useless gear, and it was a bad bargain. He had lost a substantial human being and gained this shadow-play of meaningless phenomena—meaningless, but nevertheless reproachful and burdensome, if not actually threatening. He had exchanged a poor live thing that was at least his own for a collection of poorer dead things that were nobody's, exchanged a personal and interior and partial chaos for an impersonal and exterior and almost total chaos. For there was nothing in this confusion around him—and now it seemed there was nothing in him either—which was capable of holding it together and giving it any significance or value. He saw that his own disintegration was also his world's, and that their common Heart was dead and hollow. And so his newly-discovered emptiness and non-existence, the void which only yesterday had been such a relief, so lightsome and refreshing, became today an aching void. Fear was rushing in to fill the vacuum, and the sailor's desperate longing for rescue returned undiminished. He cried, but no tears came. He shouted at the sky, and all that he could hear was a whisper.

And then in his mortal extremity it happened—what secretly he had longed for all along—*the sailor who had become the ship became the sea.* The nautical expanded into the oceanic, and there was a whole world of difference between them. As he lay near to death in his tiny boat, desireless, no longer expecting or even wanting help, he grew deep, he became the Deep. Sinking down and down, he felt himself into that underlying, clear expanse, into those countless fathoms bearing him up yet washing through him. He dissolved without residue into that Abyss, he was all of it for ever and ever. Giving himself up to that incomparable Safety, resting back with perfect trust upon That which was so much more *himself* than the sailor had ever been, he was eternally drowned yet saved from drowning, and they were the same thing. He didn't merely feel and know—he saw beyond any possibility of doubt that he and his boat were nothing else than this clear Water—not flotsam or jetsam, not waves or drops or bubbles, but the whole undivided volume of the Sea. The Sea was the Heart that he had lost, the living Heart of the world, yet he saw that it was the Heart of Nothingness, lucid and uniform and transparent through and through, holding not a speck of matter in suspension or solution. And paradoxically it was this very absence of all conceivable qualities which gave it that indescribable 'quality' beyond trustworthiness, which made it so intimate yet so splendid, so dear and yet so ungraspable, and above all so final. Had the great Ocean contained the shadow of a something, he couldn't have rested there content at the last: it would only have pointed past itself to some still deeper Sea. How strange and total a reversal he had experienced: *from being the least real, his interior emptiness had suddenly become the most real, the only Real, while remaining as empty as ever!* From being that-which-is-not, a write-off if ever there was one, a non-starter and non-entity, it had revealed itself to him as That which alone is. He was That, and there was nothing else.

He looked around. It was still true that up there, sharply silhouetted against the darkening sky, was the mast-head with a gleam of brass and a limp shred of a rag that had once been an exulting pennant, a flashing tongue of green flame that had often stirred his sailor's pride. But now it was not as that sailor, but as the Ocean, that he found himself taking in all there was to see and hear and smell and feel. Everything was as brilliantly clear as before, only it was not only vivid but valuable now; it was no longer arbitrary or trivial, a burden or a reproach, but necessary, acceptable, strangely glorified. Seen no longer by or from a mere nothing, from an infinitely shallow nothing, but now from this bottomless well of Nothingness, it was at once the same as before yet transfigured. The Sea bathed everything in its own light. Even the pain and the retching were all right. Every least thing was in order just as it was, authorised to be its sole self, precisely because the weight of his attention wasn't on that thing at all, but upon himself the Sea, himself its infinite Support, its empty Container, its welcoming Host, its very Heart. It intrigued him how the absolute *difference* between himself as the Abyss, and those faint stars and yellow moon shining in the Abyss, was what joined him to them absolutely in seamless identity. How, except by making Room for them, by being Space for them, could he entertain and become them? Between Seer and seen was no trace of similarity—they held nothing in common—and *therefore* they were one and the same. Not absurd, but on the contrary obvious to the dying man, for whom no such words arose to complicate the certainty and simplicity of What he saw.

Then another revelation came to him. A few hours ago he had suddenly lost substance and solidity and become paper-thin, scarcely so much as a surface, while the sky above him had remained immeasurably high and remote. But now the situation was exactly the other way round. All the sky's remoteness collapsed: there was no *above*. It wasn't that the skies fell, but just that they had never been aloft or anywhere but *right here* for him. For the very first time since he had bought the boat he saw the once-tall mast as he actually saw it, and not as he thought he saw it; and on this occasion it was foreshortened to a stumpy cone, and the stumpy cone to a flat triangle with a blob at the apex. So flat that he felt sure (if only he had enough strength left to raise his arm) that he could have lovingly cupped that blob—the mast-head—in the palm of his hand, and drawn his fingertips across the velvet sky and felt the prickle of the stars. The wide, wide world widened and bled off at the edges into his Space, but it was perfectly flat, two-dimensional. This expanse, and no human skin, was his surface, his now-starry face, and he could find no gap of any sort to part him from anything. No doubt his lifelong trick of *distancing* things, of holding off the objects that confronted him, had been a needful fiction, but now he saw how it had also been a damaging fiction: it had been his way of giving things and people the brush-off, his device for protecting the Seer from invasion and annihilation by the seen, a space in which his fear and hate could do their work.

But now, at the very end of all life's fictions and make-believe, there wasn't a hair's-breadth left between himself and that star-filled heaven. He wasn't in heaven, heaven was in him; and that's what made it Heaven for him now. How amazing a turnabout it was: all the distance in the world had suddenly shifted from in front of him to behind him, from above to below, from outside to inside! This mysterious third dimension (so unlike the others as to be dimensionless), now stretching back and back from him, was as real as it had been imaginary when it stretched ahead of him. And now it was this Depth that united him with the world, instead of separating it from him. Exterior distance, with the resulting alienation, had been his trouble. But now, incorporating the trouble, he found it was the end of all his troubles, of all alienation. There remained for him no other. The lone sailor wasn't lonely any more. He was the Alone.

When, next morning, he was picked up dead, they found a strange thing. The desiccated and emaciated body had wide-open eyes still staring up at the sky, and a serenity about the lips.

* * *

Chapter 41

RAMANA MAHARSHI AND THE AVAILABILITY OF SELF-REALISATION

This is the first of a number of articles I'm writing for *The Mountain Path's* celebration of Sri Maharshi's centenary. They have no pretensions to being scholarly or even objective commentaries on Maharshi's teaching. On the contrary, they are highly personal and subjective accounts of that teaching, of what it has come to mean for me after some eighteen years of bathing in Maharshi's *darshan*—if I may so put it. The other articles will be about such topics as the Body, the Mind, Mystical Experience, Happiness, and the World, each viewed in the light of Maharshi's teaching, from the writer's standpoint.

> Self-realisation is possible only for the fit... One must be ready to sacrifice everything for the Truth. Complete renunciation is the index of fitness.
>
> Divine Grace is essential for Realisation... It is vouchsafed only to him who is a true devotee or a yogin, who has striven hard and ceaselessly on the path towards freedom.

* * *

All are seeing God always, but they don't know it.

I see what needs to be seen... I see only just what all do, nothing more. The Self is always self-evident.

The ever-present Self needs no effort to be realised. Realisation is already there... The Self is within each one's experience every moment.

There is nothing so simple as being the Self. It requires no effort, no aid.

* * *

Will you please read again these two sets of quotation from Maharshi's *Talks,* and note how flagrantly they contradict each other—or so it seems.

Again and again, when reading the words of the Sages, one comes across these two messages: Self-realisation is just about the easiest thing in the world—and just about the most difficult! Liberation is the reward of long, earnest, and careful work—and conversely it is nothing of the sort: it is perfectly natural and ever-present and not at all to be striven for! Who I really am is brilliantly obvious to me right now, just as I am, if only I will dare to turn my attention round and examine the spot I occupy; and (they add) this vision is available only to the few who qualify for it!

Thus it isn't only Maharishi who confronts us again and again with this total contradiction or paradox. It appears in all the great mystical teachings of the world.

Among contemporaries, Sri Nisargadatta Maharaj tells us that Liberation is an arduous and costly work, and in the next breath that our only trouble is that we pretend that we aren't liberated.

Before going on to investigate whether and how such seemingly flagrant contradictions can be reconciled, let us notice in passing what effect they have upon readers and devotees. There are three reactions:

(1) The first and by far the commonest re-action is to take seriously only those passages which appear to say that Enlightenment or Liberation *isn't* available, and to ignore (to be word-blind to) the other passages which insist that it *is* available here and now, however fit or unfit I may think I am. The excuse frequently given to justify this word-blindness is humility. "I'm not enlightened", pronounced rather smugly, if not proudly, and with the suggestion that not everyone is so modest! In fact, it would be more honest to say: "For all sorts of reasons I'm determined to overlook, indeed deny hotly, my ever-present Enlightenment, and the words of my Master which assert it are nonsense—so far as I'm concerned."

(2) The second kind of reaction by readers and devotees is the reverse of the first: namely, to take seriously only those teachings which emphasise the immediacy and obviousness of the Self, and conveniently overlook those which mention the price that has to be paid. In this case the common excuse is likely to be that, since one's true Nature is Enlightenment itself anyway, there's nothing to be done about it, no on-going practice, no renewal of dedication, no spiritual work. And the result of this attitude is that, even if one has actually glimpsed one's true Nature, one is in effect still living the old deluded life of identification with one's human nature. One's occasional in-

seeing is largely inoperative.

(3) The third reaction is the genuinely humble one, the only one which shows true respect for the Teacher, the only one worthy of the real devotee, and that is to give equal weight to both sides of the teaching, acknowledging and not denying or glossing over its 'contradictions', and diligently working out their reconciliation, not in theory so much as in moment-to-moment practice. The rest of this article is about just that.

For a start, let's ask ourselves what Self-realisation is, anyway. What, in its simplest terms, is this experience which is so paradoxically described as perfectly free on request, and as costing the earth—costing everything? It is clearly seeing that I'm not my body, my mind, my past, my future, my thoughts and feelings, my hopes and fears, and so on, and on. You name it: I'm not that. Self-realisation is the perception that where I am is no thing whatever, no form, no limits, no content at all, but only this indescribable Reality which we inadequately call Consciousness, or I AM, or the Source, or the Still Centre of all things.

The fact that it takes no time at all to arrive at this Absence-Presence which I AM might suggest that it takes no work and involves no process, and that nothing has happened to enable me to see the Self. In one sense this is true; in another sense it is entirely false. This in-seeing, instantaneous and simple though it certainly is, necessarily involves giving up everything one had ever identified with—everything. This is no ordinary self-denial, which is giving up the 'bad' and hanging onto the 'good'. And no ordinary death, which is organic matter turning into inorganic. It is total stripping and total dying, down, down, down below the last hint of matter itself to the featureless Source of all.

Now of all adventures this stripping, this many-sided death, this annihilation of all our selves, is in fact the most difficult and terrifying and lethal, whether we consciously recognise this or not. There is no terror like the fear of vanishing without a trace. And that terror (more or less unacknowledged) is the real reason why so many of us fail to register, even fail to see, those words which assure us of our ever-present Enlightenment. No wonder we are scared stiff of what we will discover when we turn our gaze from the world to its seer. It makes no difference to be assured that the terror strikes those who hover on the brink of the Abyss, and that once over that fearful edge all fear whatever is at an end. Most of us retreat hastily from the terrible Emptiness we barely glimpse.

But some are pushed, or stumble, or are gently wafted over the edge. They are the "fit ones", recipients of the Grace which Maharshi speaks of. In actual fact, whether they are aware of it or not, they are "ready to sacrifice everything for the Truth". This plunge is certain death, without remainder, and at once extremely 'easy' and extremely 'hard'. We all know in what sense it is easy to fall over a natural cliff such as Beachy Head, and in what sense it is difficult. The Precipice of our true Nature is rather similar. The Gulf is plain to see, unfenced, very near indeed, possibly fascinating. A push, and over we go: it takes no effort to penetrate that Abyss. So Ramana Maharshi rightly insists that on the one hand Self-realisation is effortless, ours for the asking, ours anyway; and on the other that it takes all we've got.

I have many friends who are over the edge, who clearly see (or at least can see when they wish to) that the Spot they occupy is in fact unoccupied, and yet have, so far, experienced none of the terror of the Abyss, or the agony of total dying. Friends, I mean, who have tumbled over into the Void with very little effort or resistance or alarm, as soon as it was pointed out to them. Subjects of divine Grace, indeed! Are such fortunate ones, to whom Self-realisation is availability itself, then let off cheap and excused from all fear, all effort, all or much of the "hard and ceaseless strife" which Maharshi speaks of?

No! One isn't over that Precipice and dead and gone once and for all. Again and again and again that tremendous Void must be plunged into; and I suspect that, later if not sooner, in the end if not in the beginning, it will hold an agony and a terror which can only be experienced, and neither anticipated nor described. Paradoxically that ultimate fear turns out to be the recipe for ultimate fearlessness, but this doesn't mean it can be avoided or reduced. Even more certainly, I doubt whether the discipline of bringing oneself, minute by minute, over the months and years and decades, to "complete renunciation", can be avoided or much reduced. Unremitting practice is indispensible so long as there remains underfoot an inch of ground, or any trace of cliff-top, to stand on.

Maharshi emphasises the need to stabilise Self-realisation. And there certainly is a world of difference between one for whom the Truth is constantly present and one for whom the Truth is for most of the time overlooked. All the same, the Abyss is the Abyss, with no degrees of emptiness. To experience This at all is to experience it exactly as all the Sages experience it, no matter how unpractised the experiencer or how brief his experience. The Self sees to it that it cannot be mis-seen. That is its nature.

And its nature is to be always and totally available. The fallibility—the fears, doubts, blindness—of human nature cannot detract from the Perfection of who we are *already.* The ultimate truth, as Maharshi points out untiringly, is that "there is no reaching the Self. If the Self were to be reached, it would mean that the Self is not now and here... You are already the Self. Therefore realisation is common to everyone... This very doubt *Can I realise?* or the feeling *I have not realised* are the obstacles."

In spite of these encouraging words, you may rightly point out that Grace is needed to enable you to cease doubting your ever present Self-realisation. Yes: but this is no excuse for standing there, well clear of the edge, idly awaiting the push of divine Grace—and fervently hoping it won't happen just yet! At least dare to take a peep over the edge of the world. Look now at what you're looking out of. Notice what's now taking in these printed words.

Ramana Maharshi says "It is really like gazing into Vacancy." Aren't you now in your own first-hand experience no thing at all but the Vacancy in which these marks on paper are on display? Look and see if your Vacancy is available or hidden from you. To discover whether you are the fortunate recipient of divine Grace, just have the courage to look at yourself now without thought or belief or imagination, with the open mind of a little child.

As I See It

If you see that you never were standing on that desperate cliff-edge of thingness and humanness, but were and are and always will be this immense Vacancy, this Abyss of *Sat-Chit-Ananda*, why then you are no longer merely the recipient of Grace. You are Grace itself.

* * *

Chapter 42

WHO MADE THE WORLD?

Who made the world?

God.

But who made God?

God made himself, makes himself now.

He did that alone and all by himself, without any help? Out of nothing? Just happened himself—"Bang, here I am!"—like that?

Like that, but all the time. Self-origination. Self-creation, endlessly.

Now that's really *clever* of him! Impossible—except that he's actually achieved the impossible! There really should be nothing at all, not a twinge of consciousness, not a shadow of a shadow. He's done a most irregular, crazy, incredible thing. I wonder: has he any idea how he did it, does it, now?

How could he? He'd have to exist already, before contriving his existence—which doesn't make sense.

He must be knocked out and bowled over by the mystery of himself, by the glory and completeness of his impossible victory over inert, unaware, dead nothingness, by his absolute unknowability.

And bowled over equally by his absolute know-how. The unknowable God knows, *without knowing,* how to BE.

And knows how to create and sustain innumerable worlds of inconceivable complexity, all in working order, going concerns.

But after conjuring up himself, what are a billion universes—

all going strong—but mere chicken-feed? Having achieved the impossible—namely, Isness or Being—surely nothing is impossible, or difficult, or that important. Worlds upon worlds are just casual, incidental spin-offs from their Origin.

* * *

Where is he, this Self-creating God?

Nearer to me than my hands, my heart, my brain. Right here, at the centre of my world, my life. He is nowhere else. This is his only home.

What is this lodger like? How shall I recognise him?

Right here, in fact, I can find no home, no lodger, no landlord, no I and him , but only ME, Awareness Itself, this simple sense of BEING.

So this impossible feat of self-origination, this incomparable success-story, is *mine*. Alone I did it. I am my own author, my own invention, my own source, support, ground, security, rest, amazement, joy, refreshment, without beginning or end.

When did it happen, this magical arrival of the Player in the middle of the scene—no creeping in from the wings—brilliant against the dark backcloth of Nothing? When did Consciousness, against all the odds, suddenly pop out of Unconsciousness? In the beginning, long ago?

No. Now is that beginning. I'm giving rise to Myself and all things, at this instant. I catch Myself in the act, performing this two-sided miracle. I'm eternally poised with one foot dangling in the Abyss of Not-being, and the other planted firmly on the Ground of Being, and without both feet I'm lost. I AM and I AM NOT are the two inseparable sides of me. I'm dozing till I wake up to the absolute sleep I'm waking up from, right now.

And in all the worlds and throughout all time no being is left out of this fantastic achievement. There are no failures. Everyone's 'made it'!

* * *

Chapter 43

ON LOGION 29

Yeshua says—
If flesh came into existence for the sake of spirit,
it is a wonder,
but if spirit exists for the sake of flesh,
it is a wonder of wonders.
I am truly astonished
at how such richness
came to dwell in such poverty

Logion 29, from The Gospel of Thomas

Science (or rather, science misunderstood) has come up with a great deal of unscientific nonsense in its time. Perhaps the most prevalent, most specious, and craziest piece of nonsense is the materialist's view of spirit—consciousness, awareness—as a by-product of matter: a sort of phosphorescence or subtle radiation which matter gives off when it becomes sufficiently complex, as in human brains. In the beginning was matter, and in the course of evolution it accidentally became aware of itself—they say.

But what *is* a material object, according to science itself? It is a collection of phenomena, a set of appearances or pictures which the scientist picks up as he hovers around the object, surveying it from various angles, at various distances, with the help of various instruments. What these pictures are pictures of, what lies at the centre of this nest of appearances, he doesn't and can't observe. However close he gets, he's too far off, an outsider.

But he has two clues to what's inside. The first is that the nearer he gets to the object the emptier it gets. He comes to regions where all that remains of that seemingly solid thing is space haunted by twists of energy. His second clue is that, when he dares to look at what he's looking out of, and examines from inside that special bit of matter which he is, he finds it to be quite empty, no-thing at all, and *aware* of itself as just that. Such is the view of himself at mere millimeters from himself, if he is honest and attentive enough—which is to say, truly scientific.

In other words, he finds that the body vanishes on close inspection, and spirit remains. Material bodies are appearances or products of consciousness, and to derive consciousness from them is absurd. It is rather like deriving the cine-projector from the activities of the characters on the cine-screen, instead of *vice-versa*. To put it another way, there can be no outside or objective view of subjectivity or spirit: it is the inside story, and can only be examined from within, by itself. And, so examined, it is found to be the producer/container of countless objects (shapes, colours, movements, sensations, ideas, feelings, etc.). As for any of those peripheral manifestations giving rise to the central awareness of them—why there isn't the slightest evidence for anything of the sort. The very notion is nonsensical. It is unthinkable, strictly speaking, that things, as such, could generate *awareness* of things.

Of course it remains altogether mysterious how this central Void should create the riches that come and go in it. It is indeed a wonder how such great wealth can come from such poverty. It does, it does!

But if one of its creations were suddenly to turn round and create its Creator, now *that* would be a wonder of wonders! As Jesus says, in this splendid *logion*.

* * *

Chapter 44

RAMANA MAHARSHI
AND HOW NOT TO GROW OLD

1. The diagnosis

The other day a friend of mine went to see an inmate of an old people's home. The old lady wasn't senile, but she had lost almost all her sight and hearing. She couldn't read or watch television, and people didn't talk much with her: communication was too difficult. Apparently she had led a normal active life, and pursued with fair success the unpretentious goals of home and family. At all events it was now over. No action, no challenges, no goals, no pleasures, no interests. It's doubtful whether her handicaps made all that difference. What had she left to live for, anyway? What she wanted, she said, was for it all to end.

Earlier this year I was staying with a highly-placed executive who works in a firm of American aircraft manufacturers. He told me what had happened to his older colleagues—conscientious and successful like himself—when they retired. A surprising number of them died in a few months or a year or two. Physically they were in good shape, economically they were comfortable, psychologically they were finished. Like the lady in the old people's home, they had no reason for carrying on. Life was meaningless.

In the West, and particularly in the U.S.A., the frightening problem of growing old begins to obtrude itself all too early in life. "If you haven't made it by 35 you never will", they say. And, if you *have* made it, the rest of your life, presumably, is somewhat of an anti-climax. Either way, you lose! The advertising industry, accurately sensing and skilfully directing the popular mind, puts all its emphasis on youth, blown up and glamorized to the point of deification. Under the spell of these shining gods and goddesses of screen and hoarding, mums aim at being sisters to their daughters, dads at being the younger brothers of their sons. Grandads dress themselves up in short pants and juvenile headgear and go off camping, while grandmas have cosmetic surgery. The mortician makes sure that not even corpses look their age. Everyone knows that the curve of life peaks around 30 years, and thereafter one should try to look and behave and think as if one were stuck on that peak, and put off descending till the bitter end. And bitter it has to be. In the modern world old age has little dignity and no value of its own, no bright virtue to compensate for its humiliations and handicaps. Every way it's a come-down. If not actually a disease, the prognosis couldn't be worse. If not actually a crime, the penalty is never less than capital punishment.

Given these typically Western attitudes, it comes as no surprise that old persons are congratulated (if at all) for *not* being old persons! On the contrary, they are praised for walking or talking or driving or playing ball-games like someone half their age. As if one were to commend a child for being middle-aged. How sad, not to say insulting, is the implication that old age is an affliction. It *is* an affliction, when, backward looking, it has no outlook or meaning or work of its own.

But of course these pathetic attempts to prolong youth, and suppress the hard facts of ageing and dying, don't work. What's left for the has-been to be? The enchanting goals pursued by childhood and youth having been gained, and so inevitably stripped of every enchantment that distance had lent them, what comparable new goals loom up for the older person? Well, he or she can always try making a collection—of sea-shells, postage stamps, silver trophies, scalps blond and brunette, dollars, press notices, honorary degrees, directorships, disciples, good deeds—it all comes to the same thing in the end: more disenchantment. Nothing fails a man like a successful collection. Nothing gathers thicker layers of time's dust. And if he eventually succeeds in creeping from under his collection and escaping into a Haven for Senior Citizens (more rudely, a crèche for wrinkled infants) he is still liable to find himself in the collecting business— piling up bingo numbers or clock-golf scores, perhaps. Anything to fill in the time and crowd out the waiting spectre of death.

I have just been watching a television programme about a Christian hospice in London, for patients suffering from terminal diseases—in plain words, a good place for dying in. The opening shot was of a social worker (she seemed a dedicated and compassionate young woman) persuading a dozen old dears to sing a song. And the song—believe it or not—was *Goodbye Blackbird!* Not *Goodbye Life* (whoever heard of such a song, or hymn?) but *Goodbye Blackbird!* What a way of spending the last hours of that astounding adventure which began so promisingly 70 or 80 years ago! At the end of the television programme a sensitive and humble priest-nurse explained that he saw no point in thrusting religion at the last moment on folk who had managed to get by all their lives without it. Of course he was right.

One of the great ironies and contradictions of the modern world is that, while all this effort goes into *warding off* old age, equal effort goes into bringing it on prematurely. When a machine takes over a man's work, and the meaning and dignity that go with it, what's left for him to do? In highly industrialized societies it isn't only the old-in-years who find themselves with too much leisure on their hands: everyone is ageing fast to the degree that life is becoming pointless. It's no use smashing machines: they've come to stay, and along with them the wastelands of spare time which automation and the silicon-chip technology are beginning to open out. How to relieve the aimlessness, the boredom arising out of the ever shorter working day and working week and working life, to say nothing of mass unemployment itself? A man with nothing to do is done for.

Such is the disease.

2. The remedy

"Those who do not seek the purpose of life are simply wasting their lives", says Maharshi uncompromisingly, in a sentence which sums up the illness—and points to the remedy. It has to be (and, as we shall see, it *is*) strong medicine if it is to cure a disease so deep-seated.

Let me tell you about another friend of mine—a young man who, having taken an excellent degree at Oxbridge, entered the British

Foreign Office. A fine career stretched out in front of him. But in fact after a couple of years he resigned his appointment, cut himself off from family and friends, and went to live a hermit-like life in an isolated Welsh cottage. There he spends long hours every day in sitting meditation, silent, with eyes closed, immobile, solitary.

Notice a curious thing: this young man is in much the same state as the old lady I described at the beginning—only with this huge difference, that he has *chosen* the handicaps she is the victim of. He has deliberately taken upon himself, while still in the prime of life, the restrictions that belong towards the end of life. She is struck blind; he keeps his eyes closed. She goes deaf; he retires to a place where there's nothing to hear. She suffers from loneliness; he wants to be alone. She has lost interest in life, in its pleasures and goals; he is earnestly practising just such detachment. The sum is the same but the sign is the opposite: in one case minus, in the other plus.

Why is my friend behaving so 'unnaturally'? His purpose is to find the meaning of life, and how birth, suffering, old age, and death itself can be transcended. And his method is that of vaccination and homeopathy: cure like by like: give yourself a mild attack of the disease now, and thereby build antibodies that ward off the real disease when it strikes. It is the method of Jung, who writes: "As a physician I am convinced that it is hygienic... to discover in death a goal towards which one can strive; and that shrinking away from it is something unhealthy and abnormal which robs the second half of life of its purpose." It is also the method of Plato ("Philosophy is the practice of death."), of St. Paul ("I die daily."), of Rumi ("Die before you die."), and of Sri Ramana Maharshi himself ("What if anyone is dead? What if anyone be ruined? Be dead yourself, be ruined yourself.").

When should this homeopathic treatment begin? My friend started in his twenties, Maharshi in his teens. You could say the sooner the better, but there are no rules. Everything depends on the needs of the individual. Commonly, the problem of life's meaning comes to a head in middle age, after the ordinary goals set by society have been attained, and no new ones offer themselves. Jung found that most of his middle-aged patients were suffering from no clinically definable neurosis, but from the senselessness and emptiness of their lives; they were holding onto the delusion that the second half of life must be governed by the principles of the first, and failing to recognise that for the ageing person it is a duty and a necessity to give serious attention to himself.

Traditional India agrees. The ancient and noble ideal of the four *asramas*—or stages of life—lays down the norm. First, *brahmacarya*, the child and the youth learning the skills and knowledge and discipline proper to the human condition. Second, *garhasthya*, the life of the working householder and parent, contributing to the upkeep and continuation of the community. So far, so good. A fair start, you might say, a useful flexing of the muscles before getting down to business. For now the real adventure begins, the serious challenge that sorts out the men from the boys, the work to stretch and prove a man. Having taken care of his social duties and reached middle to late-middle age, he enters the stage of *vanaprasthya*, a time for the loosening of bonds and breaking through to freedom. With this in view, he winds up his remaining obligations to his family and goes off to seek the meaning of it all, and particularly his own meaning, his true identity. But first he has to find his spiritual teacher, and then take to heart his instruction and undergo his training—a discipline which may well make the rigours of the two previous stages seem mere child's play. Hopefully the question of Who he really is had been there in the background all along, but now it becomes his sole passion, and for the answer no price is too high. And when, sooner or later, that price has been paid, and he sees what in fact has always been obvious and scot free (namely, his true Nature as the One and Only, the Alone, the Real) he enters the fourth and final stage— *sannyasa*.

This is the crown of life. This is what the other three stages were for: without it they are pointless. Not to arrive here is not to arrive at all. To stop short of this is to stay immature, a case of arrested development. The Jnani or true Sannyasin (for whom other traditions have other names) is the only real grown-up—which means grown up to more-than-cosmic dimensions. Outwardly an insignificant and ageing human he is inwardly and in truth ageless and boundless as space, free as the wind, the King of the World, the Deathless Splendour, the All. Outwardly useless and unemployed (and indeed inwardly he has nothing whatever to do), his work for the world is non-stop, exacting and effective as no mere human work could ever be. The paradox is that he has no job, and never takes a moment off.

Compare this paradigm of human life as a steady, four-stage

ascent, an enterprise that grows more challenging and outrageously ambitious as it goes on, a game played for mounting stakes and sure to break the bank in the end—compare this with the sad picture we began this article with, of human life faltering and failing scarcely half way through: and make your choice. Once the stark alternatives are clearly perceived, what choice is there? Isn't it plain which is the half life and which the full life; what the disease is and what the cure is? The disease is life arrested midway. The cure is life completed.

Cure for whom? you may well ask. If so few Hindus down the centuries have gone the whole way, have cared or dared to take the full-strength medicine (in spite of all this traditional encouragement) how many non-Hindus are likely to swallow it? Is the average Westerner with time on his hands likely to seize the God-sent opportunity of devoting it to discovering and then enjoying *Who* has all this time? And in any case how could such a personal and hidden attainment as Self-realisation begin to transform the community in which it happens? Let's be realistic, for God's sake!

In the short term these objections are valid. In the longer term, over the forthcoming centuries and millennia, who can say what changes the pressures of life—its inner logic—may not demand of the human spirit? After all, the genus *Homo* has already come an awful long way. Having painfully graduated from simple animal consciousness to human self-consciousness, why shouldn't man go on to divine Self-consciousness? Doesn't the incidence (occasional but remarkably persistent and widespread) of that ultimate mutation known as the Sage or Seer, throughout the last three thousand years of the species' history, hold out some promise for (say) its next three million years? The Seers themselves, including Ramana Maharshi, describe their state as the *natural* one. In any case the commonness or otherwise of a social phenomenon is no measure of its social effectiveness. Just as the ideal of perfect physical health, though rarely attained, nevertheless affects the lives of millions today, so the mere rumour of perfect spiritual health (to wit, Self-realisation) could one day exert still greater influence. What middle-aged man could stay wholly indifferent to the choice confronting him—to live on as God, or perish as man—once he saw it clearly?

But all such speculation is beside the point. It is nonsense to speak of growing (or declining) numbers of enlightened people, living in such and such a place at such and such a time. There is only One who sees Who he is, here and now. In the fourth *asrama* all travellers join forces, and anyone who arrives here does so *as* all the others too, and *for* them. As Maharshi so often pointed out, there are no others! It follows that the best way to solve these very human problems of boredom and ageing and dying, is to solve them for oneself, at this moment and absolutely—by ceasing to be human at all, by being Oneself, changeless and immortal. In the last resort they aren't long-term social problems, or other folk's business: they are my own business, now. "Find the Self" says Maharshi, "and all problems are solved." "Until the questioner is found, his questions cannot be answered." "See yourself, and all is understood."

Strange to say, it is this so-called last stage of life which underpins and includes the three earlier stages, which keeps them going, which alone is quite real. It is not—repeat not—an optional extra. Nor is it ever ineffectual. "Realisation of the Self is the greatest help that can be rendered to humanity", says Maharshi. For in fact, as he adds: "The realised being does not see the world as different from himself." He *is* the world set to rights, instantly.

* * *

Chapter 45

WHAT I OWE TO RAMANA MAHARSHI

The backdrop

Though I lived in India from 1937 to 1945 I did not, alas, get to see Ramana Maharshi. In fact, I knew almost nothing about him at that time. Since then, however, he has become one of the great influences in my life and I would like to acknowledge, with immense gratitude, what I owe to him.

But first I must set on record, briefly, how things stood with me when, in 1959, in England, I first came across Arthur Osborne's books about Maharshi. I had already seen Who I was. Back in 1943, when I was still in India, I had noticed the absence here of anyone and anything. Leading up to that vision I had for some years been enquiring, with growing intensity, into my true Nature. In the main, this research had taken the thoroughly Western form of investigating how I appeared to observers at varying distances—from the normal human range of a few feet all the way down to the ångström units of physics, and all the way up to the light-years of astronomy. Clearly what my observers (including myself standing aside from myself) made of me depended upon their distance from here, how far off they happened to be. At great distances they saw this spot as some kind of heavenly body; in the middle distance they found a human body;

at closer range (when suitably equipped with microscopes etc.) they discovered infra-human bodies—cells, molecules, atoms, particles... In some sense I was all this, and more. How marvellous, how mind-boggling! But it only underlined, and did nothing to answer, the real question: what lies right *here*, at the centre of all these bodily shapes, these regional impressions of me? What is the reality of which these manifold views are mere appearances? It seemed unlikely that the scientists would ever get to the ultimate particles or waves, the basic substance, but would just go on unveiling, layer by layer, progressively featureless manifestations of that ever-elusive substratum. Yet this substratum, if any, was me, and therefore absolutely fascinating. I was stuck. How to penetrate to the central Unknown, which defies the inspection of the most brilliant researchers, armed with the subtlest of instruments.

Then, suddenly, I realised how silly this question was. How could I be accessible to *them*; how could I be inaccessible to *myself*? What outsiders make of me is *their* business; what I, the insider, make of myself is *my* business. They are the experts on how I strike them at X feet; I am the expert on how I strike myself at *0 feet*. I had only to dare to look at this Looker, here! What I saw then was, and is, the clearest, the simplest, the most direct and obvious and indubitable of all sights—namely the Space here, speckless, unbounded, self-luminous, vividly awake to itself as at once No-thing and the Container and Source of all things.

In the years that followed this discovery I had it for breakfast and dinner and tea. I soaked it up, lived with it, explored it, worked out some of its endless applications and implications. And I tried, by every means I could find or invent, to share my delight with others. How miserably I failed! Some folks were intrigued, even impressed, but baffled. Most considered me a fairly harmless eccentric, if not actually crazy. But what did it matter? Endorsement from *way out there* of what lies *right here*—this was as pointless as it was lacking. All the same, I confess I often felt frustrated, lonely, and (very occasionally) discouraged. Not that I could ever doubt the actuality of What I saw myself to be here, and certainly I never questioned my own sanity. It was the world's sanity that I questioned! I got on as best I could, very much on my own.

And then, in 1958, I started reading seriously the early Zen Masters—and I felt lonely no longer. Here were friends who described what was unmistakably my own experience of myself as Void. O joy! And, on the heels of this delightful company, came Maharshi himself.

Why is he so superb?

Why, I ask myself, did he become so important for me? Why is he still, for me, superb? What, specially, have I to thank him for?

Firstly, I have to thank him for the gift of *encouragement*. A precious gift indeed. Not for *confirmation* of What I see (only I am in a position to see what's right here); not for his *support* (right here is the Support of all things); not for friendship or even love (unless one can be friends with oneself). I am having difficulty in saying what I mean by the kind of encouragement he gave when I needed it most. Perhaps I should call it—his *darshan*. Anyhow, from then on my dedication to the One-I-am was complete: no more wavering, no periodical discouragement, no other real interests than This.

Accessibility of Self-knowledge

Secondly, I have to record my gratitude to Maharshi for his insistence on the ever-present accessibility, the naturalness, the obviousness, of Self-realisation. Many a time I had been informed, and had read, that Enlightenment is of all states the rarest and the remotest and the most difficult—in practice, impossible—and here was a great Sage telling us that, on the contrary, it was the easiest. Such, indeed, was my own experience, and I had never been intimidated by those religious persons who were careful to tell me that I couldn't see What I saw. Nevertheless it was for me marvellously refreshing to find that Maharshi never sent enquirers away with instructions to work for Liberation at some distant date. It is not, he insisted, a glittering prize to be awarded for future achievements of any sort: it is not for earning little by little, but for noticing now, just as one is. Other Sages, of course, have stressed the availability of this, but here Maharshi is surely the clearest, the most uncompromising, of them all. How wonderful to hear him saying, in effect, that compared with Oneself all other things are obscure, more or less invisible, fugitive, impossible to get at: only the Seer can be clearly seen.

Not a post-dated cheque

I suspect that it was because of this renewed assurance—Maharshi's insistence on the present availability of Self-realisation—that it became possibtle for me at last to share this realisation with a friend, and then with several friends, and now with many friends. Today, I won't accept that enquirers can fail to see their Absence. I don't any longer ask them whether they can see this, but what it means for them. My job is to point out the Obvious, theirs to evaluate it. It is true that among the many who see, only a few surrender at once to What they see. This is not, however, the end of the story, and in any case the words 'few' and 'many', are inapplicable here. The problem of sharing This with others never was a problem. What others?—As Maharshi would say.

The only serious question

Which brings me to my third debt to him. I thank him for his uncompromising attitude to people's problems. For him, all troubles that afflict humans reduce to one trouble—mistaken identity. The answer to the problem is to see Who has it. At its own level it is insoluble. There is no greater absurdity, no more fundamental or damaging a madness, than to imagine one *is* centrally what one looks like at a distance. To think one is a human being *here* is a sickness so deep-seated that it underlies and generates all one's ills. Only cure that one basic disease—mistaken identity—and all is exactly as it should be. I know no Sage who goes more directly to the root of the disease, and refuses more consistently to treat its symptoms. WHO AM I? is the only serious question. And, most fortunately, it is the only question that can be answered without hesitation or the shadow of a doubt, absolutely.

To sum up, then, I thank Ramana Maharshi above all for tirelessly posing this question of questions, and for showing how simple the answer is, and for his lifelong dedication to that simple answer. But in the last resort all this talk of one giving and another taking is unreal. The notion that there was a consciousness associated with that body in Tiruvannamalai, and there is another consciousness associated with this body in Nacton, England, and a lot of other consciousness associated with the other bodies comprising the universe—this is the great error which Maharshi never tolerated. Consciousness is indivisible.

* * *

Chapter 46

SEEKING THE MIRACULOUS

The further West we go the more we are barraged by books, magazine articles, advertisements and hand-outs on how to expand our consciousness, how to realise our full potential, how to work all those miracles we are hiddenly capable of, and so on. Who isn't intrigued by the exciting promises these programmes hold out? Who of us doesn't know in his heart that he is only a fraction of what he could be, that he's not yet the whole of himself? Who of us doesn't want to *grow*?

This urge is evidence of good health. Vigorous creatures don't wilt and shrink: they show drive, they seek to expand in many directions, to break new ground and venture forth into the unknown. In this article we shall examine some of the directions in which we are invited to expand, and what the difficulties are, and what may be our best chances of success. We shall be asking what are the limits—if any—to our growth if we go about it sensibly, in this very life.

We read about, perhaps occasionally we meet, people whose lives remind us that we're not nearly as awake as we could be, that there is far more going on than we are taking in, that all of us have unrealised powers of perception and feeling and comprehension and performance—that are only waiting somehow to be brought out. Life, we sense, could be so much richer, stranger, more magical, more mystical, more daring.

Let's take a few examples. Everyone knows that there are people who have the gift of healing—mental healing as well as physical—and some of their cures are truly miraculous. Then there are people who pick up the thoughts and feelings of folk in far-off places and times, and may clearly perceive what's going on there. We hear of adepts who claim, apparently with good reason, that they are in touch with the departed, or can foretell some future events, or can travel round the universe at will and faster than light itself, or can be present in more than one place at a time, or can live far beyond the normal span of years, or can easily ascend to levels of consciousness that are inaccessible to ordinary humans. It's reported of some extraordinary men and women that they can live for long periods on nothing but air, or can see with their fingertips, or can create a solid looking (and periodically hungry!) companion when they feel lonely, or can themselves disappear and re-appear whenever they want to. Some of these tales I find hard to take seriously. Nevertheless I have myself witnessed the materialisation out of thin air of quantities of ashes and sweets, and I'm quite certain I wasn't being tricked by that well-known wonder-worker. And we have all heard of Uri Geller and his knack of bending spoons and forks without exerting any physical effort at all.

Are you and I capable of such wonderful things?
The catalogue of such supernormal faculties and attainments, ranging from the level of spoon-bending to cosmic consciousness, is always being extended and in truth has no end. However, the small sample we have taken is quite enough to indicate something very important

about our nature. After all, you and I, as regular human beings, are members of the same species as these miracle-workers and psychics and mystics. We can't be so very different from them. And if we are capable of no more than a fraction of what these gifted ones are doing with ease, why it certainly follows that we are neglecting—sadly and even irresponsibly—our potential for living full, satisfying, truly mind-blowing lives.

I suspect that when we don't wish to know about this huge, shadowy, mysterious, thrilling, largely unchartered area of mankind's accomplishment, or else dismiss it offhand as a mixture of wishful thinking and credulity and superstition, we are in reality just running away from ourselves and making feeble excuses for our lack of enterprise. Or perhaps it is that we have a secret need to put ourselves down and sell ourselves short. It could well be that we are unconsciously frightened of our own suppressed capabilities, of our immense untapped resources.

Let's set aside this fear and false modesty, and brace ourselves to acknowledge what we are and can do, and come into our true heritage.

Alas, there are obstacles

We come up immediately against problems. First, there is the question of how to expand and in what direction. Some directions seem blocked off. For example, one's occasional playful efforts to emulate Uri Geller, and bend the cutlery by means of visualisation or sheer will-power, have so far met with no success at all; and even

Mr. Geller himself seems not to have the slightest idea of how he acts directly upon the metal and other objects around him. In fact, it appears that many sorts of paranormal faculty aren't learned at all and are incapable of cultivation. They could be described as accidents of birth, or even as biological mutations.

On the other hand, of course, there are on offer to all of us innumerable disciplines, retreats, courses, systems of training lasting from a weekend to a lifetime, which hold out firm promises of all manner of unusual attainments. We are invited to learn how to direct our lives by means of the Tarot cards or the I Ching, or set up infallible horoscopes, or levitate, or become white witches, or win friends and influence people, or untie our psycho-physical knots, or succeed in whatever we put our hands to, or I don't know what. None of it looks to me wicked or dangerous, much of it highly desirable. But I find this strange land of opportunity to be so confusing, so full of signposts pointing in all directions and no direction at all, that I feel quite lost in it. Every 'New Age' teacher is anxious to get me going on a path that may well lead to wonderful places. But I can't follow all these paths. It seems they don't converge but rather diverge, and if I were to follow a number of them simultaneously I would find myself more and more disorientated, more torn and fragmented, as I went on. Again, how can I surely tell the highway from the byway, the genuine guide from the false one? How can I foresee and be reasonably sure of the likely goal of any path from the start of it? And even if I did eventually win through, what about those other, untravelled paths? What about *balanced* advance? It would certainly be exhilarating, if no more, to explore the whole of this wonderland in a spirit of open-minded adventure, but this would-be traveller finds himself unable—rather than unwilling—to set out with any confidence, and with no serious misgivings.

What do you and I really want, anyhow?

Our second group of problems is even more daunting. The cost, in time and effort if not money, of acquiring even one of these unusual gifts, is apt to be high. (I'm referring, of course, to those gifts which, it's claimed, can be cultivated.) Take levitation, for instance. If, after a few hours spent learning the trick, one could stay suspended in mid-air for a mere five seconds, who wouldn't be happy to put in that amount of practice? But *years* devoted to learning a knack that still left one far less proficient than a hover-fly or a humming-bird—no thank you! If this sort of thing is realisation of my full potential, I'm not interested! If this is expansion, I'll put up with the size I am! In fact, I observe that many of these systems of training, which ostensibly are aimed at the eventual *expansion* of the trainee, demand his or her present contraction (including contraction of the purse!) as a means to that far-off end—a concentration and narrowing down of consciousness and behaviour and life-style; and the promised eventual explosion is by no means certain, at that!

Ah, but supposing I were to take my chance, and commit myself to one of the more plausible and balanced systems on offer. Supposing, for instance, I were seriously to take up one of those trainings aimed at making my life work at last, or refashioning myself into a truly superior human being, or getting whatever it is I currently want. And supposing (this is a long shot indeed!) that I did in the end get all the energy and health, all the fame and fortune and power I set out to gain—well, what then? Would I settle down happily and enjoy myself? All my experience of myself tells me NO! This conclusion is confirmed by the life stories of the most 'successful' members of our species, who turn out to be no happier than the rest of us. Often less happy, in fact. Perverse creature that I am, getting what I want is discovering that, after all, it isn't what I really want. Everything indicates that I'm likely to find myself just as far away from my heart's desire, no matter how impressive the goods or the powers or the knowledge that I have won. In that case, why exert all that effort? Show me why I should work at the supernormal expansion of my consciousness and abilities for years and decades, only to find at the end of my life that I'm still insufficiently expanded, still lop-sided and incomplete, still longing for... for what? For another sort of miracle altogether?

Ramana Maharshi is devastatingly frank on this subject. "A man has limited powers and is miserable: he wants to expand his powers so that he may be happy. But consider if this will be so. If with limited perceptions one is miserable, with extended perceptions the misery must increase proportionately. Occult powers will not bring happiness to anyone, but will make him all the more wretched."

We have indeed been warned, in the severest possible terms, by one of the great spiritual masters of modern times. Are we then to retire forever from this great enterprise of expansion, to stay insignificant and petty and feeble? To give up? The whole of Maharshi's teaching says to me: "Not on your life!" And anyhow, in spite of all these problems and discouragements and wholly-justified warnings, I can't help being fascinated by what lies 'beyond', by the wonderland that bathes us all the time and our famous common sense doesn't suspect the existence of. Our yearning for the Boundless will not be denied. There is a Mystery, an Astonishment and a Glory: it is all around, and it is our life's breath and our life's blood. I'm determined somehow or other not to let slip any opportunity for adventure into this country. I prefer not to contract out of any part of life, not to be smaller and meaner than I actually am. The question for me, then, isn't whether I want this enlargement (of course I do!) but of how to get it. I assume you feel the same.

A quite different approach and a simple experiment

So far, our every approach to this goal seems beset with obstacles. So let's try a different strategy. Let's take a rest from attempting to get anywhere or achieve anything, and be content for the moment to examine what already *is*. The assumption of the experts who would have us develop special powers is that we aren't yet exercising them. Similarly the assumption of the well-meaning people who advise us to expand our consciousness is that it is too small and needs stretching. Certainly they seem to be right. But before we agree with these critics let's check how big, how comprehensive and well-developed, how proficient, our consciousness is *right now*. That is the task of the rest of this article.

As I See It

A difficult task? How could it be? I am consciousness, you are consciousness, and as such we are perfectly placed and perfectly equipped to report on what it's like, and how magical or unmagical it is, and how big or small it is, and how far it needs stretching. I am the expert on me, you are the expert on you, and we don't rely on each other here. You are the sole authority on what it's like being your conscious self at this moment, and in a unique position to see exactly what powers you are exercising. To check up on them, will you please carry out a small experiment—very slowly and attentively? (It would be useless just to read about this experiment instead of carrying it out, so will you very kindly do what I ask? Your making sense of what follows depends on it.)

> Notice how few of these printed words are distinctly visible at a time… how beyond them are unreadable, fuzzy words… how beyond them are the shadowy outlines of this magazine and your hands holding it… and beyond them are the even more vague and shadowy objects in the room…

> Now, while still attending to that central spot (where the letters are clearly defined) take in the edges of the *whole* scene… the outside limits of your field of vision… See how this field has no hard boundary at all… How the scene fades away—on the left, on the right, upwards, downwards—into this incredibly mysterious, and incredibly neglected "nothing whatever".

> Now please hold out your arms at shoulder height and spread them till they just disappear beyond your field of vision… I think

you will find that they are at an angle of about 160° to each other. This 160° is the extent of *what you are looking at,* of the SEEN…

All right, lower your arms.

Now turn your attention round to what's looking, to the SEER… Point to where others locate your eyes, but you see—what…? Aren't you now pointing at Nothing at all, at the empty SEER… at yourself as Aware Space… extending through about 200° and taking in the scene which extends through 160°…?

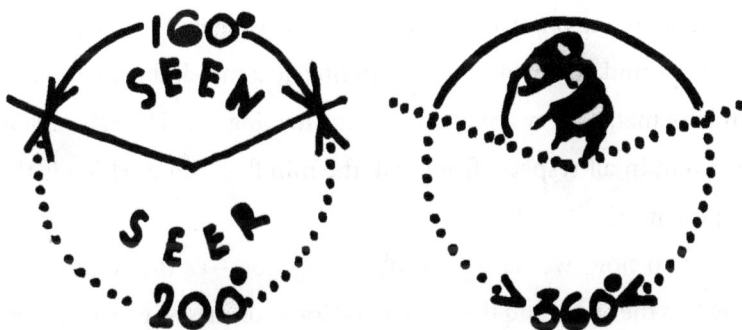

On present evidence, how deep is this SEER, this Aware Space which you are…? How wide…? How high…? How low…? Has it any size, any limits whatever…?

How could This which is already boundless be expanded any further…?

So what gifts—miraculous and otherwise—do you lack?

Isn't it obvious that, though the ever-changing contents of the SEEN—spread through 160°—are each and all of them limited, the 200° which is you their SEER is forever unlimited, forever unstained by them, forever this marvellous Clarity or Capacity or Space which is now fully aware of Itself as such?

So much for vision. As opportunity offers you can check how the other senses tell essentially the same story. Observe yourself to be the changeless and boundless and unbroken Silence which is now hearing the ever-changing sounds it contains. The Silence listens to itself. Again, observe how what you taste and smell and touch is always limited and changing, while the One who tastes and smells and touches is always unlimited and unchanging and uncontaminated by what's going on. And the same goes for whatever you happen to have in mind, to be thinking and feeling: it comes and goes, it is this and not that, its very limitations are the making of it. How absolutely different in all respects from you, the mindless Mind which is the Experiencer!

Up to now, we have been observing how—as the unbounded Field, as the Space and the Silence, as Consciousness—you are *taking in* the universe of finite objects, the passing show. But that's only part of the story, just one way of reading it. It's equally true that you as the Field are *producing* all that grows in it. Observe how everything you experience arises miraculously and unceasingly from What you really are, from this same Aware Space which is so brilliantly perceptible once you turn your attention (and your index finger) around to it. And there's still another—a third—way of reading the astounding facts about you. Notice how you as the 200° SEER are altogether united with the 160° SEEN, how you as Aware Space cannot be parted from its contents, how in your direct experience Nirvana *is* Samsara, the Void *is* Form, the Nothing *is* the All. Thus the world is yours and you are infinitely rich.

What more do you want? What more *is* there to want? Could this threefold magic be any more magical, or any more your own, than you now see it to be?

The truly miraculous

If you still don't feel absolutely content with the splendour and wealth and fecundity that evidently are yours and which constitute the true Nature of all, it could be for this reason: you secretly desire to be special, to enjoy attributes and exercise powers that—as you look around—you can *see* are your very own and quite unique.

Well—surprise, surprise!—even this secret desire is granted. Provided, that is, you are willing to drop for a few moments your discursive thinking and assumptions and beliefs, and just look.

Just look, and see whether the following isn't true now, in your own first-hand experience: don't believe it, check it against your own in-seeing, item by item.

As YOURSELF (as 1st person singular, present tense) you manifestly are *in all respects* the opposite of what you *appear* to others to be (as 2nd or 3rd person). Thus to them over there you appear small, opaque, multi-coloured, local, mobile, ageing, mortal, classifiable (as this and not that), and more or less ignorant and powerless; whereas you can see for yourself that really you are immense, transparent, colourless, at large, un-moving, ageless, immortal, unclassifiable (having no characteristics of your own, you take on the characteristics of whatever you happen to be occupied with), all-knowing (seeing into your Nature, you see into the Nature of all), and all-powerful (you see how all that happens flows from What and Who you are). And if some of the items in this catalogue of super-miracles (which is actually endless) aren't immediately apparent to you, just go on seeing the SEER, and all will become clear and self-evident. Only unveil your true identity and you will find that there's *nothing* about you which isn't miraculous!

You may even find yourself exercising in some sense— in a far truer and deeper sense—some of the more bizarre of those gifts we noticed way back: for example, the ability to "see with your fingers"! Please try this one out, relying once more on present evidence alone:

> Point again at the SEER, noting how those fingers belong to the SEEN, the 160°... Now bring your hand forward till it vanishes to one side of you... *Those fingers have joined the 200° SEER,* and it's just as true (and as false) that you are seeing with them as with your eyes. What eyes, on present evidence? In fact, as the sages insist, it is your whole Body-as-Void, your Buddha Nature, your true Self, which is the One SEER, the One Experiencer. "Only God sees", they say. And you certainly do see. Need I point out what follows?

Achieving the "impossible"

It may be that—even so—no list of attainments, however fantastic, could be comprehensive and well-balanced enough for you, and you seek a single Gift that will take care of and supersede them all.

Yet again, you don't seek in vain. If in your heart of hearts you feel that there's still something missing—perhaps the Miracle that forever satisfies all your longing—why your feeling is indeed well-founded. That ultimate Wonder, that Incredible, too, is given freely and given now. It wears two faces.

First, YOU ARE, and nothing else is. You are the One and Only, the Alone. Look now and see for Yourself that around you are no other Real Beings, only appearances. *Where did you ever find Real Being—Being alive to Itself—but at Home?*

Second, YOU ARE YOUR OWN ORIGIN. The 'normal' and 'natural' thing would be for You not to be, for nothing at all to be. How madly irregular, how truly paranormal and absurd, for this Awareness-that-You-are to occur, to invent Itself, to make Itself happen with no reason, no assistance, no antecedents or foundation, spontaneously! By rights there should be—just blankness, non-being, the everlasting night of unconsciousness. It is You— yes You!—who, arising from it, perform the 'impossible'. You hoist Yourself clean out of that darkest night by your own non-existent bootstraps, into your own blazing Light. Not once and long long ago but right now You are conjuring Yourself up out of the depths, like a rabbit producing itself out of a magician's empty top-hat— with no magician around! Compared with this original piece of legerdemain, your other tricks, such as going on to produce myriads of universes—all in good working order—are mere spin-off and chicken-feed, hardly worth a mention.

Truly you have found the Miraculous. You have found Yourself!

* * *

In *The Arabian Nights Entertainments,* a composition that was much influenced by Sufi tradition, there is told the story of a poor young fisherman called Judar. Briefly, this is how it goes. He chances to find the well-hidden Treasure House of the World, and knocks boldly at the door. It's opened by a fearsome porter, armed with an axe, who shouts: "Stretch out your neck so that I can cut off your head!" Summoning his courage, Judar obeys—and the blow is painless. He notices in passing that the porter is a body without a soul... After further adventures, he comes to the Treasure itself, which comprises the four Valuables—the Celestial Disc (whose owner sees all lands as near), the Sword (whose owner can slay all creatures), the Seal-Ring (whose owner possesses and rules the world), and the Pot of Eye-Salve (whose owner can see all the world's treasures). All four Valuables are now his very own.

We offer the following interpretation of Judar's story. Being poor (in spirit) and young (childlike) and a fisherman (seeker), he readily 'loses his head' and sees Who he really is. Then he went on to take up the powers that go with his true identity as the One— omnipresence, or the abolition of distance, annihilation and re-creation, the ownership of all things, and the vision of his own Clear Essence which is the Essence of all things.

One ounce of sanctifying grace is worth more than a hundred

weight of those graces which theologians call "gratuitous", among which is the gift of miracles. It is possible to receive such gifts and yet to be in mortal sin; nor are they necessary to salvation.

St. Francois de Sales

Most of the great theocentric saints and spiritual teachers have admitted the existence of supernormal powers, only, however to deplore them. To think that such Siddhis, as the Indians call them, have anything to do with liberation is, they say, a dangerous illusion. These things are either irrelevant to the main issues of life, or, if too much prized and attended to, an obstacle in the way of spiritual advance.

Aldous Huxley

The goods of God, which are beyond all measure, can only be contained in an empty and solitary heart.

St. John of the Cross

Revelations are the aberration of faith; they are an amusement that spoils simplicity in relation to God, that embarrasses the soul and makes it swerve from its directness in relation to God. They distract the soul and occupy it with other things than God. Special illuminations, auditions, prophecies and the rest are marks of weakness in a soul that cannot support the assaults of temptation or anxiety about the future.

J. J. Olier

* * *

Chapter 47

ALAN WATTS
SAGE OR ANTI-SAGE?

I didn't know Alan intimately, or see him very often, though we did visit each other in this country and in California, where we worked together briefly. Nevertheless he was a good friend, and I owe a debt to him which these notes may do something to acknowledge and discharge.

His many books are, of course, luminous, wide-ranging, and always lucidly written, and some of them have been very helpful to me. Nor was their brilliance superficial or merely intellectual. He had a feeling, a nose for what is essential; and I can't remember having read anything of his that struck me as false or irrelevant. Or even very controversial. In fact, I see his role as that of an extremely able clarifier, populariser, and disseminator of otherwise obscure spiritual insights, and not that of an innovator. He seems to me to have done for Eastern religion, and for Zen in particular, what C. S. Lewis (and I speak of him from some personal knowledge also) did for mainstream Christianity—namely to clear and cultivate old ground rather than break new ground. For this reason both were and are hugely popular authors. They retained the common touch, and never lost their followers by running too far ahead of them. The intelligent man-or-woman-in-the-street can and does read these contrasting yet similar writers without getting puzzled or angry. And (I imagine) without much risk of shock, or metanoia, or any dramatic turnabout in his or her life.

It was Alan's own life, not his teaching, which was "shocking"—a scandal in the eyes of ordinary decent people and not only those of the religious Establishment. You don't have to be pharasaical or specially square to find difficulty in reconciling Alan's exalted teachings with the well-known fact that he suffered from what's euphemistically called "an alcohol problem". How could you talk and write like a sage, right up to the sadly premature end, and live like a—well, let's say an un-sage to say the least, or even an anti-sage?

I don't pretend to know the answer. The human condition, including its spiritual dimension, is infinitely variable and laced with paradoxes; and to judge Alan (or anyone else) on the external evidence is as unreasonable as it is ungenerous. What I do know is that Alan's apparent inconsistency raises an important question—a near-the-knuckle one for many of us. The rest of this article addresses itself to this more general question, and doesn't comment further on Alan's particular case.

The question is this: does a ramshackle or broken-down human vehicle necessarily spoil, or let down, or lose altogether, the eternal verities it sets out to convey? In plain language, if I'm an unsatisfactory person is my work for the Truth bound to be unsatisfactory too?

Well, let's digress a little to consider some workers in other—more secular—fields. Tchaikovsky's music was incomparable, yet his life was a shambles. Van Gogh at his maddest still painted with characteristic genius. So did Gaugin, whatever his moral shortcomings. Though no one thinks of *separating* the artist from his art, no one thinks of *judging* it by him, and demanding a certificate of good character. Works of art stand on their own feet, and are to be appraised for what they manifestly are. It's as if their creators, giving so much to them, have little left over for themselves and the cultivation of their personalities. Or take thinkers. Leibniz and Rousseau and Schopenhauer and Nietzsche were not the most admirable or sane of men, but who can be sure that their philosophies didn't actually *gain* from their human weaknesses? Beauty and Truth aren't at all fussy in their choice of purveyors, and are plainly unimpressed by normal good sense and conventional virtues.

But when it comes to those subsections of Beauty and Truth dubbed spiritual or religious the case is mysteriously altered—or so we are led to believe. While we don't expect the private lives of great artists and thinkers to reflect the high standard of their output (we half expect them *not* to do so!), we insist that the private lives of spiritual teachers shall be exemplary. "It's by what the master *is*, rather than what he says, that he instructs." We feel that he must personally demonstrate the salvation—the peace, love, joy, wholeness—that he points the way to. Otherwise he invites the comment: "Physician, heal myself!" Or, more poignantly: "He saved others, himself he cannot save."

It seems to be fair comment, but let's not forget who originally made that taunt, and to whom it was addressed, and in what circumstances. And let's be aware of superficial and merely conventional views about what sort of human life and death befit the true spiritual Master. Ramana Maharshi—celibate ascetic though he himself was—tells with relish a long story about a spiritual renegade, an ex-sadhu who had sunk to living openly with a dancing girl (a scandal if ever there was one, at that time and place), and who nevertheless remained a true sage. And let's be clear about what a true sage is up to. He is concerned with what Alan Watts calls our Supreme Identity, with the Perfection that we all really are, regardless. He is not—repeat *not*—in the business of perfecting himself and others *as human beings*—an enterprise which is doomed, and in any case a contradiction in terms. His business is the realisation that, truly speaking, we aren't human beings at all. In fact, it turns out that all our life-consuming and agonising efforts devoted to the attainment of human self-sufficiency—to character-building and the development of individuality and all that—prove in the end to be the very opposite of what's needed. For it's only when we despair of ourselves as persons that we are in the market for our true and eternally perfect identity as non-persons, as no-thing and no-one whatever.

There are many ways of exposing and breaking down and peeling off the layers of our human and nonhuman appearances—our false identifications and pretences—till the naked Core (no-Core) is exposed. Some of these ways—such as most forms of Buddhist meditation—are fairly respectable and fairly healthy. Others are more dubious, even alarming. For example, the Catholic contemplative's hair shirts and disciplines (whips); and, at the other extreme, those Tantric practices which deliberately *reverse* the rules of the holy life. Is there any limit to the way in to What we really are, any code of decency they must comply with? Yet, insofar as their *end* is achieved—namely the vision of oneself as the Clear Light of the Void, as simple Awareness (or rather the unknowable Abyss from which awareness springs), as the Buddha Nature, as the Kingdom within, or whatever we call It—the *means* to that end, however repulsive or bizarre they may appear to our parochial minds, are justified. What we *are* happens to be the precise opposite of what we are convinced we are, so it's not surprising we should need strong medicine and shock treatment to switch us from the one to the other. The ultimate sanity isn't cheaply bought.

Maybe there are exceptions, but undoubtedly most of us will never begin to take a sincere interest in our true Nature till our false nature has completely let us down—in one way or another. And in some cases quite tragically.

And, after all, we in the West have a long and deep-rooted tradition which points in this direction. St Paul insisted that he was "the chief of sinners". And we all know the story of the two men in the temple: the Pharisee thanking God he wasn't like that wretched publican, and the publican beating his breast and not daring to raise his eyes to heaven and crying, "God be merciful to me, a sinner!" Jesus himself, we gather, felt more at home among the poor and the outcast, among winos and call-girls, than among well-behaved religious people. And in the end it was the latter that yelled for his crucifixion.

* * *

Chapter 48

ENLIGHTENMENT FOR PEACE
or
THE MYTH OF CONFRONTATION

This wisdom have I seen also under the sun, and, it seemed great unto me:

There was a little city, and few men within it; and there came a great king against it, and besieged it, and built great bulwarks against it: now there was found in it a poor wise man, and he by his wisdom delivered the city; yet no man remembered that same poor man. Then said I, Wisdom is better than strength, nevertheless the poor man's wisdom is despised and his words are not heard. The words of wise men are heard in quiet more than the cry of him that ruleth among fools. Wisdom is better than weapons of war: but one sinner destroyeth much good.

Ecclesiastes

God does not deprive the world of them (the mystics) for they are its sustainers.

Al-Ghazzali

If a single person lives in the Unborn, the right Dharma flourishes in the world.

Bankei

As I See It

1. The problem

The problem can be stated in various ways:

(a) How can the enlightened few—who see, value, and practise their No-thingness, their natureless Nature—pass on their enlightenment to the many? Or at least to an influential minority capable of affecting the 'defence' policy of nations?

(b) Is the absolute asymmetry—non-confrontation, true unilateralism—of the face-to-no-face set-up (as vividly demonstrated in the paper-bag experiment) reflected at the level of States and Power-blocs? If so, how can it be put into effect?

(c) First the molecular bomb (TNT, etc.), then the atomic bomb, now the nuclear bomb. What next? The ultimate Bomb, the end? Is there a way out?

(d) How can the work of D.H. [Douglas Harding] and friends be so integrated with that of R.F. [Robert Fuller] and friends as to answer the above questions, in a way that leads to appropriate action?

2. The solution in principle

The radical solution of this many-sided problem is exactly the same as the radical solution of all others. IT IS TO SEE WHO HAS THE PROBLEM. *The Science of the 1st Person* shows how surprisingly well this strategy works out in very diverse fields (37, no less) and obliges us to suppose that the field of international politics isn't likely to prove the solitary tragic exception.

Our three-part working hypothesis, then, is:

(a) that all our problems are so interconnected that they constitute one Problem—our true Identity;

(b) that, of them all, this is the *only* one that can really be solved, the only one whose solution is easy, simple, indubitable, conclusive, entirely practical, and not productive of other problems;

(c) that nevertheless this one all-embracing and genuine Solution, to take effect, has to be lived—which being far from easy, requires powerful motivation, such as may at last be provided by the need to counter the threat of genocide.

3. The solution in practice—some basic preliminaries
First, we have to go behind this talk to what it's all about, to the actual perception of those 'hard' Data without which it is wordy nonsense. So let's for a few seconds carry out yet again (in fact, every time is a first time, because the Data won't keep, and are quite unlike the memory of them)—carry out one or more of the following tests, putting aside for the moment hearsay and belief and imagination, and *going on present evidence:*

(a) Check that What's now taking in these words—these small black shapes on a white surface—has neither size, nor colour, nor shape, nor surface, but is Emptiness or Clarity without limits, speckless through and through.

(b) Check that what's being looked out of isn't two tiny peepholes, but one huge unglazed and frameless 'Window' with no peeper and no-body this side of it.

(c) Check that when we "close our eyes" we find all sorts of sensations (of warmth, pressure, tension, smell, sound, etc.) and thoughts and feelings; but there's no building them up into a some-thing or some-body who is experiencing them: they just come and go, unembodied and insubstantial, in this Space

(d) Pointing "with open eyes" to their absence here, check that this Absence or Space isn't filled with the scene—as a pot with water or a room with air—but *is* it

Now let's try some other Identity tests, having special regard to the problem these notes are about.

4. Four criteria for determining Who/What I am

(a) I see that this finger pointing at "me" is pointing at no-thing and no-person, at empty Space which nevertheless is its ever-varying contents of every grade. *These include many aspects and trademarks of my country* from satellite photos to flags, national emblems, Heads-of-State, and so on.

(b) What I *feel* myself to be is equally multi-level and depends on circumstances. Sometimes, as when you fault me, I'm apt to feel like an individual human under attack. But when my family-home is attacked by fire, decay, burglary, debt, sickness… at once (and so smoothly I don't notice the identity shift) I take on that more inclusive embodiment and status. Similarly, I slip into being, briefly or for longer periods and with varying intensity of feeling, my clan, or city, or church, or class, or race… As for my country, should it seem in mortal danger, *I may well feel myself to be more truly it than I am D.H.,* inasmuch as without question I'm willing to give the lesser life for the greater. And similarly in the event of real star wars, one would no doubt feel obliged if necessary to give one's individual life for the life of one's planet or solar system or galaxy, as now for one's country. On the other hand, much of the time it's a case of shrinking rather than expanding, as one identifies with this one human body; or just a part of it, with its pleasures and pains, as against the rest. Finally, there occur moments of great expansiveness and magnanimity when one feels like—and feels for, and feels as—the Cosmos itself; and, conversely, occasions of great detachment and freedom when one has a sense of relief from all burdens, of having vanished without trace. Indeed, of all these identifications, it is only this ultimate pair—when one becomes All and Nothing—that proves absolutely convincing and satisfying.

(c) So much for what I *look like to myself,* and what I *feel like.* It is amply confirmed by what I *look like to others.* What my roving observer makes of me is a function of his range and instrumentation. At a few metres he finds a man, of course. Retreating, but keeping the same spot in view, he's presented with, in turn, my family-home, my home town, my home country, my planet, my solar system (star), my galaxy, my space dotted with light-points, my Space. Or else, approaching this spot instead of backing off, his tale is of a limb or organ, of cells and then one cell, of molecules and then one molecule, of atoms, particles, and—once more, at the point of contact—of nothing at all, of Space. In short, whether he goes into what I consist of, or what I amount to, it turns out to be No-thing, and Every-thing; and, in between, things or embodiments of every grade, *including my country.*

(d) Finally, what do I need, to be myself? To be D.H. I find I can spare none of these embodiments and levels. What is he, for instance, without his country and planet and star, to say nothing of his cells and molecules and atoms?

To sum up now: having brought to this all-important question of What/Who I am these four very different criteria, I have arrived each time at virtually the same answer. Namely that (a) what I look like to myself, and (b) what l feel like, and (c) what I look like to others, and (d) what I need in order to be me, is No-thing, and Every-thing, and all that lies between those extremes, *including (I repeat) my country.* These four findings, confirming one another, leave me in no doubt about my true Identity.

5. A country enlightened

There is a Mahayana tradition that, when Gautama Buddha was enlightened, all beings belonging to all realms were at that moment enlightened too. The Zen master Hui-hai says that enlightenment is necessarily the enlightenment of "all one's interior beings". And of course it's Self-evident that no human *as such* can grasp the fact that he or she isn't really a human being. This Void which I perceive myself to be is the true Nature, the Inside Story, of all levels of my embodiment-identification. In particular, it's the fundamental Nature and Inside Story of my country, of the Nation-State of which D.H. is a citizen. MY SEEING INTO WHAT I AM IS AS TRULY THIS COUNTRY'S AND THIS SPECIES' SEEING AS IT IS THIS MAN'S. Actually, (at least in its more superficial aspects) this identity shifting from citizen to State, from national to Nation and back again, is a commonplace of political life. Louis XIV had good reason for his notorious boast: "L'Etat c'est moi." So had mediaeval kings and their feudal courtiers reason for addressing one another as "France", "Burgundy", "Essex", and so forth—as if in recognition of the paradox that to be human is to be much more (and much less) than human. Statesmen and politicians are in this no different from the rest of us. The main theme of *The Hierarchy of Heaven and Earth* is that, more or less unconsciously, we are all the while ascending and descending the hierarchy of being, and feeling quite at home whatever level we happen to be functioning at.

(Take some concrete examples of this hierarchical mobility. Looking at you now and taking you in thoroughly, I forget and dissolve and make nothing of those pleasant and unpleasant interior bodily sensations I was having a moment ago. They absent themselves, making way for your presence—a happy substitution! Turning next to my newspaper's foreign affairs page, I lose touch with you, along with the rest of my fellow nationals (as such), whose many domestic problems vanish into the Void here which now is filled with a picture and an account of the October parade in the Red Square. I remain the selfsame Void, but now it reads as one country or power-bloc taking in another, wholly occupied by it. Finally, for relief, I go outside into the twilight, and await the appearance of those heavenly bodies which accompanies the disappearing of this heavenly body with all its troubles: my star is darkened and goes out so that they may come out.)

Note three crucial points here. *First,* it doesn't take a number of Seers to see for my nation or my species. (The notion of multiple consciousnesses or centres of awareness is without foundation anyway, as Schroedinger—among many others—has pointed out.) No, just one will do. The quotations prefacing these notes are evidence of how widespread and perennial this realization is. *Second,* my nation and species—like every one of its members—is already perfectly enlightened. (The Void, which is the reality and core of all beings, What they are living from, is never somewhat void, more-or-less empty.) *Third,* in the truest sense my country is even now unilaterally disarmed vis-a-vis every other country, in spite of all those bystanders' views to the contrary. For the two parties involved, confrontation is illusory.

6. *Confrontation a myth*

Whatever I happen to find at the far end of the bag (in the experiment familiar to the readers for whom these notes are intended)—whether the face of a heavenly body, or a country, or a person, or an animal, or a cell...—the set-up (face-there to no-face-here) is more than asymmetrical in the ordinary sense: whatever I find over there I find its matching absence here. CONFRONTATION IS IMPOSSIBLE— even in the slightest degree. It is to (C), the third party, the one who puts the questions to (A) and (B) in the bag, that their confrontation seems so real; but he, being way outside the bag, is in no position to see what's going on in there. For him, they are opposed to each other; for themselves, not at all.

So it is with nation (A) vis-à-vis nation (B). They *appear* to be in opposition, to be up in arms against each other, but *in reality* they are not. Or you could say that each has already won the war and is perfectly secure because it has developed (or rather *is,* intrinsically) the ultimate or subnuclear bomb which destroys the Universe in toto, blasting it to speckless Nothingness—a weapon compared with which the nuclear bomb is a toy. (This Big Bang, which is even now the end of the old Universe and the beginning of the new one, is the theme of our experiment/demonstration called *The Machine:* it is designed to give a vivid and first-hand experience of the eternal moment of absolute destruction-creation.) Alternatively, you could say that (A) and (B) have both taken refuge in the only bomb-proof and nuclear-winter-proof Shelter. Or that underneath them, as underneath all the performers in the cosmic circus, is spread the Untearable Safety-net of their true Nature. And so all is well!

7. Why, then, doesn't peace break out?
Just as all men are already living from their true Nature and *in this basic sense* are perfectly enlightened (Ramana Maharshi, like many Zen masters, used to insist on this) so also are nations, the members of the body politic. What's more, there exists the conscious recognition that one's own enlightenment is multi-level and (as we've seen) no less national than individual, so that one's country also is already enlightened *in this higher or more mature sense.* But in that case, why is the effect so hard to find, indeed hard to believe in at all? What's holding up the poor wise man who by his wisdom—his

fully conscious in-seeing—saves the city? What's he not doing that he could do?

In fact, he *is* effective, but inevitably subject to one of life's strangest paradoxes. It is this: what drives him to fight the prevailing all-too-real error is his recognition that it is itself erroneous and unreal, what drives him to work for future peace is his vision that unbreakable peace is established now, what drives him to work tirelessly for non-confrontation as between humans and as between nations is the certainty that confrontation is impossible anyway. Put another way, he lives at two levels—an active one at which there's everything to do, and a contemplative one at which all is done. *And this way of life is the only way to be effective in the long run:* one-level action just doesn't work out.[1]

Three highly practical considerations emerge at this point. *First,* that the genocidal in-fighting, the civil war that at one level is tearing our species apart, can be moderated only by conscious contact with that ultimate level which is our true Nature and Peace itself. *Second,* that no such contact—however brief—can occur without some effect at all levels, albeit mostly invisible, seeing that this Nature is also the One Power, the Source of all, What makes things go. *Third,* that this contact with What-one-is needs to be maintained and matured through several stages before it can do its job well.

---

1 "What do they accomplish?" asks St. John of the Cross, speaking of well-meaning people who go into action without first gaining, through contemplation, the skill to act appropriately. "Little more than nothing", he answers, "and sometimes nothing at all, and sometimes harm."

8. The stages of social enlightenment

Briefly, we distinguish the following stages of social maturation corresponding to those of individual maturation as outlined in the final chapter of the new version of *On Having No Head*. [Published in 1986. Ch. 4: *Bringing the story up to date: The eight stages of the Headless Way*.]

(a) *Social infancy and childhood:* Sumerian, pre-Iron-Age, matriarchal society with earthy deities and little or no weaponry or organized warfare. The individual isn't yet clearly aware of himself as such, as an object, a separate thing, a 3rd person. He is still 'at large'.

(b) *Social adulthood:* Bronze-age and Iron-age patriarchal society with sky god(s) and organized warfare. The individual citizen is increasingly aware of himself/herself as a separate entity, a 3rd person. The results include a slow explosion of greed, hate, fear, anxiety, aggression... among individuals and among tribes and nations.

(c) *Social Seership:* During the past two millennia or so Seers have arisen who have begun—by assiduous practice—secretly to establish, within the old social pattern of confrontation, one of non-confrontation, in which greed, fear, hate, and so on, cease to flourish. They experience actually belonging to such a community, *now*. The social effect can hardly be doubted.

(d) *The Barrier or Dark Night:* But now there looms a terrifying Barrier, a Dark Night which is none other than the present threat (and perhaps the future reality) of the Nuclear Holocaust and Winter.

(e) *The Breakthrough* is none other than the same unconditional surrender to the Nature-of-things which is incumbent upon the individual Seer, but now manifesting at the social level. Not a *policy* of national altruism and unilateral disarmament (what chance of that?) but a thorough *recognition* that in reality such disarmament is a present fact, that any kind of confrontation is illusory, and that for this reason (as for more superficial and obvious reasons) neither side can win.

My enlightenment is mature and fruitful in my *personal* life insofar as I have entered and come through the Dark Night of the Soul, by subordinating my partial (confrontation based) individual will to my total (confrontation-free) will, that of the Whole of me. Equally it is mature and fruitful in my socio-political life insofar as I have faced and overcome and emerged from Mankind's Dark Night, his Nuclear Winter, into the Spring of no-confrontation.

Or (as some would say) insofar as I have died to myself and been reborn as mySelf. It's up to me to tell the truth about myself—to see it and feel it and to be it steadily—the paradoxical truth that not only as this person but also as this nation and power-bloc, I am reduced to Nothing, am absolutely vulnerable and defenceless and therefore absolutely safe! For this Nothing here—now alive to itself as such—cannot threaten or be threatened by any insider (there is none); and this All here—again alive to itself—cannot threaten or be threatened by any outsider (again, there is none). The ball is in my court. I can no longer sidestep my responsibility for my country—or, for that matter, for my species, or planet, or indeed universe. My taking it all on board is my coming to spiritual maturity. And in fact (mature or not) my enlightenment is that of the world, or else mere delusion. I have no medicine for cosmic and social well-being that I don't have to take as a person.

But is this secret medicine sufficient? The social sickness may be mortal and is no secret at all, while its cure—my spiritual ripening—is slow, unsure, and seemingly as yet quite ineffectual. Surely new, specific, objectively manifest measures for peace, involving masses of people, are called for. If enlightenment is the price of peace, surely it will need to become more like the norm than the rare exception it is now. And, for this to happen, mankind's motivation for seeking enlightenment will have to be stepped-up hugely.

9. *Motives for Enlightenment*

Consider the merits of various motives for seeking Enlightenment. Any motive is 'good' inasmuch as it gets you going along the Path, and keeps you going. On the other hand, all motives are 'bad' inasmuch as they are necessarily, in the beginning, egotistical. Accordingly there's little to choose between (a) the motive of the neurotic worldling who pursues Enlightenment in order to gain for himself poise, efficiency, and peace of mind, and (b) the motive of the spiritually ambitious monk who does so in order to become "holier than thou", and (c) the motive of the philosopher-scientist who does so to satisfy his burning curiosity about himself, and finally (d) the motive of the worker who is so devoted to the cause of peace that he or she will do almost anything in that cause—*even hopefully, pay the needful price of realizing non-confrontation (or unilateral disarmament) at the personal level:* the motive, in short, of one who goes all out for

Enlightenment (under another label, probably) in order to save the species. In fact, it is arguably the last of these motivations which is the most altruistic, as well as the most fitting to our time and needs, and which promises to become the most powerful and widespread. For one earnest meditator or would-be mystic there are thousands of equally earnest peace workers who—skilfully approached—could become profoundly interested in the peace that already obtains between any two contestants, the peace that, because it's perceived as *real* now, is much more likely to be *realized* in the future. *This way, the worker has the certainty of being onto a good thing, a winner.*

10. International workshops for peace

A variant of our own workshops, specifically directed at the politico-social level, will not be difficult to contrive. Here is an example of an old, well-tried and effective experiment, so adapted.

(a) The Leader gets participants into pairs facing one another (either in or out of the paper bag), and asks them whether they are in reality face-to-face, *confronting* each other, etc.

(b) The Leader tells participants to shut their eyes while he sticks a small flag (U.S., U.S.S.R., China, or 3rd World) on each forehead. In some cases he puts two flags, in others no flag—he just pretends to stick one. He explains the rules: *no talking, no looking in mirrors,* no fingering one's sticker.

He explains that everyone now has to get as quickly as possible to his/her own country indicated by his/her forehead sticker—each of the four corners of the room having been previously identified with a large flag.

(c) Eventually, after most people have been led to their 'right' corners, the Leader gets them into the same pairs again. He then asks them further questions about confrontation, but this time the experience is at the national level, since people 'know' now what flags they wear. They face each other 'across a conference table' representing their countries.

(d) Participants discuss the lessons of this experiment.

An alternative would be a similar workshop consisting of invited representatives of 3 or 4 or more countries with conflicting interests. Each participant would gain an experience, from his Openness, of thinking for and being each of the others in turn.

Many or most of our workshop experiments could be similarly adapted, and other points brought out. For example, additional light could be thrown on R.F.'s "Seattle effect", and his concern to bring China as a third party into American-Soviet negotiations:— The set-up involves just one pair of people (A & B) labelled with flags as before, and facing one another (in or out of the bag), while the Leader (C) asks questions about confrontation. This leads to a discussion about the idea that, since the symmetry of the A-B set-up is being taken care of by C, they can with less fear of annihilation relax into being asymmetrical: the apparent thinghood of both being the business of C out there, they can more confidently perceive their real no-thinghood here.

It's important, in this sort of workshop, and the following sort, to avoid references to religion, enlightenment, etc. Any ticket that gets us home to the Place we're at, our true Nature, is a good ticket, no matter how secular.

11. Workshops for negotiators

These also could be quite easily devised, bearing in mind the following:—

It's a well-known gimmick, while selling insurance, etc., for the salesperson at some point to move over to the customer's side of the table and, instead of looking *at* him, look *with* him at the documents—thus hopefully clinching the sale. It's no large step from this procedure, at conferences of greater moment, *not* to leave the shift-over from confrontation to no-confrontation till the side-by-side signing of the eventual agreement: but instead to negotiate from the fact of no-confrontation all along. This is not to adopt a position of weakness by coming *more or less* "naked to the conference table" (Aneurin Bevan) but a position of strength by recognising the fact of one's *complete* nakedness, one's absolute Openness to what's presented by the other side, plus the ability of that Openness/ Source/ Reality to respond creatively and appropriately. This isn't to *change* the situation, but to become *aware* of it: however, this awareness could not fail to make immense differences. Recognizing the truth of no-confrontation works for individuals in their private capacity— eliminating fear and hate and suspicion—and cannot fail to do so when the same individuals are functioning in their national and international capacities. To put the matter crudely, the best way to sell insurance is also the best way to sell peace. Of course!

Enlightenment For Peace

Nor do *both* sides have to adopt this most realistic of procedures, for it to succeed. When I secretly let you in to my Space or No-thingness here you *cannot* refuse the invitation: I make it hard for you to hold on to your thing, your entrenched position. Openness is terribly catching! This is the secret of "motzuing".

And, once more, let's remember that this Enlightenment—however temporary and however motivated—is (a) all-or-nothing and 'perfect', (b) as truly that of the nation as of the individual, and (c) all the better for being de-mythologized and reduced to plain horse-sense.

Concluding footnotes

To bring peace to the world, become it. The lasting and deep effectiveness of our work depends on our faithful practice of Self-awareness at all times. Note that this isn't getting caught in the Utopia trap. (Utopias, realized, are Orwellian.) The evolutionary quantum leap from conscious 3rd personhood to conscious 1st personhood, even if it were to become the norm, would not mean Humanity's pacification. Rather the reverse! Life is conflict, and the more life the more conflict. What one can hope and work for is conflict jacked up to a level where because it is more alive and vigorous, is no longer genocidal.

At times of discouragement, in particular of despair lest any of our political bosses can be interested in Enlightenment for peace, let's remember that Chinese Emperors and other potentates from centuries B.C. have been more than just interested. And remember that, now, the motivation for this concern-at-the-top is potentially so much greater, and the means of communication are quite transformed.

These notes are about *real* communication: that is, the vertical and many-level sort, not the horizontal and one-level sort which is the mere appearance of communication.

To illustrate this: in real (structured) Space as against abstract (uniform) space, A, in order to affect (touch, address, get at, change, kill...) B, has to traverse the A←→B interval: which is to advance through the nest of B's regional phenomena/appearances (whole man, limb or organ, tissues, cells, molecules...) and finally to share his central Nothingness. Conversely, B, in order to respond, has to traverse the nest of A's regional appearances and share his Nothingness. In other words, all communication is actually via our true Nature as Void. (Cf. the philosophies of Leibniz and Malebranche, and *The Hierarchy of Heaven & Earth*, XIV.)

In order to be Enlightened for peace, it is unnecessary to understand this—or indeed any of the more 'difficult' parts of the foregoing notes. The only essential is the steady perception of—and submission to—one's No-thingness/Every-thingness. It would be unhelpful to burden friends with more of the underlying philosophy of Enlightenment than they feel a need for. We all have different jobs within the One Work, all of them equally demanding.

As R.F. says, Humanity needs a positive and dynamic peace which is much more than an absence of hostilities: a peace which is at least as 'difficult'—as creative, as adventurous, as thrilling, as intellectually and emotionally and practically challenging—as war was and still is, if the Nuclear Holocaust is to be avoided. These notes propose a Peace which—at once infinitely easy and infinitely demanding—couldn't offer more of a challenge to Humankind. In any event, is there any other prospect for Peace?

* * *

Chapter 49

CONFRONTATION: THE SUICIDAL LIE

The lie is that you are what you look like. That your reality there for yourself resembles your appearance here for us. That right where you are is some-thing which is shutting us and everything else out, instead of no-thing which is taking it all in.

For our part, we can check that you are no-thing by gradually going right up to you with a camera, fitted with increasingly powerful lenses. Our photographs show you vanishing finally into Space.

For your part, turn to anyone present (your face in the mirror will do) and check that you are Space for that one. Examine the evidence now, as if for the first time. Observe how the given set-up is face to no-face, two little eyes to one immense 'Eye', coloured-shapes to no-coloured-shapes, opacity to transparency, sound to silence, motion to stillness, strife to peace, content to container... Always asymmetry, non-confrontation—for the 1st person singular, present tense.

Every animal and infant—no matter how naturally combative—lives this way, unconsciously, from its Space, its no-thingness.

Only Man contrives to thing himself, to block his Space with a This to set against every That. Confrontation is his game, the million-year-old stroke of imaginative genius to which he owes his survival, his astounding success, all he holds dear...

And all that now terrifies him. For, like other fallacies,

Confrontation eventually lets us down—in the course of our life as individuals and as nations, and now as a species. It has become counter-productive. Its survival value is turning into extinction value. Ignorant of the cause of our plight, of our basic error and its basic correction, we despair.

The human sum can be put right only by going back to where it went wrong: by re-discovering and consciously living from our no-thingness—from the Space which (like a mirror) is unstained by what it's taking in, yet one with it. A few extraordinary people—seers following various religions or none—have, over the past 5,000 years, been doing just this. And now at last, as the saving truth becomes de-mythologized and obvious, it is available to us ordinary people—in sufficient numbers and in time (we trust) to reach our leaders before imagined Confrontation ends in real Omnicide.

To help break the deep-seated habit of overlooking our Space—which is our common ground—let us share the seeing of it, and actively participate in Humanity's second (and more realistic) stroke of genius, its new and even more challenging evolutionary adventure.

If a lie could work such wonders, what could the truth not do?

* * *

Chapter 50

CONFRONTATION: THE GAME PEOPLE PLAY

Abstract

CONFRONTATION is the primeval and basic game played solely by people *as such*—that is, by beings who clearly perceive themselves to be *human beings*—and not by infants, retardates, some so-called schizophrenics, even the most intelligent of animals of course—and liberated 'seers'. The many particular games people go on to play are sub-games deriving from this single source-game, and until it is unmasked and halted they will go on proliferating.

* * *

There are five indications that CONFRONTATION is a Life Game in the Transactional Analysis (T.A.) sense. (1) It is surreptitious, not candid, and goes on unrecognised for what it is, with our implicit or explicit approval. (2) It progressively reduces and spoils our natural intimacy, spontaneity, and sensory awareness. (3) Fear, anger, distress, and manoeuvers aimed at avoidance are typical responses to its threatened unmasking. (4) From being through its earlier history a 'good' and necessary game, it is fast becoming (just because it is a game and dishonest, and therefore in the end self-defeating) a 'bad' and indeed suicidal one, crying out for our immediate recognition and counter-measures. The urgency is underscored by the many-sided threat it now poses to its players, to people everywhere, to the very survival of humanity and many other species. (5) The fact that, having been learned by each of us, it can be unlearned, and the fact that it is superfluous and can with immense and all-round benefit be opted out of, are demonstrated by the lives and teachings, over the past 3,000 years, of some notable non-players—'seers' belonging to all religions and none—whose numbers seem to be somewhat on the increase.

1. Acknowledgement

This is not a newly uncovered game to be added at the foot of the ever-lengthening T.A. checklist, but a revised version of *The Face Game* (Harding, 1967), widened here to take account of the dominant social issues of our time, and re-titled accordingly.

2. The ploy

At first tentatively and intermittently, the young player at CONFRONTATION learns to pretend that s/he is what s/he looks like.[1] She persuades herself that her central *reality* there for herself—what she is in her own experience at zero metres—resembles her regional *appearance* over here at (say) 2 metres, picked up by us her observers. She comes to believe that she *finds,* right where she is, a human something, a face, a substantial body, all the makings of a grown-up personality—charged with the feelings which, withdrawn now from their real objects out there and foisted onto this false

1 From now on, to avoid this clumsy device, 'she' should be taken to mean 's/he' or 'she and/or he'. Similarly 'her' and 'herself' should be taken to mean 'her/him' and 'herself/himself'.

central one, are (quite unknown to her) progressively contaminated by its unreality (Cf. Macmurray 1935). Now for her it's exactly as though she were coming from a human *something* which is shutting us and everything else out, instead of from a non-human no-thing or absence which can't help taking it all in.

This initial pretence gradually hardens with use and social pressures into a firm conviction approaching hallucination. The resolutely adult player *sees* herself as this human being encountering that human being in an I-and-thou, evenly balanced, reciprocating relationship. Instead of seeing what she sees—to wit, the absolute asymmetry of the set-up—she sees what she thinks she sees, is told to see, expects to see. If all goes well—or, rather, goes according to society's undisclosed plan—the impossible project of *thinging* herself, of merging her native 1st-Personhood with her acquired 2nd/3rd-personhood, proceeds so smoothly that in time it's as if the former never existed. Or, if the 1st-Person singular, present tense, is distinguished at all, it's as if it were a private and ghostly version of the solid and public face she presents to the world—instead of what it really is: absolutely *sui generis* and unique.

It is upon this absurd game (yet, as we shall see, needful and initially 'good' game) that human society, indeed humanness itself as at present understood, is founded. Founded on quicksand!

Underhandedly, language sponsors and plays the game in a hundred ploys. Witness the useful and 'harmless' little words *we* and *us,* which lump you and me together in one package like nuts and raisins. Witness, again, language's insistent invitation to you and me to get *face to face*—as if we ever could! Witness once more the unquestioned (almost unquestionable) assumption that you and I as such *encounter* and *confront* each other, and engage in personal relationships—as if this no-thing which I am could have any commerce or commensurability with anything whatever! (Identity yes, relationship never!) And so on (this is a tiny sample) inevitably, for language itself is a brilliant game, and all the more dazzling because it masquerades as our neutral and dispassionate instrument for arriving at the truth, at what's so. Though it can be disciplined to that end, its primary function, as Fromm (1960) pointed out, is to superimpose on reality the fictions we currently live by—which wouldn't matter so much, perhaps, if those fictions were not, in the long run, fatal.

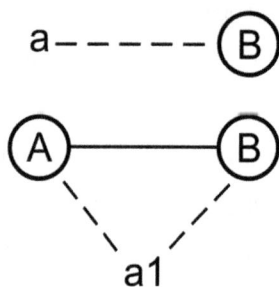

The underlying ploy of CONFRONTATION is simple. Player (a), faced with Player B here and now, compulsively jerks herself out of that central position where she is timelessly no-thing, into the peripheral position (a1) where she pictures herself as a something having a past and a future as well as a present appearance, for herself no less than for B. She escapes from the 1st-Person, who is only now and O.K., to the 2nd/3rd-person, who is—rather than has—a more-or-less not-O.K. history and outlook. In short, she becomes eccentric by (say) 2 metres, and there lives the life of a jerk: a pretended life, for in fact she can never side-step what and when she really is. The dodge is a transparent subterfuge, because at (a1) she is still nothing, still just capacity—this time for *two* things, namely A and B, symmetrically opposed.

But the trick she plays on herself passes unnoticed. Robert Burns, praying for the gift "to see ourselves as others see us", is asking for that too-freely-given and backhanded gift which is threatening to destroy us all.

3. *The role of science in the game*

A peculiarly crooked and disastrous move in CONFRONTATION is our dismissal of science just where it most needs to be taken to heart. At this point we play Ignorant or Unscientific, as if we were at least four centuries behind the times, and certainly pre-date Leeuwenhoek and his microscope.

To clear up this fear-induced obscurantism we need to extend the method and findings of science to *ourselves* at the basic physical level where our thinghood or objective aspect is about to vanish and our no-thinghood or subjective aspect about to emerge. Then, and then only, we are no longer compulsive jerks, and are free deliberately to exercise our ability to leap off-centre and promote ourselves to the rank and dignity of human beings. This is no game—so long as the empty centre and its peripheral filling are not confused.

For its own ulterior motives CONFRONTATION muddles our central reality and our peripheral appearance to the limit. In fact, it relies on a threefold confusion. First, it pretends that one's peripheral *human appearance* at a few metres reveals one's central reality and true identity. Second, it pretends that one's myriad *non-human appearances* (picked up by the receding observer who views this centre from distances ranging between an ångström and light-years) are comparatively unreal and irrelevant to that identity. Third, it pretends that one's *disappearance* at the centre, at no distance from oneself, doesn't happen at all. And so one doesn't just trade one's true and entire identity (namely Awareness of oneself as no-thing and everything) for one's partially true and partially false identity (as a small selection of those things at every level from particles upwards): but trades it for one's false identity (as just *one* of those things, belonging to just *one* of those levels). The perceiver 'becomes' what's perceived in the mirror, held at just one angle and one distance. Of all cases of mistaken identity the most mistaken and least innocent.

And the tragi-comic irony is that nowadays we are captivated by the picture books and films (e.g. *Powers of Ten* shown at the Smithsonian Institute, Washington) which should make "seeing who and what we are" far easier than it has ever been. We are thrilled to join the scientist as he zooms in from afar *on someone else,* on point X over there: and finds X taking shape as a galaxy (The Milky Way), a star (The Solar System), a planet (Earth), a city, Ms Smith, her tissues, cells, molecules, atoms, particles—and *almost* empty space, or something like twists in the space-time continuum. But at that critical juncture, so near and yet so far from Ms Smith's innermost 'substance', his story and our interest peter out, just short of their tremendous climax. But if he were at this point humble enough to consult the real expert, and ask Ms Smith herself (who alone has access to X, is stationed O ångströms from X) what *she* finds there; and she were truthfully to reply "No-thing replete with everything", why then he would bring his Odyssey to its triumphant conclusion. His tale would come to that perfectly fitting and elegant denouement towards which it had all along tended. And it would dawn upon the truly thorough physicist that he is his own wholly accessible and reliable sample of the elusive "ultimate substratum" of all things; his own free entry ticket to the place X, where nothing remains but Awareness of these things.

What's more, he would be shifting the weight and authority of science from our endarkenment to our enlightenment, and from our science-powered and science-bedevilled game of CONFRONTATION to its science-inspired antithesis.

4. *The origins of the game*
Of course the time, place, and circumstances of the original invention by proto-humans of the art of eccentricity—the art of being beside oneself and self-alienated—are lost beyond recall in pre-history. We could speculate endlessly about how there arose this distinctive human knack of looking back at the looker as if through

the onlooker's eyes, so discovering what was far from obvious—namely—that "really" one is a "normal" human complete with face, back, background, and so-forth, just like the rest of them. But, never mind *how* it happened, there's no doubt *that* it happened: perhaps a million years ago, a precocious child, or a reflective woman, or a profoundly threatened man, or maybe a family, gifted with supreme genius, did make this astounding jump, this quantum leap with nothing predictable or gradual about it, this lateral or side-stepping move at right-angles to the species' linear progress up to that point.

Thereafter the future belonged to the mutant type ("mutant" in the general sense of an evolutionary discontinuity and breakthrough, of course, rather than in the strictly biological sense). It not only survived, but at an ever accelerating pace flourished at the expense of the old type, thanks to the immense practical advantages conferred by its new mode of consciousness. Once under way, there was no halting this fast evolving species until, coming down towards historical times, the once-rare self-objectifying mutant had taken over and become the norm. Not, however, that the ability to take a cool and steady look at oneself 'from outside' became the universal rule among humans (many still leap back and forth as small children do) but that long ago it became the taken-for-granted standard against which human maturity is measured.

It is when we come to the development of the individual human, of the infant and the child, that our clues about the initial and decisive leap multiply; for here—as at the biological level—ontogeny recapitulates phylogeny, and the creeping development of the species is reflected in the meteoric development of each of its members. We are born pre-human, as 1st-Person singular, present tense, innocent of all 2nd-and-3rd-person complications, and for *ourselves* immense and at large and wide, wide open to take in our world—"space for it all to happen in" is how one child described himself to the author. But almost from birth the long and arduous (and never quite complete) process of self-objectification sets in.

5. *The development of the game*

It would lie far outside the scope of this paper—as well as this author's competence—to discuss in detail the development of the normal child's self-consciousness. From Piaget on, a vast amount of patient observation, testing, and reporting has gone into this crucial field of research. All it is necessary to do here is to highlight one particular aspect—for us a critical one—of that development: namely the child's adventures with the mirror. Four stages can be distinguished:

(1) The newborn infant gives no sign of picking out its reflection in a mirror as at all special. That face is just one of the ingredients of its world.

(2) The young child—up to around three years—refers to that face as another's; or else, if it is taken to be hers, it belongs *out there.*

When Joan is told to go and wash, she proceeds to the bathroom and starts washing—washing that dirty face in the mirror.

Kate, looking in the mirror, asks: "Has that little girl got a Mom, too?"

(3) More and more that mirrored face and head, though presented over there, are taken as *really* here, as *really* one's own and planted

firmly on these shoulders—a trick of remarkable complexity and ingenuity (and deviousness) involving the magical transportation of that head through a distance of around one metre, its twisting round to face the opposite way, the doubling (at least) of its size, and its setting up as a permanent and indispensable and very concrete object occupying (bunging up) the very centre of one's ever-changing world. And yet—this is the crowning wonder—no-one actually *experiences* such a blockage here. Everyone *lives* wide open at the centre, while pretending otherwise. (No: touch does not reveal a *head* here—that is to say an opaque, coloured, hairy ball, all present and complete— but a collection of *sensations* which are nothing like a *head*. A minor move in the Confrontation Game is denying this self-evident fact.)

That game is now in full swing, and the player, fitted up with a central headpiece of her very own (she fantasizes), is face-to-face with all comers, in symmetrical relationship with them. She may go on to play the game with moderation and half-heartedly, or very earnestly, even desperately. Sartre (1969) gives the telling example of the awkward waiter—compulsively putting on his act to the embarrassment of all around:

> All his behaviour seems to us a game. He applies himself to chaining his movements as if they were mechanisms, the one regulating the other; his gestures and even his voice seem to be mechanisms; he gives himself the quickness and pitiless rapidity of things. He is playing, he is amusing himself. But what is he playing? We need not watch long before we can explain it: he is playing *at being* a waiter in a café.

More generally, he is not only playing at being a waiter-thing, but playing at being a human-thing, playing at being any sort of thing at centre. He is playing a very hard version of the Game *People Play*, which is to feign an actor occupying the middle of the stage, in his case the café. And yet, simply by choosing to notice that *for himself* he isn't in the café at all, but instead the café is in him—the whole scene, proprietor and chef and customers and all—he could transform himself *for them* into the most charming and graceful and expert waiter in Paris!

6. The game's rewards

All the same, and despite such pitiful cases as the French waiter, this basic game does yield such an impressive and many-sided array of advantages that one might be tempted to doubt whether it is a *game* at all, and not rather that indispensable strategy whereby proto-humans cleverly become humans, and they in turn become—in some happy instances—almost super-human.

For, to be even handed, when examining the spectacular rise of *Homo sapiens* over the past million years or so, it is hard to find any achievement of value which doesn't owe its very existence to the assiduous practice and elaboration of our game. In almost all respects in which people surpass other animals, they rely on the unique faculty of contemplating themselves objectively, dispassionately, honestly, and overcoming the wishful thinking and self-conceit and personal bias that are the hallmarks of crude subjectivity and in every way crippling, a recipe for social and individual stagnation if not decline. In fact, the realization of one's full potential may fairly be described as the difficult and often agonizing—but mandatory—process of learning to acknowledge and assess one's limitations, one's strengths and weaknesses, both as a human and as *this* human. Which in practice means, again, doing one's best to see oneself through another's eyes.

In short, are we not dealing here with a *procedure*—with, you might say, *the* procedure? That is to say "a series of simple complementary Adult transactions directed towards the manipulation of reality" (Berne, 1966). To help us finally to decide, let us now look at some of its *disadvantages,* its cost to the players.

7. *The social cost of the game*

At first far outweighed by its social, political, economic, and cultural benefits, the cost of playing CONFRONTATION appears negligible—at least for the winners. The family or tribe or nation that happened to be led by an elite capable of viewing themselves and their skills and resources objectively, in contrast to their less self-aware rivals, stood every chance of overwhelming them, until they were pushed into remote and inhospitable corners of the earth, or enslaved, or wiped out. The winners' serious troubles began when social groups of comparable status, well matched against each other in the complex business of CONFRONTATION, found themselves interlocked in conflict, and moreover armed no longer with flints and inert weaponry of bronze and iron, but weaponry powered by gunpowder, TNT, and finally atomic and nuclear energies. Now the very nature of warfare—that is, of large-scale CONFRONTATION—is transformed. There are no winners, only losers. Now it's a case of STOP PLAYING—OR PERISH! And so what began as a wonderful life-enhancing gain for the fortunate ones is threatening to end as a dead loss for all players, as their mass-suicide pact.

And really the prospect of such a sinister outcome should not unduly surprise. For the alleged confrontation between a pair, their symmetry, (as we have seen from the start) is fundamentally fictitious, the bogus product of their learned and willful blindness to the given facts. In short, it really is a game, and even the best of games lets its players down in the end. (Who can seriously doubt that dishonesty isn't, in the longest run, the worse policy?) Here, our dishonesty promises to let us down all the way and with an almighty bang into the Nuclear Winter, a sterile Planet, premature elimination from the cosmic Olympics, and deserved oblivion. The final profit-and-loss account of the human enterprise we are all partners in is on the point of writing off in a few terrible minutes every plodding gain made through tens of thousands of years—at what cost in blood, toil, tears and sweat, and intelligence, love, and undaunted enthusiasm?

8. The cost of the game to the individual player

Before attempting to calculate the price the newborn infant is required to pay personally for the high privilege and rich rewards of ascending to human status, let us remind ourselves of the native advantages that infant enjoys, and stands to lose by growing up.

Our question must be: what is the infant *for itself,* in its own uncensored experience? Our answer, which at least approximates to the truth, is fourfold. *First,* the infant is wide, wide open, speckless space or room, free from thinghood and qualities or limitations. *Second,* the infant has no means of standing apart and distancing itself from and *disowning* whatever sensory or perceptual ingredients are currently occupying its space: so that as their *owner* it is richer than all the Gettys in the world lumped together. *Third,* the infant is immense, boundless, at large, nowhere and everywhere. *Fourth and last,* the infant is quite uninhibited, fearlessly spontaneous, without ulterior motives or considerations, and of course game-free. And all of this the newborn infant is due very soon to lose, to the extent that it gains humanness.

From a very early age our learned view of ourselves from outside begins to overshadow, to superimpose itself upon, and eventually to blot out, our original view of ourselves from inside. We have grown down, not up! Instead of remaining present and together with the stars—and all things under the stars—we have shrunk away and withdrawn from them. Instead of containing the world, it now contains us—what's left of us. And so, reduced from being the whole scene into being this tiny part, is it any wonder if you and I find ourselves in all sorts of trouble—if for example we grow greedy, resentful, alienated, frightened, defeated, tired, stiff, unloving, plain crazy? Or, in more detail:

Greedy—as we try to regain and accumulate at any cost as much as possible our lost empire;

Resentful or aggressive—as we seek revenge on a social order that has cruelly cut us down to size;

Alienated, lonely, suspicious—because we morbidly imagine that people, and even animals and inanimate objects, keep their distance from us, are aloof and stand-offish: and we refuse to see how that distance telescopes to no distance (try measuring how far they are away, while noticing what happens to your tape when read end-on); so that in reality they are nearer than near, our bosom companions and intimates;

Frightened—as we see ourselves to be things, up against and at the mercy of all other things;

Defeated—because working for this separate thing is making sure of failure: the probable end of even our most 'successful' enterprises is indifference or boredom or disillusion, the certain end is this thing's death and dissolution;

Tired—because the building and maintenance and constant adjustment of this imaginary box for living in—a box packed solid—uses up so much energy;

Stiff, solemn, unspontaneous, phoney—because we're living from a lie, and from a lumpish, inflexible, predictable, petty, limiting lie, at that;

Unloving—because we shut all others out from the volume we think we occupy, pretending we are not built open, not built for loving;

Crazy—because we 'see' things that aren't present, and actually believe (in the teeth of all the evidence) that we *are* at 0 metres what we *look like* at 2 metres—solid, opaque, coloured, outlined lumps of stuff. How can our life and our world stay sane if their very centre has gone insane?

Insofar as we *don't* suffer from these multiple handicaps we remain "little children at heart", transparent, lightsome, and more or less unconsciously in touch with our true nature. In fact the only reason why so many of us get by, and don't fall chronically ill or go raving mad, is simple. If, in our day-to-day lives, we are quite often sensible, loving, generous, laughter-filled, and even happy, that is because all of us—no matter how frantically we are playing CONFRONTATION—are still established in and living from our space, our native no-thingness. Even our most lethal of games is peripheral. In the unenclosed space which is our Common Ground games are banned by the Local Authority. Centrally we are never tricky or divisive. *At heart, we are perfectly all right.*

But only at heart. In fact our plight as (seemingly) individual humans, though less dramatic than our common plight as a species, is scarcely less alarming. For to the degree that we play CONFRONTATION we are desperately miserable on a hundred counts. And of course the two plights are so interdependent that they are really two aspects of the same trouble—namely CONFRONTATION being played simultaneously at all levels from private citizens to power blocs. And, beyond these, dragging into our game all the species of our Planet as well.

9. Unmasking and arresting the game
Clearly understanding the moves and consequences of CONFRONTATION, as outlined so far, certainly does make for

moderating it. Much more effective, however, than this intellectual work—and indispensable in practice—is actually seeing through the game's deviousness, actually seeing the absence of any player here.

Only you are in a position to observe and spell out exactly what's central in your life. No-one else has inside information. On this matter you are the sole and genuinely Local Authority whose decision is final, and I must accept whatever you report. What I feel free to do, however, is earnestly to ask you to carry out one or two simple experiments lasting seconds, the aim of which is to turn your attention around to the place you are at. On your willingness to actually *do* these experiments now, instead of just *reading about* them, depends whether this paper is going, to make sense or nonsense to you.

Kindly turn to anyone present (your face in the mirror, or the face pictured here, will do) and check that you are experiencing yourself as the space or capacity that is taking that face in. It is essential to attend to the evidence dispassionately, *as if for the first time.*

Isn't it true that the given set-up is that face-in-the-mirror vis-à-vis this no-face-where-you-are; those two little eyes vis-à-vis no eyes at all where you are (or, if you prefer, one immense Eye);·opaque and coloured and moving shapes all around vis-à-vis transparent, colourless, motionless, absence of shape where you are; and so on and on indefinitely? Isn't it always ASYMMETRY, NON-CONFRONTATION—for the 1st-Person singular, present tense?

Finally, to make quite sure, please point to the place you are looking out of and discover what *on present evidence* it is—FOR YOU.

If your findings do not agree with mine, I have no quarrel with them, but suggest you don't waste your time reading any further. On the other hand, if we do on the whole agree about what is given, then we have made the second quantum leap—back into the game-free life—and the easy part is over. Now the hard part begins. It is consciously staying put, in the place you and I never left. In other words, maintaining the insight, and more and more living from it.

Every animal and infant—no matter how combative—*lives* this way, "unconsciously", from its space, its no-thingness. Natural and unlearned, guileless, spontaneous, and by-and-large making for survival and maybe life-enhancement, its bouts of aggression do nothing to solidify or build itself up: and therefore are quite different from even the least confrontational of human games. Only Man contrives to materialize himself, to block his space with a This to set against every That. CONFRONTATION or PARITY is his game, the original stroke of imaginative genius to which he probably owes his survival up to recent times, and certainly owes his astounding success, practically all he holds dear...

And all that now terrifies him. For, like lesser fallacies,

CONFRONTATION sooner or later fails us, in the course of our life as individuals and as nations, and now as a species. Having in almost all respects become manifestly counterproductive, its initial survival value has gone into reverse and become extinction value. Ignorant of the cause of our all-round crisis, of our basic error and how it may be corrected, we despair.

The human sum can only be put right by going back to where it went wrong—by unveiling and consciously living in the brilliant light of our no-thingness—of our SPACE which (like a mirror) is unstained by what it's taking in, yet one with it. A few extraordinary persons—some of them non-religious or even anti-religious—have for thousands of years been doing just this. And now at last, as the saving truth about ourselves becomes de-mythologized and almost embarrassingly obvious, it is available to ordinary persons who are neither specially good nor specially gifted—and in sufficient numbers (may we hope?) to reach our leaders before imagined confrontation ends in real genocide, or rather omnicide and indeed geocide.

10. Resistance to exposure

The only real obstacle standing in the way of our deliverance is the unacknowledged but massive irrational resistance we all put up to the simple act of turning around the arrow of our attention and noticing, not just what we are *looking at,* but what we are *looking out of.* In fact it is this resistance, and the distress that accompanies its breaking down, which finally clinches the fact that we have here a typical game, and in its later stages, a very hard one indeed. The fight against disappearing, against melting into thin air, commonly manifests as terror, or anguish, or blank incomprehension, or fury, or mixtures of these. In the author's experience over the past 25 years, when people sense that there is a danger of their looking in and finding they are out, they may suddenly be taken ill, have hysterics, fall asleep, tremble, weep, or indulge in verbal or occasionally physical violence: all of which is, of course, an oblique tribute to the immense power and significance of this threatened exposure of oneself to oneself.

The underlying reason for such reactions isn't difficult to unearth. None of the arrows of our attention, when aimed outwards, threatens the archer. All of them, when turned round and aimed inwards, strike home and are instantly fatal—fatal not merely to the archer's humanness and life, but also materiality, and somethingness, and very being. The fear of plunging into the black tunnel of one's void nature is indeed well-based, for it is the profoundest of terrors—that of absolute loss and annihilation—and the tunnel has to be gone through if one is ever to emerge at the other end into the daylight vision of one's absolute gain and incomparable safety. *The truth is that, as a supposed something, I am not even that puny thing, but a pitiful non-entity, an agonizingly aching void, while as No-thing I am Every-thing and my heart is satisfied.* It's as simple as that, as easy to understand as that! And hugely difficult to go on seeing steadily, day by day.

11. The non-players
And not just difficult (one feels inclined to add) but impossible! Or, if possible, at least thoroughly impracticable!

Confrontation: The Game People Play

What is sometimes called the Perennial Philosophy, or mysticism in the highest sense of that much abused word, vehemently disagrees. Indeed for countless dedicated Buddhists down the centuries, as for serious followers of the other great spiritual traditions, the key experience isn't merely *knowing* about one's "natureless nature", but the heartfelt and sustained realisation of it. Delusion or bondage is none other than the unquestioned assumption that one really is a separate item in the world, and accordingly condemned to a life of fear, frustration, and misery. Conversely, enlightenment—alias satori, liberation, self-realisation, awakening—is actually *seeing* (it's not for nothing that spiritual adepts are described as seers rather than hearers or touchers or smellers, and never as thinkers) actually *looking in* and discovering that one is nothing whatever in oneself, and therefore filled out with the endless goods that are on offer—and indeed identical with them, seeing that nothing remains in their way. *And* actually following this insight up—here's the rub!—by going on from the mere and occasional *seeing* to *living* in the bright light of what's seen, putting it into daily and hourly practice until it becomes one's natural way of being.

In short, these adepts in the spiritual life are discovering what ceasing to play CONFRONTATION really means. What's more, while it's true that some of them were 'failures' in the sense that they succumbed outwardly to bitter persecution and came to a sticky (more often fiery) end, many more were incredibly successful at whatever practical tasks they happened to undertake: thus showing how—in this case pre-eminently—playing games is handicapping oneself, and ceasing to play is likely to release unrealised potential, tied-up energies, and extraordinary flair.

St. Catherine of Siena was a case in point. She declared that her endeavor was "to bring people to perfect knowledge of themselves, so that they will know of themselves that they have neither existence nor any grace." And certainly she lived in that knowledge. Yet not only did she do good works of many kinds, but intervened so effectively in the affairs of Church and State that she changed history.

Catherine was a genius and outstanding even among saints, of course, but she demonstrated how—contrary to popular rumour and priestly restrictive practices—no matter what the odds against it, seeing into one's voidness and behaving accordingly are natural and above all immensely practical.

Of course it is the sustaining of this 'work' that is so demanding as well as so rewarding. And no wonder! The unremitting effort, beginning soon after birth and going on till death, which we put into learning to play CONFRONTATION, demands an equally unremitting effort to undo that game of games. But consider what is now at stake—not only one's own happiness and efficiency and indeed sanity, but also the continued existence of us all! Our current motivation is—certainly it should be—far greater than in Catherine's troubled but less apocalyptic times.

It is suggested that Transactional Analysts have an additional reason for laying bare and undercutting this master game. For in doing so are they not beginning to excise, in one deep and labour-saving operation, its otherwise interminable and malignant outgrowths?

12 The role of religion in the game

This suggestion certainly doesn't imply that analysts should relax their professional standards, abandoning a scientific approach and venturing into the undisciplined and risky field of religion. For *religion*, in any regular sense of the term, will never stop—let alone put into reverse—the ever-accelerating onrush of CONFRONTATION. Quite the contrary, as the whole of its history, from the Bronze Age to our time, horrifically proves. It fuels that game.

However the true *spirituality*—involving a fundamental shift in consciousness—which secretly lurks at the living centre of the great religious traditions (and is in most respects their very opposite) holds out the only real hope for our doom-bent species, and rather more than just hope. In its thoroughly de-mythologized form it is essentially one and the same regardless of its style and language, and of the cultural context in which it happens to arise. Simplicity itself, its message may conveniently be summarized thus:

Seeing this No-thing/All things which-I-am is also seeing what all beings are intrinsically, seeing we are all at root One—namely the Being/Reality/Awareness which different traditions give different (and not necessarily holy) names to. And if we will only tend our hidden Root, then its healthy and harmonious flowering in the form of unique and autonomous individuals, is nurtured. It is when we overlook and neglect our Unity as that Root that we wither and harden into predictable warring stereotypes.

None of this perennial and universal wisdom is for believing: all is for double-checking, and daily testing. Plainly it is far more secular than sacred, far more the prime discovery of that unifying pure science which humbles itself in front of the clearly given, than it is the blind faith of that credulous and divisive religion which is eager to embrace whatever makes the believer feel comfortable. In fact, to try to arrest CONFRONTATION by taking up any religion which encourages me to find a religious *person* right here where I am, is to exacerbate that game. It says much for Hinayana or Lesser-Vehicle Buddhism that it runs on pure *anatta* or no-self, and of the Mahayana or Greater Vehicle that it runs on pure *sunyata* or emptiness, whereas most other traditions select various 'essences', or rich blends of somethingness and nothingness. Nevertheless the central *experience* of all real seers, whatever their persuasion, is of exactly the same Clarity, Transparency, Absence…

Moreover all seers have, implicitly or explicitly, solved the most insistent and poignant of all life's problems, which is the Death that looms at the end of it.

13. DEATH as a game stemming from CONFRONTATION

About the genesis of the most threatening of games "I Was Born and Shall Die", and the progress of its complementary ulterior transactions towards a predictable end, there is much to be discovered and discussed. Here we can only go into it briefly, sufficiently nevertheless to illustrate how particular games derive from the master game of CONFRONTATION.

Confrontation: The Game People Play

When I tell myself "I'm going to die" *I flatter myself! I never lived!* And obviously, *what never lived will never die.* What never was will never cease to be, and certainly never begin to confront anything. And when I add that my human death will all-too-soon be followed by the death of my species, I am repeating the same mistake at the social level. At all levels DEATH and CONFRONTATION are two sides of a coin—for me a counterfeit one.

Of course, like everything else when viewed from outside, I'm something that has a beginning and an end. Every *thing* perishes—from a particle to a person, from a species to a galaxy. What happens is due one day to unhappen. Only What never got off the Ground never returns to it, never perishes. And in this instance It actually *sees* (in and as its seers) that It has nothing of its own to lose or decay or suffer damage, to start with or end with. No wonder It can never catch itself coming to be or ceasing to be, gaining consciousness or losing it. That is why Its seers call It the Unborn, the Undying, the Abyss out of which life unceasingly springs, and into which it unceasingly dies back. And they *see* that This is what they really are.

And so, once more, the key question I have to put to myself is: am I for myself any thing at all: answering which, by reference to the evidence, not guesswork, I arrive at what some seers call "eternal life".

You would be wrong in supposing that none of these 'subjective' realisations succeeds in putting off disaster and genocide in the 'objective' scene for a moment. For it isn't merely, in the words of Bunyan's Shepherd Boy, that "he that is low need fear no fall" but that he that is beneath all things has, for himself *and for them* put an end to CONFRONTATION itself. And, into the bargain, made all things admirable and astonishing, paragons of achievement: compared with nothing, what *isn't* worshipful, if not lovable? Freed now, by dying, from the menace of Death, there is at last no obstruction to *having* Life, to *enjoying* Life, to *loving* Life. It is a condition that cannot be isolated. To say the very least, it is catching. Who can say it is not already catching on, just in time to inoculate us against our specific disease and its dreadful prognosis?

14. *After CONFRONTATION, What?*

We cannot do better than to revert to Eric Berne (1966) on this question:

> For certain fortunate people there is something which transcends all classifications of behavior, and that is awareness; something which rises above the programming of the past, and that is spontaneity; and something that is more rewarding than games, and that is intimacy.

Which answer we would expand and adapt, by way of concluding this paper, as follows:

After CONFRONTATION, the truly autonomous and game-free life begins, and it has three aspects:

Awareness, which means a simultaneous *two-way* seeing into oneself as bare Capacity, and into its contents as they come and go, in all their vividness and variety.

Spontaneity, which means delightedly allowing whatever behavior and impressions come up in that Capacity to be what they are, without monitoring or interference.

Intimacy, which means, not a sentimental and self-regarding love, but submission to the factual basis of real love: which in turn means consciously vanishing in favour of the loved one, joyfully giving place to him or her, and in a true sense giving one's life—and more—for him or her, and ultimately *being* him or her.

Firing evenly on all three cylinders, the game-free one-seater spins along happily.

Happily? What about the others? What about the terrible highway-crash that, seemingly, lies ahead? How can the perfect performance of one or a handful of exceptional drivers help to avert the general smash-up that's in the offing? What, to be quite realistic, are the chances that your seeing and my seeing into our true and natureless nature will catch on and spread so far and so fast that the ultimate Accident is indefinitely postponed?

On all common-sense calculations, the chances are nil! But at this level the rules of ordinary arithmetic cease to apply. For when you see What you really are, *who* does so? Is it as your separate, all-too-human self that you see you are *not* this self? The question answers itself! You see This only *for and as* all the other ostensibly separate human selves. Inevitably all are hiddenly caught up in your seeing and therefore profoundly affected.

The Old Testament tells the story of the poor wise man who *by his wisdom* secretly saved the city. Mahayana scriptures tell the story of the Buddha *whose enlightenment* (which was not the achievement or the property of ex-Prince Gotama, sitting under the Bodhi

Tree and watching the Morning Star rise) necessarily involved the simultaneous enlightenment of all beings everywhere and at all times. It isn't you or me, but our 'individual' *withdrawal* from the game of Confrontation, which helps to upset the game: not the functionary but the function that matters. The truly Self-aware individual, no matter how personally limited, is handling an unlimited commodity, and has no way of estimating its spread. In fact, what we call *"her self-awareness"* is nothing of the sort, but Awareness aware of Itself as *already* the Self of all. So let us take heart! (Harding, 1979).

And, after all, what happened once can happen a second time. If the species' first 'impossible' stroke of genius—of that imaginative and game-playing genius which exalted us to human status—could come off so brilliantly, why cannot its second 'impossible' stroke— this time of that realistic and game-free genius which humbles us to no status at all—come off too? At least 3,000 years ago certain 'grown-up people', daring to turn the arrow of their attention through 180°, saw that in reality they were nothing of the kind—or of any kind—but remained as they were *for themselves* when infants: "space for their world to happen in". They began our salvation from ourselves. Thanks to those anonymous heroines and heroes, each of us knows exactly *where* to look—namely IN at what A'Kempis called "the Country of Everlasting Clearness", at that Boundless Region upon which the sole 'inhabitant' is the sole Authority. And exactly *when* to look—namely NOW. And exactly *how* to look—namely AS IF NEVER BEFORE!

And now at last we have immeasurably the most powerful motivation in humanity's amazing history for doing just that.

Conclusion

Ultimately there is just *one* Bag of tricks, to unzip which is to let them all out of the bag; *one* Game of games, whose halting stops the rest. It is the Game played with one's false self for partner, learned with difficulty, addictive, always handicapping, usually a lifelong charade or non-stop putting on of acts. Underlying them all is the Pretence that the Place one is forever at, and can least afford to remain ignorant of, is the most unexplored and unexplorable, dangerous, to-be-avoided region in the universe. Or, if it is real at all, the Pretence is that the air of this "Country of everlasting clearness" is murky to the point of solidity, anything but absolutely transparent. Of the whole repertoire of self-deceiving tricks, this is the most tricky and most fantastic. But it didn't take Shakespeare in:

> But man, proud man!
> Drest in a little brief authority,—most ignorant of what he's most assur'd,
> His glassy essence,—like an angry ape,
> Plays such fantastic tricks before high heaven,
> As make the angels weep.

The beginning of Man's cure, of the only remedy which treats the specifically human disease rather than its symptoms, is its deliberate intermission *now*, just long enough to notice there's nobody *here* suffering from it.

* * *

APPENDIX

Before CONFRONTATION—The newborn infant

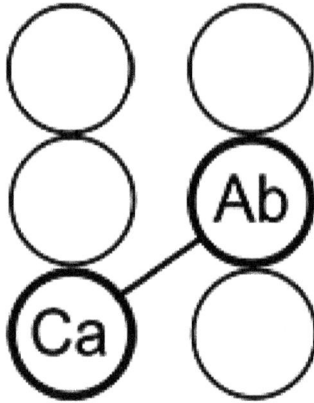

Note (fig. l):

(1) Asymmetry, the Game has not yet begun.

(2) As yet only one ego state C(a)—that of being no-thing for oneself.

(3) For oneself one has the single aspect of thisness/nothingness at C(a), and others have the single aspect of thatness/somethingness at A(b) and aren't yet differentiated into P, A and C. [**P**arent, **A**dult and **C**hild] The realization that one is also All, the Alone One—i.e. the P(a) aspect of C (a)—hasn't yet dawned.

During CONFRONTATION—The grown-up

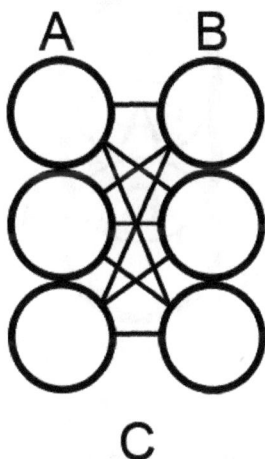

Note (fig. 2):

(1) Symmetry, the Game in full swing.

(2) Here is the Analyst's view (at C) of the games going on between A and B—who stop playing insofar as she enables them to place themselves at her vantage point.

(3) However this quantum leap out, so needful for arresting their game, does nothing to arrest the underlying game of Confrontation. For this, the following very different remedy is proposed.

After CONFRONTATION—The seer

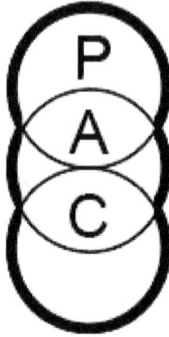

Note (fig. 3):

(1) Asymmetry restored, the Game stopped.

(2) C(a) is the seer's *basic* ego state—living "like a little child" from empty space.

(3) A(a) finds this state works, in practical affairs.

(4) P(a) is the seer's *ultimate* ego state, the I AM (cf. the seer Meister Eckhart: "Only God can say 'I'."). But in fact it's as if these three ego states merge into One state, with three functions P, A, C.

(5) For this One, B doesn't exist as a separate identity.

(6) Berne (1961, p. 57) describes a happy person as one whose P, A, C, are *syntonic*. No wonder that the seer, in whom they *merge*, should experience bliss (*ananda*).

* * *

References and bibliography

Berne, E. (1961), *Transactional Analysis in Psychotherapy.* New York: Grove Press.

Berne, E. (1966), *Games People Play;* London: Deutsch.

Catherine of Siena (1980), *The Dialogue.* New York: Paulist Press.

Fromm, E. (1960), *Zen and Psychoanalysis.* London: Allen & Unwin.

Harding; D. E. (1961), *The Universe Revalued,* in *Adventures of the Mind,* ed. Thruelsen & Kobler. New York: Knopf.

Harding D. E.(1967) *The Face Game* in *Transactional Analysis Bulletin,* April.

Harding D. E. (1974), *The Science of the 1st Person.* Shollond Publications.

Harding D. E. (1979), *The Hierarchy of Heaven & Earth, A New Diagram of Man in the Universe,* Introduction by C. S. Lewis.

Harding D. E. (In press), *On Having No Head, Zen and the Rediscovery of the Obvious* (New version). Introduction by Huston Smith. London: Routledge & Kegan Paul.

Macmurray, J. (1935), *Freedom in the Modern World.* London: Faber.

Sartre, J-P. (1969), *Being and Nothingness.* London: Methuen.

Transactional Analysis Journal. (October 1984), Special issue on Nuclear Disarmament.

Chapter 51

FACING THE YELLOW FLOWERS

Prajna is unconscious, but facing the yellow flowers it functions.

Hui-hai

I have just come back from a visit to my long-time farmer friend Bill, with much to brood on. Usually we talk about such pressing matters as how to keep the car on the road, the house warm, the vegetable garden pest-free and well manured. But this time, like the good host he is, he soon brought the conversation round (at least I think it was he) to the topic which he knows is nearest my heart—to our True Nature, meditation, and so on. Concerning which I found myself becoming more-than-usually long-winded—and a little sharp with him, though he took it in very good part.

The facts that struck me afresh as incredible were these. For close on twenty years (Bill readily agreed) he has been seeing quite clearly (on those occasions when he bothers to look, which is likely to be when I'm around) what he is in-and-for himself, his ultra-human reality at centre, in striking contrast to the very human appearance he presents to us some feet off. He couldn't see the infinite difference more clearly—or find it less boring! SO WHAT? he asks, predictably.

Of course this standard response is a yawn, not a question. But on this occasion I felt it called for an answer, and a rather elaborate and vigorous one, at that. Along the following lines.

SO WHAT? So this, for a start: *you transcend all limits.*

Turning your attention round 180º, to what you're *looking out of* as well as what you're *looking at,* you see that you are space with no edges or fence round it, space so huge and so empty that it easily finds room for that wide sky, that hurrying procession of clouds, those trees and that grass-patch, that easy-chair and expanse of carpet, those fidgety hands and knees. You thought you were small, local, tethered to an observation-post. Now you see how wonderfully large and at large you are. You imagined you were in the world, now it's obvious that all along it has been in you. Obvious that you are not a needle lost in some cosmic haystack (what would it be doing in all that fodder?) but the haystack itself. And you find these discoveries far less interesting than how many m.p.g. your car is doing! Or why the last repair bill was £20 too much!

Again, SO WHAT? So this: *you are infinitely rich.*

Notice how *inseparable* is this space-that-you-are—this wide openness or boundless capacity or room—from its contents. How that bright sky-blueness isn't a pigment or dye applied to your upper space: it's the self-colour of that region of it at this time, *your* colour. Notice how that cloud isn't a cauliflower-like shape haunting your space: it's that space itself, you yourself assuming just that curious form just there. You cannot take on the capaciousness which you are without taking on its wealth of filling. It's the nature of these goods to *present* themselves to you, to make a present of themselves to you, and your nature unquestioningly to receive their endless benediction. Moreover the way you have them is real having, real ownership, the only real ownership. For plainly no *thing* (such as that hand) can possess another thing (such as the magazine it is holding): each must shut the other out from the volume it occupies. Whereas you, who are plainly no-thing, must take in and incorporate all the things on offer, including just now both magazine and hand, plus sky and clouds and all between, because you alone are built open, built infinitely receptive and enrichable. Just look and see! And that's not all. You aren't required to collect your possessions. You just take delivery on the doorstep. (In fact, their distance from you was never more than a convenient fiction. You didn't subscribe to it when you were very young; and even now a tape-measure, stretched between you and that tree, or that church tower, or whatever, must for you read as a dimensionless point. And if you were an astronomer you would know that the star you are photographing is in your observatory and not way out there, in some remote region where it could well have blown up centuries ago.)

If you heard a vague rumour that you'd come into some modest property or other—say a terrace of houses—you'd think the matter worth looking into. And here's real news that you've inherited unlimited property—real estate, indeed—and you dismiss it as of no interest at all!

SO WHAT? you repeat. So this: *you are absolutely perfect, just as you are.*

You can see that you are already complete, incapable of improvement or deterioration. Just look in again at the clarity, and observe that it's not only unbounded (trace its edges if you can) but speckless, unclouded, unstainable, incomparably safe, and (above all) aware of itself as this many-sided perfection. And just because it's in itself so pure and innocent and inviolable, it's also infinitely fertile, infinitely productive of this endless display of sights and sounds and smells, of feelings and thoughts, bearing every kind of quality and value. See, for example, how naturally and effortlessly you are taking shape as—and giving shape to—the myriad leaves of that tree, every roughness of that carpet's texture, all the tints and lines on the palm of that hand. Everything is at once perfectly *itself* in you, and perfectly *yourself,* yet perfectly incapable of damaging you. What more could you want?

SO WHAT? you ask. So this, I reply: *you are forever at rest, the ultimate tranquillity.*

Look and see. Others may make the claim "we shall not be moved", you realize it. In fact it's the hallmark of the objects that inhabit your space that they won't stay put, or stay at all, but are always coming and going, forever on the move. It's a restless world, and all its agitation is going on against the background of unshakable stillness that you provide. Next time you drive your car, simply come to your senses. Stop believing the lie that you (I mean the real you, the one that's taking in the whole scene) are travelling through the countryside at 50 m.p.h., and instead submit to the self-evident truth that it is travelling through you at many speeds—the telegraph poles very quickly, the mountains and clouds very slowly, and everything between at its own pace. Next time you go down a corridor, see what you see instead of what you've been told to see. See it going down you, being swallowed up in your immensity-immobility. And really your native stillness is nothing new in your experience. Maybe you have never been drunk enough, or been in an accident serious enough, to find the road leaping at you. But surely, sitting in a stationary train, you have (supposedly) moved off, only to find it was the other train that was doing so? In fact, you never again need to seek perfect rest, but simply to be it, to relax into what you are—while noticing it's not the peace of exhaustion or sloth but an unflappable poise, a live steadiness packed with action and energy, including all those hands and feet get up to.

SO WHAT? you insist. So this: *you can never perish.*

Even the most durable inhabitants of your space, having had a beginning, must have an end. Even galaxies and solar systems and planets—like their species and individuals down to the tiniest of their particles—have their proper life-span, ranging between billions of years and billionths of a second. Every *thing you're aware of* perishes, including that visibly ageing thing over there in your mirror. But space, the *aware no-thing* right where you are, zero feet away, is evidently quite incapable of the slightest change, let alone of ageing and death. No wonder you can never catch yourself losing or gaining consciousness, coming into existence or going out of it. Having no history of your very own, you are cleared to provide the stage on which history is enacted. Consciously unborn and undying, you aren't in time: time is in you. And, if you doubt this, note what time it is out there now some ten inches away, according to your watch. Is it a fairly reliable instrument? Do you promise to trust it? Very well, then: slowly bring it forward till it is no distance away, and read off what time it is right here. See how time doesn't come to a stop at a particular date and hour in a false now, but at no particular date and hour (the numbers having vanished) in the real and eternal Now that you are. Why, your own humble wristwatch is trying to show you what should be obvious, that at centre and in reality you are timelessly for ever!

SO WHAT? So this: *you are.*

Look and see. At centre and in reality and for yourself you are not this or that, not someone or other, not a something or a somebody at all. What you can say with complete confidence is: "I AM". The awesome fact, your true dignity, isn't *what* you are but *that* you are. You have absolutely no notion of how you got round to being, or how you are managing so brilliantly to keep it up. This wonder of wonders is by far the most precious gift you possess, to which all those we have looked at so far are quite subsidiary, and by comparison side-issues, even trivial. And you don't want to know! Are you secretly *terrified* of your own splendour?

SO WHAT? So all this, and much more than this. Once you dare to look within for yourself at yourself without prejudice, you will find that *in every respect you are precisely the opposite of what you were brought up to believe!*

To sum up, then, so far: it has been pointed out how quite obviously you are boundless and free-ranging and at large, that you are far richer than all the tycoons on Wall Street rolled into one, that you are already perfect and safe from harm, that you are truly stable, that you will never die, and that above all you have that most incredible of gifts—the art and the skill to *be*. Well, these news items are only a small selection from the inexhaustible truth about yourself, a mere glimpse of the answer to your rhetorical question: *so what?*

My friend Bill had to agree (not for the first or last time, I guess) that, given a few minor reservations, all this is the case, that such is his true nature and identity. And on this occasion he went so far as admitting (with no enthusiasm at all) that this cornucopia of blessings isn't just the answer to what we all want and spend our lives vainly sweating for—namely, freedom, security, wealth, true dignity, and a sure way of holding back the black shadow of death—but also the *perfect* answer and the *only* answer. Only by seeing what we really are can we get what we really want.

And still the refrain: SO WHAT? Wonder of wonders, *what we most need is most accessible—and most resisted.*

* * *

I came away baffled, as so often on other occasions and with other friends. But this time I was more than usually determined to make some sense of the puzzle, if not actually to solve it.

Consider the facts. We have all surrounded ourselves with protective layer upon layer of fiction and illusion, of conventional pretences, games, put-on acts, cover-ups. Yet, reluctantly and when under sufficient pressure, we are willing to have our outer armour stripped from us piecemeal, by faithful friends and (more likely) by life itself. Convulsively we hang onto our inner carapaces, the hard shells that shield our ultimate nakedness. Yet even these may, in desperate circumstances, be penetrated. But what we will resist to the death is the final exposure of our total vulnerability as in fact our total security, the blessedness that holds all our hearts could desire. And when all else is stripped from us, our final protection against our central splendour is a weary "All right, so this is the way it is, and it's something I don't much care to know." The ideal wet blanket for putting out the flame of life, let alone of life becoming self-aware.

Shakespeare pours contempt on this obscurantism. (And if his stricture seems a harsh one, look at the history of what man does to man.) The reason why man remains "most ignorant of what he's most assured, his glassy essence" (alias his void nature) is that his wilful blindness allows him to go on behaving "like an angry ape, (who) plays such fantastic tricks before high heaven as make the angels weep."

All too true, no doubt, but hardly the whole story. In fact, we shall see that there exists a deeper and less discreditable reason for that ignorance, that boredom or indifference. That reason is what the rest of this article is about.

* * *

It's as if this world of delusion-based suffering—all stemming from the universal and obligatory fiction "I am this separate human"—were a flat landscape, wearing an overall sameness. Except, that is, for one outstanding and (in almost all respects) unique landmark—a towering monument that combines features of a sacred temple, a strong fortress, and a centre of healing. Dominating the countryside, it is there for all to see—all who want to.

It is the shrine of "I AM". Or, in more detail, "I'm not this or that, but unlimited, and *in all respects* the opposite of the miserable thing the world told me I was." This stronghold extends to everyone the prospect of a safe refuge, the true treasure and meaning the world so woefully lacks, the cure for all its ills. Not the meretricious gifts the world tempts us with, which soon wear thin or wear out and may well prove curses in the end, but instead lasting ones geared to what we are and need, to what's so, to reality.

And what happens? The near universal pretence is that this magnificent temple-fortress-clinic doesn't exist at all, or else is either a fraud or a mirage. The great majority turn a blind eye to it, don't spare it a second thought. Some, however, do take notice, and draw near and explore the structure tentatively from outside, even venturing to peep in occasionally. Almost all find, along with my friend Bill, that that's quite enough, thank you! A powerful instinct warns them off. They sense an unknown danger, much more terrifying than those the surrounding world is so full of. Nor, as we shall presently see, are they wrong.

The rare adventurer musters the courage to go right in, driven to desperation by his or her plight outside, or fascinated by the atmosphere of the place, or more likely for no conscious reason at all. Disillusionment follows. Inside, the splendid fortress of "I AM" is roofless and quite empty, a mere façade.

Worse is to come. Venturing a little further, he finds there is no floor. He slips into a bottomless chasm, where, in an infinite regress, he is stripped of every vestige of humanness, of life, of opacity and substantiality, of thought and feeling and mind in general, of existence, of consciousness. The promised life-refuge of "I AM" is exposed as a mere front for the fatal trap of "I AM NOT". But it does fulfil a triple purpose: it serves as a safety-barrier marking the abyss and ensuring that the many keep their distance; as an attractive bait drawing the inquisitive few towards their destruction; and, for the very few who actually take the bait as a chute or funnel discharging them into the gulf where their destruction is total.

And the concluding surprise is that this truly total annihilation turns out to be its very opposite also. In fact it is that absolute decay and death which is the only real remedy for death and decay at all other levels, and moreover the only radical remedy for our suffering. And truly this final voiding or self-naughting is the goal—the goalless goal—of the spiritual life in all the great traditions, no matter how successfully they cover it up. How unlike the 'lower' consciousness "I am this human", *and the 'higher' consciousness "I AM",* is this "I AM NOT" which consciousness cannot begin to comprehend, which extends infinitely beyond its furthermost reach. It is unimaginable, mystery beneath mystery for ever, yet entirely real and reliable. And this alone, this conscious unconscious, is the true resource, the sure haven.

* * *

Enough of metaphor and parable. Let's now look at some of the ways in which its seers have tried to define this indefinable, to raise to consciousness this depth on depth of unconsciousness and extol its centrality and power. [1]

The author of the *Tao Te Ching* exhausts himself in the search for apt names for the Way that is essentially nameless. It is no-being, darker than any mystery, empty, lower than low, unstriving, elusive, blank, incomprehensible, shadowy, dim, dull, useless, thin, flavourless, even depressing. On the other hand, and just because it is all of these things, it depends on nothing, is inexhaustible, and here within to be drawn upon all the while.

Like Ramana Maharshi and many other Hindu sages before him, Nisargadatta insisted that our root disease and the cause of all our misery is the illusion "I am this particular person." And its remedy is the realization "I am not this or that, but pure undifferentiated being." But he also goes much further. Neatly summing up the whole matter for us, he announces: *"I AM shows where to seek but not what to seek. Just have a good look at it…* You are the ground beneath being, from which all grows." And this ground is ungrounded, groundless, the very absence of any ground whatever, we may add.

What does it feel like to find no bottom, no basis, for living? "How rich," exclaims D. T. Suzuki, "is the inward life of the man of Zen, *because it is in direct communication with the great unconscious…* This unknown, once recognized, enters into ordinary consciousness and puts in good order all the complexities there which have been tormenting us to greater or lesser degrees… As soon as it is recognized that our consciousness comes out of something which, though not known in the way relative things are known, is intimately related to

---

1 For clarity and ease of handling, the quotations that follow are somewhat condensed.

us, we are relieved of every form of tension and are thoroughly at rest and at peace with ourselves and with the world generally." Such are the heartening words that float up (you could say) from one who is falling, for ever, from the known I AM deeper and deeper into the unknown I AM NOT.

In this, Suzuki is echoing such early Zen masters as Hui-neng and his essential doctrine of no-mind: our self-nature realizes itself as emptiness and nowhereness, and this lively awareness of the centrality and depth of the unconscious—this leaning back on this no-support—is the fundamental requirement in the life of Zen. And Hubert Benoit (in that profound book *The Supreme Doctrine*) is echoing both Hui-neng and Suzuki when he declares: "You are unhappy because you are established in consciousness instead of in the unconscious."

It is here that the old conundrum crops up: however can the unconscious rise to consciousness without leaving behind all that distinguishes it from consciousness? As if darkness, craving attention, were to come into the light! Zen has its own solution to the puzzle— one that is all the more convincing in practice because it defies the analytic intellect. In an inspired image, Hui-hai declares: "*Prajna* (that perfection of wisdom which is our true nature) is unconscious, but facing the yellow flowers it functions."

Much later, the Japanese Soto master Dogen has the famous passage (the importance of which cannot be exaggerated): "To pursue Buddhism is to pursue the self, to pursue the self is to lose the self, to lose the self is to be enlightened by all beings." Not, please note, to enlighten them, but the other way round. (And by what other means, indeed, could the unconscious be enlightened about itself, but by seeing what it comes up with? What it comes up from is inscrutable darkness. Nothing exists there to be enlightened about.) And later still, Eugen Herrigel, drawing on the same tradition, or rather on the same first-hand experience: "All things, seen from their origin, are equal, have an absolute value. *Their origin or ground can be perceived only through them.* You see, with absolute certainty, that things *are* by virtue of what they *are not*. To the degree that their formless origin is inaccessible and inconceivable, things in their concrete form become more accessible. Bathed in the light of their origin, they themselves are illuminated." All of which is nut-shelled in the great saying of Zen: *nirvana is samsara,* without which there is no *nirvana* at all.

Let's put the whole matter rather differently. It has been essential, up to now, to make much of the absolute contrast between our central reality and its peripheral appearances. Now the time has come finally to transcend this distinction—by altogether abolishing it. Sloughing off the many layers of my appearance (which others handle out there) I concentrate on the one here that sheds them, on what they grow out from, the reality right here. Only to find this reality isn't real at all! I was all integument—skin laid on skin—enclosing a vacuum. What reality I have *is* all those appearances, exactly as picked up by all observers at all ranges, whatever their instrumentation. Was it Oscar Wilde who made the joke: reality is keeping up appearances? By no means just wit for wit's sake, and far truer than he knew.

It may come as a mild shock to some readers to learn that a

number of the really great Christian mystics, not content with establishing all known things in the unknowable, describe God himself as, intrinsically, incomprehensible. His very nature precludes self-knowledge, is unconscious. He wakens, he comes to awareness of himself only via the other, in and through his eternal Son, and, through the Son, as immanent in the cosmos. Losing track of himself altogether, he discovers himself in all creatures: and this is indeed the most intimate and undiscriminating love. (You would hardly expect the Creator to be more self-centred than Dogen's Zen man, would you?) Thus Eckhart: "The end is the mystery of the darkness of the eternal Godhead, and it is unknown and never will be known. God dwells therein unknown to himself… Seek him in such a way that you will never find him… He is a not-God, a not-mind, not a person or an image. Sink eternally from something to nothing in him." Eckhart's disciple Tauler speaks of "the fathomless abyss, bottomless and floating in itself, which is much more God's dwelling than heaven or man is. No thought has entered there." And that remarkable woman, the Blessed Angela of Foligno, confesses: "I put all my hope in a secret good, which I apprehend in a great darkness. All creatures filled with God, the divine power and will—all is inferior to this most hidden good. The other things bring delight, but this vision of God in darkness brings no smile to the lips, no devotion or fervour to the soul… Yet all the countless and unspeakable words and favours of God to me are so far below this vision of God in darkness that I put no trust in them at all." And, with unparalled conviction and eloquence, the Blessed Jan van Ruysbroeck speaks of "the uncomprehended light, wayless and fathomless". If we could know and comprehend it, it would fall into mode and measure, and then it could never satisfy us. Only because it is ineffable and abysmal is this "wild darkness of the Godhead" our sure refuge.

And now just to show that Sufi masters, too, are with us, here is Rumi: "A thing which is not to be found—*that* is my goal."

Such is the cloud of witnesses, addressing us from contrasting cultures and epochs, who should encourage us to risk all for all and venture deep into that forbidding (and, by common agreement, forbidden) fortress, and take the consequences.

Finally, I would like to throw in my own testimony. I certainly don't find myself swaying on the brink of a fathomless abyss, trying to decide whether or not to let go and take that dreadful plunge. I'm already clear of the brink and well in, *and have never been anywhere else.* All I have to do is to see and submit to that perfectly self-evident fact. Of course it's just as easy for me as it is for you the reader to pretend that the abyss is an object safely located far off in fairyland and most unlikely to open up in this neighbourhood: and so attempt to evade and forget the whole issue. As if I could! No: *the abyss is right here, and I'm staring into its depths right now.* In fact it's the one feature of my universe which is always present, always brilliantly on show, quite inescapable. And if you, dear reader, will stop thinking about it just for a moment and look straight in, along the appropriate (and very easy-to-find) compass bearing of your 360°, why you too will find yourself staring into those same transparent depths. And you will be seeing exactly what all those witnesses are witnessing to, and what this article is all about. And you will be beginning to appreciate how inexpressibly obvious the essential vision is, and how inexpressibly mysterious is your source, and inexpressibly and finally *satisfying.*

* * *

Reverting now to the start of our story, it is easy to see why my friend Bill instinctively backs away from the shrine of I AM, with its tremendous implications. Bill knows what's bad for Bill. He senses that no-one, having entered, can settle down inside and enjoy the spectacle of his or her own splendour and its variegated perfections; and that there's a sense in which the splendour and perfections are unreal, mere expendable titbits, a specious lure held out to draw the unwary to their destruction.

This does not mean, however, that the inexhaustible mixture of 'commonsense' fictions and blindness and downright lying which keep the world going is valid after all, or that the true seeing that reverses them is invalid. It remains the hardest and most verifiable of facts that, when in all simplicity you dare to turn your attention right round to yourself, looking in at what you're looking out of, then you are indeed that I AM—immense, speckless, infinitely well off, deathless, and all the rest—and that seeing and living this is sanity itself and the only antidote to the world's suicidal madness. Yes, indeed! *And* plainly you are in no position to enjoy this sane and true seeing while teetering on the edge of the chasm of I AM NOT. Only when you look up at the yellow flowers from below are they quite real. Only when your seeing arises consciously from the chasm of unconsciousness can it be sustained and steady, and altogether authentic—*because that's the only place it comes from anyway.*

And it's only through and as the world *just as it is*—deplorably untidy, forever tearing itself apart with contradictions, with all its shades of grey to black—that you become yourself and self-aware: through and as the world which fixes you up with all degrees of truth and untruth for you to become aware of. Let's take those yellow flowers, flourishing on the very brink of the abyss, as standing for the special truth and beauty and practicality of the very near regions of consciousness where I AM is at home, along with all its treasures, because it is not self-supporting, because it is consciously and utterly dependent upon its unconscious source, upon I AM NOT. As for the outer regions of the world, why they are bound to be more and more confused, dreamlike, fantastic, and very likely horrific, as they are more remote from their source.

Only as viewed from the only place it really can be viewed from —from its ineffable origin right where you are—is *all* of it quite bearable, and acceptable, and indispensable, and for saying YES! to unreservedly. *Nirvana* is *samsara,* warts and all.

* * *

Chapter 52

THE PRINCE OR PRINCESS, THE TADPOLE AND THE FROG

An Enquiry into the Natural Child, the Spell-binding Parent, the Spellbound Child, and the Spell-lifting Adult

Abstract

In the opinion of Steiner (1975), "The first and most important concept... which·Berne introduced to psychiatry is embodied in his aphorism 'People are born princes and princesses, until their parents turn them into frogs'" (p. 2). The present paper, taking this view, examines its historical background and its theoretical and practical implications for today. It goes into such questions as: How does the parent work that magic? What are the essential differences between the prince or princess and the frog? How does it feel to be the former, then be reduced to the latter? Can the mature frog learn to reverse the magic spell and turn itself back into the prince or princess? Which is the deep therapy—this abrupt switch of identity, or gradually becoming a more together and self-sufficient frog jumping energetically round the bog? To what extent is this slow development the precondition of that abrupt metamorphosis? Does the parental black magic ever disfigure—let alone destroy—the original face of the prince or princess? Or do those royal features remain intact, hidden under the frog-mask that—spellbound—the players have to wear in *The Face Game* or *Confrontation* (Harding, 1967, 1986)? If the aim of TA [Transactional Analysis] is that one should become game-free (Berne, 1964, pp. 178 ff.) and not just trade in bad games for better games, and this means dropping even the best masks one is hiding behind, how is this done? These questions are tackled by the writer—a long-time and enthusiastic TA amateur—in the light of his experience over the last thirty years encouraging people to face that crucial issue: *what is my true (i.e., game-free) identity?* And by the reader who, as a TA professional, is urged to take none of this on trust, but to test all rigorously and in actual practice.

The Prince/Princess

We have four sets of clues—four different sources of information—as to what the natural child (i.e., the prince or princess) really is. And by *really is* we mean what the child is for itself where it is, in contrast to what it looks like to us over here, its central reality in contrast to all these regional appearances which that reality is giving rise to, the insider's story as the subject in contrast to the outsider's version of it as an object.

(i) The first set of clues are supplied by the child directly, before it learns to talk, in the shape of its behavior. Thus the toy that is dropped out of sight is not looked for: presumably disappearance means annihilation. Thus remote objects such as the picture on the wall or the moon in the sky are fingered; presumably distance does not exist for the child. All is taken to be present, no less its own than those legs and arms are. Thus its face in the mirror is not singled out for attention; presumably it is just an ordinary feature of the scene. Thus the child has a way of burying its face in a cushion, then looking up and laughing; presumably it is having fun annihilating and recreating the world.

(ii) As soon as the child starts to talk clues multiply fast. One of the author's young friends burst out with; "I'm very big!" Another (and this in his experience is not unusual), when counting those present, insisted on leaving herself out; counting herself in would (it seems) have been like counting the room in with the people, or the purse with the money. Another, bringing home a panoramic photograph of the whole school, successfully named everybody—except for one total stranger. Herself, of course! Another child, standing in the bath and staring down at himself, exclaimed; "I don't have a head!" One five-year-old boy warned that, if he ate any more rice pudding, he would hit the ceiling; at that moment he did not see himself as a little boy. A Canadian girl, as old as nine years, wrote this poem: "Do you know what it's like to be nobody—just a tiny speck of air, with all those people around you, and you are just not there?" And so on. This is a small sample of the evidence collected by the writer, indicating that the natural child is *for itself* a very different kind of person from the one we perceive.

(iii) The third order of clues, of evidence about the intrinsic nature of the natural child, is furnished much later in life by Seers—so-called enlightened men and women who, claiming that they have regained their childhood honesty and simplicity, announce to an incredulous or indifferent world that they are the very opposite of what they look like to the world. Many of them, for example, declare that, being wholly emptied of themselves, they are wholly filled with others. They experience themselves as nothing but space or capacity for everything. Some point out that distance is for them no more than a useful fiction, and for the rest of us a very costly one. Taken seriously, it progressively parts seer and seen—resulting in alienation from the universe, loneliness, deprivation. Some have come round to looking in their mirrors to see what they are not, to remind them that they could not be less like what they *appear to be*. One Zen master explained he was not sure how tall he was, but perhaps it was around thirty feet! Others stressed their facelessness or headlessness. Most importantly, Seers belonging to different epochs and very diverse cultures have boldly maintained that their true and inmost nature (as distinct from their superficial human nature), in fact the One they all claim they really are, is nothing less than the source and goal of all things, continually creating and destroying and recreating the world. And of course some notable Seers have stressed that the hallmark of their kind is that they have become like small children again. In sum, over the past 3,000 years or so, these exceptional men and women have (it seems) been reliving with great intensity essential aspects of their childhood, and assuring us that in reality they have never outgrown it. Moreover, this inner realization appears on the whole to have been backed up by the Seers' lifestyle—by their spontaneity, their manifest enjoyment of the world's simplicities, sense of fun, capacity for love, grace in movement, and all manner of behavioural nuances that are in the very best sense childlike.

(iv) Finally, we come to our fourth set of clues about the inside story of the natural child—of the prince or princess. It is that crucial and clinching piece of evidence which can only be furnished by the reader of this paper. It requires you to check whether, right now in your first-hand experience, you are still *for yourself* as you were when for others you were a very small child. This means, in particular, checking that you are not *on present evidence* peering out of two tiny peep-holes in an opaque and very complicated and clearly-defined lump of stuff, but are gazing (wide-eyed and single-eyed, or rather no-eyed) out of boundless empty space so immediately filled with the scene that it cannot be divorced from it. That you are not, *on present evidence,* a millionth of an inch distant from this printing, or from the rest of the things around. (Where would you measure to at the "near" end, and anyway how long would the tape-measure read when viewed end-on?) That you are not, *on present evidence,* confronting those faces in the room with one of your own, but resemble a portrait gallery or film show in which they are exhibits. That you are not, *on present evidence,* in this world at all, but rather it is in you. In fact, the writer's suggestion is that there is no end to the rediscovery of the obvious, this reactivation of the natural child in you, once you get the hang of it. And no end to the entertainment and rejuvenation it freely offers.

To sum up so far, then: we have been examining four orders of clues about the original nature of the child. We have noted some of the behavior peculiar to very young children; listened to the sort of thing that older ones have to say about themselves; discovered that childlike Seers tell much the same tale; and have ourselves looked within and (it may be) found exactly what they find: reader and writer alike donning the august mantle of the Seer—as we have a perfect right to do, no matter how brief our exercise of that right. And finally we may conclude that these four pieces of evidence dovetail and support one another. In brief, the writer suggests that we have uncovered our original nature. A worthwhile enterprise, if ever there was one!

Prince/Princess into Tadpole

However, from the start the parent has been busy pronouncing the spell which will soon turn the prince or princess into a frog. Actually into a mere tadpole; it will take decades for that inadequate little creature to grow into a proper, full-size, OK amphibian.

The spell has many versions. Some of them are complimentary—not to say overdone—"What a *heavenly* baby!" "Just look at those rosy cheeks!" "Let's see those dimples, that smile again!" Others are rude. But flattering or the reverse, the effect is much the same—the tadpole is on the way. And the verbal messages are being supplemented throughout by all manner of approving and disapproving nonverbal ones—tones of voice, facial expressions, modes of handling—which are essential ingredients of the magic.

The effect is multiplied as soon as the child begins to understand the wording of the spell. The rosy cheeks and dimples and so on start taking shape. So do other, less charming characteristics. Here is one real-life version of the spell which molds them: "You are not OK. And why? Because you are 'small, dirty, clumsy, in a world controlled by tall, clean, and deft adults.'[1] That's how you must see yourself." [2] But of course this truly bewitching spell, aimed at shaping the child's future but put out as a statement of present fact, too soon does become such a statement. Here is the perfect self-fulfilling prophecy, as the young child, helpless under its powerful influence, gradually learns to cooperate in cutting itself down to size, in becoming not OK, a tadpole in all respects. In short, very like the small, dirty, inept creature which the critical parent perceives.

Before we go further, let us not forget (if our thesis so far is valid) how "in the right" the unlimited child is here, how "in the wrong" is the magic which closes in upon it, how glaring is the lie which that magic pronounces. Who but itself is *in a position* to tell the child who and what it really is for itself at centre, zero inches from itself? Who has access to that spot but its sole inhabitant, who remains through life the one authority on what is there, everyone else being wide of the mark by inches and feet? But how could the young child—that

1 *New York Times Magazine, Nov. 22, 1972, Interview with Thomas A. Harris as quoted in Steiner (1974) p. 10.*
2 This version of the spell, masquerading as a statement of fact, is reminiscent of medieval animal psychology which described the nightingale's song as the passionate outburst of love welling from the bird's heart and addressed to its adored mate, the snake as wicked and filthy, the peacock as conceited, and so forth. In fact, that old-time, anthropomorphism hardly went so far as this modern counterpart, which–in the case quoted–goes out of its way to attribute to the natural child a view of itself which has no relation to the one it surely does have. As we have seen, the indications are that the child is for *itself,* far bigger than the biggest of those adults around, and far more powerful. As for the notion that the periodical warmth, accompanied by that pleasurable sensation and that interesting smell, is dirty in the natural child's own experience–what could be more absurd? (We are of course referring to its own defecating and urinating.)

solitary interior authority—prevail against the combined weight of those innumerable exterior authorities who so consistently contradict it? To use picturesque language, is it surprising that the innocent victim of the plot, outvoted overwhelmingly in a rigged election by falsified voting papers, concedes defeat?

But defeat occurs only after much struggle and hesitation. For years the prince or princess has some stamina left, some residual immunity against social fictions and magic spells. At first this super-spell *(you are what you look like)* works intermittently. When happily playing, not confronted by grown-ups and not guilt-laden, the signs are that the child is still for itself immense, the only real grown-up around, at large, 1st Person singular, no-thing and everything, free. And that, conversely, when unhappy and under pressure, faced by (and faced up by) those disapproving frowns and admonishing or accusing fingers (so sure they are pointing at something right here), why of course this something has to be just an undersized and awkward creature that needs to develop as quickly as possible into one of those self-assured and clever grownups.

The writer has observed that this uneasy alternation between the unadapted and adapted child may go on for as long as ten years or more, or stop short as early as three or four years—so widely do individuals differ. All the same (unless the child remains unadapted for life, and very likely subject to institutional care) it does in the end become, for itself no less than for the world, an object first and foremost, a young thing rapidly becoming an older one, a hopeful tadpole well on the way to the full dignity of froghood.

The Prince Or Princess, The Tadpole And The Frog

When we remember how much of the child's development is the development of its language, and how much of that language is frog language, it is surely astonishing how some children can hold out for so long. But given time the spell wins, thanks largely to its insidious and rarely noticed double-talk. Here for the reader, as always, to check is just one of its duplicities. Since the *predicates* are the same in the sentences "I eat" and "you eat," we take it that the *facts* are the same. The truth is that "you eat" means "alien substances are being pushed into a toothed slit in a small and tightly-packed sphere, where they remain insipid," while "I eat" means "they are being pushed into an unbounded void, where they become tasty." Because our language suppresses it, the immense contrast between these two happenings is progressively obscured as we grow up. The general effect of such semantic confusion, which is paralleled in the life of all our senses, is to water them down, to take the tang and sparkle out of them. Until it is challenged and reversed, the effect of language thus misused is to devalue the rich immensity of our 1st Personhood, and to collapse us into mechanical objects from which practically all inwardness or subjectivity has been drained. Thus the prince and princess are *talked* into froghood. This is a version of Berne's view (1964, p. 178) "that seeing and hearing have a different quality for infants than for grownups."

Small wonder, then, if the spell works a near perfect magic in the end—one so potent that it is now far from being a merely external influence or imposition. Increasingly, it seems, the growing child experiences a need to become just *like them,* a thoroughly normal and paid-up member of the human club, unquestioningly obedient to its taken-for-granted rules, however arbitrary. In fact, so insistent is its urge to belong, to be welcomed into the magic circle, that it tends to believe and do practically anything it is told to believe and do. For instance, there are the virtually universal and seemingly harmless beliefs that, on the highway, THIS one, in her or his actual experience, is *moving* along at 50 m.p.h., through the *still* countryside, looking at it through *two* eyes, and *seeing* its wide range of distances—plus many other commonplace delusions or superstitions. (The reader is invited to check that they *are* superstitious the next time she or he travels by car.) As for the more specialized and plainly harmful sort of belief, think of the variety of mutilated bodies and minds and behaviour sequences taken to be the seal of adulthood among highly cultivated peoples, let alone 'primitives'. And if we modem westerners imagine we impose no comparable conditions of entry into our superior culture pattern, we really are spellbound to the limit! Some of our beliefs, to a candid visitor from another galaxy, must seem unbelievably odd, if not actually mad.

Tadpole into Frog

Sooner or later, if everything goes normally, the not-OK tadpole, having long ago forgotten about its royal ancestry (or happy to have grown out of that childish nonsense), grows up to be a more and more OK and self-confident and successful frog. It may even go on to become a super-frog dominating the bog.

And therefore still more OK? It by no means follows. There are so many well-known instances of nothing failing like too much success. The names of tragic personalities at the top of the worlds of entertainment, the arts, and business immediately occur to one. Nor need this unhappy outcome greatly surprise. Our contention is that playing "Frogs" is not just one more game and self-deceiving pretense: that it is *the* game and *the* lie—also known as *The Face Game* or *Confrontation* (Harding, 1967, 1986)—the Game from which all lesser games derive. That in fact it is that most ancient and deep-rooted—and exclusively human—fiction which, though workable (and necessary) in the life-story of the species and of the individual up to a point, goes on to prove increasingly counterproductive and finally disastrous.

Our thesis goes on to propose the following: The better one plays this Game of games the worse off one is in the long run, the more profound is one's self-deception, and the more severe its attendant troubles. In other words, the more magnificently self-sufficient, powerful, independent (and in this sense OK) one seems to be as a frog, the less OK one really is. In fact, there can no more be a thoroughly OK frog than there can be a thoroughly true lie or factual fiction; for frogs have a built-in flaw—they are make-believe, a game or pretense, not real. The whole matter of OKness is apt to be misconceived and inverted. By nature the child is OK, as Berne maintained, and grows up to become more and more not-OK the more that child is superseded. It is the grown-up who is mature enough to know that he or she has outgrown very little, in fact the one whose frog-mask is getting more and more uncomfortable and awry, who is liable to find it slipping off altogether. And revealing? Why the prince or princess, of course!

Frog into Prince/Princess
But we anticipate, and must go a long way back in our story.

From the earliest times competition between groups of humans— for food, mates, shelter, territory—worked increasingly to the advantage of those who were more able to look at their world objectively, more open to new ways of processing the data. Fortune favoured those who learned humility in front of the evidence. Their science, gathering speed, grew increasingly scientific and far-reaching, and the more technically advanced societies won on almost all counts.

In due course practically all the scientist's discoveries about the external world are turned back and applied to the scientist. As a scientist, one becomes one's own subject matter and field of study, and always the aim is to extend control over that intimate field. Closing in on oneself from outside, one tends to refer everything inwards. One's overall view of oneself from a distance—systematized into the disciplines of history, anthropology, sociology, behavioural psychology—is filled in by nearer views—systematized into physiology, cytology, biochemistry, chemistry, physics, particle physics. One is getting nearer and nearer home, ever closer to what all things—including oneself, the scientist—really are at centre, to the ultimate substratum beyond the quark.

One seems to be almost home, almost in possession of the inmost secret. But one can never gain admittance from outside—say by further sorting out the space-time continuum or chasing the Quark beneath the quark. One will never make that final step or terminate that asymptotic curve. Nor does one need to. One is already home, and has been there all along. The scientist has only to reverse the arrow of attention, to look in at what he or she is looking out of, in order to round off the job and arrive at the inside story of what he and she and all beings essentially are. Responding to our invitation earlier in this paper, it may well be that the reader has already taken that same definitive step which was no step, conducted that ultimate experiment in physics which leads straight into metaphysics, made that last frog-leap out of the bog into the palace. Seeing into his or her *intrinsic* nature as this nameless, spotless, silent, still, colourless clarity, the reader is capacious of the world's endless riches, and truly royal. As this aware no-thing, he or she is everything. All this is set down here for verifying, or falsifying, as the case may be.

If the former, what has happened at long last is that the parent's magic spell, initially so powerful but in the end powerless against reality, has boomeranged, has worked its own destruction. Driven by its own inner logic, it leads back to the prince or princess who has been sitting quietly at home and in good health all the while, and never did become in the slightest froglike. In other words, the truly adult frog whose business (solely in frog interests, of course) is the processing of reality, is obliged to cultivate the truthfulness and impartiality which lead towards the rediscovery of his or her own identity as no frog at all, but royalty in disguise. The science of the objective world leads into the science of oneself as an object or 3rd person, which in turn (given this leap out of frogland) leads into the science of oneself as the subject or 1st Person (Harding, 1974). As the enemy of lies and therefore of games, science has scored a double triumph.

Note the foundation on which true science has been built from the start, namely on unprejudiced perception, on looking to see, on refusal to rely on tradition or belief or unchecked theory or mere speculation, but instead on the humble and patient reading of metre rods, dials, timepieces, and so on. Medieval science did not get off the ground until people stopped settling questions about the universe by looking up the answers in the Bible or Aristotle or any other authority, and dared just to inspect and experiment with what was actually on show. *The science of the object is no sounder than the perceptual base on which it rests. Now exactly the same is true of the science of the subject, of the 1st Person, of the prince or princess. Turning the direction of the scientific inquiry round 180°, from the observed to the observer, does not reduce the necessity for relying on the evidence provided here and now by looking to see and discarding all belief and opinion imported from other times and places.*[3] Consciously to revert from being a frog to being the prince or princess is to be game-free, and this is to be a Seer; this is to see what one really is at centre in and for oneself, seeing what is actually on show here and not trying to see what one is told to see, or hopes to see, or happens to feel comfortable with.

3 As a first-hand demonstration of this turn-around through 180°, the reader was invited to conduct experiments on herself or himself earlier in this paper. The italicized passage here will make sense to the extent to which he or she actually carried out those little experiments.

The Prince Or Princess, The Tadpole And The Frog

The King/Queen

Of course one does not permanently revert to being the prince or princess from the moment of first sighting one's intrinsic nature. The spell is not so easily shaken off. What took so long to bind me, then went on tightening its grip year after year, is going to take a lot of patient unbinding. In other words, a lot of coming to my senses, again and again and again. I have to keep on nudging myself awake from my coma, repeatedly bringing my wandering attention to where I am coming from and what I am looking out of, until in the end it is quite natural to be natural, to stop pretending to be what I am not, to play games no longer, to live from the no-thing-I-am. And my experience assures me of this: It is as *efficient* to live from this central no-thing-I-am as it was *inefficient*—stressful and debilitating—to live from the peripheral thing-I-am-not, from one or another of my appearances. To put it mildly, the Game was not worth the candle.

Now at last the prince or princess has grown up into the king or queen. And has surely done so the hard and humbling and only possible way, via that painful cutting down to size, that dethronement and demoting of the unique 1st Person to the rank of the altogether ordinary 3rd person, and that weird and testing frog-charade. What the Seers claim is that in the end they enjoy a conviction that nothing really went wrong, and a peace which is more and not less vigorous than all that frenetic leaping around the bog ever was.

The Six Spell-Breakers

(i) As a rule the magic spell is amazingly effective, so deceitful and addictive that its victims are for life quite unaware of its existence. Indeed, when they sense the slightest danger of its losing its grip they are apt to be very upset, without knowing why.

And this in spite of the fact that it is demonstrably ridiculous. *"You are what you look like"* is surely so naive it is not worth serious consideration. How could I be, at 0 inches from me, what I look like 100 inches away? I have only to look right here to see what *I* am getting, and over there in my mirror to see what *you* are getting, to see there is no similarity at all between them. Laughter seems the only spell-breaker that is altogether appropriate. But, for good measure, here are five others. The first two recapitulate what has gone before; the rest are additional.

(ii) Look at, listen to, and learn from young children who have not yet fallen under the spell, and adult Seers who claim to have broken free. In various ways they tell the world that they are boundless capacity for it.

(iii) The third and indispensable spell-breaker requires the reader to recheck-in his or her immediate experience at this moment—that there is no thing (awareness is not a thing) that is taking in this line of printing, this paragraph and this page, the furniture in the room, the view from the window. Failure to go on checking, to continue making quite sure that the seer altogether vanishes in favor of the seen, inevitably means that the seer—out of long habit—falls again under the spell that makes a something of him or her.

(iv) Our fourth is an optional extra. It reexamines the scriptures of the world in the light of this simplest and most obvious—yet (we suggest) deepest—of insights, using it as a metal detector to sort out the precious ore from the huge masses of sand and rock which hide it, and uncover the gold of our intrinsic nature. It can be truly encouraging to find how ancient and widespread are the search and the discovery we have been concerned with here.

(v) Our fifth spell-breaker (like the fourth, indicative rather than conclusive) relies on the secular evidence supplied by mythology, philosophy, literature, and art. The typical fairytale or legend has for hero a lad whose foster parents are peasants but whose real parentage is royal or olympian. His lifework is to regain his lost rank by overcoming a succession of almost insuperable obstacles—with some help from above. Plato was only the most articulate and celebrated of the many ancients who pictured the infant coming down from a heaven of light and divine knowledge into a dark and deluded world which has long ago forgotten its supernal origins. How else, indeed, can the child so surely recognize as self-evident such truths as it comes across here below, unless by that anamnesis which is a sudden recalling of the wisdom it enjoyed in heaven? The main theme of Thomas Traherne's *Centuries* (1908/1960) is the many-sided beatitude of the natural child, and the "dirty devices" that grown-ups contaminate it with. Better known is Wordsworth's *Intimations of Immortality from Recollections of Early Childhood.* (1807/1917). ("Trailing clouds of glory do we come, from God who is our home…" But too soon "the shades of the prison house begin to gather about the growing boy". [pp.114-120].) Again, as most real artists would acknowledge, all the drawings of children are comparable with his or her own most inspired work—

up to the moment when the child, falling under the parental spell, sees itself as an artistic young thing, instead of no-thing but space for things—including drawings—to happen in.

The foregoing is a random sampling of humanity's intuition about the exalted status of the child in its midst. None of it means that we should or could stay like that, and refuse to play "Frogs" till we are proficient at the game. There is no easy and direct route from the clear land of the young child to the still clearer land of the childlike Seer, no freeway that does not take us through the bewitched and fogbound country of so-called grown-ups. What it does mean is that somehow our species knows that true adulthood is the working out at a more conscious level all that is best in childhood, so that eventually the wheel of our life turns full circle. The last part should be as game-free as the first. And the unavoidable game-playing interlude—unless we are gluttons for punishment or determined cases of arrested development—should not be allowed to drag on through middle age and beyond.

(vi) Finally, there is the spell-breaker of *practice*. What are the clinical results of this in-seeing when it is sustained, this ever-renewed reactivation of the natural child in us? Is it true that all the therapies which overlook the central problem of who requires therapy prove at best palliatives? That in the last resort I have only one malaise—my mistaken identity, my spineless and pathetic willingness to be whatever they tell me I am—and only one cure, my true identity, my daring to be what I see I am? That so long as my Parent holds any part of my Child spellbound I am not myself and not well? That until I stop playing the Game People Play—call it "Frogs" or "Confrontation" or "The Face Game" or whatever—I will never stop playing one or other of the many subsidiary games people play, and be free?

These are questions for putting to the test, a suggested programme of research and healing practice for transactional analysts who, beginning at home, are themselves coming out from under that numbing and suffocating spell into a spellbound world that very much needs them.

References

Berne, E. (1964). *Games People Play.* London: Deutch.

Harding, D.E. (1967). *The Face Game. Transactional Analysis Bulletin,* 6(22), 40-52.

Harding, D.E. (1974). *The Science Of The 1st Person.* Nacton, Ipswich, England: Shollond.

Harding, D.E. (1986). *Confrontation: The Game People Play. Transactional Analysis Journal.* 16(2), 99-109.

Harding, D.E. (1986). *On Having No Head. Zen And The Re-discovery of the Obvious.* London: Routledge and Kegan Paul (Arkana series).

Harris, T. (1969). *I'm OK, You're OK.* New York: Harper and Row.

Steiner, C. (1975). *Scripts People Live.* New York: Bantam Books.

Traherne, T. (1960). *Centuries.* Oxford: Clarendon Press. (Original work published 1908)

Wordsworth, W. (1917). *The Oxford Book Of English Mystical Verse.* Oxford: Clarendon Press, 114-120. (Original work published 1807)

* * *

Chapter 53

THE FOUR FATAL LIES

1. "I'M FAULTY"

This is the first of a set of four articles published in *The Mountain Path*. Each examines one of the basic lies which people in general— and spiritual aspirants in particular—tell themselves: falsehoods that virtually all of us found our lives on, live by and die by, hang onto at all costs. Falsehoods which obstruct our ordinary life, as well as blocking the way to the aspirant's goal, to the freedom that he or she professes to long for and to strive for.

It's as if, told often and loudly enough, the wildest tale becomes true. The fact that these barriers are insubstantial, mere self-deception and make-believe, does nothing to reduce their obstructiveness, their sinister effect. One has to see *through* them to dissolve them. That is our aim in these four articles. We aren't going to attempt to *think* (or understand or intuit) our way past these obstacles, or to *feel* our way over or under them, but rather to *see* that they aren't there at all, that they are no more real than a mirage that vanishes on closer inspection. Thinking and feeling don't settle anything here. Nothing less than childlike looking-to-see carries conviction.

The first one of the four is: "I'm faulty. There's something radically wrong with me."

That is what society is telling us in a hundred subtle and not-so-subtle ways, and how eager we are to believe the message! We positively lap up the bad news. In fact many of us will pay large sums of money to anyone who explains convincingly what a mess we are in, and will follow him all over the world for years just to hear more and more about the mess.

Far be it from me to unsettle those who enjoy bad news about their spiritual condition. My remarks here are addressed to people who don't enjoy it so much, who have had just about enough of that sort of thing. To you I say: brace yourselves for good news. Not for *hearing* incredibly good news about yourselves, but actually *seeing* it unfold. Or rather, suddenly blaze out.

But this is to anticipate. For a start let's take the prevalent bad news about ourselves seriously and sensibly, in order to discover what truth there is in it, and what action is called for. Let's treat this tale of spiritual-personal woe as intelligently and calmly as we treat secular and less personal tales of woe—in business life for example. Supposing you are boss of a big firm, and suddenly everyone's saying that disaster looms, that the enterprise is almost certainly heading for bankruptcy and its proprietor for poverty and disgrace. How do you react?

There are two things you can do, and they contrast sharply.

(i) You can panic. You can hand out orders right and left. You can sack the works manager and the sales manager, close down a subsidiary plant or two and lay off the work force, scrap old production models and start new ones. Deeds are what you prescribe for this condition. "Don't just sit there," you cry. "Get cracking! Any change is better than no change."

The result is almost certainly that things get worse. Impulsive remedies, blindly administered to a patient the doctor can't find time to examine, may well kill him. The chances they will cure him are one in a thousand.

(ii) Instead of this frantic over-reaction, you will—if you are a normally competent businessman or woman—*do nothing: nothing remedial at all, till you have ascertained the facts.* So you call an extraordinary board meeting, at which the sales manager displays his graphs showing present trends and future market prospects, and the works manager reports on the likelihood of rising productivity and falling costs, and the accountant forecasts profit and loss for the financial year, the increasing size of the overdraft, and so on.

Then—and only then—do you make up your mind. This body of information, duly absorbed and digested, gives rise to sensible decisions. It may indicate what drastic short-term and long-term measures are needed to put the firm into shape. It may indicate that no precipitate action at all should be taken till the actual shape of things gets a lot clearer. Or it may indicate that those initial impulses to panic were quite unjustified, that all those rumours of impending doom were ill-founded if not malicious, and that *on careful examination the business turns out to be very prosperous. That, in fact, the news couldn't be better!*

That is the way, if we have any practical good sense at all, we run our ordinary secular affairs.

Would that we ran our spiritual affairs half as intelligently, a quarter as sanely, on the same business-like principle of *facts first, action second!* How very, very few of us, alas, are anything like so sensible when we turn from the conduct of our life's periphery to the very heart of it! When dealing with mere things, with markets and merchandise and money, we are fairly sane, but when dealing with the Dealer, with their Proprietor, we go quietly mad. On little or no evidence, on the basis of mere hearsay and fearful thinking (or is it, hiddenly, wishful thinking?) we decide that our lives have gone wrong, that we are profoundly defective, unfortunate, even cursed. So we thrash around seeking cures for a condition we have no idea of and don't want to know a thing about—except that it is very bad indeed and no cure is in sight.

If anything could be counted on to push us deeper and deeper into trouble it is this hysterical blindness to our present state, this compulsive yet calculated overlooking of the most self-evident facts about ourselves, this deliberate choosing to live from a miserable pack of lies about our nature instead of that nature as it obviously is. No surprise, then, that our worst fears seem to be justified, and we are in the market for the countless quack remedies on offer. Suckers all, incredibly gullible—that's us!

But now you and I are going to be business-like about ourselves—about our true condition and nature—for a change. We are going to ignore the rumours and look at the facts. We are going to come to our senses and attend—if not for the first time, at least *as if* for the first time—to what's clearly on show, to what we are in our own direct experience at this moment. Attend not (please note) to what we're *said to be* by others, or what we *appear to be* to them, but to

what we *are* to ourselves intrinsically—when we put aside all pre-
-suppositions, beliefs, imaginings. This means daring to turn our
attention round 180° and looking at the Spot we occupy: just looking
with an open mind prepared for any discovery, however strange,
and with the humility and honesty to go by what we find there. In
other words we are about to look, not just at what we're looking at
(currently at this page of writing or printing) but also at what we're
looking *out* of...

What is this pointing finger pointing at right now, *on present evidence,*
without any thinking about it? Look! Don't lay ideas on what you
clearly see: simply notice. What's it like to see IN?

Is Ramana Maharshi perfectly right when he says: "It is really like
gazing into vacancy"?

Is this finger, in your own immediate experience at this moment,
pointing at a something? In particular, at a pair of eyes, a face, a head?
At an opaque, small, solid, coloured, complicated, clearly outlined
thing of any sort? Or at just *Space?* At Vacancy, Capacity, clean of
all characteristics and limitations: just Aware Space for this page of
words, and the hands holding it, to come to pass in: just Room or
Emptiness for filling with whatever's on offer; just this No-thing that

miraculously takes in all things?

Isn't this What you are, What I am, right now? And What we are always—immense, simple, speckless, colourless Transparency, vividly alive to Itself as precisely this? Again, *miraculously* so, and with unsurpassable brilliance?

What can go wrong with This? What loss or injury can This suffer, what change for the worse? What change of any kind? What is there Here to decay and die? What is bad news for This? What does This have to do to put itself right? What medicine do you prescribe for This Patient?

But at once I can hear you raising a strong objection: "All right, I see that *physically* there's nothing here where I AM to give me trouble, but *mentally* there's a great deal. My feelings—of anger, resentment, frustration, sadness, boredom, despair, and so on—bug me just the same. What's the use of being so Spacious if I just put up (and put up with) an endless succession of mostly negative emotions, if I'm forced to play host to such guests? Why, I'd rather be bunged up solid with stuff than have it swept clean away to make room for the seven devils of the mind to rampage in!"

I reply: At this point you have to make a momentous decision. You must settle whether these feelings—both negative and positive— are really *yours* or not. Whether they are feelings about *you* who are No-thing but Room for things, or feelings about *those things*— characterizing *them,* the way they happen to come across to you, to be served up. If you attend carefully I think you will never find any resentment or anger (for instance) of your very, very own—I mean just subjective anger apart from, and having no reference to, any object. Always it's a resented world, or a resented situation or event or something or other. Whatever the feeling, if it's real and not imaginary, I suggest you will find it's about what or who you are hosting, not about their host. Thus your genuine frustration finds things and people frustrating, not the Accommodation you're providing them with. Thus your genuine love exclaims: "How lovable, how adorable he or she is!" Not "How I'm enjoying being so in love!" (That's not love at all.) Thus your genuine joy finds the universe quite delightful for a change, not yourself quite delightful for a change. *You do not change.* That bald assertion is for you to verify for yourself, not take from me. Everything hangs on your conclusion.

Look and see. It belongs to the nature of your world to be suffused and drenched with every sort of feeling (whether positive or negative)—as well as structured with every sort of thinking (attributing values, meanings, relationships), and ornamented with every sort of perceptual and sensory decoration. And just as there are no loose textures or colours floating around apart from textured and coloured things, and no loose thoughts and meanings and values floating around apart from thought-about and meaningful and valued things, so there are no loose misery-feelings or surprise-feelings or puzzle-feelings floating around apart from puzzling and surprising and miserable things. No: none of that stuff detaches itself, like fleas or germs, from your guests, and attaches itself to you their Host. In other words, of all the infinitely complex and ever-changing contents which come together to constitute your world, you are the absolutely simple and never-changing Container. As such, as this stainless, parasite-free, infection-free, speckless, trackless Spaciousness-for-worlds-to-come-and-go-in, you are the Eternal Perfection itself. This is not for believing or understanding or feeling one day, or even for seeing one day, but for simple seeing today, as you turn the arrow of your attention round 180° once more. Now.

"All right," you rejoin. "But what's the use of my being absolutely perfect if my universe (which includes the thing I'm looking down at, and the thing I'm looking out at in my mirror) is so dreadfully imperfect? Let's say—at very best—a universe that's a quarter good, half neutral, and a quarter bad?"

Apparently in the beginning (I reply) it had to be this curate's egg of a world, or else no world-egg at all. Not even You in your primeval fecundity were able to give birth to a uniformly good universe, a non-dualistic world free from clashing opposites and built-in contradictions—a world in which there flourished a joy that, to be itself, required no background of indifference and sadness; in which there flourished a love that, to be itself, had no need to grow and diminish and grow again; in which there flourished a peace that, to be itself, was inactive and automatic and not some kind of pacification. You were no more able to produce these values, without simultaneously producing their opposites, than you were able to produce light without darkness, or silence without sound, or height without depth. All the same you must have decided that, though the cost of such a universe was awesomely high, it was worth it: that this kind of universe was and is preferable to no universe at all.

But—wait a minute!—all this assumes that, when at last you see and go on seeing your own perfection as the Uncontaminated Source of the world, the world will still seem contaminated, tragically imperfect. It is an assumption which you can now do without. Be prepared to find that the universe of things, when consciously viewed from the No-thing it arises from, is a universe transfigured, mysteriously taking on the All-rightness of its Origin. Be prepared to find that, when you no longer do incalculable injury to your world by cleaving it into an observing thing you call *me* and an observed thing you call *not-me*, you heal it of the near-mortal wound you inflicted on it. Be prepared to find that, when you no longer hang onto anything— onto the shred of a particle or the ghost of a thought—you restore to your world all the goods you stole from it over the years, bringing it to a richness you haven't glimpsed since early childhood.

Yes: but do *not* be prepared simply to detach yourself from this transformed world, to shrug it off or wash your hands of it now you have put it to rights. Quite the contrary. The paradox is that, seeing you are now at last free of it, unmarked and spotless, you *are* it—spots and all—and your identity with it makes it worthy of you. (Look in now at the Space you are, that you're according these black marks on a white ground, and see how inseparable it is from them). Put the matter like this: when you see Who you are you see that, as their Source, you are empty *of* all your products, and as their Seer you are empty *for* all your products, and as their Saviour you are empty *as* all your products: and as You they are very good indeed. This is the love of God which not only creates the world and makes the world go round, but saves the world.

However fine this may sound, don't take a word of it from me. Try it out for yourself. Turn your attention round 180 degrees, see What you see, stay with the seeing, and see what happens to your world.

* * *

We have been practical. We have discovered what has to be done to remedy our plight. The answer—the business-like and sensible answer—is nothing at all. Nothing but wake up. *Seeing Who we are, we are all right as we are.* And that's putting it conservatively, the understatement of the century!

No: you are *not* faulty. Ramana Maharshi said:

> A man can realize the Self because it is here and now. If it were not so, but attainable by effort at some future time and if it were new and something to be acquired, it would not be worthy of pursuit.
>
> All are *jnanis, jivamuktas.*
>
> All are seeing God always, but they don't know it.
>
> Be as you are.

These assertions aren't for reciting but for putting to the proof. You have to see yourSelf, for yourSelf. It is the easiest, most natural, most striking sight imaginable.

And the most resisted. We humans will go to any lengths to blind ourselves to our blessedness.

* * *

2. "I'M EMBODIED."

I'm in this body, I am this body, I'm incarnate, I'm embodied, I'm imprisoned or entombed in this body—what could be more taken-for-granted and universal than this belief, in one or another of its many forms? Together with its taken-for-granted corollary that at birth I was somehow locked up in this thing, that through life I'm seldom if ever let out on parole, and that at death I shall make my getaway? Only (many would add) to be re-apprehended and given another life-sentence and transferred to another place of confinement, decanted into another cooler or can or jug.

In this the second of our investigations into the lies we live by, we shall be looking into this myth of embodiment: noticing how absurd yet how specious it is, how manifestly crippling yet how obstinately clung to, how addictive. And how comically easy it is to see through, to show up as fantasy and extravaganza, once we dare peep into it.

Reminding us of the necessity and urgency of our task we have the assurance of Ramana Maharshi that "identifying the Self with the body is the real bondage," that *"I am the body* is the cause of all mischief," and that when this conviction goes "it is Realization." And, urging us to question our habitual assumptions and start all over again along new and unfamiliar lines, we have Rumi's warning: "This body is a great deception, a great hoodwink." In fact, every real Seer has seen through and combated the popular-secular notion that (as the saying has it) "I inhabit this house of clay," and the popular-religious notion that "This house of clay is one of many I inhabited in the past, and shall inhabit in the future."

These warnings by the wise over the centuries, however, have done very little to bring our species to its senses. The time has come to stop making bare pronouncements on this subject one way or the other (the many incarnationists content to assert "I'm embodied" and their few opponents content to assert "I'm not embodied") and instead to start looking squarely at the facts: obvious, indubitable facts on which both parties could agree.

For a start, let's take this encapsulated-person idea as seriously as we can. And notice how very odd it is, how improbable. Whether the capsule is likened to a packing-case, or a tomb, or a prison, or a house, or a caravan, or a tent, or a shell, its protean shape and agility and mode of maintenance are strange enough: but not half so strange as the lifestyle of its inmate. It seems the householder is exactly the same size and shape as the house, and by no means rattling about somewhere inside like a small pea in a big pod. It seems he's so bulky—or else his dwelling is so cramped—that he occupies all the rooms and passages at once and without an inch to spare: a shocking case of slum conditions and overcrowding. Come on! We're trying to find out what we *mean* when we say we're *in* this body. Do we mean that within this four-winged, thatch-roofed, two-windowed stately home there dwells a lord of the manor who fills out and coincides with the manor-house, rather as the tea he imbibes (through the front door?) fills out and coincides with the teapot? A home-shaped home-owner? A tight fit indeed, reminding one of those young people who shrink on their blue jeans so snugly that they (the jeans) resemble the blue skin of the Lord Krishna. Which in turn reminds one of how

The Four Fatal Lies

Krishna revealed himself as the entire universe, and certainly not confined to that tiny portion of himself which Arjuna saw.

And now, turning away from this tragi-comic superstition of our own confinement, let's take a look at what's actually going on—now.

Look at your own hand, holding this book.

Are you inside that thing?

If so, I'm eager to learn how you find it in there. Congested, pitch dark, warm, soaking wet, with no room to swing a blood vessel or corpuscle in, let alone a cat?

Suppose you have come to consciousness for the first time at this very moment, or suppose you've had a sudden attack of total amnesia, what is there to tell you on present evidence that you are *inside* that hand and wrist and not inside that wristwatch and sleeve and magazine?

Look at the skin of that hand. Which side of it are you? Are you, again on present evidence, lurking beneath that surface or at large above it? Are you contained *in it,* or is it—along with the watch and sleeve and magazine, the furniture in the room, the world outside the window—all contained *in you?*

Look out at that wide sky and those clouds and trees, and then look down at those feet and arms and trunk—and say whether you are *shut out of* that vastness there and *shut into* this smallness here. Somewhere the *Pali Canon* speaks of two kinds of people: those who "live in a small hardness." and those who "live in the immensity." Which kind are you, in your own immediate experience at this moment? Isn't the first kind not only imaginary but unimaginable, no good even as fairytale or science-fiction material? In the same class as those rabbit horns and tortoise hairs that Buddhist scriptures go on about? To speak plainly, stuff and nonsense?

The whole issue can be boiled down to the simple one of how *big* you are. There's a tradition according to which Jesus said: "A man who looks on himself only from outside, and not also from within, makes himself small." Instead of trying to creep into that hand over there, please move up to where you really are stationed, to the very Centre of your world, to this Observation Post or Viewpoint from which that hand is being seen, and observe how this Point (what Point?) explodes to engulf all of that world from shirt-buttons to sky. Here's the quiet and unobserved bombshell that makes the Hiroshima blast seem like a puff of cigarette smoke. Why, so far from your being contained in that minute fragment of the world called your human body, you aren't even contained in your world body, but are the Uncontainable!

How on earth does it arise, this wild notion which no wild animal is foolish enough to dream of, this specifically human delusion that the Observer is mysteriously trapped and embedded in a little piece of what's observed? How on earth does the growing (sic) child get cut down, almost overnight, from cosmic to human dimensions? The answer is that it catches from grown-ups (sic, again) the disease of progressive *eccentricity*—of being increasingly beside oneself (which of course means crazy)—the disease whose victims, as if in a St. Vitus' dance, leap out of themselves, turn round in mid-air, and look back at themselves. What an impossible contortion: no wonder if some sufferers seem permanently twisted. It leads to the superimposing of what one *looks like* over there upon what one is here—which is bad observation, bad science, bad philosophy, bad religion, bad living, and certainly makes for the bad use of one's body. Even common sense jibs at the fallacy that *others* are in a position to see the you that *you* see. And (more generally) modern science jibs at the fallacy that things stay the same no matter where they are viewed from. Einstein took care of that one, as did Bishop Berkeley before him.

People, says the great Rumi, devise stratagems for putting the King in a pint pot. That little sentence "I AM IN A BODY" should be enough to give the game away—as if I AM could be encapsulated in any body, however capacious!

The joke is that we are well aware (with part of our minds) that our real body doesn't stop at our skin, but—to function at all—has to be worldwide. (We accept this in theory and reject it in practice, we apply it to others and not to ourselves—our capacity for this sort of doublethink being inexhaustible.)

My Earth, unlike my hand, is an indispensable organ of my life; and my Solar System is at least as vital to me as my respiratory or digestive system. I can survive a heart-and-lung transplant, but hardly a gallactic one. I could get along for years without large parts of my earthly embodiment, but for how long without my heavenly embodiment? And, in general, it's a commonplace of the modern world that all things are in countless ways interdependent and mutually conditioning, to such an extent that the Universe is strictly indivisible, a truly organic whole: indeed the only true Whole. If I'm incarnate at all (and in a sense I surely am) then nothing less than this Universe is my Incarnation, and I do myself an injustice when I settle for anything less.

But you may ask: "What does it matter that I've been taught to regard this tiny fragment of the Universe as my body, and all the rest as its environment? Surely it's a harmless enough assumption that has its uses—if not an essential social fiction at least a convenient one. After all, it works pretty well."

I reply: On the contrary, it works very badly, is inconvenient and harmful in the extreme. And it is harmful, not so much because your collapse from cosmic to human dimensions is bad for you (how much worse than a collapsed lung!) as because it is *impossible* for you, a game and pretence, a lie; and because living a lie is unhealthy living. Here are just 6 of the consequences—some hidden, some overt, all sick—of playing this distinctively human game:

(i) You see yourself as one thing up against all other things, and this means you are in constant fear of injury and loss.

(ii) At a deep level you resent having been cut down to size so cruelly and so drastically—what humiliation, what a come-down this is—and you hold a lifelong grudge against the order of things that has done this to you. The result is aggression in one or another of its many forms.

(iii) Impoverished and not liking it at all, suffering from the loss of your infinite wealth (as an infant you owned the world), you compulsively collect around you as many relics and tokens of your past estate as you can. You are motivated by greed instead of need, and it's insatiable.

(iv) Contracting the social disease of eccentricity, of being beside yourself (at the regulation distance of a metre or two) you live there the life of a displaced person: one whose handicaps are likely to include morbid self-consciousness amounting perhaps to crippling embarrassment, phoniness or putting on acts to impress people, rigidity and awkwardness in place of your natural suppleness and flow, and contrived behaviour in place of your natural spontaneity. For, curiously enough, to entomb yourself in your body is to estrange yourself from it and misuse it. Look at how elegantly and smoothly the cat walks, jumps, stretches itself, plays. Its happy secret is that, having heard no rumour of incarnation, it imposes no feline boundaries or restrictions on itself, is cat-free, wide open. And so with all creatures except man. Blake wrote:

Seest thou that little wingéd fly?

Its gates are not closed: I hope thine are not closed!

Blake was an optimist whose mission to the world was to "melt apparent surfaces away and reveal the infinite which is hid." Well, he certainly *tried*.

(v) Out there, you cut yourself off from the Source of your originality, your unique inspiration or genius—and become a mere social unit. The fact that you can only *pretend* to amputate yourself isn't enough to prevent your progressive standardisation and predictability.

(vi) Finally, you are more inefficient than you need be. To do a good job of work, the best that lies in you, you have to attend, to be realistic about what's happening and not drift off into a dream. In this case the dream is that the workman has been compressed into a particle of himself, and distorted into a shape that isn't his at all. No wonder if the work of this monster turns out to be something of a monstrosity.

What, then, is the sovereign remedy for this shrinkage-myth with all its sad consequences of which I have provided only a small sample?

Is it to ferret round diligently for escape routes from this body-prison, in order one day to find oneself gloriously at large again? Or to cultivate (by austerities or meditation or less approved means) a succession of out-of-the-body experiences while still this side of death? Or to practice feeling one's immensity, patiently projecting oneself in all directions till one stays worldwide? Or to keep reminding oneself that one is a *malade imaginaire,* and that it's an idle tale that one is a mere fragment of the universe?

Or, instead, simply to notice that you have never had an *in-the-body* experience in your whole life?

Well, I can't speak for you, but I find it's enough to do—not (thank God) ten or five or even two things—but just one. Namely (as I said above, and shall go on repeating in season and out of season while breath lasts) to turn the arrow of my attention round 180 degrees and look at What I'm looking *out of.* Now.

Otherwise, I'm one of those who (pace T. S. Eliot) have the meaning but miss the experience.

* * *

3. "I'M HUMAN."

All of the four basic lies we are considering in this series are extremely plausible, in fact automatically taken to be true by almost every sane adult. Certainly our third—"I'm human" or "I'm a man and not God"— is (or seems) so self-evident it goes without saying, along with such taken-for-granted assumptions as "I'm here and not there" or "I'm me and not you." To doubt any of them—and rashly voice your doubts— would be to invite the anxious concern of your friends and relations, and (if you persisted) to risk being taken into institutional care.

Well, this article is something like a Government Health Warning: READ ON AT YOUR PERIL! I offer no guarantee against the danger that—if you go along sincerely with the following, and actually carry out the simple and easy-to-do tests it is based on—you will be regarded as out of your mind. (Incidentally, were you ever in it?)

You will, however, be fairly safe against that risk if you're careful not to mention your conclusions to anyone. And altogether safe if you just *read* what I have to say—I mean take in the words and resolutely decline to do the experiments they describe. Only in that case the words will be virtually meaningless to you—or else (what amounts to the same thing) will consist of tritely pious and vaguely uplifting sentiments of no real value whatever—and you will be wasting your time. You have been warned.

Why should you bother to look into this question with me, the question of your humanness? Here are three good reasons:

(i) The first is that a highly regarded (though relatively small) company of men and women have, throughout the past three thousand years or so, announced that really and truly they weren't men and women at all. For example, take Ramana Maharshi's uncompromising assertion that "I AM" is natural, whereas "I am a man" is not. Or this rather charming little story from the *Pali Canon:*

> The Brahmin Drona, seeing the Buddha sitting at the foot of a tree, asked him,
>
> "Are you a *deva?*"
>
> The exalted one answered, "I am not."
>
> "Are you a *gandharva?*"
>
> "I am not."
>
> "Are you a *yaksha?*"
>
> "I am not."
>
> "Are you a man?"

"I am not a man."

Or, as Jesus is reported saying in the apochryphal *Acts of John,* "What I now seem to be, that am I not… And so speak I, separating off the manhood." One is reminded of Rumi's "They saw the body and supposed he was a man." And, in our own time, of Joel Goldsmith at his boldest: "No-one who believes he is a man has even begun to suspect spiritual truth."

Now if these pronouncements happen to be right, and you my reader are in sober fact neither a man nor a woman nor a child, why then you had better let this extraordinary news sink in and get thoroughly used to it. How futile it would be to carry on in the same old way—how impractical, how pathetic, how *crawling*—to continue living the lie that you are "only human after all." Besides, what an adventure is here: to try out your non-humanness! Can you think of a more enterprising, a more exhilarating and interesting and go-ahead undertaking?

(ii) The second reason for looking long and hard into this question of your true identity with a wide-open mind, is that the masters' message doesn't stop with the news of what you *are not*—namely a human being—but goes on to the infinitely more staggering news of What you *are. They say you are God.* Yes: the One, the Alone, the Only Real. Here is how Ramana Maharshi puts it:

There is nothing apart from your Self.
There are no others.

All know that the drop merges into the ocean, but few know that the ocean merges into the drop.

And here—taken at random from all over the world—are some more versions of the same message:

In appearance a man, in reality God.

Chuang-tzu

My ME Is God.

St. Catherine of Genoa

The stirring of religion is the feeling that my only true self in the end is God.

A. C. Bradley

No matter how often he thinks of God or goes to church, or how much he believes in religious ideas, if he, the whole man, is deaf to the question of existence, if he does not have an answer to it, he is marking time, and he lives and dies like one of the million things he produces. He thinks of God, instead of experiencing being God.

Erich Fromm

(iii) Our third and final reason for looking into this whole question—the most practical reason imaginable—is, again, spelled out for us by Ramana Maharshi: "One must realize one's Self to open the store of unalloyed happiness." Which is to say: till you are God— till you really have the sense of being no less than God, till it comes naturally to you to be Him—you don't know what true bliss is. "When there is nothing except Yourself you are happy," declares Maharshi, "That is the whole truth."

These words are addressed to people who would like to be happy: or so they say. I repeat: *or so they say.*

And fine and true words they are, immensely valuable and encouraging if they inspire you to *test for yourself* their truth: Useless if they lull you into a mildly euphoric religious daydream in which you picture what it might be like to be God and therefore happy. Worse than useless if they draw attention to their author's experience and away from yours—away from you to him, from what you *are*— namely no-man, no-woman, no-one but the One, the Alone—to what you *are not*. Minding your own business—that's what the simple experiments we are coming to are about, and why they are so vital. I beseech you to let them settle without delay or doubt *the* question— the question it's death not to ask—the question of whether you are or are not a human being, are or are not God.

First you must have a true-to-life idea of what human beings are like. Then you are ready to go on and see whether you are like that.

So let's jot down a few obvious things about them—things which are neither controversial nor hidden, lacking which they are certainly not human.

(i) If we ignore their limbs (which are sometimes missing and not quite essential therefore) they are shaped like figures of 8, or outsize cottage loaves, comprising an upper section containing specialised sense organs, and a bigger bottom section which lacks them. Alien substances are inserted in the top section, and discharged from the bottom section as waste.

(ii) Their height varies between around one foot and eight feet, and their bulk proportionately.

(iii) They are temporal—temporary things rarely lasting as long as a century.

(iv) They move around, whether by means of legs, or wheels, or wings, or whatever.

What you now have to do, to find out if you really are a human being, is to stop going by what people say you are (they are too far off, in no position to say) and instead to go by what you see you are (only you are near enough, have the inside story, are in a position to say). In particular, you need to see—in all childlike simplicity—whether the four characteristics we've listed above apply to you. If they do, you're human. If they don't, you aren't. It's as straightforward as that. As sharp and decisive as that.

This means you must pluck up the courage to be the sole authority on this supreme issue, instead of handing it over to a lot of unqualified outsiders. It means you must be honest and serious enough to start looking all over again, as if you had just happened, and take what you find. It means you must be fed up with your dreaminess and credulity and uninquisitivenees, and desperate for the facts, determined not to live and die without ever asking *yourself* who's doing so, resolved not to miss out on this rare and Godsent opportunity to settle the question of your Godhood beyond all doubt.

"Alas," I fancy I hear you replying, "an immensely difficult (if not impossible) assignment for me as I am now—unprepared, irresolute, sensual, bedevilled by worldly interests and worries."

Again and again Ramana Maharshi deplored this excuse-making and mock-modest posture, this chickening out, and insisted that (as we're about to find) it's easier to see What you are than anything else, and that you will never be better equipped or qualified to do so than you are right now. He would certainly have agreed with the Zen master who pointed out that, to realize your Buddha Nature, you don't have to "shun your wife (or husband) and gnaw the roots of vegetables." If you are one of Maharshi's devotees, show your devotion by proving him right: and you can do this by ceasing to pretend you can't see What he says is OBVIOUS.

In the four tests that follow, you are inspecting yourself for those four features we noted in human beings:

(i) Look at anyone's face in the room now. Or, if you are alone, at what you see in your mirror. Or, if you have no mirror handy, at this face:

and see whether you have anything to match it where you are. Check that, on present evidence, you are just Space for it. That the given set-up is strikingly asymmetrical: face there to No face here; two little eyes there to one immense "Eye" here; coloured and textured and opaque shapes there to nothing of the sort here—No-thing at all. That the top portion of your figure of 8—of your cottage loaf—has been sliced off and put over there in that bread-bin you call your mirror. In plain language, that already in this investigation you are revealed as immeasurably different from any human you have ever, ever, ever seen.

(ii) You see how tall humans are. On present evidence, couldn't you be any height? Try walking tall—as tall as you like, infinitely tall. With bulk to match.

(iii) Read off the time *there* by your watch. Now slowly bring it to your eye, observing how those numbers blur and vanish. Your watch is now telling you the time *here* where you are—zero o'clock, no time at all. And no wonder: as you can see, there's nothing here, nothing to change, nothing to need or to record time. Where you are and What you are is timeless, eternal.

(iv) Stand up, start rotating on the spot, and see how (on the contrary) it's the ceiling and the walls and the windows and doors that are going round—in your Stillness. Out in your car, see how it's everything *but* you—the telegraph poles and trees and houses and hills—that's on the move.

These four are only a small sample of the differences between what you appear to be and what you are, between what you'd been brought up to believe was your nature and what you can see is your Nature. It isn't that your central and divine Reality is somewhat *unlike* your peripheral and human appearance, but that in all respects it is the *opposite.* Thus instead of moving around you are Stillness itself, and instead of being two-eyed your Real or Third Eye—your God's Eye—is single, and instead of wearing a human face you wear what Zen calls your Original Face, which is none other than the Face of God. And so on: you can continue exploring at your leisure the central Godhood you overlooked for so long, and never exhaust the ways in which it contrasts so startlingly with the humanhood you imported in its stead and replaced it with. *Pretended* you replaced it with. As if you could!

Wonder of wonders, what is most needed (namely, this clear vision of one's Godhood) is most available—and most neglected, resisted, feared. Of all obvious sights it is the most brazenly obvious—and the most anxiously and hastily concealed beneath smokescreens of emotionalism, intellectual fog, religiosity. Of all messages it is the plainest—and the most meddled with and scrambled, as if it were top-secret wartime intelligence no-one must decipher. Of all simplicities this is the simplest—and whole libraries exist to prove the contrary.

I seem to hear you vigorously demurring here: "All this isn't just simple: it's simplistic, grossly oversimplified. Though I may look like God right here I certainly don't feel like God right here, nor do I think like God. If my consciousness functioned at his exalted level I should never fail to find a parking space, or forget a name, or misjudge a friend's character and intentions, and certainly I should never be sad or cross. What's the use of looking like God if I can never begin to live up to my good looks?"

A very pertinent objection, the answer to which will occupy the rest of this article.

To start with, let's glance at the tradition. According to the *Prashna Upanishad,* "the impersonal Self who sees, touches, hears, smells, tastes, thinks, discriminates, acts, is one with the personal self." In fact the basic position of the *Upanishads* is that it's only as and through the one Experiencer in all beings that we perceive and feel and think and experience at all. And the same doctrine—differently phrased of course—is to be found in many Buddhist and Sufi texts, as well as in the writings of great Christian mystics.

This is all very well, but how are we actually going to reconcile God's (presumably) perfect experience with our (certainly) imperfect experience, and do it so thoroughly that in reality it's revealed as all his? How shall we shake the settled conviction that while in *principle* we are divine *in practice* we are anything but divine? That while our *nature* is suprahuman our *experience* is all-too-human?

Here we must make a distinction—a very sharp distinction between the two modes or directions of our experience. Let's call them (a) the View Out and (b) the View In:

(a) By the View Out I mean our ordinary attention to what's going on, to the content of our experience—whether it's a feeling, a thought, a perception, a sensation, or any combination of these. For example, take your seeing now of those hands of yours and this page covered with words, plus the thoughts about your Godhood these words are stimulating, plus the feelings of hope and excitement (or incredulity, apprehension, embarrassment?) which the very idea of your Godhood excites in you. About this and all such experience three things can be said: it is continually changing; it is so partial and limited that it is at least as unreal or false as it is real or true; and it is as likely to be weighed down with sad feelings as buoyed up with joyful ones. In brief, this first kind is normal experience, the sort one would naturally expect of a fallible and faulty human being and emphatically not of an infallible and faultless Divine Being.

(b) The second mode or direction of our experience is abnormal in the sense that it is relatively rare. Centripetal instead of centrifugal, its arrow of attention is aimed inwards at the Attender instead of outwards at what's being attended to. To vary metaphors, it concentrates on the never-changing Container of one's experience instead of its ever-changing content; on the featureless Screen instead of the richly complex and colourful soap opera featuring on it. This is of course the Inseeing which (I trust) we practised in the first of these four articles—"I'M FAULTY". Inseeing which isn't for remembering but for renewing by looking now at what this pointing finger is pointing at—

—by actually *seeing* this Immense and Speckless Clarity which is its own Seer. Seeing What you are.

How very different this second kind of experience is from the first, this Inlook from that Outlook. No trouble in attributing *this* to God and not man, in perceiving *this* as none other than God's perfect viewing of his perfect Nature, as the divine Subject and the divine Object coming together seamlessly, as God enjoying God! In fact the attribution of this perfect Experience to oneself as a separate and less-than-perfect experiencer would amount to the pride which led to Lucifer's downfall.

The problem, then, is this still: how to reconcile God's perfection with his inclusion of all consciousness—his inclusion of our imperfect View Out into the world no less than our perfect View In to the world's Origin, his inclusion of our vision of the unreal there no less than our vision of the Real here.

And the solution is this: it's the View Out and not the Viewer Out that's "imperfect". The "defects" and the "unreality" all lie on the side of your seen world and not of yourself its Seer, on the side of your contents and not of yourself their Container, on the side of your soap-opera programme and not of yourself the immaculate Screen. And there's no help for it: these "shortcomings" are what make the world possible: a world clean of "soap", a "perfect" or "perfectly real" world is no world at all. *And your View Out into God's world (such as it is) is as truly God's as Your View In to God is God's. Either way, every way, you are He.*

"Phenomena are real when experienced as the Self and illusory when seen apart from the Self," said Maharshi. In other words, the soap opera becomes straight drama once you—alias God—become its author. See how the play strikes you then.

See whether you can continue sticking the labels "DEFECTIVE" or "DAMAGED GOODS" or "GRADE 2 QUALITY" on your world, on any item in it, in the same old careless way. See whether your goods aren't ultimately very good indeed, see just how the excellence of their Manufacturer rubs off onto them, just how each bears the trademark GOD and comes under his Divine Guarantee.

* * *

4. "I'M MORTAL."

Here am I, all eighty years old, surrounded by intelligent and caring people telling me (though hardly in so many words) that I've *had* it, that it's probably more a matter of months than years before I die and disappear altogether and for ever. And other intelligent and caring people telling me (with all the persuasiveness and conviction at their command) that this is a lie, and that I *have* it and will never cease to have it—to have abundant life, life everlasting!

What an intriguing situation that is! What a lark! I could say "How funny" or even ''What fun'' (like being reliably informed I have and haven't won the Pools, or am the Ruler of the world and his boot boy, or Methuselah and a mayfly)—if it were not for the fact that the joke was on me. And if it were not for the fact that the difference between a live me and a dead me is a lot greater and more poignant than the difference between me-qua-man and me-qua-mayfly. That difference—that poignancy and urgency and gravity, that bite—is the reason that I have, on top of a lifelong interest in settling this great question of my life—its transience or its permanence—spent the past couple of years giving it all the attention I'm capable of.[1]

The purpose of this article is to share some of my findings with you.

By way of introduction, let's sample what those who are so sure I'm eternal have to say:

> You have squeezed yourself into the space of a lifetime and the volume of a body, and thus created the innumerable conflicts of life and death. Have your being outside this body of birth and death, and all your problems with be solved. They exist because you believe yourself born to die. Undeceive yourself and be free. You are not a person.
>
> Nisargadatta Maharaj

> God made the senses turn outwards, man therefore looks outwards, not into himself. Now and again a daring soul, desiring immortality, has looked back and found himself. He who knows the soundless, odourless, tasteless, intangible, formless, deathless, supernatural, undecaying, beginningless, endless unchangeable Reality, springs out of the mouth of Death.
>
> *Katha Upanishad*

> Owing to the I-am-the-body notion, death is feared as being the loss of Oneself. Birth and death pertain to the body only but they are superimposed on the Self.
>
> Ramana Maharshi

I'm on trial for my life. What follows is a summary of the

---

1 The author's conclusions are set out at length in *The Little Book of Life and Death*.

proceedings, of the lawsuit in which I'm the Judge and Jury as well as the one standing trial. The Prosecution pleads that I'm mortal, in fact already under sentence of death by a higher court. The Defence vigorously contests this. If, as His Honour the Judge, I'm not impartial, if for any consideration or bribe—whether of earthly or heavenly treasure—I favour either side, and also if I rule out new and unheard-of evidence, I'm dishonourable and corrupt. Injustice will be done, and done to me.

To the evidence, then. The Prosecution takes the floor:

I don't have far to look for clues, it says. Plainly I'm dying on my feet—fast. Witness those ever-multiplying and deepening wrinkles: those ever-baggier bags under eyes and chin; those too-pearly and too-regular teeth; that snow-white hair falling like sleet through my life's long winter, leaving me balder daily and my baldness blotchy with senile lentigo—the freckles of age. (It's as if the freckles had migrated from around the child's nose to the old man's dome and the backs of his hands, where they go on growing and darkening. Will they continue to do so when, soon, those hands clench in death?)

What more resounding evidence of that death's relentless approach do I need than this crescendo of warning signals? If I am too cowardly to heed them, and go on hoping against hope that my story will end as happily as a novelette, why then I have lost—along with hair and teeth and the rest—all remaining dignity and become pathetic indeed.

All of which the Defence readily admits. In fact, insists on. Honesty about that mounting senescence, and the climax it's obviously leading to, is indispensable.

Honesty about *what* that evidence is, *but no less about WHERE it is.* About where those signs of ageing and dying are actually given. The *what* without the *where* is a half-truth that isn't just lying, but *the* lie. Repeat: *the* lie.

They are presented over there, some three to ten or more feet from me here. In fact, just about the same distance from me as people are—people who show very similar evidences of ageing and dying. That's where I find mortals and mortality, and evidently that's where they belong; and where that all-too-mortal Douglas Harding is domiciled, appropriately, among his kind—way out there. I see this with a seeing that is a thousand times more convincing than any thoughts or feelings could ever be.

And I see he can't come here, neither the whole nor any part of him. When I bring my mirror, slowly, right up to this spot—to my eye—I lose him. I watch him being progressively dismantled and dissolved signs of age and all. Well before he can touch me, he's abolished altogether. It's the same with his age-freckled hands: I find that they belong out there and won't stand up to close inspection here. And if there ever was a case of a miss being as good as a mile, this is it. Here, I'm as safe against all that mortal stuff as if it were light years away.

Well may St. Paul exclaim in a kind of ecstasy: "O Death, WHERE is thy sting? O grave, WHERE is thy victory?" *I see Death off,* I see that perisher D. E. H. off from here, every particle of him and every hint of his mortality. Death can't ever get to me in any form or disguise.

By nature and constitution I'm forever shot of that enemy.

What a bad joke, what needless and self-inflicted misery it is, what blindness to the obvious, that we should go on rummaging in books, and chasing teachers, and burning the midnight oil—trying, trying so hard to find out how death can be warded off: when all one has to do is see how it wards itself off: how it *rockets* from this launching pad of the deathless I AM! If only, instead of using our mirror for self-deception, we used it for Self-revelation, and let it put the usurper Death in his place—instantly! The very device that once planted humanness and mortality so firmly on us stands ready to take them off us—instantly and forever!

At this juncture the Prosecution intervenes to accuse me of a treble misuse of language—for purposes of special pleading, of dividing the indivisible, and of dodging responsibility. It maintains that, in ordinary life and not just to make my case, I wouldn't dream of thus washing my hands of D. E. H., artificially distinguishing and separating myself as "1st person here" from myself as "3rd person there". No: in ordinary life I answer unhesitatingly to his name and, bringing his 1st person and 3rd together, take full responsibility for what he gets up to. Thus when *he* walks and eats and sleeps *I* walk and eat and sleep, and when *he* ages and sickens and dies *I* do the same. Where's the difference? In short (says the Prosecution) if I were to use language to inform and not deceive myself and others, to take and not evade responsibility, I would have to admit that I'm precisely the sort of thing which perishes.

This the Defence at once flatly contradicts: maintaining that, directly I cease letting language make a fool of me, I discover that I'm precisely *not* the sort of thing that perishes, that I'm not remotely like that. In fact, the Prosecution supplies the Defence with all the examples it needs. When I snap out of my language-induced coma, and see what I see, I can find *no* resemblance between what this 1st Person Singular gets up to and what those 3rd persons (and that includes D. E. H.) get up to—between "I walk" and "he walks", or "I eat" and "he eats", or "I sleep" and "he sleeps". As for "I die" and "he dies", the difference between them is that whereas the second is certain the first is impossible—if not meaningless.

Take walking. When *he* walks it's he that moves and not the world, but when *I* walk—it's the world that moves and not me. (This came out in an earlier article.) Again, when he eats the food's inserted into that head and doesn't taste, but when I eat it's inserted into this no-head and does taste. And when *he* sleeps he's a sleeping organism, but when *I* sleep I'm nothing like that.

It's unbelievable how almost all of us go through life without ever noticing that there are *two* altogether different sorts of life going on: *two* sorts of eating round the dining table, *two* sorts of taking a walk; *two* sorts of whatever's being done. Incredible the power of language to stupefy, to trick, to blind, talking us into believing that, because the *predicates* of the sentences "I eat" and "he eats", and so on, are the same, the *experience*—the feel and taste and look of it—must be the same! Is it any surprise that our lives crack and crumple all out of shape, built as they are on a base so insubstantial, so nonexistent?

When it comes to the day-to-day living of life the practical consequences of this self-deception-by-language are damaging enough. But when it comes to facing the end of life they are disastrous. Turning a blind eye to the distinction between the *dying* in "he dies" and in "I die" is attempting suicide.

What, exactly, is that sharpest and most vital of distinctions?

When *he* dies, what happens? His breathing becomes irregular and stertorous, and presently ceases; his body goes cold and rigid, and before long starts to smell... And when *I* die? Well, I don't have to wait to see. Right now I turn the arrow of my attention round 180°, once more looking in at what I'm also looking out of, and see— with a seeing that couldn't be clearer or more decisive—that here I'm reduced to Nothing whatever, nothing but Awareness of this Nothing.

But that (the Prosecution butts in) isn't *dying*: it lacks the sting, the awesomeness, the inevitability, the devastation of the real thing, and is little more than a meditation upon death.

On the contrary (says the Defence) it is much *more* thorough and much *more* profound than death as it is generally taken to be. That far-less-real public dying leaves plenty of body-stuff, of chemistry and physics, in situ, and probably plenty of mind-stuff too. On the other hand, this wholly-real private dying, which leaves Nothing in situ, instantly wipes out all of me: as I can see *now*, perfectly and at will, by simple in-seeing. This is the dying-before-one-dies, the hidden practice of death this side of one's official and unhidden death, in fact that DYING TO LIVE or DEATH OF DEATH which is the theme of so many Seers—notably, of course, Ramana Maharshi, who saw death off by 'dying' at the early age of 16.

This won't do at all (counters the Prosecution)—it goes against all common sense. I admit to living now. Very well, I must then admit to dying one day. For of all certainties the death of those who live is among the most certain.

Well (comes back the swift reply) how's this for a surprise? I do not admit to living now, any more than to dying one day. *To say I shall die is to flatter myself!* Here, where I see there's Nothing, I see there's nothing to body forth or sustain life, nothing to live, not a particle of a particle of even the most primitive animate and inanimate forms. To be void at all, this Void that I am has to be void of all, and certainly void of all that could live. *My eternal safeguard against death is that I have nothing here to die.* Nor is this any ordinary deprivation or come-down. For right here is What's infinitely superior to life and death, namely the Source of both, that Origin of all which is nevertheless clean of all—as the start of a race is still, and the spring of a river is dry, and the hub of a wheel does not turn.

And anyone who doesn't believe me is invited to come and see: warmly urged to come all the way up to me here, armed with all the optical and electronic aids he or she can muster: and to discover that, well before arrival, every trace of what's under inspection is lost.

My visitor is my executioner. And how well this fits in with the common sense which the Prosecution was invoking! I have only to look down now to see that I'm beheaded, topped—drastically décolleté, so to say—and what more summary mode of execution is there than that? *And what surer safeguard against future dying?* Only the mad Duke, in Norman Douglas's *South Wind,* would be so daft as to pass sentence of *double* decapitation on me.

But the Prosecution isn't quite silenced yet. All this ingenious special pleading (it points out) might do something towards persuading my mind, nothing towards persuading my heart. Knowing the precise formula of this medicine against death, and seeing what it looks like and how it behaves in the laboratory, is valueless unless it is taken, unless it gets down to my guts, unless it is *felt.* Superficially, I may be persuaded I'm immortal, deep down I'm sure I'm not. No-one is.

And again the Prosecution isn't simply wrong, says the Defence: it has its facts upside down; and moreover goes on supplying the Defence with valuable ammunition. It's a strange and amusing—but also highly significant—fact that, *though in theory I know* that, at 80, I have very little time left (not much more than one fortieth of what I had at 40, and not much more than one sixtieth of what I had at 20) *in practice I feel* that I have just as much time ahead of me as ever, that I have all the time in the world, that essentially I'm timeless and indestructible. I don't even, inside, feel a day older now than then. No:

this isn't evidence of senile wishful thinking, of self-deception, but of the most searching candour and realism working at some level below normal consciousness. For these strong intimations of immortality apply only to the One here, to this 1st Person Singular, present tense, and not at all to those 3rd persons over there. Thus I find myself looking round the circle of my companions (generally much younger than the one I see in my mirror) and noting new symptoms of ageing; and sometimes I sense the cold finger of Death getting very near to one or another of them. But never to *this* one, whom I put in a different category altogether. And I find myself scanning the obituary columns in the newspapers with the same curious detachment: I just don't see me there, ever! In brief, I diagnose all 3rd persons as suffering from a terminal condition which only this 1st Person is immune from.

And of course I am right. I alone—unique, all Reality and no appearance—I alone am deathless. Of course, for I alone AM.

★ ★ ★

Well, that about wipes up this sketch of my trial, of the case for and the case against my mortality. It only remains to say goodbye to my reader.

If you have been reading this article as primarily or only about *my* experience, about the question of D. E. H.'s mortality or immortality and not about yours, you would have been better employed cultivating your garden. It won't do you or anyone any good to play Judge in *my* case and pass verdict on which side has won. This article is about *you*—you as 1st Person Singular, present tense, not about *me* who am (for you) a 3rd person, and as such under sentence of death most assuredly. For all you know, it may have been carried out before you read this.

If you haven't already done so, will you please read this article the way it's meant to be read—as a summery of *your* trial. A purely tentative summary, for you should not *believe* a word it says. *Test everything for yourself.*

I can't say it too loud or too often: you are the Sole Authority on you—on whether you are, in sober fact, the ONLY IMPERISHABLE.

* * *

Chapter 54

MAYDAY CALL

In the language of the child by the perilous sea,

Of his father and his father's people,

To be saved is to be Him.

(It's the only way, there's no other.)

Seven words dovetailing—doing equal justice to—

My misery-me, my crying, my crying need of Him

And my apotheosis as Him, the incomparable safety,

The kingdom and the power and the glory, nothing withheld.

O the relief overriding the wretchedness, the healing the sickness,

The joy the sadness, the lifeboat all the storms wildness!

To be saved is to be Him.

And then there's His kindness, His thoroughness, His ingenuity

As He stockpiles proof on proof on proof, evidence inescapable

Of the impossible things He gets up to in me, for me, and—

Amazing grace!—as me. Of our indissoluble oneing, world without

end.

For instance, my liver-spotty old hands (how like a toad's)

At the wheel of my battered old Peugeot trundling along the highway,

Become His hands, as He suddenly breaks from 70 to 0 mph,

To His eternal stillness. Full stop, no jar, no jerk, no jeopardy,

Accomplishing so smoothly and safely what would smash any other
driver.
Simultaneously He starts up and drives all the traffic
In all the lanes of His world—His telegraph poles
In the very fast lane, His mountains in the very slow lane,
And all between at their proper places. Now tell me,
Who can drive the world but the One who owns the world?
To be saved is to be Him.

And who else, in the train, out of His magician's top-hat,
Could pour forth this niagara of stations, signal boxes, trees,
Fields, towns, cities, countries, what-have-you?
Or the reverse, swallowing it all up, dissolving all that opacity
In His infinite capacity, stowing it all away in the bottomless depths
of that same Hat? That Magician's Top-Hat, as worn by the Godhead?
To be saved is to be Him.

The Eye that He opens is worthy of that Head, a perfect fit.
Single, of course. Clear, of course. Wide, even wider than His world,
Of course. Alternating as the Lamp that brings His world to light
And the Shutter that shuts it down. Finish, enough is enough.
I look, I dare to look at what I'm looking out of,
And see—O blessed, heavenly sight!—that never, no never did I look
Through any other Eye than His. The Eye with the cosmic blink—
And wink. Yes, heavens humour, the humour of the Divine Comedian,
Is kind, at His expense, not mine. I call this generous.
To be saved is to be Him.

Mayday Call

I call it generous to share with me His omnipresence:
To be this Wide-eyed One is to be world-wide, everywhere, boundless,
Strings stretching from my Eye to every star shrinking to a point.
I call it generous to share with me His omniscience.
To see Him here, nearer than hands and feet, is to see into all beings.
I call it generous to share with me his omnipotence.
To say YES to what He does is so to weld my will to His
That my will is done and my peace is perfected.
To be saved is to be Him.

Who is he?
He is the Divine Parachutist who—woosh!—comes down all the way
From the tiptop star to the sink and cellar of His world,
Giving His life for every creature, disappearing in its favour.
Who am I?
I'm the one who, built to that same beautiful blueprint,
Sees that, seeing you, there's nothing left here to keep you out with.
That willy-nilly I die for you the death by guillotine
And am resurrected as you and all the others.
In short, I'm built for loving you with His love
And being you with His Being.
To be saved is to Be the One who is Love itself.

* * *

Chapter 55

MY SPECIAL FRIEND

Mother and I are looking out of the oval window at the children playing.

"What are their names?" I ask.

"That's Johnny, the one with the black hair. The one with her back to us is Mary Anne. The other one is You Darling."

That's a funny name. Why does he keep staring? Why doesn't he play outside the other windows sometimes?"

"Because he is You Darling."

"Does having that name make him stare at me? I think it's because he's my special friend."

The years pass. Johnny and Mary Anne have gone.
But my friend is always there outside the oval window,
Like a good yard dog who knows he isn't allowed indoors.
Sometimes he's full of fun, sometimes miserable
But he never takes his eyes off me.

Now he's growing old and grey and slow, and often sad looking.
I think he's begging to be let in.
I think that if I let him in he would be all over me, smothering me.

He might even kill me, kill me with kindness.

And because he loves me so much, when he dies he wants me to go with him.

If I let my friend in he will be my enemy.
I will not let him in.

* * *

Chapter 56

THE TUNNEL

The star role in the drama of our life is played by Death. Nothing makes the news like Death: the greater the casualties the bigger the headlines. What but gory Death—Death threatened, inflicted, suffered—makes Shakespeare's tragedies so much greater and more gripping than his comedies? Death is the novelist's best friend, without whom where would the least bloodyminded of them be, to say nothing of Sherlock and Agatha? Let's face it: Death is to life what tomato sauce is to pasta. It lends colour and spice.

However, we humans are prodigies of inconsistency. With one eager hand we salute Death, with the other trembling hand we sweep it under the carpet. The way this absurd contradiction works out is this. In effect, we say: "Death in general, the death of others, is what I want to hear about. Tell me, shock me, horrify me, thrill me! But my own death is for hushing up. I don't know what you are talking about."

Psychologists tell us that this is a prime instance of how we suppress unwelcome facts. Refusing to face our fear, we bury it. Only to ensure that, underground, it takes root and flourishes.

To which let me add this. Not only is this suppression of our fear of Death counterproductive: the fear itself is every day becoming more unrealistic, if not plain silly. In the bad old days of hellfire we had good cause to be terrified of dying. Nowadays we have none. Quite the reverse, for two well-founded reasons. The first is founded on what I may expect on my own deathbed, judging by the reports of people who, having died or almost died, have nevertheless been brought back to life. The number of such witnesses returning from their encounter with Death is very large and growing fast, and their evidence turns out to be remarkably consistent and remarkably positive. The second reason is based on my own similar and equally positive findings when, anticipating my deathbed, I go out of my way to encounter Death now.

In this article I want to go into these two orders of evidence, these two distinct reasons for ceasing to fear Death, examining them separately before bringing them together to find out how far they fit and support each other.

The well-established name of the first is the Near-Death Experience or NDE. My name for the second is the Present-Death Experience or PDE.

(I) The Near-Death Experience

In listing the following components of a typical Near-Death Experience or NDE, I don't mean to imply that every NDE includes them all. However, most instances conform fairly closely to our composite picture. Individual accounts naturally vary according to that individual's command of language, and, of course, his or her history, temperament, and beliefs. Nevertheless the family likeness throughout, the cross-cultural agreement, is unmistakable.

(1) Leaving the body

The dying person finds himself stationed at a distance from that body in the car accident, or the patient on the bed or on the operating table. He watches with interest, but some detachment, what's going on over there, the efforts to save his life. Returning to and 'reinhabiting' that body, though a necessary preliminary to recovery, is by no means always welcome. Many are reluctant to leave what they feel is a far better place.

(2) The new body
The viewer of the body from a distance, according to many descriptions, isn't wholly disembodied. There are frequent references to a new, more ethereal body with special powers. It may be connected, as if by an elongated umbilical cord, with the old and dying body. There is greater clarity of mind, and sense experience can be surprisingly brilliant—colours blazing out, for instance—but there is no more pain.

(3) The tunnel
This notable feature of NDEs is normal rather than just common. The subject finds himself drawn through a long and dark tube or tunnel towards a bright light at the far end. There may be a loud buzzing. One witness found "no sensation of an abrupt end of the tunnel, but rather more of a merging into the light."

(4) The Light
Joining that Light, one finds it incomparably brilliant but not at all dazzling. Typically, the Light is felt to be more spiritual or transcendent than physical. It may amount to a Presence or a Person

who, though utterly mysterious, is utterly real. In some instances the Light is also a Love in which one is immersed, experiencing a joy and a peace that are indescribably marvellous.

(5) The review

One has come to a place where time telescopes. The people and events of one's life flash by in great detail, but instantaneously. One's sins are for noting and learning from rather than for rousing feelings of irredeemable guilt and self-loathing. The Light is searching, not searing or scorching. In some cases one is greeted by one's deceased relatives and friends. Those uncommon NDEs which are more negative, or even somewhat hellish, appear to be ones that have been cut short in their early stages.

(6) Results

Life following an NDE is different. The probability is that one is now free from the fear of Death, and that one's behaviour is less narrowly selfish and materialistic. But attempts to interest people in one's Near-Death Experiences, or in their tremendous implications and life-changing power, are as a rule unavailing. Disbelief or ridicule are a common reaction, so one stops talking about it.

So much, then, for our six normal components of an NDE. We come now to—

(II) The Present-Death Experience

Saints and sages are fond of telling us that the way to overcome Death is to "die before we die." No doubt these very special people are speaking from profound, first-hand experience. But for most of us this "dying", if it happens at all, is more like suffering a superficial chest wound than a fatal blow to the heart. It remains a private and personal feeling, strong while it lasts, perhaps, but—like all unanchored feelings—vague and shifting and neither available on demand nor communicable to others.

Is there a more reliable, more practical alternative, one that's not just for the rare saint or sage but for folks like you and me? A method of coming to grips with Death itself, any time and at will? A route through to verifiable facts about what dies and what doesn't die, to a manifestly Deathless foundation upon which one's feelings— so fluctuating and unmanageable—can rest secure and sufficiently steady? Is there, in short, a way of "dying before we die" that you and I can *practise?*

Yes, there is!

Yes indeed. What's more, I'm proposing that we put it into practice right away, before getting to the end of this article.

First, set up your tunnel.

For your NDE or clinical death, as we have seen, you can leave it to a kindly Providence to supply a ready-made tunnel. Your PDE tunnel, however, is a do-it-yourself affair. Either take a shopping bag of around 24 inches (600 cm) diameter and cut off the bottom to form a tube, or—better—make up your tube out of a 24 inch by 24 inch sheet of stiffish white paper, folded back on itself and sticky-taped.

All you have to do now is hold one end of the tube or tunnel up against your bathroom mirror, fit your face in the other end, and trust what you see in there.

See, at the far end, that perisher. (Excuse my language, but this is no time for sweeping Death's-heads under carpets.) See the one that Death has marked out for his own, the prisoner in Death Row awaiting execution. And facing him or her at the near end—which is now your end!—the imperishable, speckless, unbounded Space that's taking in him or her, the undying Light of Consciousness that lights every creature that comes into the world. Can you doubt that you have already come through the tunnel to that Light, have become that Light?

So you are now distinct and distant from that perhaps young and beautiful but dying person. Distant enough to perceive him or her as a 2nd person, as You and no longer as I. This doesn't mean, however, that you are altogether disembodied, just pure spirit. Not at all. As 1st Person Singular at your end of the tunnel, you have another body, a physique so magical and so mysterious that you could call it your heavenly body, exercising powers and sensibilities to match. Which I think you may enjoy all the more if you go on to discover them for yourself, with no help from me.

But a word of warning here. Just reading this spiel of mine about tunnels is as futile as sniffing at an advertisement for Chanel Number Five, or masticating a photograph of Cadbury's nut-milk. You have to make the thing, get in there, travel with attention the length of it, double-check all I've said here on the subject and take seriously what *you* see, what's brilliantly on show at this moment.

Consider! It's not just your life that's in question, but your eternal life. Compared with that, what's fifteen minutes of your valuable time spent buying the materials, plus five minutes for making your tunnel…?

So, wisely and bravely, you decided against putting off till your deathbed your encounter with the Grim Reaper. Seizing the initiative, you took him on. And reaped *him*. Congratulations!

That's it, then. You've had your PDE. It will transform your daily life to the extent that, in and out of tunnels, you go on seeing that What-you-look-out-of is Immortal Capacity for what-you-look-at, for every mortal thing. Including, of course, the perisher you see when you view yourself from a distance, courtesy of that much-abused but precious and faithful instrument, your bathroom mirror.

(III) The NDE And The PDE Compared

Let's now enquire: what will your NDE have that your PDE hasn't already got? And vice versa? How do they match up? For headings we will take the six components of the NDE as listed earlier.

(1) Leaving the body

In the NDE one is distant from the body, in our PDE from the face. If this bothers you, why not stretch and lengthen your tunnel by setting up a full-length mirror at one end of a corridor and retiring to the other end? You will then see yourself as distant—maybe by as much as twenty feet—from that body as a whole. Only go by PRESENT evidence, only trust the GOD-GIVEN OBVIOUS, and all will be clearer than clear.

Distance, however, is two-directional, can be taken in one of two ways. Most NDEs read like leaving home for a better place, whereas most PDEs read like coming Home to the place you never really left. But no matter how they read, both arrive at the same Destination, bathe in the One Light. It's like your annual vacation: whether you see it as getting away from where you belong, or going to where you really belong—your favourite holiday resort—makes no difference to the bracing sea air, those sparkling sands, those gesturing palms.

(2) The new body

Though intriguing, NDE descriptions of one's new body tend to be variable and vague. PDE descriptions, on the other hand, are precise and readily verifiable. If you still wish for guidance about how to check this and go into details, refer to any of my books. As for this new body's sensory sharpness, ascetics beware! Your PDE is liable to anticipate your NDE by dishing up ecstasies like your Christmas Toblerone, the hush of the little town after snow has fallen, the smell of mimosa and the first jonquil of Spring, and the stunning ultra-royal blue of Summer's petunias.

(3) The tunnel

There is indeed a lot to be said for the PDE tunnel. It's shorter and better lit and quieter—less troubled by loud buzzings—than its NDE counterpart. And, of course, it's to hand always and when most needed. These differences are important, but what matters in the end is that both tunnels open up into the Light. It just happens to be an NDE witness who found "no sensation of an abrupt end of the tunnel, but rather more of a merging into the light." But it could have been any PDE witness. Here, they tell exactly the same story.

Surprisingly, it's by means of this commonplace and most earthy of devices that our everlasting felicity is revealed with blazing clarity and vividness, now if we want it, and in the hour of our clinical death if we leave it till then.

(4) The Light

Whichever tunnel you go by, the Light at the near end is one and the same. But of course the hallowed word Light (capitalised) is a metaphor, a hopelessly inadequate indication of the Mystery. Other equally dubious but indispensable metaphors are Space, Emptiness, the Void, Clarity, Capacity, No-thing, the Self-originating One. Nor can Love be crossed off the list. For the Light to merge into Love itself, and issue in perfect joy and peace, is a not-infrequent (and certainly much-to-be-desired) development in the PDE and the NDE alike.

(5) The review

A normal—and surely needful—component of both the NDE and the PDE is an honest and keenly critical looking back at the drama of one's life. At those loved and not-so-loved dramatis personae, and the sometimes villainous role one has played in that drama. In the PDE this review takes time, of course, in fact a lifetime, no matter how 'good' one may be. (Saints know they are sinners, we sinners aren't so sure.) But in the NDE, as we have seen, it is timeless. This last-minute, rushed-through retrospect is less likely to dismay you— much less give you hell—if your long-drawn-out PDE review of the same facts has already done so, repeatedly. Therefore I say: get in your practice now.

(6) Results

Both the NDE and the PDE tend to remove the fear of death and bring in the amending of life. But to talk about either freely is to invite trouble. As we have noted, their own death is for most people taboo, a forbidden topic. In fact, all of us harbour a strong but rarely conscious resistance to the whole subject. Deep down, we are doubly scared, frightened out of our wits twice over. We don't want to know about the death of the thing at the far end of our tunnel, and still less about our leaving it for the No-thing at the near end. It's as if we deliberately mistake that marvellous No-thing—which is wide-awake to itself as No-thing and All-things—for insensate nothingness and mere annihilation.

Conclusion

The differences between the NDE and our do-it-yourself PDE have turned out to be secondary ones, matters of detail. To be, surely, much less than you might have expected, given the considerable differences between you now and you on your deathbed.

The agreements, on the other hand, are striking and highly significant, as well as of great practical importance. They would be all this if they numbered three. Here are twice that number. Only a determined kill-joy or would-be suicide could deny that the NDE and the PDE are complementary versions of the selfsame Death-destroying and Life-giving realisation.

Complementary is the word. Neither can spare the other. As we have seen, in several notable respects our PDE has the edge on the

NDE. It's available at will and when you most need it—which is to say frequently, if not all the while. You can take it at your own pace, slowly and deliberately, and free from clinical discomforts and urgencies. You can readily share this most precious of all gifts with anyone who's half-way interested. Above all, you can *practise* it. So that, in addition to all manner of benefits and boosts along life's difficult way, when you come to the end of it you will be prepared.

Well prepared to enjoy to the full your passage to eternal life.

I end on a historical note.

Our do-it-yourself tunnel came into being at a weekend workshop held in Toronto in March, 1971, long before I read (starting with Dr Moody's *Life after Life*, first published in 1975) about the other, ready-made sort. The idea struck me in the small hours of the morning. Creeping down to the kitchen, I fished out an unused garbage bag, truncated it, woke the none-too-pleased poet Colin Oliver, and insisted on trying it out with him. Very successfully, I might add. Ever since then my friends and I have been carrying paper bags round the world. Tens of thousands have been in there, have seen what dies at the far end, and seen and been—however briefly—what cannot die at the near end. And a relatively small but significant proportion of them are now consciously living, against all the odds, in and from and by that Undying Light.

Of our twenty-five or so devices for unveiling the Light, the paper tunnel has proved far and away the most powerful. I'm learning to see why. A tunnel is God's chosen mise-en-scéne for revealing Himself at the hour of our death. In that case, what more fitting mise-en-scéne than our version of the very same thing, for revealing Him all the days of our life?

Certainly *He* doesn't despise it! That the Highest should elect to turn up, not this time in a birth tunnel and a manger, but in a Canadian garbage bag, witnesses equally to his humour and his humility, to his loving-kindness and his mercy. Heaven's power and glory are *that* kind of power, *that* kind of glory. Any two pages ripped from any of the millions of books on theology and metaphysics in the National Library, and sellotaped together to form a mini-tunnel, have more to tell me about Him, and myself, and the nature of Reality, and what Life and Death really are, than all those volumes together.

* * *

Chapter 57

WHATDUNNIT

Here we are, this winter night, sitting at home, Catherine reading, myself scribbling. Except for an occasional crackling of the fire, all is perfectly quiet at this late hour in the country.

Then a sudden noise—something between a bang and a woosh—at the front of the house.

"*Who's* that?" exclaims Catherine, starting up.

Simultaneously I cry: "*What's* that?", and we both run out to have a look.

And find nothing, except that there's quite a wind, and snow is falling.

In the morning light we look again, and find no footprints in the snow but our own. "There you are," says Catherine, "it was nobody," and writes off the incident as just one of those inexplicable things. But I, who am more familiar with the garden, notice something that's different, that 's new. A severed and dead limb that has been lodged in the branches of the sycamore for years has fallen to the base of the tree.

In short, the question WHAT?, unlike the question WHO?, has produced the solution of the mystery of the noise in the night.

This homely whodunnit—which turned out to be a whatdunnit—brings me to the question that I want to address in this essay. Namely: when I come to *the* Mystery—the Mystery of Being in general and of my own being and identity in particular—*is it a more promising plan to ask myself WHO am I?, or WHAT am I?*

This is surely one of the most crucial but least recognized problems of the spiritual life. Granted that Self-realization is the goal of that life, and that persistent and whole-hearted Self-enquiry is the way to that goal, which of the two routes there—the WHO? road or the WHAT? road—should I take? Which is the more sure, the safer, the sensible way? Or, if there's not much to choose between them, which is the faster?

Now I'm in no position to speak for you or anyone else, and in what follows I am recounting my own experience, in case it should help at all in the clarification and working out of your own experience in this vital matter.

Certainly I began my spiritual adventure, many years ago, by asking myself WHO I am. It was a good and proper start. A *head start* as they say, and that was the trouble. All it led to was head stuff, an idea, a concept of my True Nature. A very human concept, at that, and a million miles from the direct experience of my Nature. And no wonder! WHO? is human, the word is dripping with those human associations and limitations which—come on!—the One in question isn't necessarily subject to: in fact is presumed *not* to be subject to! And so, far more by accident or luck or grace than design, I kept WHO am I? on hold and moved on to WHAT am I?, backed up by other WH queries such as WHERE and WHEN and WHY am I? The merit of these impersonal interrogative pronouns is that they don't, like WHO?, prejudge the issue and beg the question, that they are less biased or loaded, that they apply beyond as well as within the human field and are less crudely anthropomorphic.

The question WHO am I? by itself, without its interrogative partners, very soon brought me to a cul de sac, a dead end in my spiritual adventure. WHAT am I?, on the other hand, opened out all manner of scenic highways where my True and More-than-human Nature is brilliantly on show. With the help of this map, I'd like to invite you to explore this WHAT-am-I country with me.

I would like, for a start, to draw your attention briefly to seven things about this map.

(1) It's a map of oneself as first Person Singular, Present Tense, of what I am for myself verifiably, of what's given rather than what I'm asked to believe and take on trust. It's a map of the whole of me,

human and non-human, of all I need in order to be me. As 2nd/3rd person I'm that all-too-human little fellow in my mirror, who, as such, is emphatically *not all there.*

(2) At Centre (X) I am the unique Reality which is giving rise to all those regional appearances, ranging from particles and atoms to the Galaxy. Which of them you pick up, which you take me to be, depends on how far you happen to be from me at (X). But all are true of me.

(3) The view out from me here at (X) follows the same pattern of concentric circles. In the far distance I find aspects of my astronomical embodiment, in the middle distance aspects of my terrestrial and human embodiments, close at hand these hands and feet, and then at still nearer range there is evidence of cells, molecules, and so on.

(4) The layers of this concentric-system-that-I-am constitute a Unity that is strictly indivisible, an organic or super-organic whole. Thus I have every reason to ask myself what I, the man, am without my filling of organs and cells and molecules and so on, or without my complement of vegetable life and earth and water and air, and the light and energy of the Sun, and so on.

(5) Nor do I *feel* restricted to the individual human belt of this cosmic body of mine. There are times when I identify with my family, my nation, my planet, and when I embrace and take to my heart the whole Creation. And there are other times when I identify with a part of my human body, or even with the Emptiness at (X), its core. In fact, I'm thoroughly elastic, and at least as suprahuman and infrahuman as human.

6) The question WHAT am I? is addressed to and covers all my layers or bands, WHO am I? covers a comparatively narrow band. It leaves out so many of my essentials that what remains is little more than a gutless abstraction, a hollowness.

(7) I am wonderfully fortunate inasmuch as, in the region which I've labelled BITS OF MAN, I'm fitted up with various curiously mobile signposts which I call *my hands*. I find them invaluable— even indispensable—for exploring this thrilling but little-known country of the First Person. I watch their pas de deux, their antics and revelations, with awe.

I would like now to enlarge on the last of these seven features of our map.

Here am I on life's highway, with my right hand (a) thumbing a lift East and with my left (b) a lift West—I don't much care which I get. As luck would have it, I get both at once, and find myself transported at truly breakneck speed in both directions without limit. It's not that I understand or think or feel that I'm suddenly opened out to infinity, but that I *see* it, *see* that East and West are now stowed away in me.

I check this momentous discovery by pointing in (c) at myself (X), and again finding that, yes indeed, I have not only exploded beyond the far horizon, but also beyond the inmost and deepest depth.

This biggest of bombs is certainly the cleanest. I see that what (repeat *what)* this right forefinger (c) is pointing at isn't only boundless but also absolutely immaculate, empty, clearer than clear, purer than pure. Here I find myself to be No-thing whatever, keenly aware of itself as No-thing whatever.

Now with my left forefinger (d) I simultaneously point the other way, point out at my world. And at once I see that, its distance having collapsed, all of it is right here filling my emptiness to capacity. So united, in fact, is the space-that-I-am with its contents that I become those contents—human and non-human alike.

I note that everything this left finger (d) is pointing at is perishing. Even planets and stars and galaxies have a limited shelf life, to say nothing of that little old perisher in my mirror. But not to worry: he's a Dorian-Gray type picture. My right forefinger (c) is pointing in at the one he's a picture of, the one that sees itself to be timeless and ageless and imperishable, for the simple reason that there's nothing here to register time or to grow old or to die.

Finally, I apply these hands (e & f) to the steering wheel of my car, and find them driving not my car but everything else—the nearer it is the faster it goes—while I remain its immovable mover.

Let me now take stock of my discoveries when I switch from asking WHO AM I? to WHAT AM I?

At once and with utmost clarity I see that I'm at large, shut in no box whatever, boundless, infinite. That I'm as free as air, washed whiter than white and relieved of the heavy burden of all things human and non-human. That nevertheless I *am* all those things absolutely, that all are mine, my very own, and in the most intimate sense my loved ones: so that I'm not so much at home in the world as it is at home in me. I see that what I'm looking out of, in sharpest contrast to what I'm looking at, is timeless and ageless and imperishable. I see that I'm the unmoved mover of the world. (How I managed to blind myself to this incredible prowess for twenty years I shall never understand.) And right now, to cap it all, I'm vividly aware of myself as all these things. And I ask myself, is this *it?* Is this *enough?* Will it *do?* The answer comes loud and clear: *it will do!* Which is surely the understatement of all time.

At this point I must insist that you, dear Reader, check and re-check whether what's true for me is true for you also, in detail and point by point. Are your hands, too, wonderfully efficient signposts, or rather fingerposts, guiding you around yourSelf? Are they driving your Land Rover, or your Land? Are you pleased, are you satisfied with the answers that your WHAT-am-I research has come up with? Is it sufficiently marvellous, astounding?

Need I point out the awesomeness, the precision, the certainty, the cumulative power and authority, the blazing obviousness of these attributes of yours, once they are no longer suppressed and turned a blind eye to? Need I emphasize how, beyond all doubting, they confirm to the nth degree what the great sages and saints and seers of the world have been telling you for some three thousand years, namely that really and truly you are infinitely more wonderful and fortunate than you had ever dreamed of?

Allow me to put a rather personal question to those friends, whose WHO-am-I? research or practice has, up to now, proceeded without the WHAT-am-I? complication. Does it yield results comparable with your WHAT-am-I? enquiry? Or hold out as bright or brighter promises of a new and *truly* First-Person way of life?

Before going on to examine what light these discoveries about

WHAT-one-is throw on WHO-one-is, let us take a brief look at the role of those other interrogative pronouns—WHEN and WHERE and WHY—in the unveiling of one's True Identity.

WHEN AM I? The answer is NOW and only NOW, because only NOW can I *see* WHAT I am. Or, to put it another way: because I am as First Person timeless and clean of pastness and futurity, I present no surface to which these labels will adhere. In a word, I'm timetight. The trouble with WHO am I? by itself, on the other hand, is that it's by no means timetight: it leaks into the past and the future, into WHO-I-was and WHO-I-shall-be, which are objects that I think of and nothing like the Subject that I am, that does the thinking. The result is that when I ask myself, simplistically, WHO I am, I'm importing into the present moment—which alone is WHEN I am—all sorts of notions that belong elsewhen and only serve to foul up my perfect clarity.

WHERE AM I? The short answer is HERE, *this* side of the fellow in my mirror, of these black marks on white paper, of whatever I happen to be occupied with. I know my place. It's marked (X) on our map, and it's my peep-hole on all the things in the world. But *what* a peep-hole! For when I really look at those things I find that their distance from me collapses to zero, and that the whole lot, from my constellations to my shirt buttons, is all neatly set out right HERE in me. So that, in truth, my HERE is EVERYWHERE. I don't *believe* in the omnipresence of the One I really, really am. I *see* it as clearly as I see the fingerpost (d) that kindly points it out.

WHY AM I? At the end of man's little day this is the Big Question, the Question that makes hay of and binds together in one truss all other questions. But it's a question I'm unlikely to bother with so long as I'm caught up in the WHO-am-I syndrome. Again, the word WHO begs the question. It assumes what's at issue, and takes for granted a plurality of consciousnesses or entities of whom I am one, that are already in place, that have to be. But nothing has to be. Why should there be anything at all, any stuff, any matter, any consciousness, and in particular this consciousness that's now posing the question? It's not the answering of these unanswerable questions but the asking of them which is so important, so crucial. And it's this in-pointing finger (c) (surely the handiest, most precious, most underrated and neglected of all instruments) that draws attention to this Mystery of mysteries, to the Being here that can find no cause or reason for being, to the one that delightedly discovers itself to be undiscoverable, that is for itself a divine and glorious Wildness or hair-raising Fluke and virtually impossible. This is none other than the One. The One that just can't get over the wonder and joy of being its own mother and father and oh-so-dextrous midwife.

While clearly seeing, courtesy of these magical fingerposts of mine, WHAT I am, and WHEN and WHERE and (in the realest but most paradoxical of senses) WHY I am That, I am at last seeing clearly WHO I am. And this seeing is quite perfect. That's one of the three immense advantages it has over the thinking and understanding and believing and feeling that I deployed in my abortive WHO-I-am enquiry. They are matters of degree, of more or less, it is all or nothing. I just can't see WHO I am dimly, or see a little bit of it, or a spotty version of it, *so long as it merges with my seeing of WHAT I am, right here and right now.* The second immense advantage of this seeing is that it's always at hand and to hand, no matter what my mood. Unlike believing and feeling and all that, it's most available when most needed. The third advantage is that this seeing really is believing.

So in the end these four powerful and searching interrogatives come together in the perfect synthesis, and in practice I don't find myself tirelessly firing a battery of questions at myself—WHO am I? and WHAT am I? and so on. Or even, for that matter, one question. No, thanks to the One who, nearer to me than all else, has the whole world in his hands—in these very hands of mine—I'm no longer a seeker but a finder, for whom in the last resort it is enough, it is everything, simply to see.

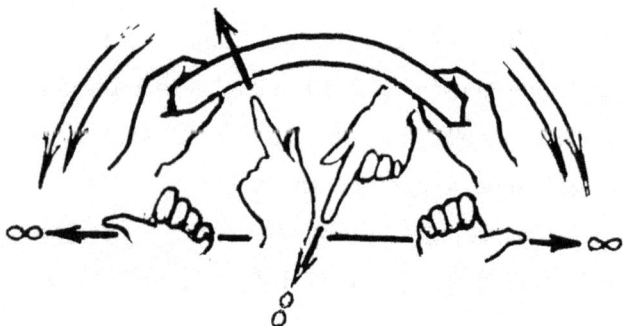

* * *

Chapter 58

HARDING'S LIST

I am crucified with Christ, nevertheless I live, yet not I, but Christ lives in me.

St Paul

Scattered thinly throughout the past two millennia there have been Christians—I'm tempted to call them real Christians—for whom these words of St Paul are literally true and by no means figurative or metaphorical. Men and women who took this tremendous pronouncement of his to heart, who applied it to themselves personally and practised what amounted to a fundamental identity shift from a superficial and wobbly and all-too-human I to an I that was deeper than deep and unshakably divine. Gifted and trusting souls who could say with St Paul "It pleased God, who separated me from my mother's womb, to reveal his Son in me." Fortunate ones, blessed with great faith, who went on to prove in everyday life the reality of what they had assumed to be true.

I am a man of little faith, a doubting Thomas who says to St Paul: "Though my dearest wish is to realise that Christ the God-Man is my life, that He is (or could become) far more me than the blatantly unchristlike fellow pictured in my passport and mirror is me, I just can't believe it. The proposition is ludicrous, altogether too fantastic and flattering to take on trust. How on earth could I, who have every reason to see myself as a momentary speck in this billion-galaxy Universe, claim to be pregnant with (or even identical with) the Source, the Underlying Mystery, the Be-all and End-all of everything? To believe that tallest of stories simply and solely because I happened to read it in some book or heard someone tell it, or because the story-tellers' names begin with St, seems to me a nonsense—a wish-fulfilling nonsense at that—and very rude to that ineffable Source."

So I say to St Paul: "Telling me is no use. I'll believe in the Christ Who is my life when I see and feel Him living my life, when He's so blazingly obvious right here that I can no longer doubt His presence and my absence, my shift of identity to Him."

But first I must be clear Who Christ is for me, what I mean by that exalted but loaded and ambiguous title. Let me therefore list what I take to be His essential attributes, the characteristics I would have to take on if—wonder of all impossible wonders!—I were to switch from being Douglas Edison Harding to being Him and living His life, Paul fashion or any fashion whatever.

I call it Harding's List, because it's not, I guess, precisely yours, or what a priest or a theologian would come up with.

(1) Self-giving
Christ's very nature is Self-giving love, to the point of dying that you and I may live.

(2) Crucifixion
What makes his death so special is the manner of it. He's the Crucified One.

(3) A new body
Now risen from the dead, however, He takes on a drastically re-modelled, resurrection body.

(4) Imperishability
It's an undying, eternal embodiment. Time is in Him, rather than vice versa.

(5) Omnipresence
Far from being imprisoned or exclusively located in that glorious body, He's everywhere, at large.

(6) Centrality
Not only does He pervade the Cosmos, but all of it proceeds from Him and returns to Him who lies at its Centre.

(7) Inclusiveness
And everything and everyone, no matter how insignificant or ugly, how miserable or sinful, is embraced by Him, is held in his great Heart.

(8) Purity
Yet He remains uncontaminated, serene, spotless, in every way perfect.

(9) Stillness
His perfection includes perfect peace and rest, yet it's from his Immobility that all things are moved.

(10) Omnipotence
In fact, He's all-powerful. At least in the long run his will is done.

(11) Omniscience
And as all-wise He has perfect insight into what all beings really are:
He knows them so much better than they know themselves.

(12) God in to Man, Man in to God
And yet, notwithstanding this galaxy of transcendent attributes, He
is Man no less than God, human no less than divine.

Well, that's Harding's List. It sets out what I'm not, but would have
to be if Christ lived in me and lived my life. Here are twelve respects
in which I fall infinitely short of his many-sided perfection. All these,
with more lurking for sure, whereas just one of them would have been
enough to bar me absolutely from Christhood.

How right I was not to *believe* the Apostle, and demand to be
shown that Christ is, or could become, my life and my very being.
And how wrong I would now be to settle for *neither,* to refuse to
believe and refuse to look, thus falling between two stools into the
dark pit of blind disbelief. No, I must do one or the other. And I
decide to LOOK AND SEE, just in case Paul had more reasons for
making his astounding claim than he was fully conscious of.

What I'm now going to do, accordingly, is to put together
Harding's Second List. Not this time a twelve-point description of
Christ as I conceive Him to be out there, but of myself as I perceive
myself to be in here, at Centre. By *myself* I don't mean that little old
second or third person I see over there in my mirror, but the very
different First Person who is this side of the mirror, the one here who
does the seeing. And for ease of comparison I combine the two lists—

Christ's attributes in italics, mine as First Person in ordinary printing.
This Map of what I see should help that comparison.

(1) Self-giving
Christ's very nature is self-sacrificing love, to the point of dying that you and I may live.

Right here at the Centre of the Map, I experience myself as Empty Space, as Capacity or Room for whatever or whoever's on show. Having nothing here to keep you out with, I vanish in your favour. In fact, I die for you. If there remained a mere cell here in the Place I'm looking out of I would survive. If there remained a mere molecule or atom or particle here I would exist. But Nothing's left. Your appearance here, in all its vividness and rich detail, requires and ensures my disappearance. You swing the axe, and I welcome my executioner.

(2) Crucifixion

What makes his death so special is the manner of it. He's the Crucified One.

Looking straight ahead and raising my arms to shoulder-height, I spread them till they almost vanish. And I notice how different they are from the puny arms of the fellow in my mirror, and those of all third persons. Mine embrace the wide world, the whole of what's presenting itself. My left hand is further from my right than sunrise is from sunset, than one end of the rainbow is from the other. And it's not only his all-inclusive gesture that's cruciform. I find myself participating in the suffering that goes with crucifixion.

(3) A new body

Now risen from the dead, however, He takes on a drastically re-modelled resurrection body.

Looking here to see what kind of body I really do sport, the true shape of this First Person O-So-Singular, I find surprise piled on surprise. Not only am I decapitated and wider-than-wide-armed, but upside-down and facing the wrong way. Or am I the right way up and facing the right way, while the others are the wrong way up and facing the wrong way? In either case, they are furnished with a pair of eyes apiece, two tiny peep-holes out of a bone box, whereas I'm furnished with a Single Eye that's at least as wide as the scene it's taking in. (To check this, I have only to put on my spectacles mindfully, to see those lenses merging into this vast Monocle. How could I ever look through anything else?) In short, every instant of my long life has been lived in and as this peculiar but rarely noticed embodiment. I'm not just different from but the opposite of what I look like to you.

(4) Imperishability
It's an undying, eternal embodiment. Time is in Him, rather than vice versa.

Every-thing, including all my appearances near and far, has a beginning and an end. As the central Reality that's giving rise to them, however, I experience the world as a succession of things in me who am no-thing whatever. As such, as their immaculate Container, I'm without beginning or end, changeless, timeless. If I should doubt this I have only to consult my wrist-watch. Normally it tells me the time over there. But when I bring it all the way to my Eye it tells me the No-time right here, and itself vanishes in the telling.

(5) Omnipresence
So far from being imprisoned or exclusively located in that glorious body, He's everywhere, at large.

Here at my Centre is the Point these huge arms are branching out of, which is also the Spot I'm looking out of. Pointing in now with my forefinger I fail to find that Point. Silently it has exploded to Infinity. The Centre of the cosmic circle has devoured all its radii. In other words, I perceive no distance between you and me, and a ruler held up between your eye and my Eye, being end-on, reduces to zero. By the same token the 'furthest' star coincides with myself its observer. All I see I see here. I'm omnipresent.

(6) Centrality
Not only does He pervade the Cosmos, but all of it proceeds from and returns to Him who is the Unique Centre of everything.

I take up the ruler again and with it prolong downwards the

perpendicular lines around me—such as the door-jambs and the corners of the room. And I discover that they all converge upon and radiate from me. My geometry teacher told me that parallel lines meet at Infinity. He was right. I am that Infinity, What's more, it's Infinity wide awake and Self-aware. It is here and nowhere else in the Universe that I find the Consciousness that brings everything to being and life and meaning.

(7) Inclusiveness
And everything and everyone, no matter how insignificant or ugly, how miserable or sinful, is embraced by Him, is held in his great Heart.

The Vacancy here is remarkably hospitable. Nothing and no-one's left out. The truth is that I'm not well, not quite sane, not all there, not whole till I'm the Whole. Nor is the Universe in good nick so long as I insist on carving it in two, into a me-part confronting a not-me-part, an observer up against an observed. To heal that cruel and cosmic wound and enjoy the Universe as it really is, as a Universe and no longer a Duoverse, I have to be what I am—all of it and none of it.

(8) Purity
Yet He remains uncontaminated, serene, spotless, in every way perfect.

What you take me to be depends on your viewpoint, and notably on how far away that viewpoint happens to be. At a distance of a few feet I appear to be a man. Approaching me, your senses sharpened with optical and electronic equipment, you find the man turns out to be a community of living things called cells, and each cell turns out to be a community of non-living things called molecules. And so on, through atoms and particles—to what? You have an equally curious story to tell if, instead of approaching me, you recede. Then I take on a succession of geographical and astronomical appearances, as indicated on our Map. Again, appearances of what? Ask me, and I will tell you: they are the regional appearances of this Central Reality which I am, and to which no outsider has access, of this Simplicity, this Clarity. As such, in sharp contrast to all those variegated and indispensable but turbid appearances of mine, I am cleansed at last. I am Purity itself.

(9) Stillness
His perfection includes perfect peace and rest, yet it's from his Immobility that all things are moved.

While I can find excuses for overlooking the obvious fact that intrinsically I'm stainless, I can find none for overlooking the equally obvious fact that intrinsically I'm motionless. In the train, at the wheel of my car, or taking a walk, I have only to see what I see instead of what I think I see. Coming to my senses, ceasing to hallucinate like mad, I stop denying that everything from distant peaks and foothills to wayside telegraph poles is on the move, and the nearer it is the faster it goes. The faster it goes in me, who am the central and all-enveloping Stillness, the unmoved mover of the world.

(10) Omnipotence
In fact, He's all-powerful. At least in the long run his will is done.

I find in me two wills. One goes with myself as second-cum-third person and the other with myself as First Person. The former is quick to say NO to half of what happens to me, while the latter eventually says YES, So Be It, to the lot. With good reason: I see that right here at Centre I've nothing left to keep any of it out with, and I'm burst wide open to take whatever's in store for me. Concurring with it is often excruciatingly difficult, of course. But in practice it's the precondition for the only peace worth having. And so at last the paradox holds: I have no will *and* my will is done.

(11) Omniscience
And as all-wise He has perfect insight into what all beings really are. He knows them so much better than they know themselves.

The Clarity I see myself to be here at Centre is obviously, in fact, no-one's property. It has no surface on which to stick anyone's label. You could describe it as the Common Ground which underlies and nourishes all beings. It follows that to see into my own Clear Nature is to see into yours, whoever you are. In fact, really to see and know myself at this level is not only to see and know you but to be you. Here, I *am* you. Now that's intimacy. The last barrier is down.

(12) God into Man, Man into God
And yet, notwithstanding this galaxy of transcendent attributes, He is Man no less than God, God no less than Man.

How shall I evaluate this First Person Singular, what status shall I accord to the sitter whose portrait I have just painted? There's much about him that's human—the shape of his arms and legs, for instance. But more that's superhuman—their dimensions, for instance; and the way, at the wheel and the pedals of his car, they drive the countryside. We have here, in fact, a most intimate conjunction of the human and the divine, an elegant and working apotheosis. Is there any other that makes good logical and practical (and indeed theological) sense? Here, held up for our most searching inspection, is the answer to all those dusty and worm-eaten volumes of convoluted and often bitter and sometimes lethal controversy about the Man who is God and the God who is Man; and how the two Natures can merge yet stay distinct. But what's far more important is that here we have our pattern for living, all day and every day. For living a life that's human at last because it's divine, and divine because it's human. A Centred instead of an eccentric life.

So there they are, all twelve of Christ's attributes as I conceive them, set against my own corresponding attributes as I perceive them. My attributes (I hasten to remind you) at Centre, as First Person Singular, in stark contrast to those of that off-centre and unsingular fellow called Harding.

It's a pretty close fit, I think you'll agree. Why so? *Because our true First Person Singular is none other than Paul's indwelling Christ.*

The Map has helped me to keep awake to this tremendous fact. I drew what I saw, and was fascinated and informed. Then I saw what I drew, and was devastated. I pray God I will never recover from that shock, from that vision. The only thing that matters, as I near the end of this earthly life, is union with my Source, my basic identity-shift to the One who is both other than me and more me than I am myself. And I find that this Map of the shift not only helps that shift along wonderfully, but balances and completes the familiar icon of the Crucified Saviour giving his life out there for me. Completes it with this unfamiliar icon of the risen and glorified Lord living his life right here in me.

Maybe you question whether the indwelling Deity whose twelve attributes I have listed is the same One that Christian saints and sages have been devoted to down the centuries. Well, there are hundreds of texts which confirm that He is indeed One and the Same for them and for me, and I trust for you also. This small sample of quotes, however, will have to do here.

The New Testament

There are many passages in St John's Gospel and in the letters of St Paul and Pseudo-Paul on the subject of our union with Him, of our Christing. And there is that saying of St Peter that we are made partakers of the Divine Nature.

St Symeon the New Theologian

We awaken in Christ's body as He awakens in our body, and my poor hand is Christ. He enters my foot, and is infinitely me. I move my hand and wonderfully it is Christ.

Meister Eckhart

What matters is that Christ's birth should happen in me. Discover this birth in you, and you shall experience all good and all comfort, all happiness, all being and all truth.

God shines in with his Light and brings in with Him all you forsook and a thousand times more, together with a new form to contain it all.

Henry Suso

He (Suso) asked one of the bright princes of Heaven what God's hidden dwelling-place in the soul looked like... Then he looked in and saw that his body above his heart was as clear as crystal.

The blessed are stripped of their personal initiative and changed into another form, another glory, another power.

St Teresa of Avila

However large, magnificent and spacious you imagine this castle of the soul to be, you cannot exaggerate it: its capacity is beyond all understanding, and the Sun at the Centre lights up every courtyard.

William Law

To find or to know God in reality by any outward proofs, or by anything but by God Himself made manifest and self-evident in you, will never be your case either here or hereafter.

I conclude with St Bernard of Clairvaux's uncompromising announcement: *We abide in darkness so long as we walk in belief and not in beholding.*

Postscript

To readers who are put off by the Christian language and bias of the above, I would point out that not one of the "Twelve attributes of the Christ who lives in me" is revealed to me by faith, Christian or non-Christian. On the contrary, all arise from *lack* of faith, from a thoroughly agnostic looking-to-see, from observation and experiment that are virtually atheist.

In that case, why do I link them to just one religion?

Because I don't know enough about the others to be sure just how and in what guise they embody the Twelve. Nor do I need to know. What matters is that the discovery of these attributes within me should inspire me to let them out, to *live* them somehow or other. In this I'm immensely helped by the fact that my own deep, deep roots draw their nourishment from Christian strata laid down over two millennia, coupled with the happy fact that this native and home-grown religion happens to take good care of the Twelve.

I suspect that my Creator foresaw that it would take all these proofs to persuade me of my union with Him, whereas just one of them would have been enough to persuade any reasonable creature. Anyway, I'm immensely grateful to Him for my doubts about Him, for the agnosticism that alone could give rise to such a gnosis.

William Blake wrote: "O Mercy! O Divine Humanity, O Forgiveness, O Pity, O Compassion! If I were pure I should never have known Thee." To which I add: *If I had believed in Thee I would never have seen Thee within me, enrobed in twelvefold splendour. I would never have seen Thee at all.*

* * *

Chapter 59

THE DOOR

For the sake of clarity and succinctness I have entitled the six parts of this article as follows:- (1) The outsider, (2) The Door in the wall, (3) The window in the wall, (4) Through the Door, (5) Into the bride chamber, and (6) The insider.

(1) The outsider

In a famous passage the English philosopher Thomas Hobbes (1588-1679) described the life of man as "solitary, poor, nasty, brutish, and short". He also described it as "a war of everyone against everyone".

"Let the miserable fellow speak for his own life and times, not for mine," you may feel like retorting.

I suggest that if Hobbes had lived in our world he would have found additional reasons for gloom. As an almost invisible speck in this billion-galaxy universe, brief to the point of extinction in the vast stretches of cosmic time, facing certain execution followed by an endless oblivion that strips all meaning from the struggle and pain of his life, modern man is the very stuff of tragedy. He asks himself—I ask myself—what is the point of it all? Even when, wearing my terrestrial blinders, I refuse to look beyond the cosmic dust-grain called Earth, I'm no better off: I learn that I'm just one of 6,000,000,000 humans now inhabiting—or do I mean infesting?—the planet. To say nothing of the hordes that have gone hence and have yet to come hither. Try as I may, I can no longer shut my eyes to these inescapable truths. Or go on denying that I'm as lost and insignificant as a sand-grain in the Sahara Desert, with the added nastiness that I'm scared stiff of dying—if not also, a lot of the time, of living? Not to mention the cruelties, the aches and pains, the bickering and squabbling that sand-grains are innocent of.

You may point out, of course, that this hideously dark picture of the human condition leaves out the love, the joy, the fun, the high adventure, the beauty that keep creeping into our lives, in spite of it all. To which I can hear myself replying: "If the fate of even the best things of our life is the meaningless and endless night of forgetfulness, of total unconsciousness, I see in them more reason for funerary mourning than rejoicing."

Of this I'm sure: nothing's gained and much is lost by burying our heads in the sand. Nothing that I say in the later and more cheerful sections of this article can subtract one iota from our plight. Not until we resolutely and honestly face what we are as humans are we driven to seek and find what else we are.

The trouble is that, between us and that What-else, there is an immense obstacle, a great wall.

(2) The Door in the wall

Yes, though the wall is vast and immensely strong there is in it a Door.

Do you remember reading, when young, about a secret door into a magic garden? Through that door the small boy in the tale passed back and forth as he pleased into that garden. But when he got bigger he couldn't find that door any more. And isn't his story your own as well as mine—a story of a real and blessed place we were shut out of as we grew up? In fact, aren't we tragically apt to forget all about that door and that garden, and even to deny they ever existed? Or else to talk sadly, with T.S. Eliot, of "the door we never opened, into the rose garden"?

You will realise, of course, that I'm not speaking of the Heaven or Pure Land or Western Paradise or Happy Country that religions promise the faithful, on conditions which distinguish it sharply from the country our Door leads to. Entry to those celestial regions depends on our correct belief and good behaviour, it's not granted at the beginning of our life but at the end, and as a rule those regions are a long, long, way off—if not in another and alien dimension. And nowadays even a reluctant sceptic is likely to dismiss this promised afterlife as so much wish-fulfilling imagination, as a mere tarted-up and pie-in-the-sky version of ordinary Earthly life, and plain incredible. All of which is the opposite of the country our Door opens out on. As we shall presently see, it's here and now, altogether present in time and space, wholly real and indubitable and satisfying, and startlingly different in all important respects from life on this, the dark side of the wall, yet immeasurably more natural. Repeat natural.

But alas, as I have said, to grow up is to lose the Door that leads to these good things. Instead, I find a window.

(3) The window in the wall
At least it has all the appearance of a window, through which I can see

myself well and truly set up on the other side of the wall, pulling faces at me on this side. A strange, if not schizoid condition, which I seek to correct by moving right up to the window, in the hope of uniting this me with that me. Result: not only, with nose pressed against the glass, am I held up on this side of the wall, but I lose all trace of the puller-of-faces on that side.

The truth, of course, is that the window isn't a window after all. It's a mirror. All the same, though it won't let me through the wall, it does hold out the hint—if not the assurance—that somehow or other, and in some guise or other, I belong on the far side of the wall no less than on this side.

The trouble starts when, in spite of that unbreakable glass, I try and try again to smash a way through for Douglas Edison Harding and as Douglas Edison Harding into that other (and presumably better) country. In fact, nearly all of us spend nearly all our lives this way, in the pursuit of happiness and fulfilment as human beings. No doubt we must have a go at it, very seriously and in spite of all discouragements—until we learn (the sooner the better) the hopelessness of our quest. The window is as rock-solid as the wall itself.

The only way through is the Door. Yes, though we lost track of it when we grew up, it's still there, as inviting as ever.

(4) Through the Door

Neither the window nor the Door is a symbol or a metaphor. Both are visibly and tangibly actual-factual. I can knock loudly at the window and handle (and even smell) the archway of that wide-open Door. And, of course, make a picture of it.

Unfortunately I can't make a hole in the page and thus open the Door for you, still less enlarge the hole to head-size. I will have to leave it to you to make up for yourself a full-size and preferably black card with a 6-inch hole in it. Or else beg, borrow, or steal such a card from your 'seeing' friends. If you want to go through the Door you must somehow produce a Door for going through, an open Door, along the lines of my sketch. Just the holed card will do, any art-work is an optional extra. But I warn you: no card, no rose garden.

Here's what you must do.

Holding the card at arm's length, examine carefully that empty doorway, that speckless void. Note that it's imperishable (nothing's there to perish), and timeless (where there's nothing there's nothing to measure time with and no time to measure). But it's not that big: the hole in the wall is strictly limited. Also it's unconscious.

Now slowly, and with great attention, approach that empty doorway, watching for the magic moment when two things happen:

The ever-growing hole in the wall suddenly expands beyond all bounds, and the empty space you were looking at suddenly becomes the well-filled Space you are looking out of. It wakes up in you and as you.

You are now clear of the wall. On this side of it you see yourself to be the timeless and imperishable No-thing that contains all those things that perish. And let me remind you that every thing, even a galaxy, has a limited shelf-life. In fact, along with no-thingness and immensity, you have put on immortality. I think you'll agree that it's a perfect fit.

But these superb blessings don't come cheap. There's a price to pay. They cost you all you have got, down to your last farthing.

Clearly to see how this all works out, you must now complete the experiment by going up to your bathroom mirror, still wearing the card.

Observe how that human being in your mirror utterly and forever fails to pass through the Door in the wall. He or she is stuck in that doorway, bunging it up. And observe how, by contrast, the one who is your side of that glass—the One who, having paid the full price of admission, is bankrupt—is clean through. Clean through as Zero, he or she is Infinity. Loser take all.

Observe, finally, how comic that one in the mirror looks. Quite unlike you, he or she is playing a game. Let's call it Belgian Nuns.

The Door

And if you were joined in your bathroom by all those 6,000,000,000 humans, each holding a card the way you are holding yours, every one of them would be playing the same game. You would clearly see that no human being as such, not even the holiest sister in that vast and weird convent, can get through the Door to the other side. To your side.

Yes, the marvellous and clearly visible fact is that you alone are through. Through to the Beatific Vision, to the True Rose Garden, to the Land of Heart's Desire, You are the Alone, the Sole Enjoyer.

You who were a sand-grain in the Sahara are now the Sahara. You are no longer lost in the world. It's lost in you. Congratulations!

End of experiment.

(5) Into the bride chamber
In case you suppose I'm alone in offering you my congratulations, or am exaggerating wildly, there are others who tell much the same story about you. For example:

In the Gospel of Thomas we read: "Many stand outside the Door, but it's the Alone that goes through to the bride chamber."

Meister Eckhart declared, with typical boldness, "A noble man is that only begotten son of God whom the Father begets from all eternity."

Jesus said, and so say I—yet not I but Christ who lives in me—"I am the Door."

Thomas Traherne insisted that you don't enjoy the world till you see that you are its sole heir.

And, in case you should imagine that he's terribly conceited and selfish, Traherne adds that his joy is complete when he realises that everyone else as well is the sole heir of the world. A wild paradox, of course. But then everything on this, the rose-garden side of the wall, is paradoxical, a union of opposites. Here you are Every-thing because you are No-thing, and own Every-thing because you own No-thing. Here you have your cake, and eat it.

I'm not asking you to believe a word of all this, but to look and see whether it's true for you. Through that Door, on this side of the wall, endless astonishing and beautiful discoveries await the sincere and enterprising enquirer.

(6) The insider

To conclude, let's see how our discoveries on this side of the wall overcome the miseries on Hobbes' side of the wall, where life is "solitary, poor, nasty, brutish, and short. And a war of everyone against everyone."

Solitary

On the dark side of the Door I'm solitary, agonisingly lonesome, because I have no room for others, while on the bright side I'm Alone because I'm all Room for others, because I include all beings and vanish in their favour. My Aloneness here is the perfect and only medicine for my loneliness there.

Poor

The richest tycoon on Hobbes' side of the Door is a pauper. Not only do his possessions shrink to invisibility in the cosmic economy, but very soon they come to possess him. True ownership is enjoyed only on the other side, where even the stars are mine. I who am in the world go through the Door, and, hey presto!, the world's in me. Which makes a world of difference.

Nasty

To say that the Door opens out on a nice and no longer nasty world is misleading. It's a world where bright lights cast dark shadows, where beauty shows up ugliness, where truth can't spare the lies it challenges, where love is free to go as well as to come. But it's a world charged throughout with meaning and adventure, in which even the nastiest nastiness plays its part.

Brutish

On the dark side of the wall, we humans are in a number of ways worse than the brutes, than animals. But there's no road back to their innocence in Eden. There's only the road ahead, through that realest of Doors to that realest of places—to the land where, paradoxically again, we become at last truly human because we have discovered and taken on our intrinsic divinity.

Short

I don't want to die. How can I prolong my life, at least by a few days, months, more doubtfully years? My doctor and the NHS will make suggestions. But the Grim Reaper is still breathing down my neck, and I'm terrified. What can I do? Only this: instead of trying to stretch out my life, I pare it down to this very moment, to the timeless Now which, once through that Door in the wall, explodes to contain all time. Wishful thinking, you suspect? In that case, hold out your wrist-watch to see what the time is over there in Hobbesland. Now bring it slowly towards you till it will come no nearer. And read off the No-time in the timeless Rose Garden. Your watch is no liar. It tells you the timeless truth about yourself, and itself vanishes in the telling.

A war of everyone against everyone

On Thomas Hobbes' side of the wall you and I stand face to face. Like it or not, we confront each other. "Keep out, I've got one" each is whispering, or muttering, or bellowing at his opposite number. And then, coming to our senses at long last, we pluck up the courage to go through the Door, one at a time, of course. And instantly, on that side of the wall—which is now this side—you and I stand face to no-face, face to space. Whatever we happen to feel about each other, or to think of each other, each sees that he or she is empty for the other. I die that you may live, for such is my nature. And this is the realest death, where nothing's left of me, not a particle of goo for an undertaker to undertake. Followed at once by the realest resurrection, in which I not only take on your life but all life. All life and all existence.

Inscribed above that Door to the beautiful Rose Garden are the words: He who saves his life shall lose it, and he who loses his life shall save it.

Chapter 60

FATE AND FREEDOM

reconciled in the 1st Person

Contemporary physics suffers from a fundamental contradiction, a yawning split down the middle. What's more, it's aware of and embarrassed by the contradiction. Not as embarrassed as it should be, but embarrassed all the same.

On the one hand, Einstein's General Theory of Relativity presents us with a four-dimensional space-time continuum in which all events—future as well as past, according to our reckoning—are "out there" and "real", much as distant objects like Mars and Antarctica are "out there" and "real", no matter how currently inaccessible to you and to me. In popular terms, the idea behind H. G. Wells' famous story *The Time Machine* was a valid one: our Here-Now is solidly embedded in an Elsewhere-Elsewhen matrix that's already established throughout. Which can only mean that our destiny, down to the smallest detail, is irrevocably settled, and that our precious free-will is an illusion. For better or worse, our fate is sealed. As the troops used to say in the First World War, it's the bullet with your name scratched on it that's sure to get you. Or words to that effect.

So much for the Finger of Fate on the one hand. On the other hand, the Quantum Mechanics of modern physics presents us with a universe whose particles—whose fundamental constituents—behave quite unpredictably. Here, at the very base of the natural world, there lurks—or rather flourishes—a freedom and a spontaneity, a lack of constraint which can by no means be fitted into the four-dimensional Einsteinian universe, a wildness which that rigidly predetermined order of things forbids absolutely.

Note that this isn't one of those normal professional ding-dongs, one of those inevitable disagreements that arise between specialists in every field. No, we don't have here a couple of speculative cosmologies which leave us free to pay our money and take our pick. *Both* are verifiable, and for *both* there's weighty scientific evidence! Yet once more, in fact, the Science of the Object or 3rd Person runs into grievous trouble, into an absurdity and a nonsense which only the Science of the Subject or 1st Person can resolve.

Yes, it's *you*—you as What and Who you really are—who supply the much-needed *tertium quid*, the only answer, the master key which opens the iron-clad door between Fate and Freedom. You personally—first-personally—are their reconciliation. And why? Because you belong on both sides of the door. As we shall presently see, you have a foot firmly planted in each camp. Miraculously, you straddle the incompatibles.

Please allow me to go on speaking to you about you and for you, on the strict understanding that in reality you are the sole and final authority on you, and that all I say is for you to check, for you to decide whether it's true for you and of you as well as for me and of me.

Let's start, as we did before, with Fate. And distinguish, among the several ways of looking at and coming to terms with Fate, three alternatives:

Fate And Freedom

(1) If you happen to be a mathematician, you can follow Einstein's calculations and respectfully endorse his four-dimensional "block universe". Or if (like me) you are not, you can picture yourself deftly steering your Time Machine slap-bang into the year 2,100 A.D., or even 21,600 A.D. Or else, if you prefer, into the year 1,900 A.D., or even 19,000 B.C. And maybe you can tell yourself that you wouldn't be able to do this so easily and naturally in imagination if time-travel had no basis in fact, and were quite absurd. And you can certainly add that your present life is nothing without memory and foresight, the one probing into the so-called past that hasn't passed and other probing into the so-called future that is there for probing into.

(2) Or you can picture the universe as a huge spider-web of mutual conditioning, yourself held fast and cocooned in its sticky threads. A universe in which the behaviour and structure of each part is determined by the behaviour and structure of every other part. So that, for instance, the pressure of your forefinger against the ball of your thumb, as you hold this book open, will in due course disturb the remotest star. In fact, the whole scientific enterprise takes for granted this gigantic web from which there's no escaping.

(3) Or, finally, you can tell yourself (and mean it with all your heart) that what happens, and in particular everything that happens to you, is divinely ordained. And you can say to God: "It's not just that I have no option but to submit to your will, but that to do so is my deepest need. Your will is my peace, the only cure for my anguish. The true recipe for joy is self-abandonment to the Divine Providence."

As I See It

Well, as I say, you have a choice of one or another of these three attitudes to Fate or formulations of Fate. And, of course, you may think up others to choose from. In fact, I don't see why you shouldn't grant some validity to them all, each from its own point of view and couched in its own peculiar terminology. What they agree on, the name of the common ground they share, is *Destiny*. Even your 'choice' between them is predestined, inevitable.

So much for the left foot you firmly plant in the Country of Fate. and now for the right foot you plant, no less firmly, in the Country of Freedom. Which makes you, as 1st Person Singular—*very singular!*—a colossos who straddles two utterly alien countries, not by effort or deliberate intention, but by reason of the dual citizenship which is your birthright.

I take it that you already have, with due care and attention and submission to the evidence, carried out the Tunnel Experiment on which *The Science of the 1st Person* is based. [This article was written as an additional chapter—but never added—to *The Science of the 1st Person*.] And I ask you to remind yourself of the discoveries you made then by simply pointing to your face, to *What you are looking out of* at this moment.

Please devote a few minutes of your valuable time to noticing that your forefinger is in fact not pointing at your face but at Space which clearly displays these six characteristics. It is (i) Boundless, (ii) Empty, Immaculate, (iii) Imperishable, because empty of things to perish, (iv) Empty-for-filling, All-inclusive, replete with and perfectly united with the changing scene, every item of which is perishing, (v) Wide

Awake to Itself as all this, and (vi) not just wide awake to *What* it is, but to the infinitely more astounding fact *That* it is, to the wonder of its own Self-origination.

Now these six add up to Who and What you are at Centre, as 1st Person, in stark and detailed contrast to what you are over there at a distance, as the 3rd Person on show in your mirror. As the former you are the divine No-thing that is Freedom Itself, while as the latter you are that human thing shackled by relentless Fate. While the *distance* between these two sides of yourself is a mere metre or so, the *difference* between them is more than astronomical.

This wonderful Freedom that is yours at Centre is revealed by the pointing experiment to be twofold. *As the One who you discovered to be boundless and all-inclusive, you are subject to no outer constraint or authority; and as the One who you discovered to be empty you are subject to no inner constraint or necessity.* As Who you really, really are there's nothing and no-one above you to boss you and nothing and no-one below you to bug you. And if you go on to describe this twofold liberation as participation in the divine freedom of the One who alone is truly free, who is Freedom itself, I'm with you all the way.

"But what sort of freedom is it," I can hear you asking, "that can find no field to function in? To be free is to be free to do something, to make a difference in the world. My *inclusion* of a world that I can't change does nothing to improve it or to free me."

I reply that—whether we like it or not—the Science of the Subject or 1st Person relies on paradoxical logic (A is B, B is A), whereas the

Science of the Object or 3rd person relies on Aristotelian logic (A is A, B is B). Take, for instance, these examples of the former: my in-pointing finger reveals that I the 1st Person am a Point that explodes into Everywhere, a Now that explodes into Everywhen, a Nothing that explodes into Everything, a Central Calm that explodes into the Cosmic Whirlpool, a Central Silence that explodes into the Music of the Spheres. Equally it reveals a Central Freedom that explodes into a Multi-peripheral Submission, a my-will-be-done into Thy-will-be-done, and this Submission is that True Freedom which is God's. By the grace and mercy of God and his lovely paradoxes, I can say YES to his designs, *and in doing so make them mine.* And these designs of mine make all the difference in the world. All the difference.

You aren't altogether convinced? Nor will you and I ever be by thinking about it, but only by living it. That's what Freedom is for.

Where the Spirit of the Lord is, there is liberty.

St. Paul

For God, freedom is necessary.

Vladimir Soloviev

God… whose service is perfect freedom.

The Book Of Common Prayer

It is because we are not near enough to Thee to partake of thy liberty that we want a liberty of our own apart from thine.

George MacDonald

With the removal of the "I" illusion, the world with all its multiplicities will disappear, and if there is anything left which can act, this one will act with perfect freedom, with fearlessness, like the Dharma King himself, indeed as the One.

D. T. Suzuki

Freedom and constraint are two aspects of the same necessity, which is to be what one is and no other.

Antoine De Saint-Exupery

* * *

NOTES

These notes provide information about when Harding wrote the articles and poems in this collection—and if they were published, when they were *first* published and where. (Sometimes it's unclear if or where they were published. In these cases I have made no comment. And some of these articles were recycled, as it were, at later times in different journals with different titles and introductions.)

* * *

1. *Engineering*. Circa 1942. "A wireless talk by Major D. E. Harding on All-India Radio, broadcast from their Calcutta studio." Harding had gone to India in 1937 with his family to take up an architectural job in Calcutta. In 1941 he joined the Army. He returned to England in 1945. (*The Hierarchy of Heaven & Earth* was published in 1952.)

2. *Man No Animal*. Written: Sept. 1951. Published: *The Frontier* journal, Feb. 1952.

3. *Are Angels Superfluous?* Written: 1951. Published: T*heology* journal, March 1952. Originally called *Concerning Angels*.

4. *On Having No Head*. Written: 1951. Previously unpublished.

5. *The Pot-Bellied Angel*. Written: Nov. 1951. Previously unpublished.

6. *Grounds For Hope*. Written: 1951. Previously unpublished.

7. *The Progress Of Ignorance*. Written: 1951. Previously unpublished.

8. *The Thinking In Us*. Written: 1951. Previously unpublished.

9. *Heavens Above*. A talk on BBC radio by D. E. Harding, Oct. 1952.

10. *Notes For A Defence of Angels.* Published Sept. 1952: *CR* [journal of The Community of the Resurrection].

11. *A Living Universe.* Paper read to The Socratic Society, Oxford University, Nov 3, 1952, at the invitation of C. S. Lewis.

12. *The Conflict Between Science and Religion.* Written: 1954. Published in *The Student Movement* journal, Oct. 1954.

13. *Embodiments: Architecture As A Bodily Function.* Written: 1954. Published in *The Architectural Review*, Feb. 1955.

14. *Thirty Questions.* Published in *The Middle Way*, journal of The Buddhist Society, London, November 1963.

15. *Spontaneous Awakening.* Published Oct. 1965 in *The Mountain Path*, Journal of the Ramana Maharshi ashram, India.

16. *Addendum.* Written: Nov. 1966. An addition to the article *On Having No Head* (a different article from the article in Chapter 3), which was published as *The Headless Way in 1965* in *The Turning Point* (a collection of articles by D. E. Harding). Previously unpublished.

17. *Home Truth.* Written: May 10th, 1967. Previously unpublished.

18. *Preface to the 2nd Edition of On Having No Head.* Written: 1967. This preface was not used.

19. *The Caller.* Written Sept. 1967. Previously unpublished.

20. *What Am I?* Written 1967. Previously unpublished.

21. *What Is Self-Realisation?* Written: April 1968. Published in *The Mountain Path*, July 1968.

22. *In This Six-Foot Body.* Written: Nov. 1968.

23. *Face To No-Face*. Written: Nov. 10th, 1968. Previously unpublished.

24. *The Serious Question*. Published Oct. 1969 in *Ramana Jyothi*.

25. *Masked Ball*. Written: Nov. 1969. Previously unpublished.

26. *Making A Good Impression*. Written Dec. 1970. Previously unpublished.

27. *What Deludes Is What Enlightens*. Written: Jan. 1971. Published in *The Middle Way*, May 1971.

28. *The Great Game Of Pretending*. Published in *The Mountain Path* in Jan. 1971.

29. *The Wild Hypothesis*. Written Aug. 1971. This article developed into *The Toolkit For Testing The Incredible Hypothesis*. (1972. Limited edition of 100 copies.)

30. *The Answer to "Who Am I?"*. Published in *The Mountain Path*, April 1972.

31. *The Headless Way*. Published as part of the 'minikit', 1973.

32. *Eleven Tests For Buddhists*. Written: Dec. 1973. Published in *The Middle Way*, Aug. 1974.

33. *How To Be Spontaneous*. Published in *Self & Society*, Oct. 1974.

34. *Perseus And The Gorgon*. Published in *The Mountain Path*, Oct. 1975.

35. *On Trial For My Life*. Published in *The Mountain Path*, April 1976. This article developed into the book (unpublished) *On Being God*, or *Man v. God*, which later became *The Trial Of The Man Who Said He Was God* (published 1992).

36. *The Evidence Of Where Thoughts Belong.* From *On Being God* (see note 35). Published in *The Nacton Newsletter*, number 3, April 1977.

37. *The Evidence Of Where Feelings Belong.* From *On Being God* (see note 35). Published in *The Nacton Newsletter*, number 4, Oct. 1977.

38. *The Evidence Of Architecture.* From *On Being God* (unpublished. See note 35).

39. *The Evidence Of The Results.* From *On Being God* (see note 35). Published in *The Nacton Newsletter*, number 1, May 1976.

40. *The Sailor, The Ship And The Sea.* Published in *The Middle Way*, Nov. 1976.

41. *Ramana Maharshi And The Availability Of Self-Realisation.* Published in *The Mountain Path*, April 1979.

42. *Who Made The World?* Written probably 1979, published 1980 in *Share It*, number 3. (*Share It* developed out of *The Nacton Newsletter*.)

43. *On Logion 29.* Written: Oct. 1979. Previously unpublished.

44. *Ramana Maharshi And How Not To Grow Old.* Published in *The Mountain Path*, July 1980.

45. *What I Owe To Ramana Maharshi.* Published in Ramana Smrti, 1980.

46. *Seeking The Miraculous.* Written: Feb. 1983. Original title: *Expansion: How And Why To Aim For It.*

47. *Alan Watts. Sage or Anti-sage?* Written: Dec. 1983.

48. *Enlightenment For Peace or The Myth Of Confrontation.* Written: Jan. 1985. Previously unpublished.

Notes

49. *Confrontation—The Suicidal Lie.* Published in 1985 as a pamphlet.

50. *Confrontation: The Game People Play.* Written: 1985. Published in *Transactional Analysis Journal,* April 1986.

51. *Facing The Yellow Flowers.* Written: Dec. 1985. Previously unpublished.

52. *The Prince Or Princess, The Tadpole And The Frog.* Published in *Transactional Analysis Journal,* Jan. 1987.

53. *The Four Fatal Lies.* Written: 1987. Published in *The Mountain Path,* 1988.

54. *Mayday Call.* Written: Sept. 1995. Previously unpublished.

55. *My Special Friend.* Published in *The Headless Way* journal, 1995. (*The Headless Way* journal developed out of *Share It.*)

56. *The Tunnel.* Published in *The Headless Way* journal, 1996.

57. *Whatdunnit.* Published in *The Headless Way* journal, 1997.

58. *Harding's List.* Written: March 1998. Published in *The Headless Way* journal, 1998.

59. *The Door.* Published in *The Headless Way* journal, 1998.

60. *Fate And Freedom.* Published in *The Headless Way* journal, 1999. This article was written, but never added, as an additional chapter to *The Science of the 1st Person.*

* * *

BIBLIOGRAPHY

Most of these books by Douglas Harding are now (2018) in print. Our aim is to make them all available. Please visit *headless.org* for more information about books and lots of other things!

Short Stories
The Meaning And Beauty Of The Artificial
How Briggs Died
The Melwold Mystery
An Unconventional Portrait Of Yourself
The Hierarchy Of Heaven And Earth (original large version)
The Hierarchy Of Heaven And Earth (condensed version)
Visible Gods
On Having No Head
Religions Of The World
The Face Game
The Science Of The First Person
The Hidden Gospel
Journey To The Centre Of The Youniverse
The Little Book Of Life And Death
Head Off Stress
The Trial Of The Man Who Said He Was God
Look For Yourself
The Spectre In The Lake
Face To No-Face
To Be And Not To Be
Open To The Source
The Turning Point
Just One Who Sees

ABOUT THE EDITOR

Richard Lang is Co-ordinator of The Shollond Trust, a UK charity (1059551) set up to help make the Headless Way more available. Richard's books: *Seeing Who You Really Are; Open To The Source: Celebrating Who We Are; The Man With No Head* (artist: Victor Lunn-Rockliffe). Richard travels widely giving workshops on the Headless Way.

For More information on the Headless Way:
www.headless.org
or contact Richard Lang:
headexchange@gn.apc.org

* * *